FRESH
from the
GARDEN

FOOD TO SHARE
with FAMILY AND FRIENDS

Sarah Raven

photography by
Jonathan Buckley

UNIVERSE

When I decided to write a book about my favorite kind of food, the sort of things I like to cook for my family and friends, I knew there'd be a lot of ground to cover. I'd want to include the obvious holidays throughout the year, but also all those other occasions when I might feel like pushing the boat out—a long weekend, a lazy picnic, a crisp bonfire night, or a pre-Christmas drinks party.

The food I like best is simple and not too fussed over. When planning a party, I'll always try to choose food that is showy and original enough to hold its own, but easy enough that it won't stiffen up the atmosphere of the party (or take over my life). I'll aim to accommodate my guests as much as possible and, as for most of us, my friends and family have diverse tastes; some are hearty carnivores, others less keen on meat, some are cheese people, others think dessert is the highlight. As for myself—while I'll happily eat most things, my appetite changes from month to month, depending on the season and my mood. In high summer I'll want abundant greenery, whereas in the depths of winter only a stew will really hit the spot. Sometimes I have time for leisurely preparation, but just as often I have no time at all, so need to get my act together fast.

The seasonal differences have always been important to me, and the best occasions are about marking the turning points in the calendar with the latest harvest. I look forward to the moment when rhubarb makes its first appearance in the markets, and I'm just as thrilled when this is followed by bundles of asparagus. Similarly, I love to celebrate spring by cooking luscious, tender lamb, and then pheasant and game as the year approaches its end. It's this coming and going of ingredients that keeps food exciting year after year.

So, I've tried to make this a one-stop book that you can turn to for inspiration all year round. With luck, within its four hundred recipes, you'll find plenty of dishes that celebrate seasonal abundance, and cater to every kind of occasion that you are likely to dream up.

Sarah Raven
Perch Hill, East Sussex

By the way, unless I specify otherwise:
Black pepper should always be freshly ground, and salt used
    for seasoning is flaky (I favor Maldon).
Onions, shallots, and garlic should be peeled.
All spoon measures are level.
Eggs are medium and preferably organic and free-range.
Bunches of herbs are roughly 1 ounce if small, 2 ounces if large.

SPRING

Spring is the season of change, when you move from bare and pared-down winter to new life, color, and abundance. If you go away in the middle of spring for even a week, you come back to find everything looking and feeling transformed. Plants in the garden have grown several inches, splashes of pale yellow, mauve, and blue can be seen everywhere, and new delicious vegetables have appeared. I love this sense of growth and burgeoning—the "whoosh" of spring.

In March you can enjoy lots of roots and earthy tastes, including Jerusalem artichokes, parsnips, and purple sprouting broccoli, which overlap and are then replaced by new spring crops, such as rhubarb, spinach, watercress, arugula, cilantro, and the soft green herbs at their most intense. The pheasant and partridge season draws to a close as birds start to reproduce, but then eggs are at their best, with lamb, asparagus, and elderflowers not far behind. And as we move toward the end of spring, it is time for those long-awaited first fava beans and baby new potatoes.

The food we cook in spring should reflect this transition from winter to summer—from robust-flavored, warming soups to dishes that are lighter, fresher, and sharper, requiring less cooking. While you might crave a rich and comforting oxtail stew at the start of spring, a month or two later a cilantro-thick pork curry is a better bet. And on the dessert front, delicious nutty-topped crumbles will make way for smarter, lighter tarts and meringues. These things are all delicious—but even more so when eaten at the right moment.

Spring also means Easter, by which time the days are usually much longer and lighter. It feels like we can all unwrap and venture outdoors, and enjoy a bright, optimistic feast with friends and family to celebrate the onset of the growing season. Cover your table with flowers, nests of eggs, chocolates (if you wish), and surround yourself with the clean colors of the garden.

Dukkah spice mix with spring vegetables

A fragrant alternative to celery salt, this Egyptian spice mix is delicious with eggs or a mixture of raw spring vegetables, such as radishes—like Hailstone shown here—the first small spears of asparagus, baby carrots, fennel, or celery. It's also great scattered over good bread or crostini drizzled with olive oil. Keep this nutty spice mix in a jar—it stores for several weeks.

Yields 1 (8-ounce) jar plus a little extra
* ½ cup sesame seeds
* ½ cup blanched hazelnuts
* 3 tablespoons coriander seeds
* 2 tablespoons cumin seeds
* Salt and black pepper
* Mixture of raw spring vegetables (see above), to serve

Toast the sesame seeds over a moderate heat without oil, shaking them in the pan until they turn golden brown. Tip into a food processor.

Toast the hazelnuts in a pan until they become shiny and patched with golden brown (about 3 minutes). Add to the sesame seeds.

Put the coriander and cumin seeds into the pan and toast for 1 minute, shaking so that the seeds don't burn. Add these to the other seeds.

Season the mixture in the food processor with salt and pepper, then whizz briefly until it becomes a coarse powder. Don't overprocess or you will end up with a paste. Pour into a dry, warm, sterilized jar (you can sterilize it in a very hot dishwasher, or boil it in a pan of water for 10 minutes), then seal and label with the date. Eat with mixed spring vegetables.

Popcorn and pumpkin seeds with chili and lime

Spicy and sour, this is good to serve with drinks at any time of year. For a Moroccan flavor, replace the chili powder with ground cumin and coriander, and use lemon juice and zest instead of lime. The heavier nuts fall to the bottom, so give the bowl a proper stir when serving. Eat immediately as the lime juice softens the popcorn if left sitting.

Serves 8 to 10 (makes 1 large bowl)
* ¾ cup pumpkin seeds, toasted
* ¾ cup hazelnuts, toasted
* 3 teaspoons flaky sea salt
* 1 tablespoon vegetable oil
* ½ cup popping corn
* 2 teaspoons medium-hot chili powder
* 1 teaspoon paprika
* Juice and grated zest of 1 lime (or 2 if you want it very sour)

Put the pumpkin seeds, hazelnuts, and salt into a large bowl.

Heat the oil in a large, heavy-based saucepan. When hot, add the dried corn and cover with a lid. Turn down the heat and shake the pan regularly while waiting for the corn to start popping; this will take a few minutes. When the popping has stopped, take the pan off the heat.

Remove the lid and allow the popcorn to cool slightly. Tip into the bowl containing the seeds and nuts, and sprinkle over the chili powder and paprika. Stir well.

Just before serving, sprinkle with the lime juice and zest and give one final stir to bring the nuts to the top.

Quail eggs with homemade celery salt

Perfect as canapés or a starter before Easter lunch. The celery salt transforms quail eggs and is good scattered on any roasted vegetables or fish. The salt keeps for at least a month, so you can make it in advance and pack it into a jar. Get lots of eggs—you'll find that people will eat half a dozen each quite easily.

Serves 10 to 12
For the celery salt, makes 1 (8-ounce) jar plus a little extra

* 6 quail eggs per person
* ⅓ cup flaky sea salt
* ½ teaspoon dried fennel seeds
* 1 teaspoon grated lemon zest
* 1 teaspoon grated orange zest
* ¼ teaspoon crushed white pepper
* 2 ounces or about 2 packed cups celery leaves, chopped very finely (leaves are best, but stalks or a mixture of leaves and stalks can be used instead)

Boil the eggs for 4 minutes, then leave to cool.

Put all the remaining ingredients into a food processor and whizz until quite fine (big lumps of salt won't stick to the egg). Pour into a dry, warm, sterilized jar (you can sterilize it in a very hot dishwasher, or boil it in a pan of water for 10 minutes). Seal and label with the date.

Quail eggs are beautiful, so serve them on a brightly colored plate with a small bowl of celery salt in the middle into which everyone can dip—and put out another bowl for the discarded eggshells.

Smoked salmon pâté

Quick to make and fine prepared 2 to 3 days before, this is perfect party food. Serve it on toasted heavy, flavorful brown bread; I like it best on rye. The chunks of smoked salmon in the creamy base give good texture and taste, so don't puree all the fish from the start, and the cayenne gives it a background punch. As an alternative, try it with flaked hot-smoked salmon replacing the strips of smoked salmon added at the end. That's delicious too.

Serves 8 as a starter or 12 to 15 as canapés
* 14 ounces sliced smoked salmon (you can use trimmings), or 7 ounces sliced smoked salmon and 7 ounces hot-smoked salmon chunks
* 16 ounces cream cheese
* ½ cup heavy cream
* Juice and grated zest of 1 lemon, to taste
* 1 teaspoon cayenne pepper
* Black pepper

To serve
* Warm brown toast
* Lemon wedges

Put half the salmon with all the cream cheese and heavy cream into a food processor. Whizz briefly. Add the lemon juice and zest, cayenne, and black pepper to taste. Whizz again until well mixed. Check the seasoning and adjust if necessary.

Cut the remaining smoked salmon into thin strips, or flake the hot-smoked salmon. Stir into the pureed mixture, then pack into a pâté dish or ramekin, cover, and put in the fridge for an hour or two to set.

Serve with warm brown toast and plenty of lemon wedges.

Spinach and arugula soup

You want your spinach soup to be a bright, rich green, so cook it with the lid off to retain the best color, and add plenty of fresh leaves once it is off the heat before you puree. For a more wintry soup, using spinach or chard (like the one in my *In Season: Cooking with Vegetables and Fruits* cookbook), use coconut milk rather than cream. Both versions are quite rich and filling, so don't serve them in huge bowls. Top this one with lightly whipped cream, and serve with Parmesan croûtes or Fluffy croutons (see pages 26 and 257).

Serves 6 as a starter, 4 for lunch
* 2 tablespoons butter
* 1 tablespoon olive oil
* 1 medium onion, finely chopped
* 2 garlic cloves, chopped
* ¾ pound potatoes, peeled and chopped
* 1 quart chicken or vegetable stock
* 2 ¼ pounds fresh spinach, stalks discarded, roughly chopped
* ½ pound arugula, roughly chopped
* 1 cup heavy cream, plus a little more for swirling, lightly whipped
* Freshly grated nutmeg, to taste
* Salt and black pepper

Put the butter, oil, and onion into a large saucepan and fry gently over a low heat to soften the onion (about 5 minutes).

Add the garlic and continue cooking gently for 2 more minutes, without coloring.

Add the potatoes and stock, bring to a boil, and simmer gently with the lid off until the potatoes are tender.

Stir in two-thirds of the spinach and two-thirds of the arugula. Allow to cool slightly (for about 5 minutes), then add the remaining spinach and arugula. Pour immediately into a food processor and puree.

Return the soup to the saucepan. Add the cream and nutmeg to taste, then reheat very briefly without boiling. Taste, and season with salt and pepper. To serve, ladle into bowls and swirl a little extra cream in each one.

Watercress soup

I love a peppery watercress soup, served warm or cold. This recipe has double the amount of watercress generally used and is all the better for it. Serve with Cheese and fennel seed scones or strong-flavored Crostini topped with tapenade (see pages 257 and 25).

Serves 6 as a starter, 4 for lunch
* 2 tablespoons butter
* 1 tablespoon olive oil
* 3 shallots (about ¼ pound), finely chopped
* 1 quart chicken stock, ideally homemade
* ⅔ pound potatoes, peeled and chopped
* 1 pound watercress, coarser stems discarded, roughly chopped
* ¾ cup light cream
* Salt and black pepper

Put the butter, oil, and shallots in a saucepan and fry gently until soft (about 5 minutes).

Add the stock and potatoes, bring to a boil, and simmer for 15 minutes.

Add half the watercress and continue to cook for a further 5 minutes. Take off the heat, allow to cool for 5 minutes, then add half of the remaining watercress (leaves only so that they wilt down and are not too fibrous).

Add the cream and whizz in a food processor or blender until well pureed. Season with salt and pepper. Add the remaining watercress leaves for texture. Reheat before serving.

Chilled asparagus soup

As spring moves into summer you get the best asparagus, so don't pass up on the chance of making this soup at least once or twice. Hot asparagus soup is good, but the flavor is best when chilled. It's ideal for making the day before and serving straight from the fridge.

Serves 6 as a starter, 4 for lunch
* 1 3/4 pounds fresh asparagus
* 2 tablespoons butter
* 1 tablespoon olive oil
* 1 medium onion, chopped
* 1 quart chicken or vegetable stock
* 2 teaspoons finely chopped mint
* 3 to 4 tablespoons plain yogurt or crème fraîche, plus extra for garnish
* Juice of 1/2 lemon
* Salt and black pepper

Break off and discard the woody stems of the asparagus. Cut each spear into 4 equal pieces. Blanch 8 tips in boiling water for 3 minutes, then drain and place in chilled water. Drain again and set aside for garnish.

Melt the butter in a large saucepan and add the oil and onion. Cook on a low heat for 5 minutes, not allowing the onion to brown. Add the chopped asparagus stems and remaining tips, and then the stock. Bring to a boil, reduce the heat, and simmer for 15 minutes, until soft.

Take off the heat and allow to cool for 10 min-utes. Puree the soup in a blender or food processor. Add the mint, yogurt, lemon juice, and salt and pepper and blend once more. Pour the soup into a large bowl and place in the fridge to chill.

When ready to serve, ladle into bowls and garnish with the asparagus spears and a dollop of yogurt.

Leek and potato soup

The traditional way to eat potatoes and leeks together in a soup is pureed with lots of cream in a vichyssoise. That's lovely, but I prefer this more straight-up, robust version flavored with celery leaf or lovage. It's delicious with Parmesan croûtes (see page 26).

Serves 6 as a starter, 4 for lunch
* 3 tablespoons olive oil
* 5 leeks (about 2 pounds), chopped
* 4 sticks of celery, leaves and all, chopped
* Small bunch of fresh lovage or extra celery leaves
* 1 garlic clove, finely chopped
* 1 bay leaf
* Large sprig of fresh thyme, leaves picked
* 2 cups vegetable or chicken stock (this is key to the flavor)
* 2/3 pound potatoes, peeled and cut into small chunks
* 1 1/4 cups milk
* 3 tablespoons crème fraîche
* Salt and black pepper

To serve
* Cream or crème fraîche
* Small handful of lovage or celery leaves, roughly chopped

Heat the oil in a large saucepan over a medium heat. Add the leeks, celery, lovage, garlic, bay leaf, and thyme leaves and cook for 5 minutes, stirring.

Pour in the stock and bring to a boil, then simmer for 5 minutes. Add the potatoes and milk, stir, and simmer for 10 minutes, or until the potato is tender.

Discard the bay leaf. Stir in the crème fraîche, taste, and season with salt and pepper. Serve the soup with a swirl of cream or dollop of crème fraîche and a sprinkling of chopped lovage or celery leaves on top of each serving.

Janis's luxurious fish soup

Rich, warm, and creamy, this is one of the best fish soups I've ever had, a recipe from Janis Abbott, the Dowager Duchess of Devonshire's cook. Every mouthful has a lump of shrimp or salmon, with a zip of spice. Janis has perfected this recipe over time, the key being a cauliflower base that gives body and texture without the starchiness of the more usual flour or potato.

This is a meal in itself, but quite a lot of work, and best assembled at the last minute. To save time you can make a few batches of the base and freeze it, then add the fish when you want to eat. The scallops aren't essential, but they lift this recipe into a different realm.

Both this soup and the chowder that follows are good with a fluffy white bread or Garlic bread with chili and cilantro (see page 26).

Serves 10 as a starter, 8 for lunch
* 4 tablespoons (½ stick) butter
* 3 tablespoons flour
* 1 quart liquid, approximately 3 parts fish stock (store-bought is fine), 1 part white wine
* ½ pound cooked cauliflower, pureed
* 1¼ cups light cream
* ½ pound cooked potato, finely diced
* Sea salt and black pepper
* Ground mace
* 1 pound fresh haddock, cod, or halibut (or any chunky white fish)
* ½ pound fresh salmon
* 2–3 scallops per serving, depending on their size, coral removed, cut into 2 or 3 pieces (optional)
* 1 quart hot fish stock
* ⅓ pound cooked small shrimp
* ⅓ pound cooked crayfish tails or lobster
* 2 shallots, finely chopped
* 3 small peppers, 1 red, 1 yellow, 1 green

Melt half the butter in a saucepan, add the flour, and cook gently for about 1 minute. Add half the liquid and stir to combine. Add more liquid as required until the sauce coats the back of a spoon.

Add the cauliflower puree and cream to the sauce. Tip in the diced potato. Season with salt, pepper, and ground mace to taste. Add more liquid if required, but the mixture should be quite thick.

About 15 minutes before serving, poach the fish and scallops (if using) in hot fish stock. As they turn opaque, lift them out with a slotted spoon. Skin and flake the fish. Add the flaked fish and scallops to the soup base. Poach the shrimp and crayfish tails in the stock for 2 minutes. (Don't overcook as the cooking process will continue, albeit gently, when you add the seafood to the soup.) Add the shrimp and crayfish tails to the soup.

Meanwhile, melt the remaining butter in a frying pan and fry the shallots and peppers on a gentle heat until softened (about 5 minutes). Add as much of this mixture as you like the look of to your soup. Mix gently and adjust the seasoning, if necessary. Thin with hot fish stock if required. Serve in warm bowls.

Crayfish and corn chowder

Here is one of my favorite meals-in-a-bowl for spring. The chowder is a basic fish soup, perfect for a hearty lunch. Use shrimp if you can't get crayfish, which are fine in this recipe.

Serves 8 as a starter, 6 for lunch
* 2 tablespoons butter
* 1 tablespoon olive oil
* 1 medium onion, finely chopped
* 1 small yellow bell pepper, finely chopped
* 1 tablespoon mild or medium curry powder
* 2 garlic cloves, finely chopped
* ¾ pound small potatoes, peeled and diced
* 2 ½ cups vegetable stock
* 8 ounces corn (frozen is better than canned)
* ½ pound crayfish tails in brine, drained (or shrimp)
* 2 ½ cups milk
* ¾ cup heavy cream
* 2 tablespoons chopped flat-leaf parsley, plus extra for sprinkling
* 1 tablespoon chopped fresh chives
* Flaky sea salt and black pepper
* Ground paprika

Heat the butter and oil in a large, heavy-based saucepan and add the onion, yellow pepper, curry powder, and garlic. Sauté for 3 minutes, or until the vegetables are just softening.

Add the potatoes and stock and bring to a boil. Lower the heat and simmer for 10 minutes.

Add the corn and simmer until the potatoes are just tender. Stir in the crayfish, then add the milk, cream, and herbs. When the crayfish have warmed through (2 to 3 minutes), taste, and season with a little salt and pepper.

Serve sprinkled with a little extra parsley and the paprika.

Crostini topped with tapenade

Serve 2 or 3 of these crostini per person with any of the stronger-tasting soups or stews. They're also excellent with a Fish tagine, and I love them on the side of a plate with Oxtail stew (see pages 45 and 61).

Yields 18 to 20 crostini

For the tapenade
* Small bunch of fresh thyme
* ½ pound really good olives (try to avoid the rubbery, pitted kind)
* 1 ounce of canned anchovies in oil, drained
* 1–2 garlic cloves
* 2 tablespoons capers, rinsed
* Olive oil

* Fresh white bread (a baguette works well)
* Extra virgin olive oil
* 2 garlic cloves, cut in half

First make the tapenade: pull the thyme leaves from the stalks and pit the olives. Place in a food processor with the anchovies, garlic, and capers and whizz briefly. Scoop into a bowl and add just enough olive oil in a stream to give you a thick, spreadable mixture.

Preheat a barbecue, grill pan, or grill until medium hot.

Cut the bread into finger-thick slices, drizzle them with olive oil, then toast them on both sides by your preferred method until brown and crisp.

Lightly scrape one side of the toast with the cut side of the garlic. Spread the tapenade over the toasts and serve.

This recipe makes more tapenade than you need, so put the remainder into a dry, warm, sterilized jar (you can sterilize it in a hot dishwasher, or boil it in a pan of water for 10 minutes). Seal and label with the date. The tapenade will keep for about 2 weeks in the fridge.

Parmesan croûtes

Made in a matter of minutes, these croûtes are very tasty and dress up almost any hot soup.

Serves 6 (makes 12 croûtes)
* 4 thinnish slices of white or brown bread
* 5 tablespoons butter
* Black pepper
* ½ cup grated Parmesan cheese

Preheat the oven to 350 degrees.

Cut the crusts off the bread, and cut each slice into 3 fingers.

Melt the butter in a baking tray, put in the bread fingers, and top with a grind or two of black pepper and the Parmesan. Bake in the oven until brown and crunchy (about 10 minutes).

Garlic bread with chili and cilantro

Homemade garlicky bread is lovely—very different from the stuff you buy in those cellophane wraps. My favorite version is this one, with plenty of fresh cilantro, lemon zest, and a little chili. It's delicious with the Crayfish and corn chowder or Cardamom parsnip soup (see pages 25 and 358). In fact, if you like garlic bread, it's great with almost anything.

Serves 4 to 6
* 1 baguette
* ½ cup (1 stick) softened butter
* 2–3 garlic cloves, crushed
* Small bunch of cilantro, finely chopped
* 1 large red chili, deseeded and finely chopped
* 1 tablespoon lemon juice
* Grated zest of 1 lemon
* Salt and black pepper

Preheat the oven to 350 degrees.

Slice the baguette diagonally at about 1½-inch intervals without cutting all the way through the base. You want the slices to remain joined together.

Mix together all the other ingredients and spread in between the cuts.

Wrap the baguette in foil and bake for about 10 minutes, or until the butter has melted into the bread. Turn up the oven to 400 degrees, open up the foil to expose the top of the bread, and blast in the hot oven for another 5 minutes. Serve immediately.

Roasted asparagus salad with orange

The sweetness of the roasted asparagus works well alongside the warmth of the nutmeg. Toasted pine nuts or sesame seeds are nice sprinkled over the top to make the salad a little more substantial. It's a lovely accompaniment to any meat or fish, and is good with warm Focaccia (see page 132). Roasted asparagus, cooked as described below, is also great served hot with a hollandaise sauce.

Serves 4 to 6 as a starter or side dish
* 2 pounds fresh asparagus spears, woody ends removed
* ½ whole nutmeg, finely grated
* 2 red onions, roughly chopped (optional)
* 3 tablespoons olive oil
* 4 garlic cloves, roughly chopped
* 3–4 good handfuls of mixed salad leaves
* Large handful of arugula leaves
* Small bunch of fresh mint or flat-leaf parsley, roughly chopped
* ¼ pound Parmesan or pecorino cheese
* Grated zest of 1 large orange

For the dressing
* Juice of 1 large orange
* Juice of ½ lemon
* 1 teaspoon honey
* ¼ cup olive oil
* Salt and black pepper

Preheat the oven to 350 degrees.

Place the asparagus into a large roasting pan with the nutmeg, onions, olive oil, and garlic and mix well. Roast for 15 to 18 minutes, until lightly browned. Set aside to cool.

Put the dressing ingredients into a bowl and whisk together.

Combine the salad leaves, arugula, and mint (or parsley) in a large, shallow bowl or on a platter. Scatter the asparagus randomly on top. Using a vegetable peeler, shave the Parmesan over the asparagus. Pour the dressing over the salad and scatter with the orange zest.

Ginger and mixed seed salad

Toward the end of spring, salads come into their own again, and I love the hot taste of this one. My friend Isabel Bannerman gave me a bowl of it recently and I'm now addicted. The fresh ginger makes a change from Dijon mustard and gives an otherwise ordinary salad a transforming punch.

Serves 6 to 8
* 4 good handfuls of mixed spring salad leaves, such as lettuce, watercress, and beet greens, plus some cilantro leaves and flowers as well, if you can find them
* 2 ½-inch piece of fresh ginger, peeled
* 2 heaping tablespoons mixed toasted seeds, such as pumpkin, sunflower, poppy, and sesame

For the dressing
* 3 tablespoons extra virgin olive oil
* 1 tablespoon red wine vinegar
* Salt and black pepper

Fill a bowl with the salad leaves and grate or finely slice the fresh ginger over them.

Put all the dressing ingredients into a screwtop jar, shake well, and pour over the salad. Sprinkle with the seeds and toss everything together.

Iranian herb and feta salad

Here's a starter that's as simple as it gets—bunches of all the spring herbs, a heap of feta cheese, and piles of warm pita bread. It is a brilliant way to start a huge feast, standing up with an aperitif before a long and delicious meal.

Serves 10 to 12 as a starter
* 8 ounces feta cheese
* A few chili flakes
* Small bunch flat-leaf parsley
* Small bunch mint
* Small bunch fresh chives
* Small bunch tarragon
* Small bunch cilantro
* Small bunch watercress
* 2–3 heads of Belgian endive, leaves separated
* ½ pound black olives

To serve
* 20 warm pita breads, halved and slit open
* Bottle of fruity extra virgin olive oil
* 3 lemons, cut into wedges

Crumble the feta and place in a heap on a large serving plate. Scatter over a few chili flakes. Arrange the bunches of herbs, the watercress, and endive leaves around the feta and make a pile of olives on the side.

To serve, place the platter on the table with a basket of warm pita bread and the olive oil and lemon wedges alongside. Each person takes a pita pocket and stuffs in a mix of herbs and leaves, a spoonful of cheese, and a couple of olives, drizzles it with olive oil and a squeeze of lemon, and eats it immediately.

Squid and chorizo salad

This dish looks and tastes marvelous, and the flavors of the squid, the spicy chorizo, and the salty pancetta all contrast perfectly with the punchy salad leaves.

To extract the pomegranate seeds, gently roll the fruit around a few times on the table, then slice it in half. Holding one half of the fruit cut side down over a bowl, tap the skin with a wooden spoon. The seeds will drop into the bowl without their bitter white pith.

Serves 4 as a starter, 2 to 3 as a main course
* 3 medium squid (about 1 pound)
* 2 red chilis, deseeded and finely chopped
* 2 garlic cloves, finely chopped
* 2 tablespoons olive oil
* Large bunch of flat-leaf parsley, chopped
* ¼ pound chorizo, sliced
* ¼ pound pancetta or bacon, chopped
* Juice of ½ lemon
* 3 large handfuls of spring salad leaves, such as mustard, sorrel, wild arugula, and baby leaf lettuce
* Seeds of 1 medium pomegranate (see above)

For the dressing
* 3 tablespoons extra virgin olive oil
* Grated zest of 1 lemon and juice of ½ lemon
* Salt and black pepper

Clean the squid and slit open the body tube. Using a serrated eating knife, score inside it at an angle.

Put the chilis, garlic, olive oil, and parsley in a bowl and marinate the squid in it for at least 30 minutes.

Heat a grill pan for 3 to 4 minutes (until you can't count to 10 with your hand hovering just above it). Cut the squid into manageable-sized pieces and grill for 2 minutes on each side.

Meanwhile, in a frying pan, cook the chorizo and pancetta for 5 minutes, until beginning to brown and turn crisp. Using a slotted spoon, transfer it to a bowl. Squeeze over the lemon juice.

To make the dressing, put the oil and lemon zest and juice into a jam jar, screw on the lid, and shake well. Season to taste. In a serving bowl, toss the salad in the dressing. Pile the squid, chorizo, and pancetta on top. Sprinkle with the pomegranate seeds.

Thai spiced pork with bean sprouts and cashews

Although the list of ingredients for this dish looks intimidating, you'll probably have most of them in your cupboard. It is a surprisingly quick and easy thing to make, and one of my absolute favorites when the weather starts to cheer up properly in the spring. If you are short of time, marinate the pork in a store-bought red or green Thai curry paste.

Serves 6 as a starter, 4 as a main course

For the marinade
* 2 lemongrass stalks, outer leaves removed, cut into thirds
* 1 tablespoon peeled and roughly chopped fresh ginger
* ½ red chili, deseeded and roughly chopped
* 1 garlic clove
* 1 small onion, roughly chopped
* 1 tablespoon fish sauce
* Small bunch of fresh cilantro
* Juice and grated zest of 1 lime
* 2 tablespoons peanut or olive oil

For the dressing
* 5 tablespoons peanut or olive oil
* 1 tablespoon soy sauce
* 2 tablespoons rice wine vinegar
* 1 tablespoon fish sauce
* Juice of ½ lime
* 1 teaspoon superfine sugar
* Salt and black pepper

* 2 pork fillets (about 1 pound)
* Olive oil, for brushing

For the salad
* ½ red pepper, quartered and thinly sliced
* 2 carrots, grated or julienned
* 10 ounces fresh bean sprouts
* 1 stick of celery, thinly sliced
* 1 small red onion, very thinly sliced
* ¼ cup roughly chopped fresh mint
* 5 tablespoons roughly chopped fresh cilantro
* ¼ cup cashews, toasted
* 1 tablespoon sesame seeds, toasted

Put all the marinade ingredients into a food processor and blitz to a paste. Cover the pork fillets in the paste and refrigerate overnight, or for a minimum of 2 to 3 hours.

To make the dressing, put all the ingredients except the salt and pepper into a jam jar, screw on the lid, and shake well. Season to taste.

Preheat the oven to 400 degrees and heat a ridged grill pan until you can't count to 10 with your hand hovering just above it. (Alternatively, cook on a barbecue, as this recipe is lovely served outside for a summer lunch.)

Brush the pork fillets with a little olive oil and grill for 7 to 8 minutes on each side. Transfer to the hot oven for a further 5 minutes. (For less smoke you can do the grilling in the oven too.) If barbecuing the meat, there's no need for the oven; just cook over the fire for 10 minutes on each side. Let the pork fillets rest for 10 minutes, wrapped in foil, before thinly slicing to serve.

Put all the salad ingredients apart from the nuts and seeds into a bowl and mix with the prepared salad dressing.

Place the dressed salad on a large plate and top with the sliced pork. Sprinkle the cashews and sesame seeds all over and serve.

Jane's warm chicken, pancetta, and Gorgonzola salad with mother-in-laws' tongues

My sister Jane devised this lovely salad. It's served with a plate of *ciappe*, thin ovals of crispbread, also known as mother-in-laws' tongues. These are sold in Italian delis, but they're easy to make and store well in an airtight tin. They are also great with cheese. The basic mixture can be flavored with a teaspoonful of rosemary or celery salt.

Serves 4 as main course

For the marinade
* Juice and grated zest of 1 lemon
* ¼ teaspoon cayenne pepper
* 1 garlic clove, crushed
* ¼ cup olive oil
* Sprinkle of dried oregano

* 3 medium chicken breasts, cut into finger-sized strips

For the mother-in-laws' tongues (makes 10)
* ½ tablespoon fine salt
* 1 tablespoon finely chopped rosemary (optional)
* 3 tablespoons extra virgin olive oil
* 1¼ cups unbleached flour

For the salad
* 3 good handfuls of spring salad leaves, such as arugula, mâche, watercress, and baby spinach
* Sunflower oil, for frying
* 6 slices of thick-cut pancetta, cut into strips
* 3 scallions, cut into 3 and sliced into 4 strips
* 3 tablespoons coarsely chopped flat-leaf parsley
* 3 tablespoons coarsely chopped tarragon
* 3 ounces Gorgonzola cheese, cut into small chunks
* Sprinkle of cayenne pepper

For the dressing
* 1 heaping tablespoon mayonnaise (a good store-bought one will do)
* 1 heaping tablespoon plain yogurt or sour cream
* 4 anchovy fillets, finely chopped
* Juice of ½ lemon
* 3 tablespoons extra virgin olive oil

Combine all the marinade ingredients in a bowl. Add the chicken and leave to marinate, ideally overnight, or for at least a couple of hours, refrigerated. Stir once or twice during the marinating time.

Meanwhile, make the mother-in-laws' tongues. Preheat the oven to 350 degrees. Lightly oil several baking sheets or line them with silicone mats.

Put 6 tablespoons warm water into a bowl or pitcher, add the salt and rosemary (if using), and stir until dissolved. Add the oil and stir well.

Put the flour into a mixing bowl, pour in the liquid, and mix well to form a dough. Knead in the bowl for a couple of minutes.

Place the dough onto a well-floured work surface or board and cut into 10 equal pieces. Roll each into a little sausage shape. Using a well-floured rolling pin, roll out each sausage into a long oval about 1/16-inch thick. Prick them all over on both sides with a fork, giving a very dotty effect. Place on the prepared sheets and bake for 8 minutes, until pale and golden. Allow to cool a bit, then use a large spatula to transfer them to a cooling rack.

Once the bread baking is underway, start making the salad. Scatter the salad leaves over a large flat plate.

Heat some oil in a wok or frying pan, add the pancetta, and fry, stirring from time to time. You want the meat to brown but not stick. Cook for 5 minutes, then set aside while the chicken is fried.

Drain and dry the chicken, then fry over a medium heat for 3 minutes on each side. Add the scallions and cook for a further 3 minutes. Allow to rest for 5 minutes, then scatter the mixture over the salad leaves.

In a bowl, mix together the dressing ingredients. Pour the dressing over the salad, then add the chopped herbs and Gorgonzola. Sprinkle with cayenne pepper.

Serve with the mother-in-laws' tongues, or stuffed into pita breads for lunch.

Scallion and cilantro pancakes with soy sauce

I love these Korean pancakes, sharp from spring onion and fragrant from plenty of cilantro. They're quick and easy to make—ideal for lunch with a salad, or with an aperitif before dinner.

Makes about twelve 5-inch small pancakes or six 8-inch large ones
* ½ cup unbleached flour
* ¼ cup rice flour
* Slightly rounded ½ teaspoon table salt
* 1 large egg
* 1 large egg yolk
* 1 small red chili, deseeded and thinly sliced
* Pinch of ground black pepper
* 4 drops of toasted sesame oil
* Vegetable oil, for frying
* 5–6 scallions (pale green and dark green parts only), diagonally sliced into ¼ to ½ inch pieces (reserve the white parts for the dipping sauce)
* Small bunch of fresh cilantro, roughly chopped

For the dipping sauce
* 3 tablespoons soy sauce
* 2 tablespoons rice vinegar (not seasoned)
* 1 teaspoon toasted sesame oil
* 1 teaspoon sesame seeds
* 1 tablespoon roughly chopped fresh cilantro

Put the flours, salt, egg and egg yolk, ¾ cup water, chili, pepper, and sesame oil in a bowl and whisk together (the batter will be thin). Allow to stand for at least 30 minutes at room temperature.

To make the sauce, combine the soy sauce, vinegar, and oil in a bowl, then stir in the sesame seeds, the reserved white spring onion parts, chopped finely, and the cilantro. This dipping sauce can be made a day ahead if kept covered and chilled, but add the cilantro just before serving.

Heat a teaspoon of vegetable oil in an 8-inch nonstick frying pan over a moderately high heat until hot but not smoking. Spoon in 1½ tablespoons of the batter, tilting the pan to spread it over the bottom. Scatter the scallions and the cilantro over the top, gently pressing them into the pancake with a spatula. If you don't have a small frying pan, use a 10-inch pan and add 3 tablespoons of batter.

Fry the pancake until the underside is pale golden, about 2 minutes. Turn it over and cook until the scallions are lightly browned, about 1 minute. Transfer, with the scallion/cilantro side up, to parchment paper. Lift the paper to help roll up the pancake. Transfer to a plate and keep warm, cutting the large pancakes in half.

Carry on making pancakes, adding a little vegetable oil to the frying pan each time, until you have used up all the batter.

Serve right away with the dipping sauce.

Scallion tart

This is a wonderful tart, treating scallions like mini leeks. The pine nuts give a good, crunchy texture.

Serves 6 to 8

For the pastry
* 1½ cups unbleached flour
* Pinch of salt
* 7 tablespoons cold butter, cut into pieces

* 4 eggs
* 1 cup heavy cream or crème fraîche
* Salt and black pepper
* 2 tablespoons Dijon mustard
* ½ cup grated Parmesan cheese
* 25 scallions, sliced into ½-inch pieces
* ⅓ cup pine nuts

First make the pastry. Sift the flour and salt into a bowl, then rub in the butter until the mixture resembles breadcrumbs. Alternatively, pulse in a food processor. Add just enough cold water for the mixture to bind together. Form into a ball, wrap in plastic wrap, and put in the fridge for at least 1 hour.

Preheat the oven to 350 degrees and heat a baking sheet until searing hot.

Roll out the pastry to a thickness of ⅛ inch and use to line an 11-inch round tart pan, leaving the excess draped over the sides in case it shrinks. Prick the bottom of the case with a fork, line with parchment paper or foil, and weigh this down with baking beans or rice. Place on the hot baking sheet and bake for about 15 minutes. Remove the baking beans and paper and bake the crust for another 5 minutes. Take out of the oven and trim off the excess pastry. Keep the oven on and reheat the baking sheet.

To make the filling, combine the eggs and cream in a bowl with some salt and pepper. Spread the mustard over the base of the tart, then scatter over the Parmesan. Spread the scallions on top. Sprinkle with the pine nuts, then pour over the egg mixture.

Put the tart on the hot baking sheet and cook until the pastry is turning golden and the contents are set (about 30 minutes). Serve warm.

Spinach tart

This is the best spinach tart I have tried. I use a local Cheddar cheese and serve with salad.

Serves 6 to 8
* 1 quantity pastry (see previous recipe)
* ⅔ pound spinach
* ¼ pound sorrel (or more spinach)
* Olive oil
* ¾ cup heavy cream
* ½ cup milk
* 3 eggs
* 1 teaspoon Dijon mustard
* Plenty of freshly grated nutmeg
* ½ teaspoon cayenne pepper
* ½ pound sharp Cheddar cheese, grated
* Salt and black pepper
* ¾ cup pine nuts

Make the pastry, as described in the previous recipe.

Preheat the oven to 350 degrees and heat a baking sheet until searing hot.

Roll out the pastry to a thickness of ⅛ inch and use to line an 11-inch round tart pan, leaving the excess draped over the sides in case it shrinks. Prick the bottom of the crust with a fork, line with parchment paper or foil, and weigh this down with baking beans or rice. Place on the hot baking sheet and bake for about 15 minutes. Remove the baking beans and paper and bake the crust for another 5 minutes. Take out of the oven and trim off the excess pastry. Keep the oven on and reheat the baking sheet.

Pick over the spinach and sorrel leaves, discarding any tough ribs. In a lidded saucepan, wilt the leaves in a tablespoon of oil over a medium heat, and cook until tender (no extra water is needed). To remove excess water from the leaves, place in a sieve and push the liquid out with a spoon. Chop the greens roughly.

Mix the cream, milk, and eggs in a bowl. Add the mustard, nutmeg, cayenne, and cheese, and season.

Spread the greens inside the pastry and sprinkle with the pine nuts. Place the tart pan on the hot baking sheet, then pour in the cream mixture.

Bake until the pastry is golden and the contents are set (about 30 minutes). Serve warm.

Spinach and ricotta cannelloni

Spring is the time to eat spinach, when it's at its most tender and delicious, and this classic dish is perfect for a big family Saturday lunch, or a vegetarian feast. The fresh lasagne sheets do not need any pre-cooking, but if using dried, follow the cooking instructions. You can also substitute thin slices of eggplant for the lasagne, lightly frying them before stuffing with the spinach mixture.

Serves 6

For the cheese sauce
* 3 tablespoons butter
* 3 tablespoons unbleached flour
* 2 cups milk
* ¼ pound Parmesan cheese, grated, plus a little extra for sprinkling
* ¼ cup crème fraîche
* Salt and black pepper

For the tomato sauce
* 1 onion, finely chopped
* 3 tablespoons olive oil
* 2 (14 ½-ounce) cans of tomatoes
* Pinch of dried oregano
* 2 whole garlic cloves
* Good pinch of salt

* 1 pound spinach
* 15 ounces ricotta cheese
* ⅓ pound Parmesan cheese, freshly grated
* 3 tablespoons toasted pine nuts
* 1 garlic clove, crushed
* ½ whole nutmeg, grated
* 10 fresh lasagna sheets

First make the cheese sauce. Melt the butter in a saucepan over a low heat. Add the flour, stirring for a few seconds. Whisk in the milk, bring to a boil, and allow to simmer for 5 minutes, whisking occasionally.

Stir in the Parmesan, crème fraîche, and salt and pepper. Set aside.

To make the tomato sauce, put the onion and olive oil in a saucepan and cook until soft (about 5 minutes). Add the tomatoes, oregano, garlic, and salt and cook gently for about 20 minutes, until reduced by about a third and quite thick. Remove the garlic. Set aside.

Rinse the spinach, then put it into a large lidded saucepan and cook over a medium heat (no extra water needed) until wilted. Drain well in a colander or sieve, pushing out any water with the back of a spoon or squeezing it out with your hands. Roughly chop and place in a bowl.

Add the ricotta, Parmesan, pine nuts, garlic, nutmeg, and a little salt and pepper to the spinach. Mix well.

Preheat the oven to 350 degrees.

Spread out the lasagne sheets on a work surface. Place an equal amount of the spinach mixture on each one and roll up.

Put the tomato sauce in the bottom of an 8 by 12-inch ovenproof baking dish and lay the cannelloni on top, seam side down. Pour the cheese sauce over the top and sprinkle with extra grated Parmesan. Place in the oven for 30 minutes, or until cooked through and golden brown.

Ricotta al forno

This is one of my favorite recipes from London's River Café. When I was a waitress there twenty years ago, I made this all the time and I still love it. It's rich yet fresh, and lighter than it sounds—wonderful with bread and a crunchy green salad. You can leave out the olives if you prefer. I like to add pine nuts for extra texture.

Serves 6
* 2 tablespoons butter, softened
* ⅓ pound Parmesan cheese, freshly grated, plus more for lining the pan
* 2 handfuls of fresh basil
* Handful of mint
* Handful of flat-leaf parsley
* 15 ounces fresh ricotta cheese
* ½ cup heavy cream
* 2 eggs
* Salt and black pepper
* ¾ cup pine nuts, toasted (optional)
* 12 black olives, pitted and chopped (optional)

Preheat the oven to 375 degrees. Grease a 12-inch springform cake pan with the butter, then coat the buttered surface with a little grated Parmesan. Shake off any excess.

Put the herbs into a food processor with half the ricotta and half the cream. Blend until bright green. Add the rest of the ricotta and cream, and, with the machine running, add the eggs one by one. Transfer to a large bowl, and season the mixture with salt and pepper. Add the pine nuts (if using), and finally fold in the rest of the grated Parmesan.

Spoon the mixture into the prepared pan and spread the olives (if using) over the top. Bake in the oven for 20 minutes. It should rise slightly and have a brown crust, but the center should be soft. Serve immediately.

Arugula, spinach, and walnut pesto pasta

The pesto used here is great with any type of pasta, but can also be dolloped on baked potatoes (white or sweet ones) and it's delicious with sausage and mashed potatoes. It's perfect to make in spring when arugula and spinach, rather than basil, are in season.

Serves 4 to 6

For the pesto
* ½ pound arugula leaves
* ¼ pound spinach
* ½ cup walnuts, toasted
* 2 garlic cloves
* Juice and grated zest of 1 lemon
* 6 tablespoons extra virgin olive oil
* Salt and black pepper

* 1 pound tagliatelle
* ¼ pound Parmesan cheese, to serve

First make the pesto. Put all the ingredients for it, except the seasoning, in a food processor and whizz briefly: you want a good-textured pesto. Taste, and season with salt and pepper.

Cook the pasta until al dente in boiling salted water. Drain and divide among 4 to 6 plates. Put a dollop of pesto and a good grating of Parmesan on top of each one. Serve immediately.

Pea and spinach timbale

I love the delicate flavor and texture of these neat little mounds, which are ideal as a light starter for a big dinner, or good as a side dish with chicken or fish. They look impressive but are really not a lot of hassle. Peas, chard, or spinach, or a mixture of all three, can be used for the filling, always with plenty of mint. For non-vegetarians, the timbales can be served with some crunchy prosciutto or chorizo on the side.

Serves 4
* Olive oil
* ¼ pound large spinach or chard leaves
* 1 cup frozen peas
* Small bunch of fresh mint
* 2 eggs, beaten
* ½ cup heavy cream
* 1 garlic clove, finely chopped
* 1 whole nutmeg, grated
* 1 ounce Parmesan cheese, grated

To serve
* A few black olives, pitted and roughly chopped
* ¼ pound chorizo (fried and doused with a squeeze of lemon) or 8 slices baked prosciutto (optional)

Preheat the oven to 350 degrees. Grease 4 ramekin dishes with a little olive oil.

Blanch the spinach leaves in boiling water for 1 minute (if using chard, which is tougher, blanch for 4 to 5 minutes). Plunge into very cold water, then drain and dry on a kitchen towel.

Line the prepared ramekins with 1 or 2 leaves each. They should overhang the sides, leaving enough to completely cover the top.

Boil the peas with the mint until tender (about 5 minutes). Drain, remove the mint, and put two-thirds of the peas into a food processor and pulse until pureed.

Transfer the puree to a bowl, add the remaining whole peas, eggs, cream, garlic, nutmeg, and Parmesan and stir to combine.

Pour the mixture into the prepared ramekins and cover with the overhanging spinach leaves.

Wrap each one in foil and cook in a bain-marie for 15 minutes, until just firm to the touch.

Allow to cool for 5 minutes before turning them out onto plates.

Serve with some good black olives, or some fine slices of fried chorizo dressed in lemon, or a couple of slices of baked and crunchy prosciutto slices.

Stir-fried green vegetables

This is one of the best quick and easy lunches. It looks and tastes bright, fresh, and perky. If you want some color contrast, add a very finely sliced red pepper. If you are feeding lots of people, cook in batches no bigger than the quantity below or the vegetables will start to steam rather than quick-fry and will become floppy. Serve with egg noodles, plain basmati rice, or Coconut and cilantro rice (see page 393).

Serves 4
* 3 tablespoons peanut oil
* Bunch of scallions, roughly chopped
* 3 garlic cloves, chopped
* 2½-inch piece of fresh ginger, peeled and grated or finely chopped
* 1 green chili, halved, deseeded, and sliced
* ½ cucumber or 1 medium zucchini, peeled, halved, and sliced
* ¼ pound snow peas, trimmed
* ½ pound bok choy, quartered
* ¼ pound green beans, trimmed and halved
* ¼ pound purple sprouting broccoli or broccolini, cut into pieces
* 3 tablespoons soy sauce
* 1 tablespoon fish sauce
* 1 tablespoon rice wine vinegar
* 2 teaspoons light brown sugar
* Juice and grated zest of 1 lime
* Large bunch of fresh cilantro or basil

Heat the oil in a wok, add the scallions and garlic, and stir-fry for 1 minute.

Keeping the wok over a high heat, add the ginger, chili, and all the remaining vegetables. Stir-fry for 3 to 4 minutes, until just starting to wilt or soften.

Add the soy sauce, fish sauce, vinegar, sugar, lime juice, and lime zest and bring to a boil. Simmer for 2 minutes, then serve immediately with the herbs scattered on top.

Belgian endive hearts with green mayonnaise

An adaptation of the crisp zucchini wedges in my *In Season: Cooking with Vegetables and Fruits* cookbook. It works brilliantly with the additional hint of smoky bitterness from the endive—a perfect winter or early spring starter, or a main course served with a peppery-leaved green salad.

Serves 8

For the flavored breadcrumbs
* 8 ounces bread for crumbs (you can include the crusts if they're soft)
* Grated zest of 1 lemon
* ¼ cup grated Parmesan cheese

* A little flour seasoned with salt, pepper, and 1 scant teaspoon English mustard powder
* 2 eggs, lightly scrambled
* 8 Belgian endive hearts (choose the tightest bullet ones), cut lengthwise into quarters, sixths, or eighths, depending on their size
* Peanut or sunflower oil, for frying
* 1 quantity green mayonnaise (see page 373)

First make the breadcrumbs by whizzing the bread in a food processor. Add the lemon zest and Parmesan.

Set out 3 shallow bowls, putting the seasoned flour in one, the beaten eggs in another, and the breadcrumb mixture in the last. Dip the endive pieces first in the flour, then the egg, and, last, the breadcrumbs.

Heat some oil for shallow-frying in 2 large pans. When hot, fry no more than 5 or 6 endive wedges at a time, until they're golden.

Serve as soon as all the endive is cooked, with a bowl of the mayonnaise in the middle of the table.

Salmon carpaccio with spring salad leaves

Carpaccio is good made with oily fish, especially salmon or tuna. I prefer it to gravlax, and it's one hundred percent quicker and simpler to make. Eat it with punchy-tasting baby leaves of arugula, radish, sorrel, watercress, and some finely chopped garlic chives, plus a few beet leaves, ruby chard, or red amaranth for extra color. If you want more of a main course, serve it with peeled and chopped tomato and cucumber mixed with a little crème fraîche and seasoned with salt and pepper.

Serves 6 to 8 as a starter, 4 as a
main course with salad
* 1 pound fillet of fresh salmon or tuna (skinned)
* 1 tablespoon capers, rinsed and chopped (optional)

For the marinade
* Grated zest and juice of 1 lemon
* Juice of 1 lime
* 2 tablespoons white wine vinegar
* Flaky sea salt and coarsely ground pepper
* ½ small red chili, deseeded and thinly sliced
* 1 teaspoon superfine sugar
* 6 tablespoons light olive oil

For the salad
* 3 tablespoons extra virgin olive oil
* Juice of ½ lemon
* Salt and black pepper
* 3 handfuls of mixed salad leaves

Slice the salmon (or tuna) as thinly as possible and lay out on a large plate.

To make the marinade, put the lemon zest and juice in a bowl with the lime juice. Stir in the vinegar, salt, pepper, chili, and sugar, then whisk in the oil. Drizzle the dressing over the fish, then cover and allow it to sit in a cool room or the fridge for at least 1 hour to marinate. In fact, this is fine stored in its marinade for 2 to 3 days in the fridge.

When ready to serve, combine the salad ingredients in a bowl. Scatter the capers (if using) over the salmon and pile some of the dressed salad leaves on the side.

Smokie or kipper soufflé

I love a soufflé for a party, and the best are made with fish or cheese. This version, ideally made with the famously delicious Arbroath smokies and curry powder, is a particular favorite. Serve individual soufflés in ramekins as a starter for dinner, or make a large one and serve it with a green salad and wilted spinach for lunch.

Serves 10 as a starter, 6 for lunch
* 4 tablespoons (½ stick) butter
* 3 tablespoons finely grated Parmesan cheese
* 1 small onion, finely chopped
* 2 tablespoons finely chopped fresh chives
* Pinch of cayenne pepper
* 1 tablespoon mild curry powder
* 3 tablespoons flour
* ½ cup milk
* ⅔ cup heavy cream
* 4 egg yolks
* ¼ pound sharp Cheddar cheese, grated
* ½ pound Arbroath smokies or smoked haddock, flaked
* Black pepper
* 6 egg whites

Preheat the oven to 350 degrees. Using a little of the butter, lightly grease ten 3-inch ramekin dishes or one 8-inch soufflé dish. Sprinkle some of the Parmesan into each and shake gently to coat thoroughly. Tip out any excess.

Put the remaining butter into a pan and sauté the onion and chives with a pinch of cayenne and the curry powder on a gentle heat for 5 minutes.

Using a wooden spoon, stir in the flour. Add the milk and cream, stirring constantly until the roux is thick and smooth. Take off the heat and stir in the egg yolks, Cheddar, and fish. Season well with pepper; it's unlikely to need salt.

In a clean bowl, beat the egg whites until stiff. Stir in one-third of the fish mixture, then fold in the rest. Spoon into the prepared dish(es) and bake until risen and golden brown (about 15 minutes for individual soufflés, and 25 minutes for a large one). Serve at once.

Sweet and sour trout with lemon and ginger

Quick, light, and healthy, this recipe has a lovely combination of flavors. Serve with Sugarsnap, snow pea, and pickled ginger salad and Coconut and cilantro rice (see pages 168 and 393). Sea bass and snapper make good substitutes for trout.

Serves 2
* 2 whole rainbow trout (about 1½–2 pounds), cleaned and scaled
* 1 lemon, thinly sliced
* 1-inch piece of fresh ginger, peeled and coarsely grated
* Olive oil
* Salt and black pepper

For the syrup
* 1 lemongrass stalk
* 1 red chili, deseeded and chopped
* 3 tablespoons superfine sugar
* 3 tablespoons lemon juice
* Grated zest of 1 lemon
* 1-inch piece of fresh ginger, peeled and coarsely grated
* Small bunch of fresh cilantro, finely chopped

Preheat the oven to 400 degrees. Put a piece of oiled foil into a baking pan.

Open up the fish and fill the cavity with the lemon slices and grated ginger. Place in the prepared pan. Drizzle over a little olive oil and season with salt and black pepper. Bake for 15 minutes, or until the flesh flakes easily when tested with the tip of a knife.

To make the syrup, bash the lemongrass a few times with a rolling pin to release the essential oils. Put the lemongrass, chili, sugar, lemon juice, zest, and ginger into a small pan and simmer for 8 to 10 minutes. Remove from the heat and cool for 2 minutes. Remove the lemongrass, then add the cilantro.

Carefully transfer the fish from the baking pan to plates, then pour over the syrup.

Sesame salmon with pea pesto

Here is a brilliantly easy, almost instant dish our daughter Molly had in a restaurant while on holiday in France and came back asking me to make. Try to find really good salmon. It's delicious served with pea pesto and a few minty new potatoes.

Serves 4
* ½ cup sesame seeds
* 4 salmon fillets (about ⅓ pound each)
* 1 tablespoon olive oil
* 1 tablespoon sesame oil

For the pea pesto
* 12 ounces peas, thawed if frozen, or blanched for 1 minute if fresh
* 5 tablespoons extra virgin olive oil
* Large handful of fresh basil leaves, plus a few extra to serve
* Juice and grated zest of 1 lemon
* 1 tablespoon peeled and grated fresh ginger
* 2 garlic cloves, roughly chopped
* Salt and black pepper

Spread the sesame seeds over a plate, then cake each salmon fillet in them. Heat the olive oil and sesame oil and cook the fish for 2 to 3 minutes on each side (depending on whether you like the fish rare in the middle, as I do, or cooked right through). You can also bake them in the oven for 15 minutes at 350 degrees.

In a food processor, briefly whizz the peas with the olive oil, basil, lemon juice and zest, ginger, and garlic. Season generously with salt and pepper. Transfer to a saucepan and warm through.

Scatter each salmon fillet with a few torn-up basil leaves. Serve with a dollop of pea pesto at the side, some new potatoes, and crisp salad leaves.

Moroccan fish tagine

It's worth making your own chermoula (spice base), as it's much more fragrant when fresh. Most tagines need to be slow-cooked, but not this one. It's quick and easy to do; perfect with Lemon and lime couscous or the Persian jeweled rice (see pages 297 and 67).

Serves 4 to 6

For the chermoula
* 2 garlic cloves
* 1 teaspoon flaky sea salt
* 1 tablespoon cumin seeds, toasted and ground
* 1 teaspoon hot or sweet paprika
* ½ teaspoon turmeric
* Juice of 1 lemon
* 1 teaspoon coriander seeds, toasted and ground
* Small bunch of fresh cilantro, roughly chopped
* Small bunch of fresh mint, roughly chopped
* 1 tablespoon olive oil

* 2 pounds firm-textured fish, such as monkfish or halibut, skinned and cut into chunks
* 10 small new potatoes
* 3 tablespoons olive oil
* 1 red onion, roughly chopped
* 1 red chili, deseeded and finely chopped
* 1 red pepper, halved, deseeded, and sliced
* 4 garlic cloves, finely chopped
* 20 cherry or grape tomatoes
* Salt and black pepper
* ½ cup apple juice
* Small bunch fresh cilantro, chopped, to serve

First make the chermoula. Using a mortar and pestle, pound the garlic and salt to a paste. Stir in all the other ingredients. Rub half of this paste over the fish and leave to marinate for 30 minutes.

Cook the potatoes in boiling salted water for 10 minutes. Drain, allow to cool, then cut in half and peel if you wish.

Heat the oil in a heavy-based pan or casserole and sauté the onion, chili, pepper, and garlic for 2 to 3 minutes, until beginning to soften. Add the tomatoes and cook until just softening (2 to 3 minutes).

Stir in the remaining chermoula mixture and season with a little salt and pepper.

Add the apple juice and fish to the pan. Bring to a boil, turn down the heat, and simmer gently for 10 minutes, or until the fish is cooked through. Add the potatoes (and a little water if necessary) and cook for another couple of minutes.

Scatter plenty of fresh cilantro over the top as you serve.

Smoked haddock with new potatoes in a cream chive sauce

My husband, Adam, wishes I cooked lovely old-fashioned food like this every day. You can use any white fish, smoked or unsmoked, but undyed smoked haddock is his fish of choice. You can make the sauce with lemony sorrel instead of chives—also delicious.

Serves 4 to 6
* 1 tablespoon olive oil
* 1 onion, thinly sliced
* 1 garlic clove, coarsely chopped
* 2 pounds undyed smoked haddock (skinned)
* 1 bay leaf
* 1 cup white wine
* 1½ pounds new potatoes
* 1 cup heavy cream
* 2 tablespoons chives (or sorrel leaves), chopped
* Salt and black pepper
* 2 tablespoons butter, for greasing

Preheat the oven to 350 degrees.

Heat the olive oil in a pan, add the onion and garlic, and sauté until soft but not brown. Transfer to a baking dish (roughly 8 by 12 inches). Lay the fish on top with the bay leaf, add the wine, and bake in the oven for 15 to 20 minutes, until just cooked.

Meanwhile, cook the potatoes in boiling salted water until soft. Drain and set aside to cool slightly.

Remove the fish from the dish and pour the cooking liquid, onion, and garlic into a saucepan. Heat until reduced by about half. Remove the bay leaf.

Add the cream to the reduced fish sauce, then stir in the chives. Season to taste. Set aside to infuse for about 10 minutes.

Butter an ovenproof dish (8 by 12 inches). Peel the potatoes if necessary and slice them into ½-inch chunks. Arrange in the bottom of the buttered dish. Lay the cooked fish on top, trying to keep the fillets intact, then pour over the sauce and bake for 10 minutes.

This is lovely served with a strong-flavored vegetable, such as wilted cabbage or chard.

Shrimp korma

This is one of my family's favorite meals, vastly better homemade, especially with nice fat shrimp. Serve with basmati rice, pappadam, chutney, and beer or lager rather than wine.

Serves 4
* 2 tablespoons olive or peanut oil
* 1 large onion, finely chopped
* 2 garlic cloves, finely chopped
* ¼ teaspoon chili powder or flakes
* ¼ teaspoon turmeric
* 1 tablespoon mild curry powder
* 1 (13 ½-ounce) can of coconut milk
* 1 pound raw peeled shrimp
* 1 tablespoon dried coconut
* 1 teaspoon honey or light brown sugar
* Salt and black pepper
* Small bunch of fresh cilantro, to serve

Heat the oil in a large frying pan or wok and cook the onion and garlic gently for 3 to 4 minutes. Stir in the spices, then add the coconut milk, bring to a boil, and simmer for a further 3 to 4 minutes.

Add the shrimp, dried coconut, and honey and simmer for a further 5 minutes. Taste and add salt and pepper if necessary. Snip the fresh cilantro over the top as you serve.

Teresa's pot chicken with tarragon sauce

Teresa Wallace, my twin sister's mother-in-law, is an experienced and discerning home cook. Her recipe for pot chicken is the perfect thing for a Sunday lunch with friends.

Serves 7 to 8
* Juice of 1 lemon
* 1 free-range or organic chicken, about 4 ½ pounds
* Salt and black pepper
* 2 onions, chopped
* 2 carrots, peeled and chopped
* Bunch of flat-leaf parsley, including stems
* 2 bay leaves
* Small bunch of fresh tarragon
* 3–4 stems of thyme
* 1 garlic clove, crushed
* ½ cup white wine or dry vermouth
* ¾ pound basmati rice

For the tarragon sauce
* 3 tablespoons butter
* 1 tablespoon flour
* 1 cup light cream
* 2 large egg yolks
* Chopped fresh tarragon, to taste
* Lemon juice, to taste

This can be cooked on the stovetop or in the oven. If you prefer the latter, preheat the oven to 325 degrees.

Rub lemon juice all over the chicken and season. Place in a deep saucepan or casserole with the onions, carrots, herbs, and garlic. Add the wine topped up with just enough water to cover. Put the lid on and place in the oven or simmer very gently on the stovetop for about 2 hours. Toward the end of the cooking time, take off 3 cups of the liquid and cook the rice in this. Simmer for 12 to 15 minutes.

To make the sauce, melt the butter in a saucepan and stir in the flour. Cook for a minute or so, then gradually add another 2 cups of the chicken liquid, whisking to make a smooth, thickish sauce. Add the cream and season. Stir in the egg yolks and chopped tarragon and heat through. Add lemon juice to taste.

Pour the sauce into a pitcher and serve with the chicken, rice, and vegetables.

Beer-can chicken

Although bizarre, the technique used here is an excellent way to cook a chicken, with the bird steamed from the inside at the same time as being roasted from the outside. This leaves it as moist as any chicken I've tried. Add whatever spices and flavors you fancy to the can, such as a bunch of chopped tarragon, the juice of a couple of lemons or limes, some toasted and crushed cumin and coriander seeds. They are all delicious. Use the smallest can of beer you can find, or it might not fit in your oven.

Serves 4
* 1 free-range or organic chicken, about 3 pounds
* 1 tablespoon olive oil
* 1 small can of beer
* 1 cinnamon stick
* 1 bay leaf
* 1 dried chili
* 1 teaspoon coriander seeds
* 1 teaspoon fennel seeds
* 1 teaspoon cumin seeds
* 4 strips lemon or lime zest
* Juice of 1 lemon or lime
* Salt and black pepper

Preheat the oven to 350 degrees.

Rub the chicken with olive oil. Open the can of lager and drink or pour out a little. Holding the can over the sink, as the beer fizzes when you add the first ingredients, stuff it with the cinnamon stick, bay leaf, chili, seeds, lemon or lime zest, juice, and some salt and pepper.

Stand the can in a baking pan and balance the chicken on the open top of it, with the neck of the chicken over the top of the can. Cook for 50 minutes, then take out of the oven. Allow to cool slightly before you lift the chicken off the can and pour its contents over the bird. Put the chicken back in the oven for a further 10 to 15 minutes.

Spoon off any fat and strain the juices. Reheat the slightly beery but delicious liquid and use for a gravy.

Chicken and leek pie

The pastry for this is wonderfully flaky and light. You can put it over the top of anything, but it's particularly good with chicken, tarragon, and leeks. In cold weather throw in chestnuts too. I make a similar pie with rabbit when it's in season in summer and autumn (see page 284), as well as a mixed game pie with two rabbits, two pheasants (poached for 45 minutes in 3 cups apple juice with 3 star anise, then meat removed), and 1 pound pigeon breasts.

Note that the pastry is used only on top of the pie; it's not used to line the dish.

Serves 8

For the pastry
* 1½ cups unbleached flour
* 11 tablespoons cold butter, cut into pieces
* 5 tablespoons lard or shortening
* 1 teaspoon salt

* 4 chicken breasts, skinned and cut into pieces
* 4 chicken thighs, skinned, boned, and cut into pieces
* ¼ pound shallots, peeled but left whole
* ¼ pound onions, finely chopped
* 2 bay leaves
* 4 leeks, cleaned and thinly sliced
* Salt and black pepper
* 4 tablespoons (½ stick) butter
* ½ cup unbleached flour
* ¾ cup heavy cream or milk
* Grated nutmeg
* ½ cup sherry
* ½ pound cooked peeled chestnuts, vacuum-packed are fine (optional)
* Large bunch of flat-leaf parsley, chopped
* Small bunch of tarragon, chopped
* Egg and milk wash (1 egg beaten with 2 tablespoons milk)

First make the pastry. Sift the flour into a bowl, then rub in the butter and lard or shortening until the mixture resembles breadcrumbs. Don't overwork.

Alternatively, pulse in a food processor. Add the salt, then a little ice-cold water, and pulse or mix with a knife to form a dough. Gather the pastry into a ball, cover with plastic wrap, and chill for 30 minutes.

Put the chicken pieces, shallots, onions, bay leaves, leeks, and seasoning in a saucepan or casserole. Cover with water and a lid, place over a medium heat or in the oven (preheated to 325 degrees), and cook until the meat is tender (15 to 20 minutes).

Strain off the stock, making it up to 2 cups with water if necessary.

Melt the butter in a saucepan, stir in the flour, and cook for a minute or so. Gradually add the stock, stirring to make a smooth, thickish sauce. Add the cream or milk. Season with salt and pepper and add plenty of grated nutmeg, the sherry, chestnuts (if using), and chopped herbs. Cook for 5 minutes, stirring.

Put the chicken mixture into an 8 by 12-inch rectangular pie dish and pour in the sauce. Stir to combine.

Reheat the oven to 350 degrees.

Roll out the pastry to cover the pie. Decorate with shapes cut out of the leftover pieces and cut a steam hole in the middle. Brush a little egg and milk wash all over the pastry and bake until brown (about 20 minutes).

Duck confit

In France it's traditional to store confit under a layer of duck or goose fat in jars for eating later, but it can, of course, be eaten straight away. Serve with rice, such as Fava bean pilaf (page 174) or Fig mashed potatoes and Plum sauce (see pages 293 and 366) with an arugula and avocado salad.

Serves 6
* 5 tablespoons coarse sea salt
* 6 duck legs
* 3 bay leaves, lightly crushed
* 5 sprigs of fresh thyme, leaves removed and chopped
* 10 juniper berries, crushed
* 3 star anise, crushed
* 1 cinnamon stick, crushed into pieces
* 2 teaspoons black peppercorns, crushed
* 4 garlic cloves, crushed

Scatter the salt over the bottom of a large dish. Sit the duck legs on top and cover with all the remaining ingredients, making sure they are well coated. Cover with plastic wrap and place in the fridge for a minimum of 24 hours, but 48 is even better, as the duck really picks up the flavors of the other ingredients.

Preheat the oven to 300 degrees.

Transfer the duck legs to a roasting pan and roast for 2 ½ hours. Serve with a bowl of plum sauce on the table. Keep the duck fat for cooking roast potatoes.

Duck curry

This recipe was given to me by Fiona Isaacs, who came to one of my cooking demonstrations at Perch Hill. It has become (with some slight changes) one of my favorite winter or spring dishes. It's quick, easy, and very tasty, and also works well with chicken or guinea fowl. If rendering the duck fat feels like too much trouble, just use 2 tablespoons of olive oil for frying the duck pieces. Serve with Persian jeweled rice (see page 67) and a little fresh cilantro sprinkled over the top.

Serves 4
* 4 duck breasts (total weight about 1 ½ pounds), skin on
* 2 lemongrass stalks, outer leaves discarded, thinly sliced
* 1 red chili, deseeded and finely chopped
* Grated zest of 2 limes
* 2 tablespoons red or green Thai curry paste
* 1 (13 ½-ounce) can of coconut milk
* ⅔ cup chicken stock
* Juice of 1 lime
* ⅓ pound snow peas or sugarsnap peas
* ⅔ pound fresh bean sprouts
* Salt and black pepper
* Small bunch of fresh cilantro, roughly chopped

Pull the skin off the duck breasts and fry it over a medium heat until the fat is released (about 10 to 15 minutes). Keep 2 tablespoons of the fat for this recipe and put the rest into a jar to use for roasting potatoes. Discard the skin.

Cut the duck breasts into bite-sized pieces and fry in the 2 tablespoons of duck fat over a high heat for 2 minutes, or until browned all over. Add the lemongrass and chili and cook for 1 minute. Add the lime zest and curry paste and cook for 2 minutes. Turn down the heat, then add the coconut milk, stock, and lime juice and simmer for 10 minutes, stirring a little.

Add the snow peas and simmer for 3 minutes. Add the bean sprouts and cook for a further minute. Don't let the snow peas or bean sprouts overcook—it's nice to have a bit of crunch left to them.

Taste, and season with salt and black pepper. Sprinkle with chopped cilantro before serving.

Raised game pie

A homemade version of a traditional English raised pie, packed with delicious lean game, so not nearly as "evil" as a pork-only pie. This is good fun to make and looks and tastes fantastic, ideal for a late spring Sunday lunch when you might eat outside. Serve with baked potatoes, Piccalilli (see page 102), and a mustardy dressed green salad, or take it on a picnic. It's almost as easy to make two as one, so freeze another for a later time.

The hot-water crust is the oldest and easiest form of pastry to make. It never shrinks and is very tolerant of being baked at a range of temperatures (anywhere between 325 and 400 degrees). It only goes wrong if the pastry is left to go cold before it is rolled into pies. Once cold, it's solid and unworkable. This pastry recipe was given to me by Brian Turner, the development chef for the National Trust, who I worked with at the Sissinghurst Castle restaurant.

Serves 8 to 10

For the pastry
* 2 ½ cups unbleached flour
* ½ teaspoon salt
* 7 tablespoons lard or shortening

* ½ pound lean ground pork
* ½ pound bacon or pancetta, roughly chopped
* ¾ pound pheasant breast, diced into bite-sized pieces (chicken breast, squab, and rabbit meat could be used instead)
* ½ cup dried apricots, roughly chopped
* ½ cup dried cranberries
* 1 onion (about ¼ pound), grated
* 1 teaspoon ground mace
* 2–3 teaspoons flaky sea salt
* Black pepper
* 1 egg, beaten, to glaze
* 1 ¼ cups cold chicken stock
* Large bunch of flat-leaf parsley, finely chopped
* 2 teaspoons powdered gelatin

Preheat the oven to 350 degrees. Lightly grease a 9 ½ x 5 ½-inch loaf pan, even if it's nonstick.

First make the pastry. Sift the flour and salt into a bowl. Heat the lard or shortening and ⅔ cup water in a saucepan.

Once the lard or shortening has melted, bring to a boil. Pour the mixture onto the flour and stir with a wooden spoon to form a soft dough. When cool enough to handle, turn onto a floured surface and knead until smooth. If the pastry is not to be used immediately, cover with plastic wrap or a damp kitchen towel and keep warm until ready to use.

Break off a quarter of the dough and set aside for the lid. Roll out the remaining pastry to a thickness of about ⅛ inch (I think it's best when thin) and use to line the prepared pan. You'll need to use your fingers to work the pastry up the sides until there is an ⅛-inch collar standing proud of the pan.

Put all the meat, fruit, onion, mace, and salt into a bowl, mix well, and season with a good grinding of black pepper. Spoon the mixture into the lined pan.

Roll out the remaining pastry to cover the top. Lay it over the pan and pinch the edges together with the collar. Cut a small hole the size of a penny in the middle of the pie and bake for 1 hour. Brush with the beaten egg and return to the oven for 10 to 15 minutes, or until the pastry looks well browned. Take the pie out of the oven and allow to cool for 30 minutes.

Put the chicken stock in a saucepan with the flat-leaf parsley and sprinkle the gelatin on the surface. Whisk to incorporate. Heat slowly until the gelatin has dissolved.

Slowly pour the stock mixture through the hole in the top of the pie—as much as it will take. It sinks in slowly, so leave it for a few minutes and then repeat a couple of times. You might have some stock mixture left over.

Chill the pie until firm, preferably overnight, before turning out of the pan.

Ham in hay with parsley sauce

A traditional Luxembourg dish, this is an excellent thing to cook for a party when you're feeding lots of people. The hay keeps the meat really succulent and gives it a distinctive sweet, grassy taste. Serve it simply with new carrots, minty potatoes, and plenty of parsley sauce. To give it a bit of zip, I add a chili and lots of freshly ground black pepper to the sauce. The ham is also delicious cold.

If you like, you can decrease the meat weight suggested and make the recipe to serve 4, using a 3-pound leg of ham and one bottle of apple juice, but still with plenty of hay.

Serves 10 to 12

* **7-pound (boned weight) lightly smoked shoulder of ham, boned and rolled**
* **2 quarts apple juice**
* **4 bay leaves**
* **A few black peppercorns**
* **1 large bag of hay (timothy hay is sold as rabbit feed at pet stores)**

For the parsley sauce
* **6 ⅓ cups milk**
* **1 large onion, stuck with a few cloves**
* **A few black peppercorns**
* **3 bay leaves**
* **8 tablespoons (1 stick) butter**
* **¾ cup flour**
* **1–2 red chilis, deseeded and finely chopped**
* **Large bunch of curly or flat-leaf parsley, stems removed, finely chopped**
* **Salt and black pepper**

Soak the ham in water (in the fridge) overnight.

Preheat the oven to 350 degrees. Discard the water that the ham has been soaking in. Choose a casserole that snugly fits your ham. If you don't have one big enough, use a large saucepan (with a lid), or, as a last resort, a roasting pan tightly covered with foil.

Put the apple juice, bay leaves, and peppercorns in the bottom of your casserole. Spread a good base of hay over this and sit the joint on top. Pack more hay all around the ham and right over it. Fill the casserole with more apple juice or water, covering the ham.

Cover and put in the oven for 20 to 25 minutes per pound (so about 2–2½ hours for the ham size suggested). Check every so often and top up with more apple juice or water if needed. It must not boil dry.

Remove from the oven and allow to rest for 20 minutes before carving.

To make the sauce, put the milk in a pan with the clove-studded onion, peppercorns, and bay leaves. Bring to a boil, then strain and put to one side.

In a separate pan, melt the butter and stir or whisk in the flour, allowing it to cook for a couple of minutes. Gradually stir or whisk in the strained hot milk. Add the chilis and parsley, stirring continuously, and cook for 5 minutes over a low heat. Season with salt and lots of black pepper. Serve the ham with the sauce.

Spicy pork ribs

A good-value dish to cook for a large crowd of people when you want eat-with-your-fingers sort of food. These ribs are cheap, but when made with slow-reared, high-quality pork, they are smoky, sweet, juicy, and delicious. If you're sitting down to eat, serve with Persian jewelled rice and a green salad or vegetable stir-fry (see pages 67 and 41). If you're not having plates, serve with good bread and a great plate of crudités with anchovy mayonnaise (see page 117).

The photograph opposite shows a double quantity.

Serves 4 to 6
* 2 tablespoons dark brown sugar
* 3 tablespoons light or dark soy sauce
* 2 tablespoons red wine vinegar
* 2 tablespoons extra virgin olive oil
* ¼ cup honey
* 2 ½-inch piece of fresh ginger, peeled and grated
* 1 red chili, deseeded and finely chopped
* 2 garlic cloves, crushed
* Salt and black pepper
* 8–10 large pork spare ribs (2 ¼ pounds total weight)

Put everything except the ribs in a bowl and mix well. Add the ribs, ensuring they are coated in the marinade. Cover and marinate in the fridge for at least 4 to 5 hours.

Preheat the oven to 350 degrees. Line a roasting pan with foil.

Transfer the ribs and their marinade to the prepared pan (the foil is needed because the marinade really blackens it) and cook in the oven for 45 minutes, until beginning to char. Turn regularly and baste with the marinade throughout the cooking time.

Pork meatballs with kale

These are the lightest, softest, and most delicious meatballs I've had. Add lovage if you can find it, or celery tops, for crucial flavor. Serve in a tomato sauce on a bed of wilted kale or chard chopped into fine ribbons so it's easy to eat. You can also serve them with noodles—glass ones are nice and crunchy.

Serves 6 to 8
* 1 pound lean ground pork
* ¼ pound bacon, finely chopped
* ¼ cup grated Parmesan cheese
* 2 cups fresh breadcrumbs
* 2 large eggs, beaten
* Small bunch of fresh lovage or celery leaves, chopped
* Small bunch of flat-leaf parsley, chopped
* Salt and black pepper
* Olive oil, for frying
* 1 quantity Rich tomato sauce (see page 277), to serve
* Kale leaves, to serve

Mix all the meatball ingredients together, season well, and chill for an hour or so in the fridge.

Shape the mixture into walnut-sized balls and fry in hot olive oil for 7 to 8 minutes, until nicely browned on all sides. (The uncooked meatballs also freeze well for future use.)

When all the meatballs are cooked, heat them up again in the tomato sauce.

Meanwhile, de-stem and finely slice the kale, and steam for about 2 to 3 minutes, until tender but not soggy.

Serve the meatballs and tomato sauce on a bed of kale leaves.

Pork rogan josh

A fresh and fragrant casserole with the clean spring flavors of cilantro and coriander, this is very quick to prepare, and is then slowly cooked. It's the ideal thing to shove into the oven on a low heat before going out for a good walk. Serve with plain basmati rice or Fava bean pilaf (see page 174) and a dollop of plain yogurt.

Serves 6
* 1 tablespoon olive oil
* 2 medium red onions, finely chopped or coarsely grated
* 2 bay leaves
* 1 teaspoon chili powder
* 1 tablespoon ground coriander
* 1 teaspoon coriander seeds, coarsely ground
* 2 teaspoons ground cumin
* 1 teaspoon ground cardamom, or ground seeds from 5 pods
* ½ teaspoon ground cloves
* 1 teaspoon ground turmeric
* 1 tablespoon peeled and grated fresh ginger, or 1 teaspoon ground ginger
* 1 teaspoon brown sugar
* 3 garlic cloves, crushed
* 1 (14½-ounce) can of chopped tomatoes
* Salt and black pepper
* 2 pounds boned leg or shoulder or fillet of pork, cut into cubes

To serve
* ¼ cup slivered almonds, toasted
* Small bunch of fresh cilantro, roughly chopped
* Grated zest of 1 lime

Preheat the oven to 325 degrees, or cook on the stovetop if you prefer.

Heat the olive oil in a large flameproof casserole or heavy-based saucepan, add the onions, and gently sauté, stirring for 5 minutes, until soft. Mix in all the other ingredients, apart from the pork. Add 1⅔ cups water and simmer gently for 10 minutes.

Put in the pork and stir to combine. Cover with a lid and cook in the oven or over a low heat for 1 to 1½ hours, or until the pork is tender. Stir every now and again to prevent sticking. Remove the lid for the last 15 minutes of cooking so that the sauce thickens. Taste and adjust the seasoning.

When ready to serve, sprinkle the slivered almonds, chopped cilantro, and lime zest over the top.

Liver and bacon with clove and onion marmalade

I love very finely cut and briefly cooked calves' liver. Serve it with mashed potatoes or Potato cakes cooked in olive oil (see page 61), some Sage leaf tempura (see page 69), and a dollop of clove and onion marmalade.

With the marmalade, you add red wine gradually, waiting after each addition to let the liquid reduce right down. This is also delicious on pasta with plenty of grated Parmesan. You can make it a day or two beforehand and store it in a jar or bowl in the fridge.

Serves 6

For the marmalade
* 1½ pounds white onions, thinly sliced
* 2 garlic cloves, finely chopped
* 10 cloves
* 3 tablespoons olive oil
* ¾ cup red wine
* Small bunch of flat-leaf parsley, chopped
* 3 tablespoons unsalted butter
* Salt and black pepper

* 12 slices of bacon
* 1 pound calves' liver, thinly sliced (3 slices per person)
* Olive oil, for brushing
* Salt and pepper
* Rosemary, sage, and thyme salt (see page 103), to serve

First make the marmalade. Put the onions, garlic, cloves, and olive oil in a heavy-based pan over a very low heat. Cover the mixture with a circle of parchment paper cut to fit inside your pan. This will keep the moisture in and allow the onions to cook until they are translucent and soft (about 20 minutes).

Once the onions are cooked, start to add the red wine, bit by bit, cooking more briskly until the liquid has evaporated. Remove the cloves, then add the parsley and butter. Season with salt and plenty of freshly ground black pepper. Set aside and keep warm.

Preheat the oven to 350 degrees. Heat a ridged grill pan for 3 to 4 minutes (until you can't count to 10 with your hand hovering just above it).

Put the bacon in a roasting pan and cook in the oven until crispy, but not burnt (12–15 minutes).

Brush the slices of liver with olive oil, season with salt and pepper, and grill for 40 seconds on each side. This will leave them just pink in the middle.

Serve immediately scattered with Rosemary, sage and thyme salt, putting the bacon and a dollop of marmalade on the side. (Offal is not a muscle, so does not need to rest.)

Mixed grill with potato cakes

If you have lots of carnivorous people staying over and brunch seems an option, a big plate of delicious, herby, grilled meat—kidneys, lamb chops, really good sausages, and bacon—is the ideal thing. You could add liver to the mixture if you want.

Serves 6
* 12 slices of bacon (about ¾ pound)
* 6 tomatoes, halved horizontally
* Olive oil, for frying
* 2 sprigs of thyme
* 2 sprigs of rosemary
* 2–3 bay leaves
* 12 small pork sausages (about 1⅓ pounds)
* 6–8 lamb chops or cutlets (about 1¾ pounds)
* 12 lambs' kidneys (about 1⅓ pounds), halved and membranes removed

For the potato cakes
* 2¼ pounds starchy potatoes, peeled
* Salt and black pepper
* 3 tablespoons butter (optional)
* Flour, for dusting
* Olive oil, for frying

Preheat the oven to 350 degrees.

Put the bacon and tomatoes in a roasting pan and cook in the oven until the bacon is crispy but not burnt (12 to 15 minutes).

To make the potato cakes, cook the potatoes in boiling salted water. Drain and mash, adding some seasoning and the butter, then set aside to cool (this makes the cakes stay together better). Shape the mashed potatoes into palm-sized cakes about 1 inch thick. Roll in flour and fry in hot olive oil in a nonstick pan for 5 minutes on each side, turning once.

Put the olive oil and herbs in a large frying pan and heat together for 2 minutes. Add the sausages and cook for 2 minutes. Add the lamb chops and cook for 2 minutes. Turn over the lamb and sausages and cook for another 2 minutes. Finally, add the kidneys and cook for 2 minutes on each side.

Put the food onto a large warmed platter in the center of the table so that people can help themselves.

Oxtail stew

Robust, warming, and rich, this stew has had a renaissance in the last couple of years, and is a must during the colder months of spring. Ask the butcher for the large, meaty chunks of oxtail, not the smaller bony bits at the end of the tail. Serve with mashed potatoes.

Serves 6 to 8
* 3 tablespoons olive oil
* 7 ounces smoked or regular bacon, chopped
* 3 pounds oxtail, cut into chunks
* 2 red onions, finely chopped
* 3 garlic cloves, roughly chopped
* 4 sticks of celery, thinly sliced
* 3 carrots, finely chopped
* 2 teaspoons flour
* 2 sprigs of rosemary
* 2 bay leaves
* 1 sprig of thyme
* 2 cups vegetable or beef stock
* 3 cups full-bodied red wine
* 1 tablespoon tomato puree
* 1 tablespoon Worcestershire sauce
* 1 orange or yellow bell pepper, halved, deseeded, and sliced
* 1 red bell pepper, halved, deseeded, and sliced
* 1 tablespoon peeled and grated fresh ginger
* Salt and black pepper

Preheat the oven to 325 degrees.

Heat the oil in a large ovenproof casserole. Add the bacon and oxtail and sauté until browned. Using a slotted spoon, transfer to a bowl, and set aside.

Put the onions, garlic, celery, and carrots in the casserole and sauté for 5 minutes, adding a little extra olive oil if necessary.

Return the meat to the casserole, add the flour, and stir well. Add the herbs, stock, wine, tomato puree, and Worcestershire sauce and bring to a boil.

Put the lid on the casserole and place in the middle of the oven for 2 hours. Check that the stew does not dry out during the cooking time, adding a little extra water if necessary.

Add the peppers and ginger and cook for a further 30 minutes. Season to taste with salt and pepper. Discard the herb stalks before serving.

Five-hour leg of lamb

This lamb dish is my favorite thing to cook for an Easter lunch. You can put it in the oven at breakfast-time and it will be perfect by lunch. Last time I served it with hummus-stuffed peppers and Cumin chunky fries (see page 70).

Serves 8
* 1 leg of lamb, about 5–5 ½ pounds
* 3 carrots
* 2 onions
* 3 leeks
* 4 garlic cloves

For the marinade
* 1 (750-ml) bottle of dry white wine
* 5 garlic cloves, finely chopped
* 2 tablespoons cumin seeds, toasted and coarsely ground
* 2 tablespoons coriander seeds, toasted and coarsely ground
* 5 tablespoons olive oil
* Salt and black pepper

For the gravy
* 1 tablespoon unbleached flour
* 2 cups vegetable or meat stock
* Salt and black pepper
* ½ cup port or red wine
* 2 tablespoons red currant jelly

Put the meat in a very large plastic bag with all the marinade ingredients. Toss it well. Put the whole thing into a bucket and place somewhere cool for 24 to 48 hours. Remember to turn it regularly so that the meat is fully coated in the marinade.

Five hours before you want to eat, preheat the oven to 300 degrees.

Peel and coarsely chop the vegetables but leave the garlic whole. Place in a large roasting pan. Empty the contents of the plastic bag onto the vegetables, turning the bag inside out to add the seeds to the pan.

Roast for 4 ½ hours. Transfer the meat to a warm serving plate, cover in foil and kitchen towels, and leave to rest for 30 minutes. Discard the cooked vegetables.

To make the gravy, spoon off and discard most of the fat in the roasting pan. Scrape the bits off the bottom and mix into the remaining juices. Put the pan over a medium heat, add the flour, and mix with a wooden spoon while cooking it for 1 to 2 minutes.

Meanwhile, heat the stock and add to the pan little by little, stirring all the time, until you have a smooth gravy. Check the seasoning and add the port and red currant jelly. Allow to bubble and simmer for 5 minutes.

Pour the gravy into a pitcher and serve with the lamb, which will be falling off the bone and won't need to be carved. You can just pull it apart.

Slow-cooked shoulder of lamb with rosemary and onion sauce

Rich and delicious, this slow-cooked meat is good served in two ways: either the old-fashioned British way, with crunchy roast potatoes and plenty of onion sauce, or Armenian-style, with Chickpeas in tahini dressing (see page 71). I went to university in Edinburgh, where friends and I occasionally ate at an extraordinary Armenian restaurant. We were usually served this strong-flavored, sustaining, and fragrant dish—and I loved it.

Serves 4 to 6
* 6 garlic cloves
* 5 sprigs of fresh rosemary (or 2 tablespoons cumin seeds and 1 tablespoon coriander seeds, crushed)
* 10 bay leaves
* 1 (4 ½–5 pound) shoulder of lamb, bone in
* Salt and black pepper
* 1 cup red wine

For the rosemary and onion sauce
* 3 tablespoons butter
* 1 onion (about ½ pound), thinly sliced
* 2 tablespoons flour
* 2 cups milk
* 2 tablespoons cream or crème fraîche
* 1 tablespoon finely chopped fresh rosemary

Preheat the oven to 325 degrees.

Don't bother to peel the garlic cloves: just give them a gentle bash with a rolling pin and place in the bottom of a large roasting pan with the rosemary and bay leaves. Sit the lamb on top and sprinkle with a little salt and pepper. (If doing the Armenian version, add the cumin and coriander seeds rather than the rosemary.) Roast in the oven for 2 hours, then pour in the wine. Roast for 1 more hour.

To make the sauce, put the butter into a saucepan and melt over a low heat. Add the onion and sauté until soft but not brown. Stir in the flour, then gradually add the milk, stirring or whisking to prevent lumps. Cook on a low heat for 5 minutes, stirring or whisking all the time. Add the cream and rosemary and cook for a further 5 minutes, again stirring all the time to prevent the sauce from sticking or burning. If necessary, add a little extra milk; the sauce should not be too thick. Season with salt and pepper.

Take the lamb out of the oven and transfer to a warm plate. The meat should be falling off the bone. Cover in foil while you make the gravy.

Discard the rosemary, bay leaves, and garlic left in the bottom of the roasting pan and spoon off and chuck all the fat. Put the pan over a medium heat, add a little water (or vegetable water), and bring to a boil, stirring to make a gravy.

Arrange the lamb meat in chunks on a serving plate, pour over the gravy, and serve with the rosemary and onion sauce.

Hugh's shepherd's pie

A recipe from my husband, Adam's, American pub-lisher Hugh Van Dusen, who is an excellent cook, this is a classic, old-fashioned shepherd's pie. It's a brilliant way of using up leftover lamb, nicer with small chunks of meat rather than ground.

Serves 8 to 10
* 2 ¼ pounds leftover lamb, or fresh lamb leg, cut into stewing meat size (the leg meat will need more stewing than leftover lamb)
* 2 thin leeks, thinly sliced
* 2 carrots, peeled and thinly sliced
* 3 garlic cloves, finely chopped
* 2 onions (⅓ pound), coarsely chopped
* Bunch of fresh thyme
* 2 tablespoons tomato puree
* 1 (14 ½-ounce) can of chopped tomatoes
* 1 ¾ cups beef consommé
* ½ cup red wine
* 1 tablespoon flour
* 1–2 tablespoons Worcestershire sauce, to taste

For the topping
* 2 ¾ pounds potatoes, peeled and quartered
* 2 leeks, thinly sliced
* 2 tablespoons olive oil, for sautéing
* 8 ounces sour cream
* ¼ pound Parmesan cheese, grated
* Salt and black pepper

Put all the pie ingredients into a large saucepan and bring to a boil uncovered. Simmer gently for 30 minutes to make a thick, rich sauce. Discard the thyme stalks. Pour into a large, deep pie dish (about 8 by 12 inches).

Cook the potatoes in boiling salted water. Meanwhile, sauté the leeks in the oil until limp. Preheat the oven to 350 degrees.

Drain the potatoes. Mash well and add all the other topping ingredients, including the sautéed leeks. Mix well. Spoon over the top of the lamb in the pie dish. Cook in the oven for 30 minutes.

Lamb rissoles

Another good way of using up cooked lamb. These rissoles are delicious served with still-firm, bay-flavored cauliflower and Leek, celery root, and potato gratin (see page 398). Alternatively, serve them with a Rich tomato sauce (see page 277) and rice.

For 12 rissoles (serves 6 people)
* 1 pound cooked lamb (½ small leg works well), cut into chunks
* 1 onion
* 1 ⅔ cups fresh breadcrumbs
* 2 tablespoons flat-leaf parsley, chopped, and a little more to serve
* 2 tablespoons chopped fresh rosemary
* 2 garlic cloves, crushed
* 1 egg, beaten
* Salt and black pepper
* Seasoned flour, for shaping
* Olive oil, for frying

Finely mince the lamb and onion in a food processor. Place in a mixing bowl and add the breadcrumbs, herbs, garlic, and egg. Season generously with salt (3 good pinches) and pepper.

Divide the mixture into 12 portions and shape into fat sausage shapes. Coat each one lightly with the seasoned flour. All this can be done in advance, and the rissoles can be covered and chilled in the fridge.

When you are ready to cook, heat just enough oil to cover the bottom of a frying pan. When hot, fry the rissoles for 4 to 5 minutes on each side. Add more oil as necessary—they tend to soak it up a little.

If serving with tomato sauce, pour the sauce into the pan with the rissoles and heat them together gently for about 5 minutes.

Scatter with parsley before serving.

Persian jeweled rice

The textures, color, and flavor of this rice make it an almost stand-alone dish. Where in summer and autumn I cook Fava bean pilaf (see page 174), in the winter and spring I cook this—one of my favorite things to eat with any strong-flavored fish or meat. It's perfect with Duck curry (see page 51). You can also replace the rice with bulgur wheat, and add pomegranate seeds or pink grapefruit segments. For decoration, add some primroses, pansies, or violets on top—all edible flowers.

Serves 4 to 6
* 1/3 cup dried cranberries
* 1/2 cup raisins, or a mixture of red and golden raisins with chopped dried apricots
* 1 1/4 cups basmati rice
* 2 tablespoons olive oil
* 1 small onion, finely chopped
* 1 cinnamon stick
* 1 teaspoon cardamom pods, toasted
* 1 teaspoon coriander seeds, toasted
* 2 1/2 cups hot chicken stock
* 1/3 cup pistachios, toasted
* Salt and black pepper

Put the cranberries and raisins into a bowl and pour over enough boiling water to cover. Soak for 20 minutes, then drain well.

Wash the basmati rice in several changes of cold water, until the water is no longer cloudy. Drain well.

Put the olive oil into a pan and heat gently. Add the onion and sauté until soft. Add the rice, cinnamon stick, cardamom, and coriander, stirring well to ensure all the grains get coated in the oil.

Pour in the stock, bring to a boil, then turn down the heat and cook with the lid on for 15 to 20 minutes, until all the liquid has evaporated. Take off the heat and stir in the cranberries, raisins, and pistachios. Taste, and season with salt and black pepper. Serve hot or cold.

Juliet's fava beans in parsley sauce

Here's a lovely old-fashioned dish that my sister-in-law Juliet often serves with roast lamb or beef. It's also delicious with ham.

Serves 8

For the sauce
* 4 1/4 cups milk
* 1 onion, studded with a few cloves
* A few black peppercorns
* 2 bay leaves
* 6 tablespoons butter
* 2/3 cup flour
* Large bunch of curly or flat-leaf parsley, stems removed, finely chopped
* Salt and black pepper

* 2 1/4 pounds fava beans, podded weight (frozen baby beans are fine)

Put the milk, onion, peppercorns, and bay leaves in a saucepan and bring to a boil. Strain over a large bowl. Discard the onion, peppercorns, and bay leaves.

In a separate pan, melt the butter and stir in the flour, allowing it to cook for a couple of minutes. Gradually add the strained hot milk, whisking or stirring as you do so. Cook for another 5 minutes. Add the parsley, stirring continuously. Season with plenty of salt and pepper.

Cook the beans in salted water for 2 to 3 minutes, until soft. Strain and mix with the sauce.

Sage leaf tempura

Sage leaves are ideal for tempura as the batter sticks well to their furry texture. Leave the stems on so that you have something to hold while eating them. This recipe appears in my previous cookbook, *In Season: Cooking with Vegetables and Fruits*, but as the leaves are excellent with calves' liver (see page 59), I have also included it here. Try them served with Oxtail stew too (see page 61).

Serves 8 as a snack or a side dish
* 1½ cups unbleached flour
* Maldon or other flaky sea salt and black pepper
* 2 eggs
* 1½ cups ice-cold sparkling water or cold beer
* Peanut oil, for frying
* 30–40 sage leaves, depending on size and variety

Sift the flour into a bowl with plenty of salt and pepper and make a crater in the center. Add the eggs and mix with a balloon whisk. Now whisk in the water or beer to make a not-too-smooth batter. It should be the thickness of heavy cream.

Cover with plastic wrap and keep in the fridge until you need it. The coldness of the batter hitting the hot oil gives a lighter, airier texture to the tempura leaves.

Fill a deep saucepan with enough oil to reach about one-third of the way up the side, and have a lid or splash-guard on standby to prevent the oil from spitting too much after you add each batch of leaves. Heat the oil until it reaches about 375 degrees, or until a cube of bread browns in 30 seconds.

Dip the herb leaves into the cold batter and then lower into the hot oil. Cook until pale gold and crisp. Fish them out with tongs and drain on paper towels. The leaves are at their best eaten hot with a sprinkling of sea salt and ground black pepper.

Parsnip and sweet potato chips

Sprinkled with herb salt (see page 103), these chips are good served as canapés for a small party, but don't take on frying too many. They are also a tasty addition to a bowl of soup or on top of a salad, or you can eat them with a roast pheasant or chicken.

Serves 15 to 20
* Vegetable oil, for deep-frying
* 1 pound medium-sized parsnips, thinly sliced lengthwise (use a vegetable peeler or mandoline), core flesh discarded
* ²/₃ pound medium-sized sweet potatoes, thinly sliced lengthwise (use a vegetable peeler or mandoline)
* Salt

Fill a deep saucepan with enough oil to reach about one-third of the way up the side, and have a lid or splash-guard on standby to prevent the oil from spitting too much after you add each batch of vegetable slices. Heat the oil until it reaches about 375 degrees, or until a cube of bread browns in 30 seconds. Line a bowl with paper towels.

Deep-fry the parsnip and sweet potato slices (no more than 10 to 15 at a time) until golden brown (about 2 minutes). Keep a continual eye on them as they burn easily.

Remove with a slotted spoon and drain in the prepared bowl. Sprinkle with salt.

The parsnips crisp up as they cool. The sweet potatoes are less crunchy, but still delicious.

Cumin chunky fries

Baked rather than deep-fried, these fries taste just as good, but are better for you. They are ideal with fishcakes and your own homemade tomato sauce (see page 277), and I love them with the slow-roast lamb on page 64 or roast chicken. In fact, I make them all the time. You need to use baking potatoes to guarantee fries that are wonderfully crunchy outside and soft within.

Serves 8
* 4 ½ pounds medium-sized baking potatoes, peeled
* Olive oil (amount depends on the size of your baking pan)
* 2 tablespoons cumin seeds, or finely chopped garlic, or a sprinkle of cayenne pepper, or 1 tablespoon finely chopped sage or rosemary
* 2 heaping teaspoons ground cumin
* Salt and black pepper

Preheat the oven to 400 degrees.

Cut the potatoes lengthwise into chunky chips (about 6 per potato). Parboil for 7 to 8 minutes in boiling salted water, until just soft when pierced with the tip of a sharp knife. Drain and dry for a few minutes in a colander, then shake to rough them up a bit. Set aside until you're ready to cook them.

Just cover the bottom of a baking pan with olive oil and place in the oven. After 5 minutes, add the potatoes and cumin seeds (or other flavorings), the ground cumin, salt and pepper, and a little more olive oil. Move the potatoes around in the oil so that they're well coated, and roast for 20 to 30 minutes, turning occasionally until the fries are nicely golden brown and crispy.

Potato bonne femme

I really enjoy a potato dauphinoise, but it's so rich and bad for the waistline, you perhaps don't want to eat it too often. Yet layered potatoes are the ideal things to serve with roast meat or casseroles. You can shove them in the oven at the same time and forget about them. This lighter version, with the potatoes cooked in stock and wine, is an excellent substitute for the creamy one. It has a crispy top, with meltingly soft potato underneath. The key to the success of this bake is not to have the potato slices too thick as that tends to make them get starchy.

Serves 4
* 6 tablespoons butter
* 1 tablespoon extra virgin olive oil
* 4 garlic cloves, thinly sliced
* 1 teaspoon dried thyme or 1 tablespoon fresh thyme leaves
* 1 tablespoon Dijon mustard
* 1 ½ pounds potatoes
* ½ cup vegetable or chicken stock
* ¼ cup white wine
* Salt and black pepper

Preheat the oven to 375 degrees.

Melt the butter in a 10-inch ovenproof pan over a medium heat, add the olive oil and garlic, and cook for 4 to 5 minutes. Stir in the thyme and mustard, then turn off the heat.

Cut the potatoes into very fine slices (a mandoline is best for this). Put them immediately into the butter mixture and stir thoroughly to prevent them from discoloring. Stir in the stock and wine and season with salt and pepper.

Place the pan in the middle of the oven and bake for 45 minutes to an hour, until the top is golden brown and the edges are crispy. Serve immediately.

Spicy cauliflower

Lovely spring cauliflower is used in this tasty one-pot dish. It's great with roast lamb or pork, and leftovers can be pureed to make the basis of a delicious soup—just add stock to thin it out. Add a pinch of chili flakes if you like things spicy.

Serves 6 to 8
* 2 tablespoons olive oil
* 1 tablespoon fennel seeds
* 1 tablespoon cumin seeds
* 1 teaspoon ground cumin
* 1 teaspoon garam masala
* 2 red onions, roughly chopped
* 1 large red bell pepper, deseeded and roughly chopped
* 1 cauliflower (about 1½ pounds), divided into large florets
* 2 (14½-ounce) cans of chopped tomatoes
* Grated zest of 1 lemon
* Salt and black pepper
* Small bunch of fresh cilantro, roughly chopped
* 2 tablespoons pumpkin seeds or cashews, toasted

Heat the oil in a heavy-based pan or ovenproof casserole dish. Add the seeds and spices and cook for 1 minute, stirring. Add the onions and bell pepper and cook over a medium heat for 3 to 4 minutes.

Stir in the cauliflower, tomatoes, and lemon zest. Bring to a boil, then cover and simmer as gently as possible for 20 minutes, or until the cauliflower is just tender. Stir now and again.

Taste, and season with salt and pepper. Serve sprinkled with the fresh cilantro and seeds or nuts.

Warm chickpeas with tahini dressing

I love the mixture of flavors and textures in this dish—chickpeas, plenty of cumin seeds, tahini, and parsley. Eat it with any beef, lamb, or game.

Serves 4
* 1 cup dried chickpeas, soaked overnight in cold water, or 1 (15-ounce) can of chickpeas, drained
* 2 bay leaves
* Pinch of salt
* Sprig of fresh thyme
* 2 onions, finely chopped
* 2 garlic cloves, finely chopped
* Olive oil, for frying
* Pinch of chili flakes
* 1 tablespoon cumin seeds, toasted and lightly crushed to a powder
* Large bunch of cilantro, roughly chopped
* Large bunch of flat-leaf parsley, roughly chopped
* Juice and grated zest of 1 lemon (optional)

For the dressing
* ¼ cup plain yogurt
* Juice and grated zest of 1 lemon
* 2 teaspoons tahini paste
* Flaky sea salt and black pepper

Drain the soaked chickpeas and place in a saucepan with the bay leaves, salt, and thyme. Cover well with fresh water and bring to a boil. Put the lid on and simmer for about ¾ hour, or until tender but still intact. Check from time to time that there is enough water, and top up if necessary. Remove the herbs and drain the chickpeas. Place in a large bowl and keep warm. Alternatively, you can skip this stage and use canned chickpeas, but the texture is not as good.

Fry the onions and garlic in a little olive oil until soft (about 5 minutes). Stir in the chickpeas, chili flakes, and crushed cumin seeds, and cook for another 5 minutes. Stir in the cilantro, parsley, and lemon juice and zest, if using.

To make the dressing, put the yogurt, lemon juice and zest, the tahini, and ½ tablespoon water into a small bowl and whisk with a fork. Season to taste.

Pour the dressing over the chickpea mixture while still warm and stir together. Season well.

Coffee mousse

When the weather is cooler, there's nothing better than a really intense coffee mousse—a cappuccino in a pudding. Serve in small bowls or coffee cups, with thin Walnut cookies on the side (see page 98) or chocolate-dipped walnuts. It sounds strange, but a wok is very handy for this recipe—its curved sides make the whisking process easier.

Serves 6 to 8
* ¼ cup strong ground coffee
* 2 teaspoons gelatin
* 6 egg yolks
* ⅔ cup superfine sugar
* ½ cup heavy cream

Put the coffee in a french coffee press and add 1¼ cups boiling water. Allow to brew for a few minutes, then plunge and pour the coffee into a cup to cool.

Put the gelatin in a bowl, just cover with cold water, and leave to soften.

Put the egg yolks and sugar into a large bowl and whisk until the mixture becomes pale and frothy and thickens slightly. Whisk in the coffee a little at a time. (A handheld electric whisk is best for this process.)

Pour the mixture into a large, heavy-based saucepan or wok, place over a very low heat, and keep whisking until the mixture thickens. Take off the heat and, whisking all the while, add the softened gelatin; it should dissolve easily. Continue whisking until the mixture becomes lukewarm, then leave to cool completely.

Whip the cream until thick and fold into the cooled coffee mixture. Spoon into coffee cups or small bowls and put in the fridge for at least 1 hour to set.

Bay leaf ice cream

The first time I went to De Kas in Amsterdam, now one of my favorite restaurants, I discovered their fantastic basil ice cream—the recipe is in my cookbook *In Season: Cooking with Vegetables and Fruits*. Last spring I went again and had this version, which uses bay as a cold-season alternative to basil. This is a mild-flavored ice cream, perfect with any fruit, fresh or cooked.

Serves 4 to 6
* Handful of fresh bay leaves (about 18–20), preferably very young and still juicy, cleaned and patted dry
* 1 cup sugar
* 8 egg yolks
* 2 cups whole milk
* Juice and finely grated zest of 1 lemon

Blanch the bay leaves in a saucepan of boiling water for 5 minutes. Drain and dry, then place in a food processor with the sugar and mix until very fine. Spoon into a bowl, add the egg yolks, and whisk well.

Put the milk into a saucepan over a very low heat and add the egg and bay leaf mixture, stirring constantly until it thickens enough to coat the back of a spoon. Do not let it boil.

Add the lemon zest, then pour the mixture into an ice cream maker if you have one. Freeze/churn for about 20 minutes, then pack into a plastic container and freeze for 2 hours.

If you don't have an ice cream maker, place the mixture in a shallow container and freeze until half-frozen (about 1 hour). Remove and fork through, mixing the frozen edge into the middle to break up the ice crystals. Repeat twice.

Before serving, allow the ice cream to soften in the fridge for 15 minutes.

Lemon and passion fruit meringue pie

All the elements of this pie are wonderful: the cookie-like pastry base, the fruit curd in the middle, and the meringue top with crunchy coconut bits. Serve it anytime when the weather perks up; it will make you feel that summer is on the way. If you like, decorate the pie with vibrant blue anchusa or borage flowers.

The lemon and passion fruit curd can be made in advance, and will keep in the fridge for 2 weeks.

Serves 8

For the pastry
* 1 cup (2 sticks) softened butter
* 1 cup confectioners' sugar
* 2 eggs, beaten
* 1 teaspoon vanilla extract
* 2 ½ cups unbleached flour
* Grated zest of 1 lemon

For the curd
* 12 passion fruits
* ½ cup (1 stick) unsalted butter
* 1 cup superfine sugar
* Juice and grated zest of 2 lemons
* 2 teaspoons vanilla extract
* 5 eggs, beaten

For the meringue
* 5 egg whites
* 1 ¼ cups superfine sugar
* ⅓ cup dried coconut (optional)

First make the pastry. Cream the butter and confectioners' sugar together until pale and fluffy. Gradually add the eggs and vanilla. Fold in the flour a bit at a time, then add the lemon zest and shape the dough into a ball. Wrap it in plastic wrap and chill for 30 minutes.

Preheat the oven to 350 degrees and heat a baking sheet until searing hot.

Roll out the pastry on a floured surface to a thickness of ⅛ inch and use to line a 9-inch loose-bottomed, high-sided tart pan, leaving the excess draped over the sides in case it shrinks. If any cracks develop as you put it into the tart pan, patch them up with spare pastry.

Prick the bottom of the pastry crust with a fork, line with parchment paper or foil, and weigh this down with baking beans or rice. Place on the hot baking sheet and bake for about 15 minutes. Remove from the oven and allow the crust to cool a little. Lower the temperature to 325 degrees and reheat the baking sheet.

Remove the baking beans and paper and bake the crust for another 10 minutes. Take out of the oven and trim off the excess pastry. Keep the oven on and the baking sheet hot.

Cut the passion fruits in half and scoop the pulp into a bowl. Set aside.

Put the butter and sugar in a heavy-based saucepan, place over a low heat, and stir until the sugar has dissolved (or nearly dissolved). Add the passion fruit pulp, lemon zest and juice, vanilla, and eggs. Stir until the mixture thickens. Allow to cool slightly. Pour into the crust and spread out evenly.

To make the meringue, whisk the egg whites until very stiff. Add the sugar a bit at a time and continue whisking until the whites are quite dry (but not quite as dry as with usual meringues). Fold in the coconut (if using) and spread the mixture over the curd filling. Place on the hot baking sheet and bake in the oven for 15 minutes, or until the meringue is golden. Allow to cool, then cut into small portions to serve—it is very intense and sweet.

Blood orange and grapefruit sorbet with limoncello

There is nothing better than a bowl or glass of sorbet doused with a slosh of lemon vodka at the end of a large and heavy meal. The sharp yet sweet coldness of this is perfect.

Serves 4 to 6
* **5 blood oranges**
* **¾ cup superfine sugar**
* **2 pink grapefruits**
* **Limoncello (see page 106), to serve**

Scrub and dry the oranges, then use a zester to remove the zest.

Put the sugar and ¾ cup water in a small saucepan over a low heat and stir until dissolved. Add half the orange zest and bring to a boil for 2 to 3 minutes. Allow to cool, then strain and reserve the liquid. Discard the cooked zest.

Squeeze the juice from all the oranges and grapefruits (there should be about 3⅓ cups of juice). Combine the juices with the cold syrup and the uncooked zest.

Pour the mixture into an ice cream machine and churn for 20 to 25 minutes. Pack into a plastic container and freeze for at least 2 hours before serving.

If you don't have a machine, pour the mixture into a plastic container and freeze for 1 hour. Remove and fork through, mixing the frozen edge into the middle to break up the ice crystals. Repeat twice. Before serving, allow the sorbet to soften in the fridge for 20 minutes.

To serve, put 2 scoops per person into a glass and pour a little limoncello over the top.

Rhubarb tart

A lovely tart with a fresh, sharp flavor, this always looks wonderful—the pink of the rhubarb against the gold of the saffron custard. It's ideal for any party or lunch around Easter, when rhubarb is usually at its best.

This recipe is also excellent with blackberries, black currants, or plums.

Serves 6

For the pastry
* 1 cup unbleached flour
* ¼ cup superfine sugar
* 5 tablespoons very cold unsalted butter, cut into chunks
* 1 egg yolk

* 3 eggs
* 1 cup heavy cream
* ¼ cup sugar
* Grated zest of 1 orange
* A few saffron strands
* ¾ pound rhubarb, cut into roughly 1-inch lengths
* ½ cup sliced almonds, toasted

First make the pastry. Sift the flour into a bowl and mix in the sugar. Rub in the butter until the mixture resembles breadcrumbs. Add the egg yolk and a little ice-cold water—just enough to bring the pastry together into a soft ball. Wrap in plastic wrap and chill in the fridge for 1 hour.

Preheat the oven to 375 degrees and heat a baking sheet until searing hot.

Roll out the pastry on a floured surface and use to line a loose-bottomed 9-inch tart pan, leaving the excess draped over the sides in case it shrinks.

Prick the bottom of the pastry crust with a fork, line with parchment paper or foil, and weigh this down with baking beans or rice. Place on the hot baking sheet and bake for about 15 minutes. Remove the baking beans and paper and bake the crust for another 10 minutes. Take out of the oven and trim off the excess pastry. Keep the oven on and reheat the baking sheet.

Lightly beat the eggs and mix them with the cream, sugar, orange zest, and saffron.

Arrange the rhubarb in circles inside the pastry crust. Pour the egg mixture all over it, then bake the tart on the hot sheet for 15 minutes. Lower the temperature to 350 degrees and bake for about another 10 minutes, until the filling is firm and beginning to color. Allow to cool a little, then scatter the toasted almonds over the top.

Rhubarb charlotte

I love any kind of charlotte, the crunchy buttery bread (or panettone) making a good contrast to the soft, ideally not too sweet, fruit inside. You can prepare it well in advance and warm it up (at 350 degrees)—just enough to heat through and crisp up the top—when you're ready to eat.

Serves 8
* 4 ½ pounds rhubarb, cut into roughly 1-inch lengths
* Grated zest and juice of 2 oranges
* ½ cup sugar, plus a little extra for sprinkling
* 1 good-quality, large white loaf, or 2-pound panettone, cut into slices 1 inch thick (don't be tempted to use cheap, white sliced bread)
* 14 tablespoons butter, melted
* Crème fraîche or Greek yogurt, to serve

Preheat the oven to 350 degrees.

Poach the rhubarb gently over a low heat in the orange juice and zest. When soft, add the sugar. Mash the fruit to break up any large pieces, but do not puree.

Cut the crusts off the bread and, with a pair of scissors, cut the slices into shapes that will completely cover the bottom and sides of the dish. Also cut some for the top and set aside.

Brush some of the melted butter over the bottom and sides of an 8 by 12-inch ovenproof dish. Sprinkle with a little sugar and shake the dish to distribute it evenly over the buttered surfaces. Brush both sides of the bread pieces with melted butter and lay them in the bottom and around the sides of the dish.

Spoon in the fruit mixture and cover with the remaining bread. Brush the top generously with melted butter.

Bake in the oven for at least 40 minutes, until the top is golden brown. Serve with crème fraîche or Greek yogurt.

Hot cross bun and butter pudding

The secret here is to go easy on the bread content. And it's important to use apricot jam—somehow no other flavor works as well. You can vary it by adding fruit: the pudding is excellent with cranberries, and I particularly like it with rhubarb in between the slices. This must be eaten straight out of the oven and is a recipe that you can easily double up when cooking for more people. See Hot cross bun recipe (page 90)

Serves 4 to 6
* 1 cup milk
* 1 cup heavy cream
* 1 vanilla pod, split open, or 2 teaspoons vanilla extract
* Pinch of salt
* 3 large eggs, beaten
* ½ cup superfine sugar
* 4 classic hot cross buns, each cut into 5 or 6 slices
* 2 tablespoons butter
* Small handful of golden raisins, soaked for 30 minutes in a little brandy (optional)
* 1 tablespoon apricot jam
* Confectioners' sugar

Put the milk, cream, vanilla pod or vanilla extract, and salt in a saucepan and bring slowly to a boil. Take off the heat, allow to cool slightly, then beat in the eggs and superfine sugar.

Butter an 8 by 12-inch pie dish. Butter the bun slices and arrange them in overlapping rows in the prepared dish. Sprinkle the raisins and alcohol (if using) over the slices. Remove the vanilla pod from the egg mixture and pour over the slices. Leave to rest for 30 minutes.

Preheat the oven to 350 degrees.

Put the pudding in a bain-marie and bake in the oven for 30 to 40 minutes. Remove, and spread the jam over the top. Return to the oven for 10 minutes or so to brown. Sift confectioners' sugar over the top before serving.

Pear and apple crumble

You can't go through spring without having several fruit crumbles. Make them with just apples, or add pears too, which produce much more sweet juice than apples. The topping is, of course, also delicious with rhubarb.

Serves 8
* 4 ½ pounds apples and pears (half and half), peeled and cored
* Grated zest and juice of 1 orange
* Freshly grated nutmeg
* 1 cinnamon stick or 1 teaspoon ground cinnamon
* ¼ to ⅓ cup sugar, depending on the sweetness of the fruit

For the crumble topping
* 1 cup unbleached flour
* 1½ cups roughly chopped hazelnuts, toasted
* ¼ cup rolled oats
* ½ teaspoon ground cinnamon
* ½ cup light brown sugar
* ⅓ cup dark brown sugar
* ½ cup (1 stick) cold unsalted butter, cut into chunks
* Cream or Greek yogurt, to serve

Preheat the oven to 325 degrees.

Slice the fruit and put into a shallow, 8 by 12-inch ovenproof dish. Sprinkle with the orange zest and pour over the juice. Scatter the spices and sugar all over.

To make the topping, put the flour, hazelnuts, oats, cinnamon, sugars, and butter into a food processor and pulse until the mixture resembles large breadcrumbs. Alternatively, rub in the butter by hand. This mixture can be kept in the fridge until you want it, or put straight over the prepared fruit. Bake in the oven for 30 minutes, until the topping is pale gold.

Crumble is much better served warm rather than hot, with lashings of cream or Greek yogurt.

Elderflower and milk gelatin

Unusual and easy to make in late spring or early summer, these gelatins are lovely with strawberry and rhubarb compote (see right), or just with a little honey drizzled over the top. If you can't find elderflowers, flavor the milk with lemon balm, mint, or rose petals.

Serves 4
* 2 cups whole milk
* 1 vanilla pod
* 6 heads of elderflowers
* 1 (¼-ounce) envelope gelatin
* 3 tablespoons honey
* Strawberry and rhubarb compote (see right), or 3 tablespoons honey, for topping

Put the milk into a saucepan. Slit open the vanilla pod and scrape the seeds into the milk. Add the pod too and gently bring to the simmering point. Take off the heat and allow to cool slightly, then add the elderflower heads. Leave to infuse until cooled—about 45 minutes.

Cover the gelatin with cold water and leave to soften for 10 minutes.

Strain the milk through a fine sieve, discarding the elderflowers and vanilla pod. Return the milk to a clean pan set over a low heat. Add the gelatin to the milk along with the honey. Whisk until the gelatin has dissolved.

Pour the mixture into 4 ramekins and chill for 3 hours, or until set. To serve, dip the ramekins in hot water for a couple of seconds, then turn out. Serve with fruit compote or drizzle with honey.

Yogurt panna cotta semifreddo with strawberry and rhubarb compote

Panna cotta, made with yogurt and cream, is a brilliantly easy dessert for any time from May until September, when the weather feels sunny and warm. This one is partially frozen and served with a pile of fruit compote. The compote can be made in advance and frozen until needed.

Serves 6
* 1 cup heavy cream
* ½ cup superfine sugar
* 1 teaspoon vanilla extract or 1 vanilla pod
* 2 teaspoons powdered gelatin
* 1½ cups Greek yogurt
* 2 ounces preserved ginger (or candied ginger), finely chopped

For the fruit compote
* ⅔ pound rhubarb
* Juice of ½ lemon
* Juice of 1 orange and grated zest of ½
* 2 tablespoons superfine sugar
* 7 ounces (1½ cups) strawberries (kept whole, so small ones are best)

Put the cream into a pan with the sugar and vanilla (if using a vanilla pod, split it open and scrape the seeds into the pan too). Bring gently to a boil, then turn off the heat and whisk in the gelatin until dissolved (about 2 to 3 minutes). Discard the vanilla pod.

Put the yogurt into a large mixing bowl and slowly pour in the cream mixture, whisking to combine. Stir in the ginger.

Spoon or pour into ramekins or small bowls lined with plastic wrap and allow to set in the fridge. Transfer to the freezer 1 hour before you want to serve them.

Cut the rhubarb into 1-inch pieces and put in a saucepan with the juice of the lemon and orange and the orange zest. Add the sugar and cook gently for 4 to 5 minutes. Add the strawberries and cook for 2 to 3 minutes, until soft but not totally mushy. Allow to cool.

To serve, ease the panna cotta out of the ramekins and onto plates. Pour plenty of fruit compote beside each one.

Orange and lemon cake with marmalade cream

Based on a Claudia Roden recipe, this is an ideal cake for a picnic, moist but easy to transport and slice. The marmalade cream can be spread over the top or served alongside each slice. The cake is also delicious with poached rhubarb or Cardamom and poppy seed ice cream (see page 402).

Serves 8 to 10
* Oil, for greasing
* Flour, for dusting
* 2 oranges
* 6 eggs
* 1¼ cups sugar
* 2 teaspoons vanilla extract
* Grated zest of 1 lemon
* Grated zest of 1 lime
* 1 teaspoon baking powder
* 1½ cups ground almonds

For the marmalade cream
* ⅔ cup heavy cream
* 4 ounces mascarpone or cream cheese
* 2 tablespoons Seville orange marmalade, preferably homemade
* 1 tablespoon superfine sugar (optional, depend-ing on the sweetness of the marmalade)

Preheat the oven to 375 degrees. Oil a 9-inch non-stick, loose-bottomed cake pan and dust with flour.

Wash the oranges and boil them whole for 1½ hours, or until they are soft. Allow to cool.

Beat the eggs with the sugar. Add the vanilla, lemon and lime zest, baking powder, and almonds and mix well.

Cut open the oranges. Discard the seeds and puree the whole fruit, skin and all, in a food processor. Add to the egg mixture and stir thoroughly.

Pour into the prepared cake pan and bake in the middle of the oven for 1 hour. Allow to cool before turning it out.

Lightly whip the cream. Fold in the mascarpone and then the marmalade. If the mascarpone is quite firm, beat it separately first and then fold in. Taste and add sugar as necessary.

Primrose lemon curd cupcakes

My friend Sarah Wilkin, who is a cupcake queen (see also Raspberry cupcakes on page 222), gave me this recipe. It makes fabulous cupcakes, with a gooey middle of sharp lemon curd. In fact, the recipe makes plenty of lemon curd, so if you have any left over, pour it into dry, warm, sterilized jars (you can sterilize them in a very hot dishwasher, or boil them in a pan of water for 10 minutes). Seal and label with the date. The curd will keep in the fridge for up to 2 weeks.

Yields 12 to 14 cupcakes

For the lemon curd
* Juice and grated zest of 2 lemons
* 1 cup superfine sugar
* 7 tablespoons unsalted butter
* 4 eggs, beaten

* 3 tablespoons butter, at room temperature
* ¾ cup superfine sugar
* ¾ cup unbleached flour
* 1½ teaspoons baking powder
* 1 egg
* ½ cup milk
* 2 tablespoons grated lemon zest from unwaxed lemons

For the icing
* 1½ cups confectioners' sugar
* 1 tablespoon lemon juice
* Primroses and crocuses, to decorate (optional)

First make the lemon curd. Put the lemon juice and zest into a heavy-based saucepan, add the sugar, and dissolve over a low heat. Add the butter and stir until melted. Add the beaten eggs and stir until the mixture thickens. Spoon the mixture into a bowl and allow to cool (it will thicken further as it cools).

Preheat the oven to 325 degrees. Set out a couple of muffin trays and put a paper cupcake case in each hole.

Now make the cake mixture. Put the butter, sugar, flour, and baking powder in the bowl of an electric mixer or food processor and mix until you get a consistency of breadcrumbs. Transfer to a large mixing bowl.

In a separate bowl beat together the egg, milk, and lemon zest. Add bit by bit to the flour mixture until it's fully incorporated, but don't overmix.

Spoon the mixture into the paper cases until a third full. Put a teaspoonful of lemon curd on top, then cover with another dollop of cake mixture. The cases should be about two-thirds full. Bake for 20 to 25 minutes, until the cakes are golden and the tops spring back when touched. Take them out of the tray and leave to cool on a rack.

To make the icing, sift the sugar into a bowl. Add the lemon juice and 1 tablespoon warm water. You want a thick icing, so if it appears to be too runny, just add a bit more confectioners' sugar.

Sarah W. says she likes a level cupcake, so if there's a small peak, she trims it off, then spreads a good spoonful of the icing all over the top. You can decorate these cakes with lemon rind, or primroses or crocuses, which are edible.

Chocolate cake with lime

A rich, dense chocolate cake with the sharpness of lime is the perfect pudding for Easter day. You need only a small slice with some lightly whipped cream.

Serves 8
* 6 ounces dark chocolate (at least 70% cocoa solids)
* ¾ cup (1 ½ sticks) softened butter
* ⅔ cup superfine sugar
* Finely grated zest of 6 limes
* 1 ⅓ cups ground almonds
* 4 eggs, separated

For the icing
* 3 ½ ounces dark chocolate (at least 70% cocoa solids)
* 2 tablespoons butter
* 1–2 tablespoons lime marmalade

Preheat the oven to 300 degrees. Lightly oil a 10-inch springform or loose-bottomed cake pan.

Break the chocolate into pieces and melt in a heatproof bowl over simmering water. Put the butter, sugar, and lime zest into a large bowl and beat until soft and creamy (an electric beater is good for this).

Mix in the ground almonds, egg yolks, and melted chocolate until well combined.

Whisk the egg whites until stiff. Using a large metal spoon, fold into the chocolate mixture. Pour into the prepared pan and bake in the middle of the oven for 30 to 35 minutes. Allow to cool in the pan.

To make the icing, put the chocolate, butter, and marmalade into a saucepan. Melt over a low heat, stirring gently all the while. When the cake is cooled and turned out of the pan, spoon the icing over it and leave to set.

Lemon and poppy seed kugelhopf cake

This is one of my favorite cakes, with an intense taste of lemon. I love the bundt shape of it too, which looks wonderful with unevenly dripping icing.

Serves 8 to 10
* 1 cup light brown sugar
* 1 cup (2 sticks) softened butter
* 4 eggs, beaten
* 1 ½ cups self-rising flour, sifted
* Grated zest of 2 lemons, juice of 1
* 1 tablespoon poppy seeds
* 2 tablespoons milk

For the syrup
* Juice of 1 lemon
* 3 tablespoons confectioners' sugar, sifted

For the icing
* 7 tablespoons confectioners' sugar, sifted
* 1 tablespoon lemon juice
* Lemon zest, for sprinkling on the top

Preheat the oven to 350 degrees. Lightly grease and flour a bundt cake pan or a 9-inch spring-form pan.

Put the sugar and butter into a large mixing bowl and beat together until light and fluffy. Gradually stir in the beaten eggs and flour (alternating the two). Then stir in the lemon juice, lemon zest, poppy seeds, and milk. Spoon into the prepared pan and smooth the mixture down with a rubber spatula or palette knife.

Place in the middle of the oven and bake for 45 to 50 minutes, until firm. Cool in the pan for 10 minutes.

Meanwhile, make the syrup by stirring together the lemon juice and confectioners' sugar in a small bowl. Using a skewer, prick the top of the cake and pour over the syrup. Allow the cake to cool completely in the pan. When cooled, turn out onto a serving plate.

Next make the icing. Mix together the confectioners' sugar, lemon juice, and 1 tablespoon of water and pour over the top of the cake, allowing the icing to trickle down the sides (if using a spring-form cake pan, do the same, but smooth the icing over the top of the cake with a palette knife or spatula). Sprinkle with the lemon zest.

Hot cross buns

These buns are best eaten fresh out of the oven with butter; if not, they are better toasted. The mixture of flours (half whole wheat, half unbleached flour) gives good flavor and texture. The single rising works fine and cuts down the prep time.

Yields 12 buns
* 1 teaspoon superfine sugar
* 1¼ cups warm milk and water, mixed half and half
* 1 tablespoon dried yeast
* 1½ cups unbleached flour, sifted
* 1½ cups whole wheat flour, sifted
* 1 teaspoon salt
* 2 teaspoons pumpkin pie spice
* 2 teaspoons ground cinnamon
* 1 teaspoon ground nutmeg
* ¼ cup superfine sugar
* 1 egg
* 4 tablespoons (½ stick) melted butter
* ½ cup dried currants
* ½ cup chopped mixed peel
* Finely grated zest of 2 lemons
* 4 ounces prepared pie crust

For the glaze
* 1 tablespoon water
* 1 tablespoon superfine sugar
* 1 tablespoon milk

Stir the superfine sugar into the milk and water mixture, sprinkle over the yeast, and leave for 10 minutes.

Put the flours, salt, spices, and sugar into a large mixing bowl. Make a crater in the center and add the yeast liquid, egg, melted butter, currants, mixed peel, and lemon zest. Mix well to form a soft dough, adding a little more milk if necessary.

Place the dough on a floured surface and with floured hands knead for 8–10 minutes, until the dough is smooth and elastic.

Divide the dough into 12 equal pieces and shape into buns. Place on lightly oiled baking sheets, then cover and leave in a warm place until doubled in size (about 1 hour).

Preheat the oven to 400 degrees.

Spread out the pastry and cut strips about ½-inch wide. Make a pastry cross on each bun, gluing it down with a little water or milk.

Bake the buns for 15 to 20 minutes, until golden. Transfer to a wire rack to cool.

Melt the glaze ingredients over a high heat until just boiling, then brush this over the hot buns to make them shiny. Serve warm with butter.

Easter cookies

You can cut these cookies into any shape you want, and the recipe can be adapted for Christmas if you add some ginger along with the other spices. If you want to hang the cookies on the tree, make a hole in them to thread ribbon through.

Yields about 30 cookies, depending on shape and size
* 18 tablespoons (2 sticks plus 2 tablespoons) butter, softened
* ¾ cup superfine sugar, plus extra for sprinkling
* 2 eggs, separated
* 2¾ cups unbleached flour, sifted
* Pinch of salt
* 1½ teaspoons pumpkin pie spice
* 1 teaspoon cinnamon
* ⅓ cup raisins
* ⅓ cup dried cranberries
* 2 tablespoons candied orange and/or lemon peel
* 2 tablespoons milk

Preheat the oven to 400 degrees. Lightly grease a couple of baking sheets or silicone mats.

Put the butter and sugar into a large bowl and cream until pale and fluffy. Beat in the egg yolks. Add the rest of the ingredients, except the egg whites, stirring well to make a soft dough.

Put the dough onto a floured surface and knead lightly. Roll out to a thickness of about ¼ inch. Cut into your preferred shapes and place on the prepared baking sheets. Bake for 5 to 8 minutes.

Meanwhile, lightly beat the egg whites. Brush the cookies with the whites and sprinkle with a little superfine sugar. Return to the oven and bake for a further 4 to 5 minutes, or until golden brown. Cool on a wire rack.

After Eight chocolate chip cookies

With the delicious After Eight combination of mint and chocolate, these cookies are good for serving with coffee after your Easter lunch or dinner.

Yields 12 to 14 cookies
* 14 tablespoons (1½ sticks plus 2 tablespoons) butter, softened
* ¾ cup light brown sugar
* 1 large egg, beaten
* 1½ cups unbleached flour
* Pinch of salt
* 1 teaspoon baking soda
* 5 ounces After Eight mints, roughly chopped
* 3 ounces semisweet chocolate, finely chopped, or plain chocolate chips

Preheat the oven to 350 degrees. Lightly grease several baking sheets or cover with silicone mats. (The mats are best as they ensure that the cookies don't overbrown on the bottom.)

Cream the butter and sugar in a large mixing bowl until light and fluffy. Slowly beat in the egg. Sift the flour, salt, and baking soda over the mixture and fold in. Add the After Eights and chocolate pieces and mix gently.

Place scant tablespoonfuls of the mixture on the prepared baking sheets. The cookies need room to spread, so don't put more than 4 on a sheet.

Bake for 10 minutes—they should still be soft inside. Allow to cool on the baking sheets for a few minutes before transferring with a spatula to wire racks.

Solid mini Easter eggs

Various chocolate molds—plastic, silicone, and metal—are available now in cook shops, and they come with full instructions about greasing (most don't need it) and tips on how to turn out the chocolate. You can also buy colored foil from specialty shops for wrapping the finished eggs. These small solid eggs are made in separate halves, which are then stuck together with a little melted chocolate. You can eat them as they are, or use them to fill a large hollow egg (see next recipe), tied together with ribbon.

Yields 8 eggs (depending on mold size)
* 7 ounces dark chocolate (at least 70% cocoa solids), or milk or white chocolate, plus a little extra for joining the egg halves together

For the different flavorings (optional)
* 2 tablespoons grated lime, orange, or lemon zest
* 2 tablespoons chopped roasted hazelnuts
* 3 tablespoons puffed rice cereal
* 1 pinch of chili flakes
* 2 tablespoons chopped apricots or dates
* 2 tablespoons finely chopped candied ginger

Break the chocolate into small pieces and place in a heatproof bowl set over a pan of boiling water. Heat until melted, stirring the chocolate as little as possible so that it does not become grainy. (Dark chocolate melts the best, but a mix of half milk chocolate and half dark chocolate gives a lovely mild taste.)

Add any of the flavorings (if using) and mix well.

Place the mold on a flat surface and fill each shape with the melted chocolate. Leave to set in the fridge.

When solid, turn the chocolate shapes out of the mold. Join the two halves together with a little melted chocolate.

Large hollow Easter egg

I used a metal mold (about 4 x 2 ½ inches) to make this egg. It's best made when you have a few hours to spare, as you build up the thickness of the chocolate gradually, but it's very easy and satisfying to do.

Yields 1 egg
* 3 ½ ounces dark chocolate (at least 70% cocoa solids)
* Drop of sunflower oil, if needed
* Handful of small chocolate eggs (see left)

Break the chocolate into small pieces and place in a heatproof bowl set over a pan of boiling water. Heat until melted, stirring the chocolate as little as possible so that it does not become grainy. Take the pan off the heat but keep the bowl over the hot water.

Oil the mold with sunflower oil (if the instructions recommend it). Then, using a soft, 1-inch paintbrush or cake brush, paint the inside of the mold with an even coating of chocolate. Place in the fridge to set for 15 to 20 minutes, then repeat the process, building up the egg layer by layer, until all the chocolate has been used.

Put in the fridge to set for 1 hour, then remove the egg from its mold. It is very difficult to get perfect edges with homemade Easter eggs, but don't worry—they still look good and are, I think, nicer than most store-bought eggs.

Fill the hollow egg with the mini eggs and tie a ribbon around the middle.

Arabian macaroons

These are some of my favorite "cookies" ever.

In fact, they aren't really cookies, but little mounds of delicious-tasting and -textured fruit and nuts—wonderful because they're not too sweet.

Yields 15
* 2 ¼ cups dried coconut
* ½ cup superfine sugar
* ½ cup chopped dates
* ½ cup chopped dried apricots
* ⅓ cup pine nuts
* ⅓ cup sesame seeds
* 2 eggs, beaten
* 1 teaspoon vanilla extract
* Pinch of salt

Preheat the oven to 350 degrees. Lightly grease a couple of baking sheets or line them with nonstick baking parchment or silicone mats.

Put all the ingredients into a large bowl and mix well. Leave to stand for a few minutes.

Put scant tablespoonful-sized dollops of the mixture onto the prepared baking sheets—about 7 or 8 per sheet. Bake for 10 to 12 minutes, or until golden brown. Transfer to cooling racks with a spatula. Store in an airtight container.

Butter oat tea cookies

These biscuits make a nice, light change from granola bars, good with mousse or just as a cookie with a cup of tea.

Yields 36
* 1 cup (2 sticks) softened butter
* 1 cup light brown sugar
* 1 egg, beaten
* 2 teaspoons vanilla extract
* 1 teaspoon ground cinnamon
* ½ teaspoon ground ginger
* Grated zest of 2 lemons
* Pinch of salt
* ⅔ cup self-rising flour, sifted
* 1 ½ cups rolled oats

Beat the butter and sugar together in a large bowl with a wooden spoon until light and fluffy (or blend in a processor, then transfer to a large mixing bowl).

Stir in the beaten egg, vanilla extract, ground cinnamon, ground ginger, lemon zest, and salt. Using a large metal spoon, fold in the flour and oats. The mixture will form a soft dough. Put in the fridge to chill for 30 minutes.

Preheat the oven to 350 degrees.

Lightly oil a baking tray or cover a tray with a silicone mat.

Using a teaspoon, scoop out some of the mixture and roll into a large grape-sized ball, put into the baking tray, and lightly press down with a fork.

Repeat, using up all of the mixture. These are best cooked in batches in the middle of the oven. Cook for 9 to 10 minutes until golden brown.

Turkish honey nuts

Perfect with yogurt for breakfast, these nuts are also good in cakes, granola bars, and cookies. They make an instant topping to all sorts of things—I love them with vanilla ice cream.

Yields 2 small jars
* ¾ cup hazelnuts
* ¾ cup walnuts
* ½ cup Brazil nuts, roughly chopped
* ¾ cup pistachios
* ½ cup pine nuts
* 16 ounces (2 cups) honey

Preheat the oven to 350 degrees.

Put all the nuts in a single layer on a baking tray and roast for 5 to 6 minutes. Set aside to cool.

Put the nuts in a food processor and whizz for literally a second to break them up slightly. Pack the nuts into dry, warm, sterilized jars (you can sterilize them in a very hot dishwasher, or boil them in a pan of water for 10 minutes) and pour over the honey. Seal, label with the date, and store in a cupboard, ready to eat whenever you want them.

Honey nut cookies

These crunchy, buttery cookies are a treat with any ice cream, and great after lunch or for tea. For a spicy flavor, ground cinnamon can be added to the dough if you like. You will need to bake them in two or more batches as they spread a lot.

Yields 30 cookies
* ½ cup (1 stick) softened butter
* 1 cup light brown sugar
* 1 large egg
* 1 teaspoon vanilla extract
* ½ teaspoon cinnamon (optional)
* ¼ cup Turkish honey nuts (see left)
* 1½ cups self-rising flour, sifted

Cream together the butter and sugar until pale and soft. (A handheld electric beater is good for this.) Beat in the egg, vanilla, cinnamon (if using), and honey nuts. Gradually stir in the flour to make a soft dough. Cover the bowl with plastic wrap and chill in the fridge for 1 hour.

Preheat the oven to 350 degrees and lightly oil a couple of baking sheets.

Take spoonfuls of the dough and roll into spheres the size of ping-pong balls. Place about 7 or 8 on each baking sheet, spacing them well apart. (They will naturally flatten into domes.) Bake for 12 minutes or until slightly risen and firm. Cool on racks and store in an airtight container.

Walnut cookies

These are the lightest cookies you can make, sweet but with a hint of lemon, and a fantastic, melt-in-the mouth texture. They make an ideal dessert cookie to serve with fruit syllabub, ice cream, or mousse (see page 73).

They will keep, without going soft, for a month in an airtight tin or jar.

Yields about 50 cookies
* 1 cup (2 sticks) salted butter, softened slightly
* ½ cup brown sugar
* 1 cup self-rising flour
* ⅔ cup rice flour
* ¾ cup walnuts, toasted and finely chopped (in a food processor)
* Grated zest of 1 orange
* Grated zest of 1 lemon

Preheat the oven to 350 degrees. Lightly grease a baking sheet.

Cream the butter and sugar in a large bowl with a wooden spoon (or use an electric beater) until light and fluffy. Sift in the two flours, add the chopped nuts, and beat together. Add the citrus zest and continue to beat until smooth.

Form the mixture into a dough, then break off large grape-sized pieces and roll into balls. Place them on the prepared baking sheet, flattening them slightly with the back of a fork. Bake for 8 minutes.

Remove from the oven and allow to cool and harden for 10 minutes. Using a spatula, transfer the cookies to a wire rack and leave to cool fully. Store in an airtight container.

Liz's marzipan and dried cherry granola bars

Liz Wood cooks course lunches in my school and is a bread, cookie, and dessert queen. The tartness of the dried cherries in these granola bars prevents them from being too sweet, and the marzipan adds a hint of almond.

Yields 16
* 1½ sticks butter
* ½ cup brown sugar
* 2 tablespoons corn syrup
* 1 tablespoon honey
* 3 cups rolled oats
* ¾ cup dried cherries
* 4 ounces marzipan, diced

Preheat the oven to 325 degrees. Lightly grease a shallow 9 by 12-inch baking pan.

Put the butter, sugar, corn syrup, and honey in a saucepan and melt together, stirring all the while. Take off the heat. Add the oats, cherries, and marzipan and stir well. Spoon into the prepared pan and smooth down with the back of a spatula.

Bake in the hot oven for 20 to 25 minutes, until lightly colored. Keep an eye on them as they burn quickly once cooked. Leave to cool in the pan for 10 minutes or so, then cut into squares—you should get about 16. Transfer to a cooling rack. When cooled, store in an airtight container.

Quick rhubarb chutney
with cardamom

You can use this chutney in the usual way, with bread and cheese or alongside cottage pie, but it's also good heated through and served with roast pork, duck, or grilled mackerel.

Yields 2 pint jars
* **1 cup cider vinegar**
* **2 cups light brown sugar**
* **½ cup raisins**
* **2 red onions, chopped**
* **1-inch piece of fresh ginger, peeled and grated**
* **Seeds from 20 cardamom pods**
* **4–5 star anise**
* **Grated zest of 1 lemon**
* **1 teaspoon salt**
* **2 ¼ pounds rhubarb, cut into 1-inch chunks**

Put all the ingredients except the rhubarb into a large, heavy-based pan, bring to a boil, and boil for 5 minutes. Add the rhubarb and bring back to a boil. Reduce the heat and simmer for 15 minutes, stirring occasionally.

Cool slightly and spoon into dry, warm, sterilized jars (you can sterilize them in a very hot dishwasher, or boil them in a pan of water for 10 minutes). Seal each jar and process in a boiling-water bath according to jar manufacturer's instructions. Label with the date. This chutney can be eaten right away. Once opened, it is best stored in the fridge, and will keep for up to a month.

Piccalilli

This piccalilli, a crunchy, spring vegetable chutney, is quick to prepare and make. It has great spicy flavor with the lovely taste of cumin, and good texture from all the fresh vegetables. It goes well with anything sausagey, and is ideal with Raised game pie (see page 52). It's also delicious with a sharp Cheddar cheese and Ham in hay (see page 54).

Yields about 3 ½ pounds (about 4 pint jars)
* 1 cauliflower (about 1 ¾ pounds), divided into 1-inch florets/chunks
* 3 red onions, cut into 1–1 ½-inch chunks
* 1 cucumber, peeled and deseeded, cut lengthwise into quarters, then ½-inch chunks
* 4 sticks of celery, cut into ½-inch chunks
* ½ pound green beans, topped, tailed, and cut into thirds
* ⅓ pound snow peas or sugarsnap peas, cut in half
* 1 teaspoon garam masala
* 1 teaspoon ground ginger
* ½ teaspoon chili flakes
* 1 teaspoon ground cumin
* 2 tablepoons cumin seeds
* ¾ cup light brown sugar
* 2 garlic cloves, crushed or chopped
* Grated zest of 2 limes (optional)
* 3 cups cider vinegar, plus 4–5 tablespoons extra
* ¼ cup ground turmeric
* ¼ cup dry mustard powder
* ¼ cup all-purpose or self-rising flour

Prepare all the vegetables and put into a large bowl.

Put all the remaining ingredients, apart from the turmeric, mustard, and flour, into a large, heavy-based stainless-steel pan. Stir over the heat until the sugar dissolves.

Add all the vegetables to the pan, bring to a boil, then turn down the heat and simmer for 5 minutes. Turn off the heat and let the vegetables sit in the liquid for 5 minutes (you want the them crisp, not overcooked and soft). Strain through a colander set over a large bowl. Reserve both vinegar and vegetables.

Put the turmeric, mustard powder, and flour in a bowl, add 4 to 5 tablespoons cider vinegar, and mix to make a smooth paste; a little water can be added if necessary. Add a ladleful of the reserved vinegar and put the mixture into a large saucepan. Stirring or whisking over a low heat, add all the reserved vinegar and simmer for 5 to 10 minutes (it should be the consistency of a thin white sauce). Pour the vinegar mixture over the vegetables and stir well to cover everything.

Spoon the piccalilli into dry, warm, sterilized jars (you can sterilize them in a very hot dishwasher, or boil them in a pan of water for 10 minutes). Seal each jar and process in a boiling-water bath according to jar manufacturer's instructions. Label with the date. The piccalilli will keep for 1 year. Once opened, store in the fridge.

Rosemary, sage, and thyme salt

An invaluable seasoning for grilled meats, poultry, and fish, this salt is also excellent added to cooked vegetables with a little butter or olive oil, and fantastic sprinkled on roast potatoes. Although not a long-term preserve, it will keep in the fridge for at least a month.

Yields 1 small jar
* ⅓ cup coarse sea salt
* ¼ cup fresh rosemary leaves
* 2 tablespoons fresh sage leaves
* 1 tablespoon fresh thyme leaves
* 2 garlic cloves
* 1 tablespoon black peppercorns
* Finely grated zest of 1 lemon

Put all the ingredients into a food processor and whizz briefly until combined quite finely. Put into an airtight container and store in the fridge.

Yogurt cheese balls

I love the soft, creamy consistency, and sharp flavor of these cheesy balls, which are good fun to make over a weekend. It's always surprising that the yogurt turns out solid enough to make into balls.

You can eat some straight away—served with hunks of bread or slices of tomato and sprinkled with fresh herbs and paprika—and store others in jars of olive oil. They look impressive, but are easy to make, so they are a brilliant present—particularly good with Roasted red peppers or Globe artichoke and zucchini summer salad (see pages 270 and 137).

Yields 16–20 balls (4 pint jars)
* 2 quarts plain yogurt
* 2 teaspoons salt
* 4 sprigs of thyme
* 4 bay leaves
* 4 garlic cloves (optional)
* 4 teaspoons black peppercorns
* Extra virgin olive oil

Line a colander with cheesecloth and place over a large bowl.

Put the yogurt and salt into a large mixing bowl and whisk well. Pour into the lined colander and leave to drain overnight. By the morning you should have a soft, creamy yogurt.

Shape the yogurt into walnut-sized balls, place on a large plate, and chill in the fridge for 24 hours. The balls can be eaten right away or put into 4 dry, warm, sterilized jars (you can sterilize them in a very hot dishwasher, or boil them in a pan of water for 10 minutes). Add a sprig of thyme, a bay leaf, a garlic clove (if using), and a teaspoon of peppercorns to each jar, then top up with olive oil. Store in the fridge and eat within 3 weeks.

Orange and passion fruitade

My absolute favorite soft drink when I feel like something delicious but not alcoholic. Have this once and you're hooked. You'll find yourself forever scraping out the inside of passion fruits.

Serves 4
* Pulp and juice of 8 passion fruits
* Juice of 4–6 limes, to taste
* Juice of 6 oranges
* 1–2 tablespoons superfine sugar, to taste
* 24 ounces soda or mineral water
* Fresh mint, finely chopped, to serve

Scoop all the passion fruit pulp, seeds, and juice into a pitcher with the lime and orange juice. Add the sugar and stir well to dissolve. When you're ready to serve, add plenty of ice. Top up with the soda water or mineral water, and stir some mint into the pitcher.

Grapefruit and cranberry spritzer

One of the best non-sweet soft drinks for a party. You can also add a little sparkling water to it if you like.

Yields 6 tumblers
* 2 cups pink grapefruit juice
* 2 cups cranberry juice
* 2 cups lemonade or bitter lemon
* 1 pink grapefruit, halved and thinly sliced

Mix the juices and lemonade in a pitcher full of ice. Pour into glasses and serve each with a halved slice of pink grapefruit.

Rhubarb and ginger vodka

A frozen shot of this is delicious, and it makes a fragrant drink with tonic or served over ice with a little lemonade. Try to make the mixture a month before you want it so that the flavors have time to intensify. For the best color use bright pink rhubarb, not the pale forced stuff.

Yields 1 (750-ml) bottle
* 1 pound rhubarb, cut into chunks
* 1¼ cups superfine sugar
* 1½-inch piece of fresh ginger, peeled and sliced
* 6 long pieces of orange peel (from 2 oranges)
* 1 (750-ml) bottle of vodka

Put the rhubarb, sugar, ginger, and orange peel into a large, wide-mouthed canning jar and pour in the bottle of vodka. Screw on the lid and put into a cupboard for 1 month, turning it upside down every other day.

When ready, strain into a bottle and use as suggested above. (The straining is essential or the drink will turn rather bitter.)

Limoncello

Although this takes only 10 minutes or so to make, it should be left for at least a couple of weeks before you drink it. This allows the vodka to become really infused with the flavors of the lemon zest and lemongrass. It's best served ice cold, straight from the freezer, and a splash of it is fantastic over any fruit sorbet (see pages 76 and 210).

Yields 1 (750-ml) bottle
* 2 lemongrass stalks
* Grated zest of 8 unwaxed lemons
* 1 (750-ml) bottle of good-quality vodka
* 1 cup superfine sugar

Crush the lemongrass. Put it into a large, wide-mouthed preserving jar (you can sterilize it in a very hot dishwasher, or boil it in a pan of water for 10 minutes) with the zest and pour over the vodka.

Put the sugar into a saucepan with 1½ cups water, bring to a boil, then simmer for 3 to 4 minutes. Leave the syrup to cool, then add it to the vodka mixture.

Seal the preserving jar and leave in a cupboard for 2 weeks, shaking and turning it for the first couple of days.

When ready, strain the limoncello into a bottle.

Jamaican rum punch

Rum punch can be sickly, but not this one, as it contains lots of fresh lime and orange juice. It's also the most wonderful shade of coral-orange. Serve it alongside a clear glass pitcher of Claret cup (see next recipe) for a party and you have a perfect color contrast.

Serves 4 to 6
* ½ cup Earl Grey tea, cooled
* Juice of 10 limes
* Juice of 5 oranges
* 1 cup rum
* 24 ounces ginger ale

To serve
* 1 lime, sliced
* Mint leaves

Put the tea, juices, and rum into a large pitcher or punch bowl and stir with a wooden spoon. When you're ready to serve, add the ginger ale.

Ladle the punch into ice-filled glasses and add a slice of lime and some mint leaves to each.

Claret cup

Rather like a posh sangria, this is more subtle and less sweet because it uses good-quality red wine and sparkling water instead of the usual cheap wine and lemonade. It's ideal for when the weather cheers up.

Serves 6
* 1 (750-ml) bottle of claret or Bordeaux, chilled
* 2 ounces crème de cassis (or mango juice), as a sweetener
* Juice of 2 lemons
* Juice of 2 oranges
* 1 pint blueberries
* 2 pints strawberries, roughly chopped
* A little fresh mint
* 24 ounces sparkling mineral water

Put the wine, crème de cassis, and citrus juices into a pitcher with plenty of ice. Add the fruit and mint and stir round. When you're ready to serve, add the sparkling water and stir again.

SUMMER

One of the wonderful things about summer is the possibility of leading an outdoor kind of life. With the long, bright days and the guarantee of at least some good weather, we can eat, cook, chat, and even sleep outside as much as possible.

There's nothing I like better than bringing meals out to eat in the garden—simple, light, cheery food. This is the moment for crab, shrimp, and scallops, eaten with just a bowl of herbs or lemon mayonnaise. And it's definitely the season when interesting vegetarian food rides high. You rarely get complaints from even the most stalwart meat-eaters if you serve them homemade artichoke hearts with mozzarella, stuffed zucchini flowers with honey, or garden fritto misto.

As for dessert, all you need is fresh fruit—white peaches, nectarines, strawberries, raspberries, cherries, plums, and the first of the figs. One thing I would say is that it's worth spending a little time preparing the fruit. A sweet, juicy peach is miraculous, but there's something particularly special about a plate of prepared fruit—no work, no mess, just a pure injection of texture and taste. For something showier, stick to the same principle but use the fresh fruit to make ice cream, to stuff meringues, or to top a cake or tart.

This is also the time of year to organize picnics, and for these I feel that basic is not best. You want to mark out a summer picnic very clearly from a sandwich-based everyday lunch, packed up efficiently in a lunchbox. Don't go quite as far as a portable table and chairs, but it's lovely to have a good selection of things to choose from, to eat and come back to as the day goes on.

Of course, summer is also the season for parties, and creating food for these is fun if you have things well planned. Keep it simple and do as much as possible in advance; and always remember the competition for last-minute fridge and oven space. I've had real success feeding hordes of people with the dishes that follow—marinated mozzarella with basil and prosciutto, followed by chicken tagine, Persian butterflied leg of lamb or fillet of beef, and finally basil, raspberry, and hazelnut meringues with fresh fruit, or a gooseberry meringue cake. Of course, get friends to help. The preparation, with everyone involved, is often as much fun as the actual party itself.

As well as eating in the garden, I like to go one step further and cook out there as well. I don't tend to go as far as roasting a whole pig or sheep for a party—I always end up feeling sorry for it—but there are lots of other ideas for feeding large or small groups from food on a fire or barbecue. I love lamb kebabs, or a Chinese barbecued fillet of pork. You can wrap any small fish in damp newspaper and steam it in the ashes, or grill an herb and lemon chicken souvlaki dressed in a cilantro and mint yogurt sauce.

And during the summer, I wouldn't be without my pizza oven. We use it almost every weekend at this time of year, and even more when the children are on holiday from school. Homemade pizzas, on a lovely, lazy evening, are one of my family's favorite summer meals.

Crunchy summer vegetables with anchovy mayonnaise

An Elizabeth David classic, this is one of my favorite things to eat with an aperitif, or to keep hunger at bay at a barbecue or picnic. Fresh, summery, and simple, it will satisfy guests while you get everything else laid out. Take the mayonnaise in a jam jar (which you can pour out into a bowl if you want) and lay all the vegetables around it on a large dish or wooden plate.

Serves 6 to 8

For the anchovy mayonnaise
* 2 egg yolks
* 2 garlic cloves, finely chopped
* 8 anchovy fillets, drained and finely chopped
* ½ teaspoon English mustard powder
* Juice of 1 lemon, or to taste
* Salt and black pepper
* 1 cup sunflower oil (or 1 part light olive oil to 2 parts sunflower oil)

* Bunch of small carrots, cut in half lengthwise, leaves left on
* Handful of radishes, cut in half lengthwise, leaves left on
* Handful of sugarsnap peas, strings removed
* Handful of green beans, blanched
* Small bunch of asparagus spears, blanched
* 6 baby zucchinis, blanched
* Handful of broccoli florets, blanched
* Handful of chard stems, blanched
* Handful of new potatoes, boiled

First make the mayonnaise. Put the egg yolks into a food processor or bowl with the garlic, anchovies, mustard, lemon juice, salt, and pepper and mix well. When the mixture is quite smooth, carefully add the oil in a stream while blending continuously to make a thick, smooth mayonnaise. Taste and add more lemon juice if you like.

Put the mayonnaise in a bowl in the center of a large flat plate and arrange the prepared summer vegetables all around it. Then get everyone to dip and eat.

Marinated artichoke heart and fennel salad with pecorino

Having recently had this in a restaurant in Florence, I've been reminded how delicious it is. Thin slices of raw artichoke heart and fennel marinated in olive oil and lemon juice, eaten with slivers of Parmesan or pecorino—this is perfect with an aperitif in summer. I'd eat this, from a big plate, with my fingers, but you can serve it with a glass of cocktail sticks if you want it more refined. It's best with tender early artichokes or small ones from a side stem.

Serves 8 as canapés, 4 as a starter
* 10 small globe artichokes
* Juice and grated zest of 1 lemon, plus some extra juice for acidulating the artichoke water
* 1 large fennel bulb
* 3 tablespoons extra virgin olive oil
* Small bunch of flat-leaf parsley, chopped
* Salt and black pepper
* 3 ounces pecorino or Parmesan cheese

Pick or buy your artichokes with long stems because these, as well as the hearts, are delicious if you skin them, and you also double the amount in your salad.

Strip the tough outer scales from the artichokes until you get to the soft white leaves. Cut the top off the whole thing and pare off the stringy outer third of the long stem with a sharp knife. Cut the artichokes in half and use a spoon to scrape out the choke (the nascent flower) if it has started to form. Drop the hearts straight into a bowl of water acidulated with lemon juice.

When all your artichoke hearts are prepared, dry them and slice into thin slivers and lay out on a flat plate. Chuck away any tough outer scales from the fennel and slice the remaining bulb very finely (I find a mandoline is the best tool for this). Squeeze the lemon juice over the artichokes and fennel, and add the olive oil, parsley, and salt and pepper. Leave them marinating for a couple of hours.

When you're ready to serve, slice the cheese—I use a potato peeler or mandoline—and scatter over the top.

Split pea and mint croquettes with minted yogurt

Healthy, sustaining, and absolutely delicious, I love this sort of imprecise recipe (from Crete) where you can suit yourself, adding mint one time and cumin the next. The sauce is also equally delicious using sorrel instead of mint.

Yields 12 to 15 croquettes
* 2 cups yellow split peas
* 3 garlic cloves
* 2 onions, 1 cut into quarters and 1 very finely chopped or grated
* Olive oil
* Large bunch of fresh mint, chopped, or 1 tablespoon cumin seeds, toasted and ground
* ¾ cup breadcrumbs
* 3 ounces hard sheep's cheese, such as manchego or pecorino, grated
* 1 egg
* 1 red chili, deseeded and chopped (optional)
* Salt and black pepper
* Flour, for dusting

For the sauce
* 1 cup plain yogurt
* Large bunch of fresh mint, roughly chopped
* 2 garlic cloves, finely chopped

Put the split peas in a pan with the garlic, quartered onion, a good splash of olive oil, and 3 cups water and cook, stirring occasionally, until the split peas disintegrate into a puree with a bit of texture, not smooth (about 20–25 minutes). You can add more water if it is too dry, and more olive oil to taste. Leave to cool. You can do this stage the day before.

Mix the cold puree with the finely chopped onion, chopped mint, breadcrumbs, cheese, egg, chili, salt, and pepper. Mix well and shape into croquettes. Dust in flour and fry in hot olive oil until golden brown on both sides. Drain on paper towels to absorb any excess oil.

To make the sauce, mix the yogurt, mint, and garlic in a food processor with just enough water to give the consistency you want, usually in the region of ½ cup.

Crunchy zucchinis in an anchovy crust with tartar sauce

These crunchy zucchini chunks are ideal for a starter, or as canapés for a party. You can serve them with Basil mayonnaise (see page 158) or the classic tartar sauce below, which is also great with crabcakes or fried fish.

Serves 12 as canapés, 6 to 8 as a starter

For the tartar sauce
* 1 egg yolk
* 1 tablespoon white wine vinegar
* Salt and black pepper
* 1 cup vegetable or peanut oil
* Grated zest of 1 lemon and juice of ½
* 8 anchovies, finely chopped
* 2 tablespoons capers, finely chopped
* 4 cornichon pickles (about 3 ounces), finely chopped
* 2 tablespoons finely chopped flat-leaf parsley

* 7 ounces bread or about 5 slices (brown or white, crusts removed—bread a few days old is best)
* 4 canned anchovy fillets, drained
* Grated zest of 1 lemon
* 1 tablespoon grated Parmesan cheese
* Peanut or sunflower oil, for frying
* 2 tablespoons flour, seasoned with salt, pepper, and English mustard powder
* 2 eggs, beaten
* 3 medium zucchinis (about 1 pound), cut lengthwise into thirds and then sliced into chunks about 3 inches long

First make the tartar sauce: whisk the egg yolk in a medium-sized bowl, then add the vinegar and a little salt and pepper and whisk until smooth. Slowly whisk in the oil, making a mayonnaise. Stir in the rest of the sauce ingredients and chill in the fridge.

Put the bread and anchovies in a food processor and whizz together to make breadcrumbs. Add the lemon zest and Parmesan and briefly whizz again.

Heat a ½-inch depth of oil in a deep frying pan until a small cube of bread sizzles and turns golden brown in it within 30 seconds.

Meanwhile, set out 3 shallow bowls and put the seasoned flour in one, the beaten egg in another, and the breadcrumb mixture in the third. Dip the zucchini chunks into the flour, then into the egg, and finally into the breadcrumbs. Shallow-fry them in the hot oil, just 5 or 6 at a time, until they're golden, but still with a good bite. These chunks can be made in advance and heated briefly in a hot oven to crisp them up again, so they're ideal to make as a canapé for a party.

Serve them on a big, shallow plate with a bowl of tartar sauce in the middle.

Seeded sausage rolls

Mix chopped chestnuts into the sausage meat to give it texture and a slight sweetness and top the sausage rolls with different seeds. Make these normal-sized (2 inches long) or do them smaller as a party canapé.

Yields about 24 two-inch rolls or 40 one-inch rolls
* 1 tablespoon olive oil
* 1 small red onion, finely chopped
* 1 stick of celery, finely chopped
* 1 large garlic clove, crushed
* 1 heaping teaspoon dried thyme
* 1 heaping teaspoon dried oregano or marjoram
* 4 ounces vacuum-packed chestnuts, roughly chopped
* 1 pound good-quality sausage meat
* 1 ounce Parmesan cheese, freshly grated
* Salt and black pepper
* 1 pound puff pastry
* 1 egg, beaten
* Selection of seeds, such as poppy, sesame, fennel, and black cumin, for sprinkling

Preheat the oven to 400 degrees. Lightly oil a baking sheet.

Heat the oil in a frying pan and add the onion, celery, garlic, and herbs and sauté for 5 minutes, until softened. Allow to cool.

Put the onion mixture into a large bowl with the chestnuts, sausage meat, and Parmesan and mix well. Season with a little salt and black pepper. Divide the mixture into 4 equal portions.

Roll out the pastry into a rectangle about 10 by 20 inches and about ⅛-inch thick. Cut into 4 long strips about 5 inches wide.

Roll each portion of sausage into a long sausage shape and place one in the middle of each pastry strip. Brush one side of each strip with beaten egg and roll up, keeping the seam side down. Brush the top with beaten egg and sprinkle each long roll with one type of seed. Cut into 2-inch lengths (or smaller if you want them for canapés).

Place the rolls on the prepared baking sheet and bake for about 15 minutes, or until the pastry is golden brown. These are best served warm.

Prosciutto-wrapped asparagus

This is one of the simplest and best canapés for a late spring or early summer party when there's plenty of asparagus around that tastes good and doesn't cost an arm and a leg. You can also add a wafer of pecorino or Parmesan between the ham and asparagus, or do some with and some without.

Serves 15 to 20 as canapés or 10 as a starter
* 2 ¼ pounds asparagus (about 50 spears, depending on width)
* 20–25 slices (depending how wide the slices are) of prosciutto or Serrano or Parma ham
* 3 ounces pecorino or Parmesan cheese (optional), shaved or in strips

Break off the tough woody ends of the asparagus. Cook the tender stems in loose bundles, standing them upright in the pan, or steaming them lying on their side until the thickest bit of the stem is only just cooked and still has a bite to it, but the tips are not yet collapsing (about 5 minutes, depending on the spear widths). Drain and set aside to cool and dry.

Cut each of the prosciutto slices into 2 strips (or 3 if the slices are wide). Wrap each spear in a strip of ham, adding a sliver of cheese (if using). Lay the spears out on a wide plate and serve.

Crostini with pea and basil pesto

These are ideal as canapés or as a starter for a big party meal. The topping is the most amazing bright green because the lemon in the puree stops the peas from oxidizing. Make the crostini bases from deliciously chewy Pugliese sourdough bread, if you can find it; if not, French bread is fine.

Yields 30 crostini
* 1 Pugliese sourdough loaf or French baguette
* 2 whole garlic cloves
* Maldon salt

For the topping
* ½ pound chorizo, thinly sliced (optional)
* Juice and grated zest of 1 lemon
* 12 ounces (1½ cups) peas, blanched for 1 minute if fresh, defrosted if frozen
* 5 tablespoons extra virgin olive oil
* Large handful of fresh basil leaves, and a few leaves for sprinkling
* 1 tablespoon peeled and grated fresh ginger
* 2 garlic cloves, roughly chopped
* Salt and black pepper

Preheat the oven to 325 degrees.

Cut the bread into 30 slices ½ to ¾ inch thick and bake in the hot oven for 5 to 10 minutes, until just toasted.

You can do this up to several days in advance and store the toasts in an airtight container.

Lightly scrape a garlic clove over one side of the toast and scatter with salt.

Fry the chorizo slices in a drop of oil until well cooked and just becoming crunchy. Strain to remove most of the oil that bleeds out as they fry. Toss them in plenty of lemon juice and set aside.

Briefly whizz the peas with the olive oil, basil, remaining lemon juice and zest, ginger, and chopped garlic. Season generously with salt and pepper. Put into the fridge until needed. The flavor of the pea puree improves when slightly chilled.

When you want to eat, stir the puree and spread it thickly over the toasts. Top with a slice of chorizo (if using) and sprinkle with some torn basil leaves to serve.

Parmesan lollipops

If you want to show off at a party, make these lollipops as canapés, or serve them with almost any soup. They look impressive but are easy to do.

Yields 20
* ¼ pound Parmesan cheese
* 20 woody rosemary sticks (leaves removed), 3–3½ inches long

Preheat the oven to 350 degrees. Lightly oil a baking sheet, or place a silicone mat on it.

Coarsely grate the Parmesan into a bowl. Arrange the rosemary sticks on the prepared baking sheet, spacing them about 3 inches apart. Make a little pile of Parmesan (1 to 2 teaspoons, about 2 inches diameter) over one end of each stick.

Place in the oven and bake for 3 to 5 minutes, until the cheese is bubbling and golden. Set aside to cool and solidify (about 10 minutes).

Remove the lollipops with a spatula and place in little glass vases for serving. You can crunch on them while having an aperitif, or dip them into soup.

Cream of tomato soup

Creamy, with a lovely, old-fashioned, comforting taste, this soup is best served warm and is good with toasted pita, fluffy white bread, or Parmesan and dill seed toasts and a swirl of Basil oil (see pages 359 and 208). The soup is quite rich, so don't serve it in huge bowls.

Serves 6 as a starter, 4 for lunch
* 3½ pounds fresh tomatoes, peeled (see below)
* ½ small onion, finely chopped
* 2 tablespoons butter
* ¼ cup flour
* 2 cups milk
* Salt and black pepper
* 1 cup light cream
* Basil oil (see page 208), to serve

Prick each tomato a couple of times with the tip of a sharp knife. Place in a large bowl and pour over enough boiling water to cover. Leave for 2 to 3 minutes, then strain through a colander and allow to cool slightly before peeling off the skin. Chop coarsely.

Chop the tomatoes and chuck away the cores.

In a large saucepan, sauté the onion in the butter until soft (about 5 minutes). Add the flour, stir, and cook for a further 2 minutes. Add the milk and whisk constantly until the mixture thickens.

Add the tomatoes and their juice to the pan, bring just to a boil, then turn down immediately and simmer gently for 10 minutes.

Pour the mixture into a blender or food processor and blend until smooth. Strain and return the soup to the pan. Season to taste and stir in the cream. Heat through, but do not allow the soup to boil. Serve with a drizzle of Basil oil.

Darina's pea, chili, and cilantro soup

The Irish cook Darina Allen makes the most wonderful pea soup—sweet, fresh, and zappy with chili. It's good hot or cold. We make it with cilantro or mint; both are delicious. Some small strands of crispy bacon over the top make a tasty addition.

Serves 6 as a starter, 4 for lunch
* ⅓ pound onion, finely chopped
* 2 garlic cloves, chopped
* 1 green chili, deseeded and finely chopped
* 3 tablespoons butter
* Salt and black pepper
* 1 pound peas (frozen are fine)
* 3½ cups chicken stock, ideally homemade
* 2 tablespoons chopped cilantro (or mint) leaves
* Pinch of superfine sugar

To serve
* Softly whipped heavy cream
* Fresh cilantro (or mint) leaves
* 2 or 3 strips of bacon, cooked till crunchy and broken into bits (optional)

Gently fry the onions, garlic, and chili in the butter. Season with salt and pepper and cook until soft but not brown (about 5 minutes).

Add the peas and cover with the stock. Bring to a boil and simmer for 7 to 8 minutes. Take off the heat, add the chopped cilantro (or mint) and puree in a blender or food processor. Taste, and season with a little more salt and pepper if needed, and add a pinch of sugar to bring out the flavor.

Ladle the soup into bowls and serve with a swirl of lightly whipped cream and some fresh cilantro (or mint) leaves and perhaps some bits of crunchy bacon.

Chilled cucumber soup

Made in only five minutes, this soup is just the thing for lunch on a really hot day. Eat it ice-cold. The liquid comes from the cucumbers, so it doesn't need any extra, but the consistency and temperature of the soup are best if it's made several hours before you want to eat and put in the fridge.

Serves 6 as a starter, 4 for lunch
* 1 large cucumber, ¾ peeled and roughly chopped, ¼ peeled and finely cubed
* 1 garlic clove, finely chopped
* 2 heaping tablespoons roughly chopped mint leaves, plus a few small leaves for serving
* 1 cup sour cream
* ½ cup light cream
* Salt and black pepper

Put the roughly chopped cucumber into a food processor or blender with the garlic, chopped mint, sour cream, and heavy cream. Whizz until well pureed. Taste, and season with salt and pepper. Chill until ice-cold.

   To serve, put a few cubes of cucumber in each bowl and ladle in the soup. Top with a couple of small mint leaves.

Andalusian soup salad

A fantastic, healthy meal in itself, this soup has the crunch of cucumber and intense flavor of summer tomatoes. The key thing is not to chop the vegetables too finely: the chunks should be about ½ inch across. It's also essential to start making this soup at least a couple of hours before you want to eat. It's best eaten really cold, so needs an hour or two in the fridge.

   I like to eat this with Cornbread (see page 258), or fluffy white bread and unsalted butter. (The picture here shows a double quantity of the soup.)

Serves 6 as a starter, 4 for lunch
* 3 large, ripe vine tomatoes, peeled (see page 125)
* 2 hard-boiled eggs
* 2 teaspoons Dijon mustard
* ¼ cup extra virgin olive oil, plus a little extra for serving
* ¼ cup red wine vinegar
* 2 garlic cloves, crushed
* 1 slice of stale white bread, crusts removed, torn up
* ½ large cucumber, peeled (if you want), deseeded, and chopped
* 1 red bell pepper, deseeded and chopped
* 4 scallions, thinly sliced
* 1 red chili, deseeded and thinly sliced (optional)
* 4 cups tomato juice
* Salt and black pepper
* A little fresh oregano, coarsely chopped, to serve

Coarsely chop the tomatoes and chuck away any hard cores.

   Shell the hard-boiled eggs and separate the whites from the yolks. Coarsely chop the whites and set aside.

   In a large bowl, mix the mustard, olive oil, vinegar, garlic, torn bread, and egg yolks to make a paste. Add the tomatoes and all the vegetables, then the tomato juice. Stir it all together. Taste, and season with plenty of salt and pepper. Add the chopped egg whites just before putting the soup in the fridge to chill thoroughly.

   To serve, ladle into bowls and top with a little oregano and a swirl of extra virgin olive oil, or, better still, a Basil oil ice cube (see page 131).

Summer vegetable garden soup with tarragon pesto

This pure and delicious soup is the very essence of summer—full of baby vegetables. The quality of stock is crucial to the flavor, so ideally use homemade. Top with crostini spread with tarragon pesto, made without pine nuts for a lighter taste.

Serves 6 as a starter, 4 for lunch
* 5 cups chicken stock, preferably homemade, or vegetable stock
* 1 tablespoon finely chopped tarragon leaves
* ½ cup thinly sliced baby carrots
* ⅓ pound young fava beans
* ½ cup freshly podded peas, or defrosted, uncooked frozen peas
* 6 scallions, thinly sliced
* 6 radishes, thinly sliced

For the tarragon pesto
* Small bunch of fresh tarragon, stems discarded
* Small bunch of flat-leaf parsley
* 3 ounces Parmesan cheese, freshly grated
* ½ cup extra virgin olive oil
* Salt and black pepper

To serve
* 6–12 Croûtes or Crostini (see pages 131 and 25)
* Freshly grated Parmesan cheese

Heat the stock and add the chopped tarragon. Simmer for a couple of minutes before adding the carrots and fava beans. After 2 minutes, add the peas and scallions and cook for a further 2 minutes. Finally add the radishes and take off the heat.

To make the pesto, put the tarragon, parsley, Parmesan, and olive oil into a food processor and whizz until coarsely pureed. Taste, and season with salt and pepper. Spread the mixture onto the croûtes or crostini.

To serve, put a ladleful of soup into each bowl, then top with pesto-covered croûtes or crostini and a scattering of grated Parmesan.

Crab (or shrimp) and tomato bisque

A light version of traditional fish soup, packed with flavor. For the best seafood stock, you ideally need to cook 2 to 3 crabs (depending on size) yourself, so this is perhaps a seaside vacation recipe. If you can't find live crabs, the cooking liquid of langoustines or shrimp is fine, or use store-bought fish stock as a last option.

Serves 6 as a starter, 4 for lunch
* 2 onions, coarsely chopped
* 2 tablespoons butter
* 2 tablespoons olive oil
* 2 garlic cloves, finely chopped
* 1 quart shellfish stock or fish stock
* Small bunch of flat-leaf parsley, leaves and stems coarsely chopped
* ¼ teaspoon saffron strands, soaked in a little hot fish stock
* 2 (14 ½-ounce) cans of chopped tomatoes, or about 2 pounds very ripe fresh tomatoes, peeled and chopped (see page 125)

To serve
* Light cream (optional)
* Croûtes with rouille (see page 131)
* 3 ounces Gruyère cheese, grated

Put the onions, butter, and oil in a saucepan and gently fry until soft (about 5 minutes). Add the garlic and fry gently for another 2 to 3 minutes.

Add the stock, parsley, saffron, and its soaking liquid and the tomatoes. Bring to a boil, then simmer gently for 20 to 30 minutes to cook the vegetables and reduce the stock. Allow to cool slightly, then puree in a blender or food processor.

To serve, reheat the soup, but do not allow it to boil. Ladle it into bowls and swirl a little cream into each, if you want it. Let everyone help themselves to the croûtes, sprinkled with a little grated Gruyère.

Basil oil ice cubes

Here's a really easy and useful instant seasoning: frozen cubes of oil containing fresh basil leaves. They make a great addition to a cold tomato soup (such as Andalusian soup salad on page 126) and are excellent in a bloody Mary. You can also make them with mint (for the Chilled cucumber soup on page 126), or with cilantro (for Darina's pea, chili, and cilantro soup on page 125). When used on top of hot soup, the oil, which turns cloudy on freezing, becomes clear and glossy again as it melts. Use ice cube trays that make small cubes so you don't end up with too much oil.

Yields 15 small ice cubes
* Large handful of fresh basil leaves
* 5 tablespoons extra virgin olive oil
* 3 tablespoons sunflower oil
* Salt and black pepper

Put all the ingredients into a food processor or blender and whizz for 20 to 30 seconds.

Pour the mixture into an ice cube tray and freeze. When ready to use, pop the cubes out of the tray and place one on top of each bowl of chilled soup.

Croûtes with rouille

These little slices of toast spread with garlic and saffron rouille are ideal for floating in almost any soup—and famously good with fish or seafood bisque (see page 128).

Yields 20 croûtes
* 2 egg yolks
* Pinch of salt
* 1 large garlic clove, crushed
* 1 teaspoon Dijon mustard
* 3 tablespoons sunflower oil
* 3 tablespoons olive oil
* 10 saffron strands, soaked in 1 teaspoon boiling water
* Paprika
* Lemon juice, to taste
* 20 (½-inch) slices of bread (½ French baguette)

To make the rouille, put the egg yolks, salt, garlic, and mustard into a mixing bowl. Whisk with a hand blender or by hand until frothy. Keep the whisk moving while adding the oils in a thin stream until the mixture thickens to a mayonnaise consistency. Add more oil if necessary.

Stir in the saffron, a light dusting of paprika, and the lemon juice.

Grill or bake the bread until crisp. Spread with the rouille and add one or two slices to each bowl of soup as you serve it. Alternatively, put the rouille in a serving bowl standing on a plate and surround it with the toast for people to help themselves.

Chili and feta cornbread

This crumbly bread tastes deliciously of corn with the odd zap of chili and salty lump of feta. It is lovely with any soup or fish dish, and particularly good with mussels (see pages 274 and 381). As it freezes well, I tend to double up the quantities and freeze half for another day. It's best served warm.

Yields 1 loaf (serves about 6)
* 2 eggs
* 2 cups buttermilk, or plain yogurt thinned with milk
* 3 tablespoons butter, melted
* ½ cup unbleached flour
* 1 teaspoon baking soda
* ½ teaspoon ground mace
* 1 teaspoon table salt
* 1 ⅔ cups fine cornmeal
* 2 fresh red chilis, deseeded and finely chopped, plus ½ red chili, sliced, to serve
* 4 ounces feta cheese, broken into lumps
* Flaky sea salt

Preheat the oven to 350 degrees. Line and grease a 9 by 5-inch loaf pan.

In a large bowl, whisk the eggs until frothy, then whisk in the buttermilk and melted butter.

In another bowl, sift the flour, baking soda, and mace together. Add the table salt, then gradually stir this dry mixture into the eggs.

Fold in the cornmeal a little at a time. Add the chilis and crumble in the lumps of feta. Stir well.

Pour the mixture into the prepared pan and bake for 25 to 30 minutes, until the top is firm to the touch. Leave the loaf to cool in the pan for 5 minutes before turning out on to a cooling rack. While still warm, scatter over some red chili slices and sea salt and serve.

Focaccia

A fluffy, olive-oil-rich focaccia, topped with rosemary, olives, and cherry or sun-dried tomatoes, is great with almost any summer soup.

Yields 1 loaf (serves about 8)
* 3 ½ cups unbleached flour
* 1 teaspoon salt
* 1 teaspoon sugar
* ¼ cup olive oil, plus a little extra for drizzling
* 1 (¼-ounce) packet of dried yeast

For the topping
* Flaky sea salt can be used alone, or use 2 to 3 rosemary sprigs, 6 olives, and 8 small cherry tomatoes or 3 sun-dried tomatoes cut in half (these quantities will each do a quarter of the focaccia)

Lightly oil a shallow baking tray (14 ½ by 10 ½ inches).

Put the flour, salt, sugar, olive oil, and yeast into a large mixing bowl. Add 1¼ cups warm water and mix with your hands. You want a loose, elastic dough, so don't be tempted to add more flour even if it's sticky.

Transfer the dough to a lightly floured surface and knead for 1 to 2 minutes, no longer.

Lightly oil another bowl. Put the dough in it and cover with a kitchen towel. Leave in a warm place for 1 hour, or until the dough has doubled in size.

Knock back the dough by giving it a firm punch, then use your fingertips to press it into the prepared baking tray. Cover once more with the kitchen towel and leave to rise for another 20 to 30 minutes.

Preheat the oven to 375 degrees.

Drizzle a little olive oil over the dough and, again with your fingertips, press it into the dough, which absorbs it. Now add your chosen topping. If using all 4, put them on separate quarters of the bread. If using sun-dried tomatoes, put these on the top halfway through the cooking time or they will char.

Bake in the oven for 25 minutes, or until golden; when tapped underneath it should sound hollow.

The focaccia is best served warm, straight after baking. It can be frozen, but loses its lovely soft texture and is then better toasted.

Marinated mozzarella with basil and prosciutto

This is a brilliant recipe for making inexpensive mozzarella taste like the finest buffalo mozzarella. You can use almost any herb—rosemary, torn bay leaves, thyme, or chives—and some chili flakes to add to the flavor.

Serves 6 as a starter or side salad,
4 as a main course
* 2 (8-ounce) packages of mozzarella cheese
* Small bunch of fresh basil
* 3 tablespoons extra virgin olive oil
* Grated or pared zest of 1 lemon
* Good pinch of chili flakes
* Salt and black pepper
* 12 slices of prosciutto, to serve

Drain the mozzarella, then tear into chunky strips and put into a mixing bowl. Tear up the basil leaves and add to the mozzarella along with the olive oil, lemon zest, chili flakes, and a good pinch of salt and pepper. Stir well to combine and leave overnight in the fridge for all the flavors to infuse. Take out of the fridge a couple of hours before you want to eat.

Put a couple of slices of prosciutto on each person's plate, and serve the mozzarella mixture with more fresh basil leaves scattered over the top. Almost any white bread goes well with this, but it's particularly good with Focaccia (see page 132). For a change, try serving it as part of a salad with tomatoes, basil, and artichoke hearts (see right).

Tomato, basil, and mozzarella salad with artichoke hearts

A fantastic salad to serve at a party. Use several different kinds of tomatoes—some cherry varieties, Sungold, and Gardener's Delight—as well as beefsteak salad varieties. This gives a good mix of textures and tastes.

Serves 8 as a starter or side salad,
6 as a main course
* 2 (8-ounce) packages of mozzarella cheese, marinated in basil and olive oil (see left)
* 8 grilled artichoke hearts (see page 137)
* 2 pounds tomatoes, mixed varieties
* 3 tablespoons extra virgin olive oil
* 1 heaping tablespoon capers
* 1 large green chili, thinly sliced into rings, seeds removed
* 1 tablespoon red wine vinegar or juice of ½ lemon
* 1 teaspoon superfine sugar
* Large handful (about ½ cup) fresh basil leaves (a mixture of green and purple leaves looks good)
* Salt and black pepper
* Sea salt, to serve

Prepare the mozzarella and artichokes by following the recipes indicated above.

Cut the tomatoes into different-sized chunks and slices, keeping some of the smaller varieties whole and some just halved. Put them into a bowl with the olive oil, capers, chili, vinegar, sugar, 1 tablespoon of chopped basil leaves, and salt and pepper to taste. Stir well and allow to sit for 20 minutes.

When ready to serve, lay out the tomatoes, mozzarella, and grilled artichoke hearts in separate piles on a large plate. Scatter the remaining basil leaves all over. Don't be tempted to mix it up. Sprinkle with sea salt and a good grinding of black pepper. Serve with just-baked Focaccia (see page 132).

Warm zucchini, cumin, and goat cheese salad

I like the sourness of goat cheese with zucchini—
all you need for a quick and tasty lunch with some
delicious bread. This also works well as a side dish
with broiled or grilled meat or fish.

For 6 as a starter or side dish, 4 for lunch
* 3 medium-sized zucchinis (about ¾ pound)
* Olive oil, for brushing
* 4 ounces goat cheese (the log type), crumbled
* 2 tablespoons pine nuts, toasted
* 2 tablespoons roughly chopped flat-leaf parsley

For the dressing
* ¼ cup extra virgin olive oil
* Juice and grated zest of ½ a lemon, to taste
* Dash of honey
* Salt and black pepper
* 1 teaspoon cumin seeds, toasted and ground
  in a mortar
* Seeds from 8 cardamom pods, crushed

Heat a ridged grill pan or nonstick frying pan for 3
to 4 minutes (until you can't count to 10 with your
hand hovering just above it).

Slice the zucchini lengthwise in 1-inch slices.
Brush them with olive oil and place in a single layer
on the hot grill pan—don't pack them in. Cook for 2
minutes on each side, until stripy and beginning to
soften, then lay them out in a single layer on a large
plate. Repeat this process until all the zucchinis are
cooked.

To make the dressing, put all the ingredients into
a jam jar, screw on the lid, and shake well. Season to
taste with salt and pepper, then pour over the warm
zucchini. Scatter the goat cheese, pine nuts, and
parsley over the top.

Globe artichoke and zucchini summer salad

This is an excellent recipe for the tender young artichokes that become available in the spring or, if you're growing them, the small side ones that form on the stem below the main large king. It's also a good way of using just the hearts later in the year, when the artichokes have become too big and tough for eating whole. You can cheat and buy prepared artichoke hearts in olive oil, but these tend to have quite a vinegary taste. Buying them unpickled and frozen by the bag, or even brined and canned, is better. Making your own, as described below, gives them a much sweeter flavor. Earlier in the year you can also try this combination with grilled asparagus.

**Serves 6 as a starter or side salad,
4 as a main course**

For the homemade artichokes
* 2–3 artichokes, depending on size (buy those with the longest stems, or pick with at least 1½ inches of stalk, as once pared down, these are delicious too)
* Juice of ½ lemon
* 1⅔ cups white wine
* ½ cup extra virgin olive oil
* 2 garlic cloves, left whole
* Sprigs of thyme
* Salt and black pepper

* 2 zucchinis
* 2 tablespoons extra virgin olive oil
* 2 garlic cloves
* 3 good handfuls of arugula
* Bunch of thin scallions, quartered lengthwise and separated into ribbons
* 2 tablespoons pine nuts, toasted
* ⅓ pound pecorino cheese, coarsely grated or thinly sliced
* Small handful of mint leaves, coarsely torn

For the dressing
* 6 tablespoons extra virgin olive oil
* Juice and grated zest of 1 lemon, or to taste
* 1 garlic clove, crushed
* 1 teaspoon superfine sugar
* 1 tablespoon finely chopped fresh mint
* Sea salt and black pepper

Strip the tough outer scales from the artichokes until you get to the soft white leaves. Cut the top off the whole thing and pare off the stringy outer third of the long stem with a sharp knife. Cut the artichokes in half and, with a spoon, scrape out the choke—the nascent flower—if it has started to form. Drop the hearts straight into a bowl of water acidulated with the lemon juice.

Put the white wine, olive oil, garlic, and thyme in a pan and bring to a boil. Add the prepared artichokes and poach gently for 20 minutes. Season with salt and pepper. The artichokes are delicious eaten just like this, still warm, or you can store them in olive oil in the fridge for grilling later. They will keep for a couple of weeks if kept refrigerated.

If you can't face any of this, buy canned or frozen prepared artichoke hearts. These are often better (less vinegary) and cheaper than those sold in oil.

Heat a ridged grill pan or nonstick frying pan for 3 to 4 minutes (until you can't count to 10 with your hand hovering just above it).

Slice the artichoke into 1-inch slices and grill for 3 to 4 minutes on each side until stripy. This gives them extra flavor.

Slice the zucchinis lengthwise (about 1-inch thick). Brush them with olive oil and grill on both sides until they are just beginning to soften and show stripes from the ridges.

Using a mortar and pestle or food processor, make a paste with the olive oil and garlic. Spread a little of this over one side of the zucchini as they come off the grill pan.

Cover a large plate with a bed of arugula. Add the scallions, zucchini, and sliced artichoke hearts on top.

To make the dressing, put all the ingredients into a jam jar, screw on the lid, and shake well. Season to taste with salt and pepper.

Drizzle the dressing over the salad, and top with the pine nuts, pecorino, and mint.

Greek salad with marinated onions

Having juicy, fresh, sweet tomatoes and cucumber is the making of this salad. Use fresh oregano with its strong, slightly medicinal taste, but parsley is also fine. Oregano has an intense flavor, so you don't need much. I hate that sharp, repeating thing of onions, particularly when eaten for lunch, and usually pick them out of a salad. Marinate them and they are transformed—delicious and mild.

**Serves 6 as a starter or side dish,
4 as a main course**

For the marinated onions
* 1 red onion, sliced as thinly as possible
* 3 tablespoons red wine vinegar
* 1 tablespoon port or red wine
* 1 tablespoon light brown sugar
* 2 tablespoons fresh rosemary leaves
* 2 bay leaves
* 1 teaspoon crushed juniper berries (optional)
* Salt and black pepper

* 4 large tomatoes, ideally juicy, thin-skinned, beefsteak types (about 1 pound)
* 1 cucumber (about ¼ pound), peeled
* 15 Kalamata olives, pitted and halved
* 10–15 fresh oregano leaves, plus a few extra to serve
* 6 ounces feta cheese

For the dressing
* ¼ cup extra virgin olive oil
* 1 tablespoon red wine vinegar or juice of ½ lemon
* Salt and black pepper

Start by putting all the ingredients for the marinated onions into a bowl and allow to marinate overnight. If your tomatoes are cold, put them in the sun for 30 minutes if possible. When you're eating tomatoes raw, warmth makes all the difference to the taste.

Cut the tomatoes into chunks. Cut the cucumber in half lengthwise. If it's very heavy on seeds, scoop them out with a teaspoon. Cut the remaining flesh into chunks.

Put the tomatoes and cucumber into a bowl. Scatter in the olives and marinated onions. Coarsely chop the oregano so that you can still see the leaf shape and add to the bowl. Mix well.

Put the dressing ingredients into a jam jar, screw on the lid, and shake well. Season to taste with salt and pepper. Pour over the salad and toss well.

When all is mixed, add the cheese on the top. You don't necessarily want a bit of feta in every mouthful, so don't crumble it: cut it, as the Greeks do, into decent-sized slabs and place on top of the salad. Serve immediately, scattered with a few oregano leaves.

Shrimp and smoked trout salad

Similar to the Niçoise salad principle of fish with French beans and new potatoes, this recipe uses juicy shrimp and chunks of smoked trout rather than anchovies and tuna, and sits them on a bed of lettuce.

Serves 6 as starter or side salad, 4 as a main course
* 12 raw unshelled shrimp
* 1 tablespoon olive oil
* 1 pound green beans, trimmed
* 1 pound waxy new potatoes
* 2 large handfuls of summer salad leaves or 1 crunchy head of romaine lettuce
* 30 or so small cherry tomatoes, preferably on the vine
* 2 mild red chilis, cut into thin strips (optional)
* 12 radishes, sliced
* 20 black olives, pits in (about ¼ pound)
* ⅔ pound smoked trout
* 20 capers
* Small handful of fresh basil, parsley, or chervil leaves

For the dressing
* ¼ cup extra virgin olive oil
* 1 small garlic clove, finely chopped
* 1 teaspoon Dijon mustard
* 1 tablespoon red wine vinegar
* Salt and black pepper

Heat a ridged grill pan for 3 to 4 minutes (until you can't count to 10 with your hand hovering just above it).

Brush the shrimp all over with olive oil and grill for 1½ minutes on each side. Transfer to a plate and allow to rest for 5 minutes before peeling and deveining. Cook the beans whole for 3 minutes in a large pan full of boiling salted water (to retain their color and texture). Plunge them into cold water. Drain and allow to dry.

Cook the potatoes in boiling salted water for about 15 minutes, until they're tender. Drain and allow them cool a bit. Peel and cut into chunks.

To make the dressing, put all the ingredients into a jam jar, screw on the lid, and shake well. Season to taste with salt and pepper.

Make a bed of salad or lettuce leaves in a large bowl or plate. Toss the beans in a little of the dressing and add them on the top. Add the tomatoes, chilis (if using), radishes, potatoes, and olives. Flake the trout over them, scatter with the capers, and lay the shrimp on top. Drizzle with the rest of the dressing and scatter over some basil, parsley, or chervil leaves.

Shrimp, melon, and tomato salad

This is one of my husband, Adam's, favorite suppers, which we had with friends last summer, and I've made countless times since. It has a very 1970s feel about it: a wonderful combination of shrimp with the sweetness of melon and the tang of curry powder. If you're in a hurry, you can use store-bought mayonnaise.

**Serves 6 as a starter or side salad,
4 as a main course**
* 2 sweet Galia melons or 1 large
  Honeydew melon
* 1 pound shrimp, cooked
* 3–4 cherry tomatoes, cut in half
* 5 tablespoons good store-bought mayonnaise or homemade mayonnaise (see page 117, without the anchovies)
* Juice and grated zest of 1 lemon
* 2 tablespoons bottled chili sauce
* 1 tablespoon medium curry powder
* 1 tablespoon cumin seeds, toasted and ground
* Small bunch of fresh basil, roughly chopped
* Small bunch of fresh mint, roughly chopped
* Salt and black pepper

To serve
* 1 head romaine lettuce
* Large handful of arugula

Remove the skin from the melons and cut the flesh into chunks. Place in a large bowl and mix with the shrimp and halved tomatoes.

In a separate bowl, combine the mayonnaise, lemon juice and zest, chili sauce, curry powder, ground cumin, and half the herb leaves. Season with a little salt and pepper, then pour over the melon mixture and stir thoroughly. Top with the remaining basil and mint leaves.

As a starter, I'd normally serve this on its own. As a main course, I'd scatter it on a bed of crunchy green lettuce with some arugula leaves scattered on top.

Crab and avocado salad

I can never resist a good-looking crab on a fish stall, and if it's not prepared, I love the whole process of pulling out the "dead man's fingers" or gills, excavating the brown meat, and then cracking the huge claws so that everyone can fish for their own white meat with hooks and probes as they talk. That's a fine way to eat a crab, or you can go a bit further—as in this recipe—and mix the white and brown meat with creamy avocado, plenty of lemon juice, and Basil mayonnaise. It's fantastic party food. Serve with lots of brown toast, or warm new potatoes and green beans. This is rich, so a little goes a long way. It also makes a great canapé for a party, served on small slices of brown toast.

Serves 4
* ½ pound mixed crab meat (white and brown), plus 4 crab shells (optional)
* 2 ripe avocados
* Juice and grated zest of 1–2 lemons, or to taste
* Salt and black pepper
* 1 quantity Basil mayonnaise (see page 158)

If you find live crabs (you'll need at least 4 medium-sized crabs), cook them first. Crabs up to 2 pounds in weight cook for 20 minutes, plus another 5 minutes for every extra pound. Remove the claws, then the central body armour (reserving the shell) and the dead man's fingers (the circle of gray feathery gills on the underside). Pull out the brown meat from around the edge of the shell and put it in a bowl. Excavate the white meat from all the claws. If you don't want to bother with all this, buy prepared mixed crab meat.

Peel and pit the avocados. Place the flesh in a bowl and smash with a fork. Squeeze over the lemon juice and add the zest, pepper, and salt to taste. Combine with the crab and mayonnaise and pile back into the shells, or serve from a bowl with toast.

Haloumi and summer fruit salad

I love the saltiness of haloumi, either on its own or dressed with olive oil, lemon juice, and chili, but it's even better mixed in a salad with sweet fruit—particularly mangoes, lime-dressed papaya, and figs.

Serves 6 as a starter or side dish,
4 as a main course
* 24 ounces haloumi cheese, cut into ½ inch slices
* 1 mango
* 1 papaya
* Juice of 1 lime
* 4 handfuls of summer salad leaves, including pea tips, spinach, mizuna, lettuce, and arugula
* 4 fresh figs, cut into quarters
* Large bunch of fresh mint, leaves picked and torn into strips

For the dressing
* Juice and grated zest of 1 lime
* 2 teaspoons honey
* 1 red chili, deseeded and finely chopped
* 2 tablespoons finely chopped mint
* ¼ cup olive oil
* Salt and black pepper

Heat a ridged grill pan for 3 to 4 minutes (until you can't count to 10 with your hand hovering just above it). Grill the haloumi until striped (about 2 minutes each side). Set aside on a plate.

Put all the dressing ingredients into a food processor and whizz for an instant.

Cube the mango. To do so, run a sharp knife around it lengthwise, cutting either side of the long, flat seed. Make a criss-cross pattern in the flesh, being careful not to cut all the way through the skin. Pushing against the skin with your thumbs, turn the fruit inside out so you end up with a hedgehog shape. This allows you to easily cut away the cubes of mango from the skin. Place them in a bowl.

Peel the papaya, deseed and cube it, then add it to the bowl of mango. Squeeze over plenty of lime juice so that it starts to marinate.

On individual plates lay out a base of salad leaves. Scatter the fruit, mint leaves, and haloumi on top. Pour the dressing over the salad and serve.

Warm chorizo, tomato, and bread salad with tahini dressing

You can eat this lovely warm salad for lunch or as a starter, or with grilled or barbecued fish (it's great with mackerel, see page 195) or meat.

Serves 6 as a starter or side dish,
4 as a main course
* ½ pound chorizo, sliced ½ inch thick
* 3–4 tablespoons olive oil
* Juice of 1 lemon
* 3 thick slices stale white bread
* 1 pound cherry or grape tomatoes
* 2 green chilis, deseeded and thinly sliced
* 2 garlic cloves, finely chopped
* Pinch of paprika
* 1 teaspoon ground cumin
* 3 tablespoons roughly chopped flat-leaf parsley

For the dressing
* ¼ cup plain yogurt
* 2 teaspoons tahini paste
* Juice and grated zest of 1 lemon
* Salt and black pepper

In a large, heavy-based frying pan over a medium heat, fry the chorizo in 1 tablespoon olive oil until crispy. Throw away the oil as a lot is released from the chorizo while cooking. Put the chorizo into a bowl and squeeze over the lemon juice.

Remove and chuck the crusts from the bread. Cut the remaining white parts into 1-inch cubes. Heat 2 tablespoons olive oil in a frying pan until hot (about 2 minutes). Throw in the bread and fry until crispy. Put into the same bowl as the chorizo.

Heat the remaining tablespoon of oil in the pan. Add the tomatoes, chilis, garlic, and spices and cook, stirring occasionally, until the tomatoes start to soften and release some juice. Take off the heat and pour into a salad bowl. Add the chorizo mixture, then the parsley, and mix together.

To make the dressing, combine the yogurt, tahini, lemon juice, and zest in a small bowl with ½ tablespoon water and whisk with a fork. Season to taste with salt and pepper.

Spoon the dressing over the salad, mix well, and serve while still warm.

Moroccan roasted chicken salad with green beans

Served warm, this is a delicious main course salad. It's wonderful with a few new potatoes or an Edible flower couscous salad (see page 170).

Serves 8 as a starter or side salad, 6 as a main course

* 2 tablespoons butter, softened
* Small bunch of fresh cilantro, chopped
* 1 teaspoon coriander seeds, toasted and crushed
* 1 teaspoon cumin seeds, toasted and crushed
* 2 garlic cloves, thinly sliced
* Salt and black pepper
* 1 medium-sized chicken (about 4 pounds)
* 3 lemons—2 pierced and 1 thinly sliced
* 1½ pounds green beans, topped and tailed
* Small bunch of fresh mint, leaves coarsely torn, to serve

For the gravy dressing

* Juice of 2 lemons and grated zest of 1
* 1 red chili, deseeded and finely chopped
* 1 garlic clove, finely chopped
* 3 tablespoons olive oil
* 1 teaspoon coriander seeds, toasted and finely crushed
* 1 teaspoon cumin seeds, toasted and finely crushed
* ½ teaspoon mustard powder
* 2 teaspoons superfine sugar

Preheat the oven to 350 degrees.

Put the butter, fresh cilantro, coriander seeds, cumin seeds, and garlic in a bowl, season with salt and pepper, and mix with a fork.

Loosen the skin over the chicken breast by easing your hands in between the skin and the flesh. Spread the flavored butter over the flesh just below the skin. Stuff the pierced lemons into the bird's cavity. Cover the chicken thighs with the slices.

Place the bird in a roasting pan and cook in the oven for 1¼ to 1½ hours. It is cooked once the flesh at the base of the thighs, where they join the body, is no longer pink and the juices run clear when a skewer is inserted. Cover loosely with foil and set aside to rest for 15 minutes before carving into chunks.

To make the dressing, pour the fat out of the roasting pan. Return the pan to the heat and deglaze by adding the lemon juice and scraping up all the crunchy bits from the bottom. Take off the heat and allow to cool for a couple of minutes. Add the lemon zest, chili, garlic, olive oil, coriander seeds, cumin, mustard, and sugar. Taste, and season with salt and pepper. Strain into a pitcher.

Bring a large pan of salted water to a boil and cook the beans for 3 minutes, until softened, but still a little crunchy and squeaky on the teeth. Drain, blanch briefly in cold water, drain again, and mix with half of the dressing while still warm.

Scatter the dressed beans on a large shallow plate and top with the chunks of chicken. Drizzle with the remaining dressing, scatter with coarsely torn mint leaves, and serve while still warm.

Summer garden fritto misto

This is a fabulous and versatile summer garden harvest meal—baby vegetables and the flowers and growth tips of herbs and edible flowers. In Italy they eat borage and calendula (pot marigolds) as vegetables—leaves, flower buds, and all. I realize that some of these things are tricky or impossible to find if you don't have a garden, but you can use almost any tender early summer vegetables. (I do a similar thing in the winter, see page 373.)

Although this is a fantastic and beautiful-looking summer party dish, don't cook it for any more than 10 or you'll be frying all night.

Serves 8–10 as a starter or light lunch

For the batter
* 1 cup flour
* 1 tablespoon extra virgin olive oil
* Salt and black pepper
* 2 egg whites

* Handful of young fava beans, pods the size of your ring finger
* Handful of baby or small carrots
* Vegetable or peanut oil, for frying
* Several baby zucchinis, flowers still on, halved lengthwise
* Handful of pea tips
* Handful of sugarsnap peas, strings removed
* Handful of borage flower buds and growing tips (optional)
* Handful of calendula buds and tips (optional)
* Handful of basil tips and top leaves
* Handful of sage leaves
* 2 unwaxed lemons, thinly sliced

To serve
* Lemon wedges
* Salt and black pepper

First make the batter: sift the flour into a medium bowl and make a well in the center. Pour in the olive oil, stirring as you pour. Gradually add a little warm water to loosen the mixture, stirring all the time, until you have a batter the consistency of heavy cream. Season to taste. Leave to stand at room temperature for at least 45 minutes. The warm water swells the flour and stops it from being too heavy.

Just before cooking, beat the egg whites until stiff, then fold gently into the batter.

Blanch the fava beans in their pods for 5 minutes in salted boiling water. Dry them well on a kitchen towel.

Blanch the carrots for 2 minutes in salted boiling water. Dry them well on a kitchen towel.

Fill a deep saucepan with enough oil to reach about one-third of the way up the side, and have a lid or splash-guard on standby to prevent the oil from spitting too much after you add each batch. Heat the oil until it reaches about 375 degrees, or until a cube of bread browns in 30 seconds.

Coat all your vegetables, fruits, herbs, flower buds, and tips with the batter and shallow-fry in the hot oil—only a few at a time—until they're crisp and golden. Drain on paper towels.

Serve with a slice of lemon and a scattering of salt and freshly ground black pepper.

Grilled summer vegetables with goat cheese

You can make this delicious, light summer vegetable dish in individual gratin dishes, or in one big shallow heatproof dish for everyone to serve themselves from in the middle of the table. It's good as a starter, and also as a main course with rice or crusty bread and a green salad.

Serves 6 as a starter or side salad,
4 as a main course
* ½ pound young fava beans, podded weight
* 1 large red onion, halved and thinly sliced
* ⅓ pound button mushrooms
* ½ pound baby zucchinis, halved lengthwise
* Olive oil
* 4 ounces crème fraîche
* Small bunch of fresh dill, roughly chopped
* Grated zest of 2 lemons and juice of 1
* Salt and black pepper
* 2 tablespoons butter, for greasing
* 5 ounces goat cheese

Blanch the fava beans in boiling water for 3 minutes, then drain.

Gently fry the onion, mushrooms, and zucchinis in a little olive oil for 8 to 10 minutes, until the onion is golden brown. Add the beans (peeled if large), the crème fraîche, half the dill, the lemon zest, and juice, and stir together, cooking for another couple of minutes. Season with salt and pepper and sprinkle the remaining dill over the top.

Lightly butter your dish(es) and spoon in the vegetable mixture.

Heat the broiler. Cut the goat cheese into ½ inch slices, place on top of the vegetables, and place under the hot broiler for 5 minutes, or until the cheese is melting and beginning to brown.

Fasolakia

Summer comfort food, this is an old-fashioned Greek recipe for a green bean stew, cooked until everything is glossy and soft. Have it hot for lunch or supper with some feta and crusty bread. It's also lovely eaten cold the next day, with a dollop of yogurt. You cook it slowly, but it takes less than 10 minutes to prepare.

Serves 6 as a side dish, 4 as a main course
* 2 onions, finely chopped
* ¼ cup olive oil
* 2 garlic cloves, finely chopped
* 1 pound green or Romano beans, topped and tailed or strings removed and sliced
* 2 carrots, peeled and grated
* 1 (14 ½-ounce) can of tomatoes, or 4 large tomatoes, peeled and coarsely chopped (see page 125)
* 1 tablespoon coriander seeds, crushed
* 2-inch piece of fresh ginger, peeled and finely grated
* Salt and black pepper
* Pinch of dried chili flakes
* ½ cup chicken or vegetable stock
* Large bunch of flat-leaf parsley, chopped

Put the onions and olive oil in a large saucepan and fry until translucent (about 5 minutes).

Add all the other ingredients with three-quarters of the parsley, mix well, cover, and simmer on a low heat for about 1 hour. Taste, and season with salt and pepper. Add the remaining parsley as you serve.

Zucchini "meat" balls

Although quite time-consuming to prepare, these are utterly delicious, so it's a good idea to make masses, using the grater on your food processor, and freeze some or serve them for a party. It's an ideal recipe for when you've got a glut of zucchinis and tomatoes, and it works with larger tougher zucchinis too. I make a similar thing in the autumn and winter with parsnips (see page 292).

Eat these on their own or with some slightly spiced basmati rice. This is an adaptation by my friend Teresa Wallace of a recipe from Madhur Jaffrey's *Eastern Vegetarian Cooking*. For meat-eaters, I like to serve these balls mixed up with Pork meatballs (see page 57), half and half of each.

Serves 4 (makes about 16 little balls)
* 3 tablespoons very finely chopped onion
* 2 tablespoons butter
* 1 tablespoon olive oil
* 1 pound zucchinis (about 3 medium zucchinis)
* ½ teaspoon salt
* 1 hot green chili, finely chopped
* 1 teaspoon peeled and grated fresh ginger
* 2 tablespoons chopped cilantro or flat-leaf parsley
* ⅓ cup chickpea flour
* Oil, for frying

For the sauce
* 2 medium onions, finely chopped
* 2 tablespoons olive or sunflower oil
* ¼ teaspoon turmeric
* 1 teaspoon ground cumin
* Cayenne pepper, to taste
* 2 teaspoons ground coriander
* ½ pound tomatoes, peeled and chopped (see page 125)
* 1 cup heavy cream
* ½ teaspoon garam masala
* ½ teaspoon cumin seeds, roasted and ground
* Salt

Gently fry the onion in the butter and olive oil until soft but not browned (about 5 minutes).

Grate the zucchinis and put them in a colander with the salt. Leave for 30 minutes, then squeeze dry with your hands, saving the liquid for the sauce.

Mix the zucchinis with the chili, ginger, and cilantro. Sprinkle in the flour and mix again.

Next make the sauce. Fry the onions in the oil for 7 to 8 minutes, until brown. Add the turmeric, cumin, cayenne, and coriander. Stir and add the tomatoes. Pour in 1 cup of the zucchini juice (made up with water if not enough). Bring to a boil and simmer for 15 minutes. Add the remaining ingredients, seasoning to taste with salt.

Fill a deep saucepan with enough oil to reach about one-third of the way up the side, and have a lid or splash-guard on standby to prevent the oil from spitting too much after you add each batch. Heat the oil until it reaches about 375 degrees, or until a cube of bread browns in 30 seconds.

Roll the zucchini mixture into 16 little balls. Fry them in the hot oil until they've browned all over. Drain on paper towels.

Add the zucchini balls to the sauce, cover, and simmer gently for 6 to 7 minutes, spooning the sauce over the balls as they cook. (If you prefer, the final cooking can be done in a gratin dish in an oven preheated to 325 degrees.)

Stuffed zucchini flowers with honey

You don't often see zucchini flowers for sale in the supermarket, but if you do, buy them. If you grow zucchinis, pumpkins, or squash, you'll have plenty in your garden.

This recipe might look tricky, but is, in fact, perfectly easy. The Cretan combination of the mild goat cheese with the runny honey is wonderful.

Serves 8

For the batter
* 1 cup unbleached flour
* 1 tablespoon extra virgin olive oil
* 2 egg whites
* Salt and black pepper

* 16 zucchini flowers
* ½ cup pine nuts or ¾ cup fresh or frozen peas
* 5 ounces cream cheese
* 5 ounces goat cheese, crumbly or soft (any that will mix in with the cream cheese)
* Salt and black pepper
* Small bunch of fresh thyme, leaves finely chopped
* 1 tablespoon olive oil
* Light olive oil, for frying
* Honey, to serve

First make the batter: sift the flour into a medium bowl and make a well in the center. Pour in the olive oil, stirring as you pour. Gradually add a little warm water to loosen the mixture, stirring all the time, until you have a batter the consistency of heavy cream. Season. Leave to stand at room temperature for at least 45 minutes. The warm water swells the flour and stops it from being too heavy.

Just before cooking, beat the egg whites until stiff, then fold gently into the batter.

Shake the zucchini flowers to dislodge any ants or insects that might be hidden inside, and remove the stigma from the center. If you have mini zucchinis with the flowers, slit them lengthwise two-thirds of the way up the fruit (this allows the heat to penetrate the zucchini flesh).

Toast the pine nuts or cook the peas in plenty of salted boiling water for 3 minutes. In a mixing bowl, combine the pine nuts or peas with the cheeses, salt, pepper, thyme, and olive oil.

Using your fingers, gently part the flower petals, leaving one finger inside to keep them open. Carefully stuff each flower with 2 teaspoons of the cheese mixture, sealing the pointed end by giving it a little twist.

Fill a deep saucepan with enough oil to reach about one-third of the way up the side, and have a lid or splash-guard on standby to prevent the oil from spitting too much after you add each batch. Heat the oil until it reaches about 375 degrees, or until a cube of bread browns in 30 seconds.

Coat your stuffed flowers with batter and shallow-fry them—just 3 or 4 at a time—until they're crisp and golden (you'll need to turn them while they're cooking). Drain on paper towels.

Put 2 flowers per person on individual plates, drizzle with the honey, and add a scattering of salt and freshly ground black pepper.

Moroccan spiced zucchini and goat cheese tart

A wonderfully unusual zucchini tart, with the addition of raisins and cinnamon. It's a very easy thing to cook for lots of people when the garden is bursting with zucchini.

Serves 6 to 8
* 6–8 medium zucchinis (a mixture of colors works well), thinly sliced
* 2 large garlic cloves, finely chopped or crushed
* Bunch of scallions, chopped
* Olive oil
* 1 tablespoon medium curry powder
* 10 ounces soft goat cheese
* 2 tablespoons raisins
* 1 cup light cream
* 3 eggs
* 1 teaspoon ground cinnamon
* Salt and black pepper

For the pastry
* 1 3/4 cups unbleached flour
* Pinch of salt
* 9 tablespoons cold butter, cubed
* 1 egg, beaten

First make the pastry. Sift the flour into a bowl and add the salt. Rub in the butter by hand until it resembles breadcrumbs. Alternatively, pulse in a food processor. Add the egg and a little cold water—just enough to bring the pastry together into a ball. Wrap in plastic wrap and leave in the fridge for an hour.

Preheat the oven to 350 degrees and heat a baking sheet until searing hot. Roll out the pastry to 1/8 inch in thickness, and use to line an 11-inch loose-bottomed tart pan, leaving the excess pastry draped over the sides in case it shrinks.

Prick the bottom of the pastry crust with a fork, line with parchment paper or foil, and weigh this down with baking beans or rice. Place on the hot baking sheet and bake for about 15 minutes.

Remove the baking beans and paper and bake the crust for another 5 minutes. Take out of the oven and trim off the excess pastry. Keep the oven on and reheat the baking sheet.

Meanwhile, put the zucchinis, garlic, and scallions in a heavy-based saucepan with a little olive oil and the curry powder and sweat over a gentle heat for 7 to 10 minutes. When the vegetables are soft, put them into the pastry crust. Crumble over the goat cheese and add the raisins.

Combine the cream, eggs, and cinnamon in a bowl and season well with salt and pepper. Pour this over the vegetable mixture, then bake the tart on the hot baking sheet for about 30 minutes, or until set and golden. Serve warm with a green or tomato salad.

Tomato tarte tatin

Here's a tasty and simple lunch dish, a puff pastry tart with a difference—the tomatoes halved rather than sliced, and sitting on top of a pesto rice base. Use a homemade pesto if you can, but the stuff from a jar is fine. This tart is best served warm while the pastry is crisp, but is still good cold the next day.

Serves 6 as a main course

* ½ cup long-grain rice
* Water or vegetable or chicken stock
* 3 tablespoons olive oil
* 1 onion, finely chopped
* 2 garlic cloves, finely chopped
* 1 zucchini, finely chopped
* 1 red bell pepper, finely chopped
* 3 ounces pesto
* 2 heaping tablespoons pine nuts, toasted
* Grated zest of 1 lemon
* Salt and black pepper
* 6 vine tomatoes (about 1⅓ pounds)
* 16 ounces puff pastry

Cook the rice in the water or stock until just done. Drain and place in a large bowl.

Preheat the oven to 400 degrees. Have ready a 10-inch ovenproof frying pan, ideally nonstick so that the tart turns out easily. If you don't have one, line a 10-inch tart pan with parchment paper cut to the right shape.

Heat the olive oil in your ovenproof frying pan and sauté the onion, garlic, zucchini, and red pepper until just softened (about 10 minutes).

Add the vegetable mixture to the rice in the large bowl, along with the pesto, pine nuts, lemon zest, and a little salt and pepper. Mix well.

Cut the tomatoes in half around the middle and chuck away the cores. Place them skin side down in the frying pan (there's no need to wash the pan after cooking the vegetables). Spoon the rice and vegetable mixture over the tomatoes and smooth it down, using the back of the spoon.

Roll out the pastry to a thickness of ⅛ inch and place over the pan, cutting away any excess, then gently push it down around the inside edge of the pan. Bake in the middle of the oven for 20 minutes, until risen and golden brown.

Allow the tart to cool in the pan for 15 minutes, then turn out onto a serving plate. Pinch off the tomato skins, which should come away very easily at this stage. Serve immediately with a summer mixed leaf salad.

Pizza

If we are having lots of children for a big summer meal, particularly on a warm evening, we almost always make pizza. I usually lay out a range of different toppings—Parma ham, anchovies, capers, chorizo—as well as grated mozzarella. The dry blocks of cheese are oddly better than the balls in water, which, even drained, tend to make the pizza soggy. We roll out a pile of bases—kept apart with layers of plastic wrap—and bake them on the loose metal discs from the bottom of tart pans. Everyone takes a base and creates their own topping. It's the best family meal.

Yields 8 medium-sized pizzas
* 4 cups unbleached flour, plus more for dusting
* 1 teaspoon salt
* 1½ teaspoons dried yeast
* 2 tablespoons extra virgin olive oil
* Sunflower oil, for the baking sheet

For the tomato sauce
* 3 (14½-ounce) cans of chopped tomatoes
* 3 tablespoons olive oil
* 2 whole garlic cloves
* Good pinch of salt

For the topping
* 1 pound mozzarella cheese, grated
* Selection of extras, such as 1 (2-ounce) can of anchovies, drained; 1 (3.5-ounce) jar of capers; 20 black olives; 12 slices of prosciutto; 24 thin slices of chorizo

To make the dough, put the flour and salt into a large bowl. Add the yeast, about 1¼ cups tepid water, and the oil. If your mix is too dry, add a little more water. A moist, sticky dough makes a light pizza base with a crisp crust, so don't be put off by the mess. Once the dough is well mixed (kneading isn't necessary if you don't have time), leave it to rest under a damp kitchen towel for a couple of hours. It should at least double in size.

To make the tomato sauce, put the tomatoes in a saucepan with the oil and garlic. Cook gently for about 20 minutes, until reduced by about a third and quite thick. Remove the garlic cloves, add the salt, then set aside.

Preheat the oven to at least 475 degrees (the maximum on conventional ovens) and lightly oil your baking sheets. Alternatively, if using a pizza oven, wait until it has burned down to searing hot ashes.

To make a pizza base, break off a ball of dough about 3 inches in diameter, depending on the size required, and roll it out as thinly as you can on a lightly floured surface. Transfer to a prepared baking sheet. Repeat this step to make as many bases as required.

Spread your bases with a very thin coating of tomato sauce, then cover with a light, even scattering of grated cheese and your choice of topping(s). Place in the oven and bake for 3 to 5 minutes, until the top is bubbling and beginning to brown and the base is slightly charring at the edges. Eat right away.

Summer vegetable risotto

This is one of my favorite risottos, using small, vibrant summer vegetables and vegetable stock. I like risotto soupy (Italians call this *all'onda*, which means "wavy"), but you can reduce the amount of stock for a drier, firmer consistency. I was taught as a child to make risotto by an elderly cook, Lisetta, in the Veneto town of Asolo, where risotto is eaten almost every day. The amount of butter, olive oil, and cheese is frightening, but that's what makes it so creamy and delicious. You can use almost any combination of summer vegetables.

Serves 4 to 5
* 5–6 cups vegetable stock
* 1 large red onion, finely chopped
* 1 garlic clove, finely chopped
* 3 tablespoons extra virgin olive oil
* 7 tablespoons butter
* 2 cups Arborio or Carnaroli rice
* 1 tablespoon finely chopped tarragon
* 2/3 cup white wine
* 1/4 pound baby carrots, sliced or left whole
* 1/4 pound asparagus, sliced lengthwise or into diagonal pieces
* 1/4 pound baby fava beans (podded weight)
* 1/4 pound peas or snow peas
* Bunch of scallions (about 1/4 pound), thinly sliced
* Bunch of radishes (10–12 roots), sliced
* 3–4 baby zucchinis, thinly sliced on the diagonal into ovals
* 1/3 pound Parmesan cheese, grated, plus more to serve
* Salt and black pepper

Put the stock in a pan, bring to a boil, and allow it to simmer gently.

Sweat the onion and garlic in a heavy-based saucepan with the olive oil and butter until the onion becomes translucent, but not brown (about 5 minutes). Stir in the rice and tarragon and cook for 1 minute, stirring, to coat the rice in oil. Add the wine and allow it to bubble until almost all the liquid has been absorbed.

Now start adding the hot stock, a ladleful at a time, stirring each addition until it has been absorbed before adding another one. About 15 minutes after starting to add the stock, check the rice: it should be al dente—tender but still slightly firm.

Cook the carrots in a little water in a large flat pan until tender (about 5 minutes, depending on size). Remove and cook all the other vegetables except the zucchini in the same way for about 2 minutes (radishes just 1 minute), until tender. To stop them from cooking, plunge them into cold water.

A couple of minutes before you remove the risotto from the heat, add the lightly cooked vegetables and the zucchini slices, heat through, then stir in the Parmesan. Season carefully with salt and pepper, and serve with a bowl of Parmesan on the table for people to scatter themselves.

Sea bass baked in salt

The mixture of two salts used here bakes hard, so take the whole fish hidden in the crust to the table and crack it in front of everyone. Serve with potatoes and Fennel ratatouille (see page 393).

Serves 8 to 10
* 6 pounds kosher salt
* 1½ pounds flaky sea salt
* 5½ pounds sea bass (or organic salmon), cleaned but not filleted (you might need more than 1 fish)
* 2 lemons, sliced
* Handful of fresh fennel stalks and leaves

For the salsa verde
* Large bunch of flat-leaf parsley
* Large bunch of mixed summer herbs (sorrel, basil, and mint) and 2 sprigs of thyme, leaves picked
* 4 cornichons, rinsed and chopped
* 20–30 small capers, rinsed and chopped
* 1 cup olive oil
* Juice of ½ lemon
* Salt and black pepper

Preheat the oven to 400 degrees.

In a large bowl, mix the two lots of salt with about 2 cups cold water to give a sand-castle consistency.

Fill the cavity of the fish with the lemon and fennel. Cover the bottom of a baking dish with half the salt mixture and lay the fish(es) on top. Cover them completely with the remaining salt and pat it down smoothly with your hands. If using several small fish, bake for 15 to 20 minutes; a single large fish will need about 30 minutes. Test by inserting a skewer: if the tip of it is hot to the back of your hand, the fish is ready. If not, cook for a further 5 to 10 minutes.

Crack open the salt crust by knocking it with a large carving knife or rolling pin. Pick off the pieces, taking care to brush away any loose salt from the flesh of the fish. Carefully lift the fish and place it on a platter. Remove the skin.

To make the salsa verde, chop all the herbs. Add the cornichons, capers, olive oil, and lemon juice. Season with salt and pepper to taste.

Serve fish drizzled with salsa verde.

Shrimp with basil mayonnaise

This is as simple and delicious as it gets—shrimp (or langoustines) shelled as you eat and dipped into a bright green basil mayonnaise.

Serves 8 to 10

For the basil mayonnaise
* 2 egg yolks
* ¼ cup lemon juice
* 1 cup sunflower oil
* ½ cup olive oil
* 1 red chili, deseeded and finely chopped (optional)
* ¼ cup finely chopped fresh basil
* Flaky sea salt and black pepper

* 2–4 shrimp/langoustines per person (depending on size and what else they are served with)

First make the mayonnaise. Whisk the egg yolks in a large bowl until smooth, then whisk in the lemon juice. Slowly whisk in the oils, making an emulsion. Stir in the chili (if using), the basil, and salt and pepper to taste. Leave for at least a couple of hours to let the flavors infuse, but ideally store the mayonnaise in the fridge and eat it the following day.

Bring a large pan of water to a boil. Drop the shrimp or langoustines into it a few at a time so that they are fully covered. Replace the lid immediately and—once the water has returned to a boil—cook for 3 to 5 minutes (depending on size). The little ones, which fit in the palm of your hand, need only 3 minutes, but the whoppers may need more.

Strain the shellfish in a colander, retaining the cooking water in another pan. (Don't chuck this— it's delicious. Reduce it right down and use it for making Crab or shrimp bisque, see page 128.) Allow the shellfish to cool.

Serve the shrimp or langoustines on a large, shallow plate with a bowl of mayonnaise in the center and perhaps a crunchy green salad in a strong Dijon mustard dressing.

Crab cakes with chili jam

In the summer there are few better things than crunchy-on-the-outside, soft-in-the-middle crab cakes. Perfect with waxy new potatoes and Ginger and mixed seed salad (see page 29), they're also ideal as canapés if you make them much smaller, about 1 inch across. They can be made beforehand and reheated in a hot oven for 10 minutes before serving.

I am addicted to the chili jam and eat it instead of tomato ketchup with sausages, cottage pie, and fries, but it's at its best with these fishcakes: sweet and sour and a little hot—a good contrast to the richness of the crab. The quantities below make about double the amount you need when serving the cakes for 6, but you can store the rest in a sterilized jar. The longer you keep the jam, the hotter it gets. It keeps for years in a jar and, in my experience, doesn't need to be stored in the fridge once opened.

Serves 6 (makes 12 cakes or 36 canapés)

For the chili jam
* ⅔ pound very ripe tomatoes
* 3 garlic cloves
* 2 large red chilis (seeds left in if you want your jam hot)
* 1-inch piece of fresh ginger, peeled and sliced
* ¾ cup golden superfine sugar
* 3 tablespoons Thai fish sauce
* 5 tablespoons red wine vinegar

* Olive oil, for frying
* Bunch of scallions, finely chopped
* 2 eggs
* 2 tablespoons good-quality mayonnaise
* 1 tablespoon Worcestershire sauce
* 1 or 2 mild red chilis (depending how spicy you like things), finely chopped
* Grated zest of 1 lemon and juice of ½
* 2 tablespoons finely chopped flat-leaf parsley
* 2 tablespoons finely chopped fresh cilantro
* Flaky sea salt and black pepper
* 1½ pounds fresh crabmeat
* ¾ cup fresh fine breadcrumbs
* ½ teaspoon paprika

For the coating
* 2 tablespoons flour
* 1⅔ cups coarse fresh breadcrumbs
* Lemon wedges, to serve

First make the chili jam. Blitz half the tomatoes with all the garlic, chilis, and ginger in a food processor. Pour into a heavy-based saucepan. Add the sugar, fish sauce, and vinegar, and bring to a boil, stirring slowly. Reduce to a simmer.

Dice the remaining tomatoes (to give some texture) and add them to the pan. Simmer for 30 to 40 minutes, stirring from time to time. The mixture will turn slightly darker and sticky.

Pour some into a bowl to eat with your crab cakes, and store the rest (while still warm) in a dry, warm, sterilized jar (you can sterilize it in a very hot dishwasher, or boil it in a pan of water for 10 minutes). Seal and label with a date.

To make the crab cakes, heat a little olive oil in a frying pan and sauté the scallions for 2 to 3 minutes, until just softening. Allow to cool.

Beat one of the eggs in a large bowl and mix in the mayonnaise, Worcestershire sauce, chili, lemon zest, juice, and herbs. Season generously with salt and black pepper. Fold in the crabmeat, fine breadcrumbs, paprika, and scallions, and then shape into 12 equal-sized cakes.

Place the cakes on a lightly oiled baking tray, or one lined with parchment paper, and chill in the fridge for 1 hour.

Remove the cakes from the fridge. Put the flour and coarse breadcrumbs on separate plates, and lightly fork the remaining egg in a shallow bowl. Roll the cakes in the flour, then dip in the egg, and roll in the breadcrumbs.

Put a little more oil in the frying pan and place over a medium heat. Add the crab cakes and sauté on each side for 3 to 4 minutes.

Serve with the chili jam, or tartar sauce (see page 120) or basil mayonnaise (see page 158) and lemon wedges.

Pea, scallop, and shrimp risotto

The joy of this is the contrast of the pink shrimp and scallops against the lush green of the pea risotto, and the sweetness of the shellfish against the flavor of the peas. Top with a few crunchy pea tips if you can find them. This recipe was given to me by the painter Francis Hamel, who is a wonderful cook.

Serves 8 as a starter, 6 as a main course
* 5–6 cups stock (fish, shellfish, or chicken)
* 1½ cups fresh or frozen peas (shelled amount)
* Small bunch of fresh mint
* ½ cup heavy cream
* ¼ pound scallions, thinly sliced
* 1 garlic clove, finely chopped
* 3 tablespoons extra virgin olive oil
* 2 tablespoons unsalted butter
* 2 cups Arborio or Carnaroli rice
* ⅔ cup white wine
* 12 scallops
* 1 pound raw shrimp, shells on
* ¼ cup grated Parmesan cheese
* Salt and black pepper
* Handful of pea tips, to serve

Put the stock into a saucepan, bring to a boil, then allow it to simmer gently.

Cook the peas in boiling salted water with a little fresh mint. Drain and set aside ¼ cup of them. Put the rest of the peas in a blender, add the cream, and whizz to a puree. Keep them warm and covered.

Sweat the scallions and garlic in a heavy-based saucepan with the olive oil and 2 tablespoons of the butter until translucent (about 5 minutes). Add the rice and stir to combine, coating the rice with oil. Pour in the wine and allow the mixture to bubble until almost all the liquid has been absorbed. Add a ladleful of hot stock to the rice and keep stirring until it has been absorbed; repeat, adding a ladleful at a time, until all the liquid has been absorbed.

After about 15 minutes, check the bite of the rice: it should be al dente—tender but still firm—and you should ideally have a solid-ish risotto. Take care not to overcook it or the rice goes mushy. Stir in the remaining butter and leave it to rest off the heat for 5 minutes.

Heat a ridged grill pan for 3 to 4 minutes (until you can't count to 10 with your hand hovering just above it). Add the scallops and sear for 1 to 2 minutes on each side (depending on size), until browned on the outside and very soft and creamy in the middle.

Steam or boil the shrimp for a very short time (1 to 2 minutes, depending on size) until just cooked.

While the seafood is cooking, stir the pureed peas and whole peas into the risotto and heat through, then add the Parmesan. Season carefully with salt and pepper. Pour onto a large, shallow plate, scatter with the pea tips (if using), and drape with the scallops and shrimp.

Beef carpaccio with fennel

For the best carpaccio (thinly sliced raw beef) you want very good meat. Put the piece of meat in the freezer for an hour before you carve it as this will make it much easier to slice.

Soaking the capers in red wine vinegar is an excellent tip from River Café. It reduces the saltiness of the capers and adds an extra zip to the flavor.

Serves 4 as a starter
* ⅔ **pound beef fillet**
* **2 teaspoons salted capers, rinsed, then soaked in red wine vinegar for 30 minutes and drained**
* **1 dried red chili, crumbled**
* **Flaky sea salt and black pepper**
* **A small handful of fennel tops (with their flowers if available)**
* **Extra virgin olive oil**

For the dressing
* ½ **tablespoon Dijon mustard**
* **1 tablespoon red wine vinegar**
* ¼ **cup extra virgin olive oil**
* **Salt and black pepper**

Slice the beef as thinly as you can and place a few slices on each serving plate. Sprinkle with the capers, chili, sea salt, and black pepper. Scatter with most of the fennel tops (and flowers if using).

Put all the dressing ingredients into a jam jar, screw on the lid, and shake well. Season with salt and pepper to taste.

Drizzle some olive oil over the beef, and then drizzle with the mustard dressing. Finish with a scattering of a few more fennel tops (and flowers).

Marinated fennel fillet of beef with sharp mustardy leaves

Where the carpaccio is raw, the fillet of beef here is seared so that the outside is cooked but the center is only just warm. Served with piles of punchy-tasting salad, this looks and tastes good and summery; it's also excellent cold.

You can use sirloin steaks—less expensive than fillet—cut into strips after very brief cooking, but whatever you opt for, always try to find slow-raised meat. When eaten simply like this, the quality makes an enormous difference.

Serves 8 as a main course

For the marinade
* Juice and grated zest of 2 lemons
* 1 red chili, deseeded and chopped
* Large bunch of fresh fennel leaves
* 3 garlic cloves, chopped
* ½ cup olive or sunflower oil
* 2 tablespoons fennel seeds, toasted and broken up a bit with a mortar and pestle

* About 3 pounds beef fillet, trimmed
* 5 or 6 large handfuls of mixed peppery summer leaves, such as watercress, wild arugula, mustard, and some sorrel, all refreshed in cold water and dried

For the dressing
* 1 red chili, deseeded and chopped
* Red wine vinegar, to taste
* 1 tablespoon Dijon mustard
* 2 garlic cloves
* ¼ cup extra virgin olive oil
* Flaky sea salt and black pepper
* Good handful of fresh fennel leaves, chopped (and flowers if you can find them)

To make the marinade, put the lemon juice and zest, chili, fennel, garlic, and sunflower oil in a food processor and whizz until smooth.

Add the fennel seeds, then spread over the beef fillet and leave for several hours (or overnight) in the fridge, turning from time to time.

When you're ready, bring the fillet to room temperature (an hour or so out of the fridge).

Preheat the oven to 425 degrees. Heat a ridged grill pan for 3 to 4 minutes (until you can't count to 10 with your hand hovering just above it).

Dry the fillet and brown quickly on the grill (or in a frying pan) over a high heat. Transfer to the oven and roast for 15 to 20 minutes, depending on whether you want it rare or medium. Allow to cool a little.

Meanwhile, combine all the dressing ingredients with half the fennel leaves.

Thinly slice the fillet and arrange the slices on a bed of salad leaves. Drizzle the dressing over the top and sprinkle with the rest of the fennel leaves and the flowers (if using). Add salt and pepper to taste.

Larb moo

This is a recipe from a friend who ate this pork dish when he was drilling for oil in the Golden Triangle of Southeast Asia. Give everyone their own bowl of the pork surrounded by crunchy summer vegetables cut into wide strips so that they can be used as scoops.

Serves 4
* 1 pound medium-lean ground pork
* 1 onion, finely chopped
* 2-inch piece ginger, peeled and grated
* 1 red chili, deseeded and finely chopped
* 1 large garlic clove, finely chopped
* Juice of 3 limes
* 1 tablespoon oil
* Splash of fish sauce
* Splash of soy sauce
* Black pepper
* Small bunch of fresh mint, roughly chopped
* Small bunch of fresh basil, roughly chopped
* Small bunch of fresh cilantro, roughly chopped
* 1 tablespoon coriander seed, toasted and crushed
* 1/3 cup pine nuts, toasted
* Seeds of 1 pomegranate (see page 31)
* Selection of raw summer vegetables, including romaine lettuce leaves, snow peas, peas, baby carrots, celery, Belgian endive, and radishes
* Lemon wedges, to serve

Put the pork into a large bowl. Add the onion, ginger, chili, garlic, and lime juice, mix together, and leave to marinate for 30 minutes.

Heat the oil in a wok or frying pan over a high heat. To get the meat cooked quickly and slightly crunchy, fry it in small batches—about one-fifth at a time—blasting it for 5 minutes and stirring often. Add the splashes of fish and soy sauce, then take off the heat. Add the pepper (you won't need salt) and mint, and transfer to a bowl or large shallow plate. Add the basil, fresh cilantro, and coriander seeds, and scatter over the pine nuts and pomegranate seeds.

Give each person a large plate with a bowl of pork in the middle, raw vegetables surrounding it, and a lemon wedge to one side. To serve as canapés or a starter, fill endive boats with the larb moo.

Pork and porcini casserole

With the fresh, sharp flavors of porcini, juniper, and oregano, this is perfect late-summer food. It is another excellent recipe given to me by Teresa Wallace. Serve simply with new potatoes or rice and a salad. It reheats well, so is ideal for cooking ahead.

Serves 4
* 3/4 ounce (about 1/3 cup) dried porcini mushrooms
* 1 shallot or small onion, finely chopped
* Olive oil
* 2 pork fillets, or equivalent weight of good-quality lean stewing pork, cut into chunks
* 2/3 cup dry white wine
* 2 tablespoons brandy
* Splash of white wine vinegar
* 1/2 pound fresh mushrooms, halved or quartered
* 6 anchovy fillets, chopped
* 1 tablespoon fresh marjoram or oregano
* 1 bay leaf
* 20–25 crushed juniper berries
* Salt and black pepper
* Bunch of flat-leaf parsley, finely chopped

Preheat the oven to 300 degrees.

Soak the porcini in a little warm water until they're soft (about 30 minutes). Drain through a sieve lined with paper towels, saving the liquid, and chop the reconstituted mushrooms.

Put the shallot and some oil into a flameproof casserole and cook until soft. Add the meat and brown briefly. Add the wine, brandy, vinegar, and porcini liquid and bring to a boil.

Add both lots of mushrooms, the anchovies, marjoram or oregano, bay leaf, juniper berries, and salt and pepper. Bring to a simmer, then cover the pan with foil and a lid. Put in the oven and cook very slowly for 1 to 1½ hours, depending on the cut of meat used. You want the meat to be absolutely tender, but not at all dry.

Just before serving, stir in the parsley.

Chicken tagine with almonds and apricots

This North African stew is made with a minimal amount of liquid. It takes its name from the conical dish it's cooked in, which creates its own moisture. If you don't have one, use an ordinary covered casserole instead (as shown here). The great thing about a tagine is that it is best prepared a day or two in advance and kept in the fridge for the flavors to merge. If you're going to reheat it, use thighs, not the whole bird, then the meat doesn't become dry and stringy. Serve this with Lemon and lime couscous and a Pea, fava bean, and edamame bean salad (see pages 297 and 173).

Serves 4
* 3 1/3 pounds free-range chicken, cut into 8 pieces, or 8 thighs if you plan to reheat
* 1–2 tablespoons olive oil
* 2 onions, thinly sliced
* 2 garlic cloves, crushed
* Pinch of saffron strands
* 1 teaspoon turmeric
* 1 teaspoon ground cumin
* 1 teaspoon ground cinnamon
* 1/2 teaspoon ground ginger
* 1/2 teaspoon hot paprika
* Apple juice (amount depends on size of dish)
* 1/2 pound dried apricots
* 1/4 pound whole blanched almonds
* Large bunch of fresh mint, chopped
* Large bunch of cilantro or parsley, chopped

In a heavy-based flameproof casserole, lightly brown the chicken pieces in a little olive oil. Add the onions and garlic and sauté for a further 3 to 4 minutes.

Sprinkle on the saffron, turmeric, cumin, cinnamon, ginger, and paprika, and pour in just enough apple juice to cover the meat. Bring to a boil, cover, and simmer gently for 15 minutes, stirring frequently to ensure the chicken cooks evenly and doesn't dry out.

Add the apricots and almonds. Cover and cook for a further 15 minutes, or until the chicken is tender.

When ready to eat, stir in most of the mint and cilantro or parsley, leaving a little to scatter over the top as you serve.

Chicken and black pepper Boursin kiev

The good thing about these kievs is that, unlike when they're stuffed with butter, the peppery cream cheese doesn't disappear. They're lovely hot and ideal cold for a picnic, and children always seem to love them. You can adapt this recipe in many different ways—adding garlic, blue cheese, and herbs, or a soft goat cheese to the cream cheese base—all delicious. Serve with Fava bean pilaf (see page 174) and a tomato or green salad.

Serves 4
* 5 ounces black pepper Boursin cheese
* 2 garlic cloves, crushed
* Grated zest of 1 lemon
* 2 tablespoons chopped fresh mixed herbs (parsley, chives, and rosemary)
* 4 chicken breasts (about 1/4 pound each)
* 4 slices Parma ham
* 1 1/4 cups fresh breadcrumbs
* 2 tablespoons grated Parmesan cheese
* Salt and black pepper
* 1 egg, beaten

Preheat the oven to 350 degrees. Lightly oil a baking pan.

Mix together the Boursin, garlic, lemon zest, and herbs.

With a very sharp knife, cut a horizontal pocket in each chicken breast. Be careful not to cut them in half. Fill each pocket with a quarter of the Boursin mixture, then wrap each breast with a slice of Parma ham, covering the opening.

Put the breadcrumbs and Parmesan in a bowl, add salt and pepper, and mix together. Spread this mixture over a large plate.

Dip each chicken breast into the beaten egg, then roll in the breadcrumb mixture, ensuring they are well covered. Place in the prepared pan and bake for 25 to 30 minutes, until golden brown and cooked all the way through. Some of the cheese mixture may escape slightly, but most will remain inside.

Sugarsnap, snow pea, and pickled ginger salad

Here is the perfect salad to eat with Asian food, ideal with Sweet and sour trout or Crab cakes (see pages 44 and 160). It has excellent texture as well as taste. I also like to add fava beans and edamame beans to this dish, just a handful of each. I sometimes add a tablespoon of sweet chili dipping sauce to the dressing of the salad to give it extra punch.

Serves 4 to 6, or 6 to 8 if adding extra beans
* 1 teaspoon sugar
* 1/3 pound snow peas, topped, tailed, and strings removed as necessary
* 1/3 pound sugarsnap peas, tailed and strings removed as necessary
* 1/2 pound fresh or frozen fava beans (podded weight), optional
* 1/2 pound frozen edamame beans (optional)
* 2 tablespoons finely chopped Pickled ginger (see page 331)
* Small bunch of cilantro, finely chopped
* 3 tablespoons plain yogurt
* Salt and black pepper

Bring a large pan of water to a boil, and add the sugar. Cook the snow peas and sugarsnaps in the pan for 2 minutes. (The sugar in the water helps to keep the peas a really bright green.) Drain and rinse under running cold water for 1 minute to stop them from cooking. Set aside.

If using the fava beans, cook them in boiling water for 2 minutes. Drain and rinse under running cold water for 1 minute. If the beans are large, slip off the interior skins. Set aside. If using the edamame, put them into a pan of cold water, bring to a boil, and simmer for 3 minutes. Drain and rinse under running cold water for 1 minute.

Put the snow peas and sugarsnaps into a salad bowl, add the favas (if using), the ginger, cilantro, and yogurt and toss well. Season to taste with salt and pepper.

River Café garden salad with bruschette

This salad is one of the classics of the River Café in London and it's hard to improve on—an interesting mix of summer leaves and edible flowers, served with a grilled slice of Pugliese bread drizzled with a peppery first pressing extra virgin olive oil. Serve on its own as a starter, or as a side salad with almost any meat or fish.

Serves 4

For the bruschette
* 4 slices of Pugliese or robust-textured sourdough bread
* 1 whole garlic clove
* Good, fruity extra virgin olive oil

* Selection of garden leaves, such as mâche, purslane, wild arugula, sorrel, and beet greens
* Edible flowers, such as Romano or Scarlet Runner bean, chicory, calendula, violas, arugula, and nasturtiums
* Olive oil
* Juice of 1/2–1 lemon
* Sea salt and black pepper

First make the bruschette. Grill the bread on both sides. While the bread is still warm, lightly scrape the garlic clove over one side, then drizzle with the olive oil. Put out 4 salad plates and place a slice on the side of each one.

Scatter some garden leaves over each plate and top with lots of flowers. Drizzle with a little olive oil, a squeeze of lemon, and sprinkling of salt and pepper. Gently toss the salad and serve.

Savory fruit salad

Wonderful on a hot day, this is one of the best things to eat with poached or baked salmon or chicken. You can get everything ready a bit beforehand, but don't dress it until you want to eat—its crunchy texture is crucial. Altogether, this is a glorious combination of things.

Serves 8 to 10
* 2 large cucumbers
* Juice and finely grated zest of 1 lime
* Small bunch of fresh mint, roughly chopped
* Bunch of radishes
* 2 ripe mangoes
* 1 small red chili, deseeded and thinly sliced
* 2/3 pound seedless red grapes, cut in half
* 1 cup walnut halves, roasted and roughly chopped

For the dressing
* 1/4 cup extra virgin olive oil
* 1 tablespoon sherry vinegar or balsamic vinegar
* 1 tablespoon honey
* Salt and black pepper

Peel the cucumbers and cut into ½-inch slices, then cut the slices into quarters. Place in a bowl and add a squeeze of lime juice, plus the zest and mint. Allow to marinate for about 1 hour.

Cut the radishes into thick slices.

Cube the mangoes. To do so, run a sharp knife lengthwise around them, cutting either side of the long, flat seed. Make a criss-cross pattern in the flesh, being careful not to cut all the way through the skin. Pushing against the skin with your thumbs, turn the fruit inside out so you end up with a hedgehog shape. This allows you to easily cut away the cubes of mango from the skin. Put the flesh into a serving bowl with the rest of the lime juice and the chili and stir well. Add the radishes, cucumber, grapes, and walnuts. Stir well.

Mix all the dressing ingredients in a bowl and dress the salad just before you serve it.

Edible flower couscous salad

A couscous or bulgur wheat salad makes a refreshing change from new potatoes, and goes with almost any meat or fish.

Serves 4 to 5
* 2 cups good vegetable or chicken stock
* 1 3/4 cups couscous
* 2 tablespoons extra virgin olive oil
* Salt and black pepper
* Generous handful of mint, chopped
* Generous handful of flat-leaf parsley, chopped
* Juice and grated zest of 1 lemon
* Juice and grated zest of 1 lime
* 4 ounces feta cheese
* Selection of edible flowers, such as Scarlet Runner bean, chicory, marigolds, violas, arugula flowers, and nasturtiums

Put the stock in a saucepan and bring to a boil, or mix up the bouillon. Put the couscous into a deep bowl, pour over the olive oil and stock, stir just once, then cover and leave for 10 minutes to allow the grains to soften. Only then fork it through. Done like this, your couscous should be dry, with each grain separate rather than a cloggy mush. Season with salt and pepper, then add the herbs and citrus juice and zest.

Transfer the couscous to a serving bowl. Crumble over the feta cheese and top the salad with lots of the colorful edible flowers.

Pea, fava bean, and edamame bean salad

This is an unusual and delicious salad, good for serving with meat and fish, and ideal with the Chicken tagine (see page 167). It's not hard to find edamame beans now, particularly frozen, and some supermarkets do a frozen mixed bag of fava beans, edamame beans, and peas, ideal for this recipe even out of season. Eat warm or cold.

Serves 8 to 10

* 5 ½ pounds unpodded fava beans, or 1 pound podded fava beans, fresh or frozen
* 1 cup fresh or frozen peas
* 1 pound frozen edamame beans
* ½ cup extra virgin olive oil
* 2 lemons—juice of 1 and grated zest of 2
* 3 garlic cloves, chopped
* 2 teaspoons cumin powder
* 2 teaspoons toasted cumin seeds
* 2 mild red chilis, deseeded and finely chopped
* 1 small red pepper, cut into small chunks
* Salt and black pepper
* Good handful of fresh cilantro, chopped
* Good handful of fresh mint, chopped
* 20 black olives, roughly chopped

Pod the fava beans if necessary, and cook them in a large pan of boiling salted water for 2 minutes. Drain and rinse under running cold water for 1 minute. If the beans are large, slip off the skins. Set aside.

Cook the peas in the same way as the fava beans, then drain and set aside.

Put the edamame beans into a pan of cold water, bring to a boil, and simmer for 5 minutes. Drain and rinse under running cold water for a minute.

Put both lots of beans into a large, heavy-based frying pan, adding the oil, lemon juice and zest, garlic, cumin powder and seeds, chilis, and red pepper. Cook over a low heat for about 10 minutes, stirring occasionally and not allowing the beans to brown. Take off the heat, season with salt and pepper, and allow to cool in the pan.

Spoon the beans into a serving bowl with all the juices from the pan. Stir in the cilantro, mint, and peas and sprinkle over the olives. Season to taste.

Fava bean pilaf

A delicious and simple summer rice pilaf, this is very easy to throw together. I love it with Chicken and black pepper Boursin kiev, and it's perfect with Turkey tonnato for when you're feeding lots of people (see pages 167 and 435). Also serve as a vegetarian supper with pomegranate raita (see page 374) and pappadams.

For extra texture you could add some cooked wild rice to it as you serve. While this is at its best warm, it is also good cold—ideal for a picnic.

Serves 8
* 2 ¼ cups basmati rice
* ¼ cup wild rice (optional)
* 6 cardamom pods, lightly crushed
* 5 star anise
* 1 cinnamon stick
* 12 peppercorns
* 10 cloves
* Pinch of mustard seed
* 1 tablespoon peanut oil
* 2 tablespoons butter, plus 2 tablespoons for serving
* 1 onion, finely chopped
* 2 ½ cups hot water or chicken stock (or vegetable bouillon for vegetarians)
* 3 bay leaves
* ½ pound baby fava beans (podded weight)— frozen are fine
* Flaky sea salt and black pepper

Rinse the basmati rice well in cold water and leave to soak for 30 minutes.

Cook the wild rice in a pan of boiling salted water for about 25 minutes. Drain and set aside.

Toast the spices in a pan, then add the oil and butter. Add the onion and cook until softened but not brown (about 5 minutes).

Drain the basmati rice and add to the pan, stirring to coat well with the oil/butter and spices. Pour in the hot water or stock and bring to a boil. Add the bay leaves, stir, and cover with a tight-fitting lid (cover with foil first if your lid is not tight). Do not stir while cooking.

Simmer on a low heat for 10 minutes (this can be done in the oven if you want at 325 degrees). Take off the heat and leave for 5 minutes. When you eventually remove the lid the rice will have absorbed all the liquid.

While the casserole is resting, cook the fava beans in salted water for 2 to 3 minutes, depending on size.

Fork 2 tablespoons of butter through the spiced rice, fluffing it up. Add the wild rice. Drain the beans and stir into the rice. Taste, and season with salt and pepper. Pour into a large shallow bowl and serve immediately.

Potato and leek salad

Potato with chives is a classic combination, but even better is waxy salad potatoes with more substantial thinly sliced leeks and a scattering of capers. This is the perfect salad to eat with chicken or fish and a good dollop of chutney. Cook and then peel them, as it's quicker and easier this way round. Serve warm or cold.

Serves 6 to 8
* 2 ¼ pounds small new potatoes
* 3 leeks (about 1 pound)
* 3 tablespoons olive oil
* Salt and black pepper
* 2 tablespoons capers, drained

For the dressing
* 6 tablespoons extra virgin olive oil
* Juice and grated zest of 1 lemon
* Small bunch of fresh mint, stalks removed
* 1 tablespoon Dijon mustard

Cook the potatoes in boiling salted water until just done (15 to 20 minutes, depending on size). Drain and allow to cool, then peel.

Slice the white and green parts of the leek as thinly as you can (a mandoline is good for this). Heat the oil in a large frying pan and cook the leeks on a gentle heat for about 10 minutes: do not allow to brown. Take off the heat and set aside to cool.

Put all the dressing ingredients into a food processor or blender and blend until smooth.

Combine the potatoes, leeks, and dressing in a large bowl. Taste, and season with salt and pepper. Scatter over the capers and serve.

New potatoes with shallots, peppers, and cream

When you've had one too many days of eating plain boiled new potatoes, this excellent dish comes to the rescue. You get the lovely waxy richness of the potatoes, but with the added oomph of shallots, peppers, and cream. It was a chance throw-together by my friend Matthew Rice when we were on holiday in Normandy, where the cream is so fantastic. The result is rich and delicious, excellent with roast chicken, and good on its own with almost any salad. It's best served warm, but also good cold.

Serves 8
* 3 tablespoons olive oil
* 3 tablespoons butter
* 1 pound shallots or red onions, finely chopped
* Bunch of scallions, sliced (keep the green and white parts separate)
* Large sprig of thyme
* 2 large red bell peppers, cored and deseeded
* 1 teaspoon salt
* Black pepper
* 1 teaspoon sugar
* 2 ⅔ pounds small new potatoes
* 1 cup of heavy cream or crème fraîche
* Bunch of flat-leaf parsley, coarsely chopped

Put the olive oil and butter in a heavy-based pan, add the shallots, white parts of the scallions, and the thyme and slowly braise for about 20 minutes, until the onions are transparent.

Break the peppers into 1 ½ to 2 inch chunks, not strips, and fry with the onions until soft.

Add the salt, plenty of pepper, the sugar, and green parts of the scallions and continue to fry for 2 to 3 minutes.

Meanwhile, cook the potatoes in boiling salted water until tender (about 15 to 20 minutes, depending on size). Drain, then peel and chop them roughly. Add to the frying pan. When you're ready to eat, add the cream and heat through. Sprinkle with the parsley before serving.

Potato and chard salad
with pea pesto

This bright green salad looks as good and fresh as it tastes. Serve it plain, or scatter it with thinly sliced and crispy chorizo. It's ideal for eating with almost any barbecued meat (see pages 187–91).

Serves 6 to 8
* 2 ¼ pounds small new potatoes
* 1 pound Swiss chard or spinach, stemmed and sliced into ribbons

For the pesto
* 1 ½ cups peas, thawed if frozen or blanched for 1 minute if fresh
* 5 or 6 tablespoons extra virgin olive oil
* Large handful of fresh basil leaves, plus a few extra for sprinkling
* Juice of 1 ½ lemons, grated zest of 1
* 1 tablespoon peeled and freshly grated ginger
* 1 garlic clove, roughly chopped
* Salt and black pepper
* ¼ pound chorizo, thinly sliced (optional)

Cook the potatoes in boiling salted water until tender (about 15 to 20 minutes, depending on size). Drain and allow to cool, then peel.

Put the chard or spinach into a large lidded saucepan and cook over a medium heat (no extra water needed) until wilted. Drain well in a colander or sieve, pushing out any water with the back of a spoon.

Put the peas in a food processor or blender with 5 tablespoons olive oil, the basil, juice and zest of 1 lemon, ginger, and garlic and whizz briefly. Season generously with salt and pepper. Put into the fridge until needed. The flavor of the pea puree improves when slightly chilled.

Fry the chorizo slices (if using) in the remaining tablespoon of oil until well cooked and just beginning to turn crunchy. Drain them in a sieve to remove the oil that bleeds out as they fry. Toss them in the remaining lemon juice and set aside.

Put the potatoes into a large serving bowl, add the pea puree, and then the chard or spinach, and stir to combine. Top with the chorizo (if using) and sprinkle with some torn-up basil leaves to serve.

Beet horseradish

This is excellent with almost any fish (such as Mackerel in a fennel-seed oatmeal crust, page 195) and very good with rare roast beef. If you can't find fresh horseradish root, use 2 tablespoons of good-quality horseradish to about the same amount of crème fraîche (or to taste).

Serves 6
* 4 medium-sized beets (around 1–1½ pounds)
* Grated horseradish, to taste (it's difficult to give an exact quantity as fresh horseradish strength varies hugely)
* A little grated lemon zest and juice
* 1 tablespoon balsamic vinegar
* 2 tablespoons Greek yogurt
* 2 tablespoons heavy cream or crème fraîche
* 1 teaspoon mustard powder
* Salt and black pepper

Cook the beets in boiling salted water until soft (about 30 to 40 minutes, depending on size). Drain and cool a little, then peel. Grate on the coarse blade of a grater.

Peel and grate the horseradish. If you want it very strong, grate it just before you eat. It has highly volatile essential oils, so its strength soon fades. It also oxidizes quickly, so mix it with the lemon juice immediately to prevent it from discoloring. Add the vinegar, yogurt, and enough cream to make a creamy consistency. Add the mustard powder, salt, and pepper.

Combine the horseradish mixture with the grated beets. Sprinkle with the lemon zest and serve.

Potato puttanesca

Here we have a hot potato salad dressed in a sauce usually served with pasta—melted anchovies, black olives, capers, sun-dried tomatoes, chili, onion, and garlic. Potato salad is definitely nicer with no peel, so cook and then peel the potatoes. Eat this on its own with Parmesan shavings over the top, or with any strong-flavored meat or fish. It's ideal for a barbecue.

Serves 6 to 8
* 2¼ pounds small new potatoes
* Large bunch of flat-leaf parsley, coarsely chopped
* Black pepper
* ¼ cup Parmesan shavings, to serve

For the sauce
* 4–5 tablespoons olive oil
* 1 large red onion, finely chopped
* 1 red chili, deseeded and finely chopped
* 1 garlic clove, finely chopped
* 1 (2-ounce) can anchovies
* 2 tablespoons roughly chopped sun-dried tomatoes
* 2 tablespoons roughly chopped black olives
* 2 tablespoons capers

Cook the potatoes in boiling salted water until tender (about 15 to 20 minutes, depending on size). Drain and allow to cool, then peel.

To make the sauce, heat the olive oil in a frying pan, add the onion, chili, and garlic and cook on a medium heat for 5 minutes. Add the anchovies and cook for another couple of minutes, until they've melted.

Add the tomatoes, olives, and capers and cook just long enough to heat through.

Put the potatoes into a large bowl and stir in the sauce. Scatter lots of parsley over the top, folding some of it in. Taste, and season with a little pepper, and scatter with Parmesan shavings.

Eggplant and mozzarella stacks

These molten, layered cheese and eggplant stacks
are among my favorite things to cook on an open
fire. The eggplant and sauce are cooked in advance,
so all you have to do when you're ready to eat is
make up the stacks, which is very easy. They look
and taste fantastic. Serve with a green salad and
some good bread.

Serves 4 to 6 (makes 8 stacks)
* 2–3 large eggplants, cut into ½-inch slices
* Olive oil, for brushing
* 2 (8-ounce) packages of mozzarella cheese,
  sliced to match the eggplants
* Small bunch of fresh basil, to serve
* Basil oil (see page 208), to serve
* Sourdough bruschette (see page 168), to serve

For the sauce
* 2 (14 ½-ounce) cans of chopped tomatoes
* 3 tablespoons olive oil
* 2 whole garlic cloves
* Good pinch of salt

Preheat the oven to 325 degrees.

Brush the eggplant slices with olive oil and roast
in the oven for 10 minutes, until beginning to soften.

Meanwhile, mix the sauce ingredients together
in a saucepan and cook over a low heat for 20
minutes, until reduced by about a third; the sauce
should be thick and rich. Remove and discard the
garlic cloves.

Soak 8 wooden skewers in water for about 20
minutes while you get the fire going. Or, use fresh
rosemary sprigs as skewers, as shown in the picture
opposite.

Spread the eggplant slices with a little tomato
sauce, then stack them up, alternating them with
mozzarella slices—about 3 to 4 slices of each per
skewer. Push a skewer or rosemary sprig through
each stack of eggplant and mozzarella.

Cook in a cast-iron skillet on the stovetop or grill
until the stacks are heated through and the cheese
is beginning to melt but not collapsing.

Serve scattered with torn-up basil leaves and
a drizzle of Basil oil and some delicious bread or a
sourdough bruschette cooked on the grill.

Baked feta with thyme and tomatoes

Simple to throw together and chuck on the fire or in the oven, this is Cretan shepherds' food—simple, imprecise, and always delicious. Dip into the parcel with raw carrot or celery chunks, or warm flatbread (which you can heat on the stones around the fire).

Serves 6 to 8
* 1 pound of feta cheese, broken into roughly 1-inch pieces
* 20 small cherry tomatoes
* 20 capers
* 15 Kalamata olives, halved and pitted
* 2 tablespoons olive oil
* 6 sprigs of thyme

Pile everything onto a large square of foil, wrap securely, and place in or near the fire or a very hot conventional oven for 10 to 15 minutes, until the cheese is bubbling and browning on top (look inside to check).

Barbecued fava beans with pecorino

This is a dish I had with an American friend of mine, Stephen Orr, who cooks the fava beans over a wood fire and then serves them as an appetizer while the rest of the meal is being cooked.

Serves 4
* 25–30 fava bean pods
* Flaky sea salt
* 1 lemon, cut into wedges
* 1 (3-ounce) lump of pecorino cheese, slivered

Put the whole bean pods on a very hot open grill 8 to 10 inches above the flames (depending on the heat). Once they are soft and blackened on both sides (about 5 minutes), transfer the pods to a plate. Allow to cool a little, then serve as they are for people to shell themselves.

To eat, squeeze some lemon juice over the pods and dip each bean in a little of the salt, then wrap one or two beans together in a sliver of pecorino.

Zucchini and mascarpone frittata

This is a recipe shown to me by Rose Gray, co-founder of the River Café in London, using squash growth tips as well as zucchini. If you don't have access to these tips, plain zucchinis are fine. Frittatas are brilliant things for cooking outside on a fire as each one is so quick and easy to cook. You ideally need one or two 8 by 1½-inch-deep frying pans, each perfect for an individual frittata.

Yields 1 frittata (serves 1–2)
* Handful of squash growth tips and tender baby leaves
* 1 or 2 zucchinis (about ¼ pound), sliced ½–1 inch thick
* Handful of mint, finely chopped
* 1 tablespoon mascarpone cheese
* 3 large eggs, lightly beaten
* 2 tablespoons freshly grated Parmesan cheese, plus a little extra for serving
* Salt and black pepper
* Olive oil, for frying

Boil the squash tips, baby leaves, and zucchini in salted water for 3 minutes. Drain and cool a bit, then roughly chop.

Combine the cooked vegetable in a bowl with all the remaining ingredients. Heat a little olive oil in a frying pan and pour in the egg mixture, using a fork to distribute it evenly. Lower the heat, cover, and cook for 1 to 2 minutes, or until the eggs are just set. Sprinkle with a little Parmesan before serving.

Stuffed sweet red peppers

Sweet red peppers stuffed with cream cheese and pine nuts are delicious served with barbecued meat, or as part of a mixture of starters with Barbecued corn (see page 247).

Yields 8 pepper halves
* 4 sweet red peppers
* 7 ounces cream cheese or goat cheese
* ⅓ cup pine nuts, toasted for 3–4 minutes
* 1 tablespoon finely chopped thyme leaves
* 2 tablespoons extra virgin olive oil
* Salt and black pepper

Slice the peppers in half lengthwise—including the stems—and scrape out the seeds.

Mix the remaining ingredients together and use a teaspoon to fill the peppers with the mixture. Don't stuff them too tightly or they won't cook evenly.

Put them on a hot grill pan or barbecue skin side down and cook them for 10 minutes, until the undersides just begin to char. They may pop and jump slightly on the heat, so you need to watch them.

Skewered new potatoes

Serve these skewers with any barbecued meat or fish, scattered with Rosemary, sage, and thyme salt (see page 103), or doused with a little garlic and herb butter, melted over them as soon as they come off the fire.

Serves 6–8
* 1 ¾ pounds new potatoes
* 1 pound small pickling/boiling red or white onions
* ½ pound cherry tomatoes
* Olive oil, for brushing
* Salt and black pepper

Pick 8 rosemary stems or soak 8 wooden skewers in water for about 20 minutes. Alternatively, use metal skewers.

Meanwhile, parboil the potatoes for 10 minutes in boiling, salted water. Add the onions for the last 5 minutes of cooking time. Drain and leave to cool a bit, then peel the onions.

Thread a potato, a tomato, and an onion onto the skewers in that order, repeating until almost full. Brush with olive oil, scatter with salt and pepper, and cook on a rack over the fire or in a grill pan for 3 minutes on each side.

You can also cook these skewers on a baking tray in a conventional oven (preheated to 400 degrees): simply drizzle with olive oil, scatter with Rosemary, sage, and thyme salt (see page 103)—a little before cooking and a little after they've come out of the oven—and roast for 20 minutes.

William's burger recipes

William is my middle stepson and a really good cook. Burgers are one of his favorite things, and he says that it's not what you put on the burger, but what you put in it that matters. He has suggested two variations on his basic burger recipe: "ploughman's," which is rich and smoky with a hint of sweetness; and "tangy," which has a sharp and interesting flavor. To make either of these, just add the extra ingredients to those in the classic burger recipe. It's important to use ground beef with a decent fat content as this tends to create more flavor and give the burgers a nice moistness.

Serve with Skewered new potatoes (see left).

Yields 10 to 12 burgers
* 2 pounds ground beef (15–30% fat)
* 1 large onion, finely chopped
* Handful of flat-leaf parsley, coarsely chopped
* 3 garlic cloves, finely chopped
* 1 egg
* Salt and black pepper

For the ploughman's burger, add
* ¼ pound sharp Cheddar cheese, grated
* 3 tablespoons Dijon mustard
* ¼ cup onion marmalade

For the tangy burger, add
* 1 tablespoon finely chopped thyme leaves
* 6 pickled onions or shallots, coarsely chopped
* 2 tablespoons capers

Using your hands, combine all the burger ingredients in a bowl. Mold the mixture into burgers about 1 inch thick and 3 to 4 inches wide with your hands. Cover them and place in the fridge for a couple of hours: this helps them hold together.

Heat a barbecue (or grill pan, if cooking indoors on a stovetop) until you can't count to 10 with your hand hovering just above it. Cook the burgers on it for about 4 minutes on each side (medium-rare), flipping them as few times as possible.

Lamb kebabs with spiced eggplant sauce

Middle Eastern lamb kebabs flavored with cumin and mint are lovely eaten any day for supper, but they're particularly good cooked on an open wood fire or barbecue.

Serves 4

For the marinade
* 2 tablespoons olive oil
* 2 garlic cloves, finely chopped
* Juice and grated zest of 1 lemon
* 1 tablespoon cumin seeds, toasted and roughly ground
* 1 teaspoon coriander seeds, toasted and roughly ground

* 2 ¼ pounds lamb fillet or boned leg cut into chunks

For the sauce
* 1 large eggplant (about 1 pound)
* 2 tablespoons extra virgin olive oil
* 1 red onion, finely chopped
* 2 sticks of celery, finely chopped
* 1 green chili, finely chopped
* ⅔ cup vegetable stock
* 2 tablespoons tomato puree
* 2 tablespoons crème fraîche
* Small bunch of fresh mint, chopped

Mix all the marinade ingredients together in a large bowl. Add the lamb chunks and smother with the marinade. Cover and leave at least overnight in the fridge. Preheat the barbecue until you can't count to 10 with your hand hovering just above it.

Thread the lamb onto 4 metal skewers, not too tightly packed. Cook on the barbecue (ideally with the lid closed) for 5 minutes on each side. (You can also cook these kebabs for the same amount of time in a hot grill pan on a conventional stovetop, or in the oven at 325 degrees.) Take them off the barbecue to rest for 5 minutes before serving.

To make the sauce, cut the eggplant in half lengthwise. Make small, shallow slashes into the flesh and brush 1 tablespoon olive oil over each half. Place in the oven at 350 degrees for 15 to 20 minutes, or grill them for about 10 minutes on each side, until the flesh is soft and beginning to char.

Meanwhile, in a large pan, sauté the onion, celery, and chili in a little olive oil for 10 minutes on a very gentle heat until soft.

Scoop the softened flesh out of the eggplants. Mix with a fork into a chunky paste and add to the onion mixture. Add the stock and tomato puree and heat gently. Stir in the crème fraîche and heat through. Take off the heat and stir in the mint.

Serve the lamb kebabs with a dollop of sauce, or put the sauce in a bowl for people to help themselves.

Persian butterflied leg of lamb

My favorite marinade for this barbecued lamb is a Persian mix of yogurt, chili, mint, and lemon. Also delicious is a combination of rosemary, garlic, olive oil, and lemon; or go for a Moroccan flavor, with ground cumin and cinnamon, crushed coriander seeds, olive oil, garlic, and paprika. I also love Thai-flavored lamb, with coconut milk and green or red Thai curry paste; or Indian, with fresh grated ginger, turmeric, cumin, and garam masala. One by one, try them all over the summer. This makes excellent, simple, and delicious party food.

Serves 8
* 1 (4 ½-pound) leg of lamb, boned and butterflied

For the marinade
* Small bunch of fresh mint, chopped
* 3 garlic cloves, finely chopped
* 2 red chilis, deseeded and finely chopped
* Juice and grated zest of 2 lemons
* 1 cup plain yogurt
* 6 tablespoons extra virgin olive oil
* Salt and black pepper

Try to buy the leg of lamb already boned and butterflied by the butcher. If you can't, cut out the bone and flatten the joint yourself.

Mix all the marinade ingredients together in a bowl large enough to hold the lamb. Slash the fleshy side of the lamb with shallow cuts, then smother it with the marinade. Cover and leave overnight in the fridge.

Preheat the oven to 400 degrees.

Place the joint in a roasting pan and put in the oven for 30 minutes.

Meanwhile, heat the barbecue until you can't count to 10 with your hand hovering just above it. Transfer the lamb to the hot barbecue (ideally with the lid closed) and cook for a further 15 minutes on each side. (You can do the whole cooking process in the oven if you want, lowering the temperature to 325 degrees after 20 minutes, and cooking for a further 30 minutes.) Rest the lamb for 10 to 15 minutes before carving.

Chicken souvlaki with cilantro

My daughter Molly has loved this dish—warm pitas packed with fragrant chicken and grassy cilantro—ever since she was small.

Serves 8

For the marinade
* Small bunch of mint, chopped
* 3 garlic cloves, finely chopped
* 1 red chili, deseeded and finely chopped
* Juice and grated zest of 1 lemon
* 1 tablespoon coriander seeds, crushed
* 1 teaspoon turmeric
* 1 cup plain yogurt
* ¼ cup extra virgin olive oil
* Salt and black pepper

* 6 chicken breasts (about 2 pounds), cut into cubes
* 8 warmed pita breads

For the dressing
* Large bunch of fresh cilantro, plus extra for serving
* 1 cup plain yogurt
* Juice and grated zest of 1 lemon
* 2 tablespoons extra virgin olive oil

Mix all the marinade ingredients together in a bowl.

Add the chicken cubes to the bowl and smother with marinade. Cover and chill overnight. For an intense taste of lemon, marinate for 2 to 3 days.

Preheat the barbecue until you can't count to 10 with your hand hovering just above it.

Thread the chicken chunks onto 8 metal skewers, not too tightly packed. Place on the barbecue and cook for 5 minutes on each side. (You can also cook these kebabs for the same amount of time in a hot grill pan on a conventional stovetop, or in the oven at 325 degrees.) Take them off the barbecue and leave to rest for 5 minutes.

Push the chicken off the skewers and into a bowl. Put all the dressing ingredients in a food processor and whizz to form a smooth green sauce. Pour over the chicken and mix well. Stuff several chunks into a pita bread with some fresh cilantro, and serve.

Char sui pork

This style of barbecue is one of the things I will always order when I go to a Chinese restaurant—and it's easy to make. Serve on top of Stir-fried green vegetables (see page 41) or with a green salad and a mound of rice. I love searing it very quickly on a wood fire, and it's delicious cooked on a grill pan indoors. It's also good cold, sliced thinly.

Serves 6

For the marinade
* ½ cup soy sauce
* ¼ cup dry sherry
* 2 teaspoons five-spice powder
* 2 teaspoons brown sugar
* 2-inch piece of fresh ginger, grated
* 4 garlic cloves, crushed
* 2 cooked beets, pureed or grated

* 2 ¼-pound fillet of pork
* ¼ cup honey
* 1 teaspoon five-spice powder

Mix all the marinade ingredients together in a bowl and add the pork, smothering it with the mixture. Cover and leave to stand in the fridge for at least 3 hours, but preferably overnight. I have sometimes left mine marinating for 2 to 3 days.

Heat a ridged grill pan for 3 to 4 minutes (until you can't count to 10 with your hand hovering just above it).

Stir together the honey, 3 to 4 tablespoons hot water, and the five-spice powder. Scrape the marinade off the pork, then brush both sides of the meat with the honey mixture. Grill it for 7 to 8 minutes on each side until cooked right through. Remove from the heat and allow to rest for 15 minutes. Slice the pork thinly and serve.

For even quicker cooking, slice the pork before you cook it and sear each thin slice for less than a minute on each side.

Scallops cooked on the fire

Scallops are among the most delicious things to cook on a fire and eat outside; they cook perfectly in their shell "dishes." Serve them with simply cooked new potatoes, or better still with Potato and chard salad with pea pesto (see page 176), plus a crunchy green or sliced tomato salad.

Serves 4
* **12 scallops, with shells**
* **Salt and black pepper**
* **1 red chili, deseeded and finely chopped**
* **Small bunch of flat-leaf parsley, finely chopped**
* **Extra virgin olive oil, for drizzling**
* **Lemon wedges, to serve**

Open the scallop shells, removing everything inside with a short, sharp knife, then pulling off and discarding all but the white flesh and orange coral. Replace the scallop and coral in the shells. Season with salt and pepper.

Scatter a little of the remaining ingredients, except the lemon wedges, over each scallop in its shell and put them on a rack over the fire. Cook for about 3 minutes, until the flesh becomes opaque.

Serve the scallops with wedges of lemon.

Mackerel in fennel-seed oatmeal crust

Very fresh mackerel, with their eyes bright and sparkly, are an emblem of summer. Roll them in fennel-seed flavored oatmeal and cook on a fire—there's no better way to eat them.

Serves 6
* 4–5 tablespoons steel-cut oats (enough to cover a dinner plate)
* 1 tablespoon flour
* 2 tablespoons fennel seeds
* Salt and black pepper
* 6 very fresh medium-sized mackerel, cleaned and heads left on
* Olive oil, for frying
* Beet horseradish (see page 178), new potatoes, and green salad, to serve

Combine the oats, flour, fennel seeds, and plenty of salt and pepper, then spread out the mixture on a large flat plate.

Dampen the skin of the mackerel and roll them in the oat mixture.

Heat plenty of olive oil in a couple of frying pans and cook the mackerel for about 5 to 7 minutes on each side (depending on the size of the fish).

Serve with a dollop of beet horseradish, some new potatoes, and a green salad.

Trout or mackerel in a newspaper parcel

An old friend, Andrew Wallace, showed me this ingenious and reliable way of cooking fish in a wood fire. If you're out fishing, this is the best way to eat any small to medium-sized fish you catch.

Allow 1 fish per person
* 1 small to medium-sized trout or mackerel
* Salt and black pepper
* 2 or 3 sheets of newspaper

Wrap your fish in some newspaper and soak it in the river (or sea) for a couple of minutes. Put your parcel into the ashes of a wood fire. When the paper begins to dry enough to catch on the fire, your fish should be done. Season and eat.

Summer terrine

Strictly speaking, a terrine should have slices of bacon around it, but you can do this recipe with or without. This is an incredibly easy and versatile dish, excellent for picnics with a green salad and potato salad, and delicious served as a starter with some salad leaves and Horseradish cream (see page 267). I also love it with Bruschette (see page 168) and a topping of coarsely chopped basil, parsley, or mint. It can be made, then wrapped and stored in the fridge for 2 to 3 days. It also freezes well, but then it's better to leave out the bacon.

Serves 8
* 4 slices of bread from a small whole wheat loaf (about 4 ounces)
* 1 egg, beaten
* 2 teaspoons Dijon mustard
* ¼ cup milk
* Olive oil
* 1 onion, finely chopped
* 2 sticks of celery, finely chopped
* 1 red pepper (or ½ red pepper, ½ yellow pepper), finely chopped
* 3 garlic cloves, crushed
* Grated zest of 1 lemon
* 1 pound ground pork
* 1 pound ground beef
* 1 tablespoon chopped fresh sage
* 1 tablespoon tomato puree
* 1 tablespoon Worcestershire sauce
* 1 teaspoon dried thyme or oregano
* ½ teaspoon ground ginger
* ½ teaspoon ground nutmeg
* ½ teaspoon ground cloves (optional)
* Salt and black pepper
* 8–10 slices of bacon (optional)

Preheat the oven to 350 degrees. Lightly oil a loaf pan.

Cut the crusts off the bread. Tear the soft parts into small pieces and place in a large bowl. Add the egg, mustard, and milk and stir well to combine.

Heat a little olive oil in a large shallow pan and add the onion, celery, pepper, and garlic. Sauté for about 5 minutes, until the vegetables are soft. Tip the contents of the frying pan into the bread mixture. Add all the other ingredients up to and including the ground cloves (if using), and stir together really well. Season generously with salt and pepper.

Line the prepared pan with the bacon (if using). Spoon in the meat mixture, lightly smoothing it down with a fork. Put the pan onto a baking sheet and place in the middle of the oven for 45 minutes, until the meatloaf feels firm to the touch and the sides have begun to pull away from the pan. Allow to cool, then serve warm or cold.

Falafel

I love falafel—little balls of spiced, mashed chickpeas—either on their own, with Red pepper and feta salad or Grilled eggplant (see page 200 or 268), or packed into pita bread with shredded lettuce and sliced tomatoes in a tahini-flavored yogurt dressing (see page 144).

Yields 35 balls
* 1 pound dried chickpeas
* 3 garlic cloves
* 1 small onion, cut into quarters
* Small bunch of flat-leaf parsley, stalks removed
* Small bunch of fresh cilantro
* ½ teaspoon cayenne pepper
* 1 teaspoon turmeric
* 1 teaspoon ground coriander
* 2 teaspoons ground cumin, toasted
* 2 teaspoons cumin seeds
* Juice of ½ lemon
* Grated zest of 1 lemon
* 1 tablespoon salt
* ¼ teaspoon black pepper
* 1 egg, beaten
* 1 teaspoon baking soda
* 4 cups vegetable oil, for deep-frying

Soak the chickpeas in cold water for 12 hours. Drain and put them into a food processor with all the other ingredients up to and including the black pepper. Whizz until combined but not pureed. Add the beaten egg and baking soda. Put the mixture into a bowl and allow to stand for 30 minutes.

Shape the mixture into 35 balls and allow to stand for a further 30 minutes.

Fill a deep saucepan with enough oil to reach about one-third of the way up the side, and have a lid or splash-guard on standby to prevent the oil from spitting too much after you add each batch. Heat the oil until it reaches about 375 degrees, or until a cube of bread browns in 30 seconds.

Put a batch of balls into the oil without overcrowding and cook for about 4 minutes, until golden brown. Drain on paper towels and keep warm while you cook the rest.

Chicken breast stuffed with garden herbs

One of the simplest and most delicious recipes in this book, given to me by a friend, Kitty Ann. The chicken is good served warm with rice, green beans, and the Sugarsnap, snow pea, and pickled ginger salad (see page 168). It's also brilliant for a party buffet or picnic, neat and easy to pack.

Serves 6
* 6 skinless chicken breasts
* ⅓ pound mixed garden greens, such as spinach, chard, arugula, and watercress, coarsely chopped
* 1 small bunch (about 1 ounce) fresh tarragon, coarsely chopped
* 2 garlic cloves, finely chopped
* 12 ounces cream cheese
* Grated zest of 1 lemon
* Salt and black pepper
* 1 cup vegetable or chicken stock

Preheat the oven to 350 degrees.

Cut the chicken breasts almost but not quite in half, slicing horizontally through their fattest part. Open them out between two sheets of plastic wrap, then bash them gently with a rolling pin. You want to flatten them to a thickness of about 1 inch.

Put the greens and three-quarters of the tarragon in a food processor or large bowl, add the garlic, cream cheese, lemon zest, salt, and pepper, and whizz briefly or mix with a wooden spoon.

Spread the mixture evenly over the flattened chicken breasts. Roll them up and pack into a baking pan. Pour in enough stock to come about a quarter of the way up the chicken breasts. Put into the middle of the oven and bake for 30 minutes, or until the chicken is cooked all the way through.

To eat hot, transfer the chicken to a plate and keep warm. Add the remaining tarragon and stock to the juices in the baking pan and simmer gently for 5 minutes. Pour the sauce over the chicken breasts. Allow to rest for 5 minutes, then serve with rice, green beans, and a crunchy salad.

For a picnic, allow the chicken to cool completely, then put in the fridge for a few hours before packing in plastic containers. (There is no need to make a sauce for the picnic version of the recipe.)

Focaccia open sandwiches

I don't like huge amounts of bread, so I am not that keen on sandwiches, even for a picnic, but these open slices of focaccia, flavored with ground cumin and coriander or toasted, coarsely ground seed, don't feel like sandwiches. Top them with smoked salmon, Parma ham, or beef. It's really worth trying to find some fresh horseradish root—as an alternative to mustard—to grate over the top of the smoked salmon or beef sandwiches.

Yields about 8 slices
* 1 loaf of focaccia (see page 132)
* Extra virgin olive oil
* 2 teaspoons ground cumin
* 1 tablespoon coriander seeds, toasted and ground
* Salt and black pepper

For the toppings
* Cream cheese, a small bunch of fresh dill, and smoked salmon

or
* Mozzarella, Parma ham, and a small bunch of fresh basil

or
* Rare beef and fresh horseradish root

Heat a ridged grill pan for 3 to 4 minutes (until you can't count to 10 with your hand hovering just above it).

Slice the bread into chunks ½ inch thick. Drizzle with olive oil and sprinkle each slice with the cumin, coriander, and salt and pepper on one side.

Grill on both sides for 2 to 3 minutes, until toasted, then add whichever topping you fancy.

Red pepper and feta salad in a jar

Buy several sweet red peppers at a market and make several jars of this delicious mixture—ideal for a picnic, and a welcome present. If you like things spicy, add a hot chili to the mix. With a splash of balsamic vinegar, it is excellent added to some salad leaves for lunch with a hunk of bread; and it's lovely with spaghetti for a quick supper. This is not a long-term preserve because it hasn't been cooked in vinegar, but it's all the nicer for it.

Yields about one 16-ounce jar
* 5 sweet red peppers
* 4 ounces feta, cut into small chunks
* 1 sprig of fresh rosemary
* 2 fresh bay leaves
* 2 garlic cloves
* 1 teaspoon mustard seed
* ½ teaspoon whole black peppercorns
* 1 teaspoon fennel seeds (optional)
* About ¾ cup extra virgin olive oil

Heat a ridged grill pan for 3 to 4 minutes (until you can't count to 10 with your hand hovering just above it). Add the red peppers, turning occasionally until all sides are slightly blackened and blistered (about 10 minutes in all). Put the peppers into a plastic bag or large bowl covered in plastic wrap and leave to steam for 10 to 15 minutes. Remove the stem, skin, and seeds, and tear the peppers into large pieces.

Heat the grill pan again and sear the pepper flesh for a couple of minutes. This gives it nice stripes, which look good in the jar.

Put the peppers, feta, rosemary, bay leaves, garlic, mustard seed, whole black peppercorns, and fennel seed (if using) into a dry, warm, sterilized jar (you can sterilize it in a very hot dishwasher, or boil it in a pan of water for 10 minutes). Cover everything with the olive oil, then seal, label with a date, and eat within 2 weeks. Keep in the fridge.

Sweet red pepper and feta tart

A well-filled and colorful tart is always an appetizing thing to give friends for a summer lunch, and this one, with a mound of sweet red peppers and a zap of feta saltiness, is ideal. A generous slice served with new potatoes and a crunchy salad of lettuce, arugula, and watercress will make everyone happy. This is an adaptation of a tart in my Christmas book, with more abundant contents. Served warm or cold, it is practical for a picnic, transported in its tart pan. The amount of peppers sounds over the top, but once cooked, they reduce down a lot.

Serves 6 to 8

For the pastry
* 1½ cups unbleached flour
* Pinch of salt
* ½ cup (1 stick) cold butter, cut into cubes
* 1 egg yolk

* 1 large onion, chopped
* 2 tablespoons olive oil, plus extra for drizzling
* 8 red peppers, or a mixture of red and yellow
* 2 ounces canned anchovies, chopped
* 2 garlic cloves, crushed
* 1 tablespoon balsamic vinegar
* 2 teaspoons superfine sugar
* 20 black olives, pitted and halved
* Small bunch of fresh thyme, leaves stripped and chopped
* 1¼ cups light cream
* 4 eggs, beaten
* Salt and black pepper
* 10 ounces feta cheese

First make the pastry. Sift the flour and salt into a bowl and rub in the butter by hand until the mixture resembles breadcrumbs. Alternatively pulse in a food processor. Add the egg yolk and a little iced water, just enough to bring the pastry together into a ball. Wrap in plastic wrap and chill in the fridge for an hour.

Preheat the oven to 350 degrees and heat a baking sheet until searing hot.

Line an 11-inch loose-bottomed tart pan with the pastry, leaving the excess draped over the sides in case it shrinks.

Prick the bottom of the pastry crust with a fork, line with parchment paper or foil, and weigh this down with baking beans or rice. Place on the baking sheet and bake for about 15 minutes. Remove the baking beans and paper and bake the crust for another 5 minutes. Take out of the oven and trim off the excess pastry. Keep the oven on and reheat the baking sheet.

While the tart crust is cooking, in a heavy-based saucepan, sweat the onion in olive oil for 5 to 10 minutes over a gentle heat, then set aside.

Heat a ridged grill pan for 3 to 4 minutes (until you can't count to 10 with your hand hovering just above it).

Halve and deseed the peppers, then grill them until they are beginning to blacken. Put them into a plastic bag, seal tightly, and leave to steam for 10 minutes.

Peel and slice the peppers, then put in the saucepan with the softened onion. Add the anchovies, garlic, a drizzle of oil, the balsamic vinegar, and sugar and cook over a gentle heat for 5 minutes. Remove from the heat and add the olives and thyme.

In a separate bowl, combine the cream and eggs, and season well with salt and pepper. Spread the pepper mixture inside the pastry crust, crumble over the feta, and pour the cream mixture on top. Place on the hot baking sheet and bake for about 30 minutes, or until the tart is set and golden.

Asparagus and Gruyère tart

There are plenty of summer tarts that are best eaten warm, but this one is also good cold, and when asparagus is at its best is one of the most delicious picnic things for early summer. Serve with dressed leaves and any potato salad (see pages 175–78).

Serves 6 to 8

For the pastry
* 1½ cups unbleached flour
* Pinch of salt
* 9 tablespoons cold butter, cut into cubes
* 1 egg yolk

* 1 pound asparagus
* 2 tablespoons butter
* 1 tablespoon oil
* 2 ounces Parmesan cheese, grated
* ½ pound Gruyère cheese, grated
* 3 eggs
* 1 cup heavy cream
* 1 teaspoon Dijon mustard
* Salt and black pepper

First make the pastry. Sift the flour and salt into a bowl, then rub in the butter by hand until the mixture resembles breadcrumbs. Alternatively, pulse in a food processor. Add the egg yolk and a little cold water, just enough to bring the pastry together into a ball. Wrap in plastic wrap and chill in the fridge for an hour.

Preheat the oven to 350 degrees and heat a baking sheet until searing hot.

Line an 11-inch loose-bottomed tart pan with the pastry, leaving the excess draped over the sides in case it shrinks.

Prick the bottom of the pastry crust with a fork, line with parchment paper or foil, and weigh this down with baking beans or rice. Place on the baking sheet and bake for about 15 minutes. Remove the baking beans and paper and bake the crust for another 5 minutes. Take out of the oven and trim off the excess pastry. Keep the oven on and reheat the baking sheet.

While the tart crust is cooking, wash the asparagus. Cut off and discard the woody bases. Break off the spear tips. If you bend them, they break naturally where the tender flesh meets the tougher part. Put the tips aside, then slice the stalks thinly at an angle, creating long ovals. Place in a pan with the butter and oil and sauté gently until tender (about 5 minutes).

Scatter the Parmesan inside the pastry crust (this absorbs any liquid, so keeps the base firm). Place the softened slices of asparagus on top of the Parmesan and sprinkle over the Gruyère cheese.

Heat a ridged grill pan for 3 to 4 minutes (until you can't count to 10 with your hand hovering just above it).

Grill the asparagus tips for a couple of minutes to char slightly and bring out their sweet taste (they might need longer if the tips are thick).

Mix together the eggs, cream, mustard, salt, and pepper and pour into the pastry crust. Arrange the asparagus tips on top. Place on the hot baking sheet and bake for 30 minutes, or until the tart is set and golden.

Party plum tart

A firmly set tart like this is one of the easiest desserts to transport for a picnic when you are feeding lots of people, and always delicious in summer when plums are at their best. This tart is best served just warm, but is also excellent cold, with a generous dollop of cream. A Summer berry Bakewell tart and Basil meringues with fresh fruit (see pages 214 and 210) are also perfect for big party picnics.

Serves 8 to 10
* 12 plums, halved and pits removed
* 3 tablespoons Cointreau
* 1 cup superfine sugar, plus 1 tablespoon extra
* 1¼ cups unsalted butter, softened
* Juice of 1 large lemon
* Grated zest of 2 lemons
* 2 cups blanched whole almonds, coarsely ground
* 1 tablespoon flour
* 2 eggs
* 1 teaspoon vanilla extract

For the pastry
* 2 cups unbleached flour
* 14 tablespoons cold unsalted butter, cut into cubes
* 3 egg yolks
* ½ cup confectioners' sugar
* Pinch of salt

Put the plums in a bowl and add the Cointreau and 1 tablespoon superfine sugar. Mix and leave to marinate, ideally overnight.

To make the pastry, sift the flour into a bowl and rub in the butter until the mixture resembles coarse breadcrumbs. Alternatively, pulse in a food processor. Add 2 egg yolks, the confectioners' sugar, and salt and mix/pulse again until the pastry comes together into a ball. Wrap it in plastic wrap and chill for 1 hour.

Preheat the oven to 350 degrees and heat a baking sheet until searing hot.

Line the base of a loose-bottomed 11-inch tart pan with baking parchment (the rich pastry can stick). Roll out the pastry ⅛ inch thick and use to line the prepared pan, leaving the excess draped over t he sides in case it shrinks.

Prick the bottom of the pastry crust with a fork, line with parchment paper or foil, and weigh this down with baking beans or rice. Place on the hot baking sheet and bake for about 15 minutes. Take it out, remove the baking beans and paper, and leave to cool for 5 minutes. Brush the pastry crust with the remaining egg yolk and bake for 5 more minutes to create a hard base. Allow to cool, then trim off the excess pastry. Lower the oven to 300 degrees and reheat the baking sheet.

Using an electric mixer, cream the butter and the 1 cup of superfine sugar until the mixture is pale. Add the lemon juice and zest, ground almonds, and flour and beat to combine. Add the eggs, one at a time, mixing well. Finally, add the vanilla extract and juice from the marinated plums.

Spoon this mixture into the pastry crust. Push in the halved plums (there should be enough to be almost touching each other) and bake on the hot baking sheet for 40 to 50 minutes, until golden brown. Cover with foil if the top is browning too quickly.

Baked vanilla and lemon cheesecake with marinated strawberries

An unbeatable summer dessert. Serve chilled—it needs to be really cold.

Serves 8
* 10 Graham crackers (about 5 ounces)
* 3 tablespoons butter, melted
* 16 ounces cream cheese
* ⅔ cup superfine sugar
* 1 tablespoon flour
* Juice and grated zest of 2 lemons
* 2 eggs, plus 1 yolk
* ¾ cup sour cream
* 1 tablespoon vanilla extract, or seeds scraped from 1 vanilla pod
* Heavy cream, to serve

For the marinated strawberries
* 16 ounces fresh strawberries
* 2 tablespoons Cointreau
* Juice and grated zest of 1 small orange
* 1 tablespoon finely chopped fresh mint
* 2 teaspoons superfine sugar or honey

Preheat the oven to 325 degrees.

Put the Graham crackers into a small plastic bag and bash them gently with a rolling pin, or whizz them for a minute in a food processor. Mix with the melted butter and press into the bottom of an 8-inch springform cake pan to cover the base.

Put the rest of the cheesecake ingredients into a large bowl and beat or whisk together until light and fluffy. Pour on top of the cookie base.

Place the pan on a baking tray in the middle of the oven for 40 to 50 minutes, or until firm and very slightly wobbly in the middle. Turn off the oven and leave the cheesecake in it to cool as this prevents it from cracking. (Don't worry if cracks slightly.) When cooled, remove from the pan and place in the fridge to chill.

Hull and halve the strawberries. Place in a bowl with the Cointreau, orange juice and zest, mint, and sugar. Allow to marinate for at least 30 minutes. To serve, spoon the strawberries over the top of the cheesecake and pour cream on the top.

Poached fresh apricots with cardamom

These sweet apricots are at their best very cold, straight from the fridge, delicious with yogurt, thick cream, or on top of vanilla ice cream. Apricots are better lightly cooked than raw. A sprig of rosemary is a good alternative to cardamom.

Serves 4
* 1 cup apple juice
* 1 vanilla pod, split open
* 8 cardamom pods, lightly crushed
* 7 tablespoons superfine sugar
* 1½ pounds fresh apricots, halved and pitted
* 1 tablespoon Cointreau (optional)

Heat the apple juice, vanilla pod, cardamom, and sugar in a saucepan until the sugar has dissolved. Add the apricots, reduce the heat, and simmer gently for 3 to 5 minutes, or until tender but not too soft. Transfer just the fruit to a serving dish.

Boil the syrup until it has reduced by half. Take off the heat, stir in the Cointreau (if using), and pour over the fruit. (The apricots are wonderful for breakfast with yogurt, but leave out the Cointreau.) The vanilla and cardamom pods can be strained out if you wish, but I leave them for people to remove, as I like the look of them.

Strawberry and basil ice cream drizzled with basil oil

One of my favorite ice cream recipes in my *In Season: Cooking with Vegetables and Fruits* cookbook is strawberry and black pepper ice cream, and this is an adaptation of it. The basil really brings out the flavor of the strawberries, and the basil oil is a surprising and excellent sauce. This recipe will make much more oil than you need for one batch of ice cream, but you can use it on Tomato, basil and mozzarella salad (page 135), or drizzled over Eggplant and mozzarella stacks (page 181) or Cream of tomato soup (page 125).

Serves 6 to 8

For the basil oil (makes about 2 ½ cups)
* Large handful of fresh basil leaves, without stalks
* 2 cups mild olive oil

* 32 ounces strawberries
* Small bunch of fresh basil, plus a few extra leaves to serve
* Juice of 1 orange
* Juice of 1 lemon
* 1 cup heavy cream
* ¾ cup superfine sugar

First make the oil: blanch the basil leaves briefly, then put them into ice water. Pat dry on a kitchen towel. Put the oil in a food processor, add the basil, and process for 5 minutes. Transfer to a jar and leave in the fridge for 1 week.

Strain the oil through cheesecloth, then pour into a dry, warm, sterilized bottle (you can sterilize it in a very hot dishwasher, or boil it in a pan of water for 10 minutes). Seal and label with a date. It keeps for a couple of months. Once open, store in the fridge.

To make the ice cream, hull the strawberries and puree three-quarters of them with the basil and citrus juice in a food processor. (Keep a few basil leaves for scattering when you serve.) Add the cream and sugar, mixing well. Taste, remembering that the flavor is milder when frozen than at room temperature, so add more basil if necessary.

Pour the mixture into an ice cream maker if you have one. Freeze/churn for about 20 minutes, then pack into a plastic container and freeze for 2 hours.

If you don't have an ice cream maker, place the mixture in a shallow container and freeze until half-frozen (about 1 hour). Remove and fork through, mixing the frozen edge into the middle to break up the ice crystals. Repeat twice.

Before serving, allow the ice cream to soften in the fridge for 15 minutes. When ready, scoop it into individual bowls and sprinkle each serving with the remaining strawberries and one or two basil leaves.

Place a bottle of basil oil on the table for everyone to drizzle over their serving.

Raspberry ripple ice cream

An all-time favorite, this should be made whenever you have access to lots of raspberries. The more fruit, the more intense the taste, so halve the amount below if you want something milder and creamier. (If you leave out the raspberries entirely, the recipe makes fantastic vanilla ice cream.) The finished result is rich, so most people won't need more than a couple of scoops.

Serves 8 to 10
* 2 ½ cups whole milk
* ½ cup superfine sugar
* A few drops of good vanilla extract
* 7 ounces (½ can) sweetened condensed milk
* Pinch of salt
* 2 cups heavy cream
* 2 cups raspberries, to serve

For the raspberry puree
* 2 cups raspberries
* 1 cup superfine sugar

Put the milk, sugar, and vanilla in a saucepan and bring to the boiling point. Remove from the heat and cool. When lukewarm, add the condensed milk, salt, and cream.

Pour the mixture into an ice cream maker if you have one. Freeze/churn for about 20 minutes, then pack into a plastic container and freeze for 2 hours. If you don't have an ice cream maker, place the mixture in a shallow container and freeze until half-frozen (about 1 hour). Remove and fork through, mixing the frozen edge into the middle to break up the ice crystals. Repeat twice.

To make the puree, whizz the raspberries with the sugar in a food processor, then strain them or push them through a food mill.

When the ice cream is hardening, but before it freezes solid, add the raspberry puree and fold it in with a fork; avoid mixing it up too much. Freeze completely.

Before serving, allow the ice cream to soften in the fridge for 15 minutes. Give each person a couple of scoops of topped with plenty of raspberries.

Black currant mousse ice cream

The taste of pure black currants is so intense that they are best eaten in a mousse or ice cream—best of all in a softly frozen mousse made an hour or two before you want to eat. The purple ice cream topped with some passion-fruit pulp, a few frozen black currants, and their bright green leaves looks marvelous.

Serves 6
* 1 pound black currants
* Juice of ½ orange
* 2 cups confectioners' sugar
* 1 cup heavy cream

To serve
* 3 passion fruits
* A few whole stems of black currants, frozen
* A few black currant leaves, frozen

Put the black currants in a saucepan with the orange juice and cook until soft. Press them through a strainer to extract the seeds. Add the confectioners' sugar to the fruit. Whip the heavy cream to soft peaks and fold into the puree.

Pour the mixture into an ice cream maker if you have one. Freeze/churn for about 20 minutes, then pack into a plastic container and freeze for 2 hours. If you don't have an ice cream maker, place the mixture in a shallow container and freeze until half-frozen (about 1 hour). Remove and fork through, mixing the frozen edge into the middle to break up the ice crystals. Repeat twice.

Cut open the passion fruits, scrape the seeds and pulp into a bowl and break up a bit with a fork.

Before serving, allow the ice cream to soften in the fridge for 15 minutes. Serve 2 or 3 scoops per person with the passion fruit pulp drizzled over the top. Decorate each plate with 1 or 2 whole stems of frozen black currants and a few black currant leaves.

Raspberry and Valpolicella sorbet

Rose Gray demonstrated this fantastic recipe at one of our Perch Hill cookery classes last summer. It's wonderfully easy to make, light and not too sinful, with intense flavor.

For 10
* 4 cups raspberries
* 1 cup Valpolicella
* Juice of ½ lemon
* ½ cup superfine sugar
* ¼ cup heavy cream

Place all the ingredients in a food processor and pulse-chop to a liquid.

Pour the mixture into an ice cream maker if you have one. Freeze/churn for about 20 minutes, then pack into a plastic container and freeze for 2 hours. If you don't have an ice cream maker, place the mixture in a shallow plastic container and freeze for 1 hour. Remove and fork through, mixing the frozen edge into the middle to break up the ice crystals. Repeat twice.

Before serving, allow the sorbet to soften in the fridge for 15 minutes.

Basil, raspberry, and hazelnut meringues

Served with summer fruit, these meringues are perfect for a party. Ideally, make one batch with hazelnuts, and another batch with basil, adding whole raspberries to some of both for a wonderful splotch of pink through the white meringue.

Yields about 10 (3- to 4-inch) meringues
* Peanut oil, for greasing
* 4 egg whites
* ½ cup granulated sugar
* ½ cup superfine sugar, plus a little more for the whipped cream
* Pinch of salt
* Grated zest of 1 lemon
* 2 cups raspberries
* ½ cup hazelnuts, chopped and toasted until golden, or a good handful of basil leaves, roughly chopped
* 1 cup heavy cream

Preheat the oven to 225 degrees. Rub a trace of oil over a sheet of parchment paper and use to line a baking sheet. Alternatively, use oiled baking parchment or a silicone sheet.

Beat the egg whites until stiff and really dry—longer than you would for any other recipe that includes whipped egg whites. Continue beating while you add the granulated sugar, 1 tablespoonful at a time, until the whites regain their former stiffness.

Using a metal spoon, lightly fold in the superfine sugar, salt, lemon zest, a small handful of raspberries and the hazelnuts or basil leaves, being careful not to knock out the air. Put tablespoonfuls of the mixture on to the prepared baking sheet and place in the oven for about 2 hours, until crisp but slightly gooey in the middle. Turn off the oven and, with the door open, leave the meringues in it until completely cooled.

When ready to serve, whip the cream until thick. Add about 1 teaspoon superfine sugar, or to taste. Use to sandwich the meringues together. Serve with the remaining raspberries.

Lemon tart topped with raspberries

There are few better things than an extremely lemony tart, but when it's topped with fat, sharp raspberries, it is sublime. I much prefer it to the more classic crème pâtissière that is often served with raspberries.

Serves 8 to 10

For the pastry
* 1¼ cups unbleached flour
* ½ cup (1 stick) cold unsalted butter, cut into cubes
* 3 egg yolks
* ¼ cup superfine sugar
* Pinch of salt

* Juice and grated zest of 6 lemons
* 6 eggs
* 1 cup superfine sugar
* 1 cup heavy cream
* 2½ cups raspberries
* 1 tablespoon honey, warmed, to glaze
* 1 cup heavy cream, softly whipped, to serve

To make the pastry, sift the flour into a bowl, and rub in the butter until the mixture resembles coarse breadcrumbs. Alternatively, pulse in a food processor. Add 2 egg yolks, the sugar, and salt and mix/pulse again until the pastry comes together into a ball. Wrap it in plastic wrap and chill for 1 hour.

Preheat the oven to 350 degrees and heat a baking sheet until searing hot.

Line the base of a loose-bottomed, 11-inch tart pan with parchment paper (the rich pastry can stick). Roll out the pastry ⅛ inch thick and use to line the prepared pan, leaving the excess draped over the sides in case it shrinks.

Prick the bottom of the pastry crust with a fork, cover with a round of parchment paper or foil, and weigh this down with some baking beans or rice. Place on the hot baking sheet and bake for 15 minutes. Remove the baking beans and paper and allow the pastry crust to cool for 5 minutes. Brush the crust with the remaining egg yolk and bake for 5 more minutes to create a hard base and prevent leaks of the runny filling. Trim off the excess pastry and allow to cool.

Lower the oven temperature to 300 degrees and reheat the baking sheet.

Put the lemon juice and zest, eggs, sugar, and heavy cream in a bowl and beat together. Place the tart pan on the hot baking sheet in the oven, then pour in the lemon mixture so you don't have to move the brimming tart: this avoids spillage. Bake for about 30 minutes, until set and springy.

Leave to cool for 30 minutes before topping with the raspberries, either heaped up or placed neatly in circles. Brush with the warm honey, to glaze.

Serve with the softly whipped cream.

Summer berry Bakewell tart

You can use almost any berries for this tart—mulberries, if you have a tree, or blackberries, loganberries, or raspberries. Out-of-season, frozen mixed berries are fine too. This is a recipe for one large tart, but it can also make eight individual tarts if you wish.

Serves 8
* 18 tablespoons (2 sticks plus 2 tablespoons) butter
* 1¼ cups sugar
* 2 cups blanched whole almonds, coarsely ground yourself (for more texture and taste)
* Juice and grated zest of 1 lemon
* 3 eggs
* 1 cup fresh berries
* Toasted sliced almonds, for sprinkling (optional)
* Cream or crème fraîche, to serve

For the pastry
* 1¼ cups unbleached flour
* ½ cup (1 stick) cold unsalted butter, cut into cubes
* 2 egg yolks
* ¼ cup superfine sugar
* Pinch of salt

First make the pastry. Sift the flour into a bowl and rub in the butter until the mixture resembles coarse breadcrumbs. Alternatively, pulse in a food processor. Add the egg yolks, sugar, and salt and mix/pulse again until the pastry comes together into a ball. Wrap it in plastic wrap and chill for 1 hour.

Preheat the oven to 350 degrees and heat a baking sheet until searing hot.

Line the base of a loose-bottomed, 11-inch tart pan with a silicone sheet or baking parchment (the rich pastry can stick). Roll out the pastry ⅛-inch thick and use to line the prepared pan, leaving the excess draped over the sides in case it shrinks.

Prick the bottom of the pastry crust with a fork, cover with a round of parchment paper or foil, and weigh this down with some baking beans or rice. Place on the hot baking sheet and bake for 15 minutes. Remove the baking beans and paper and allow the pastry crust to cool for 5 minutes. Trim off the excess pastry.

Lower the oven temperature to 300 degrees and reheat the baking sheet.

Using a food processor or electric mixer, cream the butter and sugar until pale. Mix in the ground almonds, lemon juice, and zest, then add the eggs one by one.

Scatter two-thirds of the berries into the pastry crust, then spoon in the almond mixture. Place on the hot baking sheet and bake for 40–50 minutes, until golden brown and macaroony-looking on the top.

Scatter with the flaked almonds, if using, and serve warm with cream or crème fraîche and the remaining berries.

Peaches in sweet rosé wine with lemon verbena

Apart from looking beautiful, this summer dessert is exceptionally easy to make. If you can't find lemon verbena (or verveine, which can be dried), use lemongrass or lemon balm. You could also add raspberries once it has cooled, and serve it with vanilla ice cream for a delicious peach melba. The small flat or white peaches (or nectarines) tend to have the best and sweetest flavor.

Serves 4 to 6
* ¾ cup rosé wine (a sweet Zinfandel is the best)
* 2 teaspoons superfine sugar or honey
* 10 lemon verbena leaves (or 2 lemongrass stalks, outer leaves removed, chopped quite finely)
* 2 teaspoons vanilla extract
* 2 strips of lemon peel, removed with a potato peeler
* 4 ripe peaches (about 1 pound), or 8 to 10 of the small, flat, very tasty variety
* Vanilla ice cream, to serve (see page 209 and exclude the raspberries)
* 2 tablespoons slivered almonds, toasted, to serve

Put the wine, sugar, lemon verbena, vanilla extract, and lemon peel into a saucepan and bring to a boil. Take off the heat and allow to cool for 5 minutes for the flavors to merge.

Meanwhile cut each peach into segments and put them into a serving bowl.

Pour the wine mixture over the fruit and give it a good stir. Cool for a couple of hours in the fridge. Serve with vanilla ice cream and top with the almonds.

Gooseberry meringue cake

For a big summer party you can't beat this dessert. It's an adaptation of Tam's mocha meringue cake in the *In Season: Cooking with Vegetables and Fruits* cookbook. I love the sourness of the gooseberries in contrast to the meringues and cream. Bought meringues are fine here as they need to be quite dusty and dry. For a children's party, do this recipe with strawberries. It's also good with rhubarb in the spring.

Serves 8 to 10

For the meringues
* 6 egg whites
* 1¾ cups superfine sugar
* Pinch of salt

* 2 pounds gooseberries
* 2 cups superfine sugar
* 10 heads of elderflowers
* 3 cups heavy cream
* 1 tablespoon superfine sugar

Preheat the oven to 225 degrees. Grease a baking tray or line it with parchment paper.

To make the meringues, beat the egg whites until very stiff and dry. Slowly add the sugar bit by bit, and the pinch of salt, beating all the while, until the egg white regains its former stiffness. Dollop tablespoonfuls of the meringue mixture onto a greased baking tray and bake for 2–3 hours, until the meringues are dry.

Wash and dry the fruit, then place in a pan with the sugar and elderflowers. Cook over a gentle heat for 5 minutes, stirring carefully as you want some of the fruit to retain its shape. Allow to cool completely, then drain the fruit, keeping the juice to use at the end. Discard the elderflowers.

Put the cream in a bowl, add the sugar, and whip into soft peaks. Fold into the gooseberries.

Break up the meringues and fold into the gooseberry mixture. Pour into a large loaf pan and freeze for 24 hours before use.

Eat the cake almost straight from the freezer as it melts quickly. Serve with the remaining juice poured over the top.

Melon soup

This is a fantastic, refreshing summer dessert. Serve chilled with a scoop of vanilla ice cream.

For 4
* 1 cup Beaumes de Venise or another Muscat wine
* 1 cinnamon stick
* 1 vanilla pod, split open
* 1 tablespoon honey or superfine sugar
* 1 pound cantaloupe melon flesh (1 medium melon)
* Vanilla ice cream (see page 209, but exclude the raspberries), to serve

Put the wine and cinnamon into a saucepan. Scrape in the vanilla seeds and add the pod. Warm gently but don't allow to boil. Add the honey and stir until it has dissolved. Leave to infuse and cool.

Pulse the melon in a food processor and add to the cold wine mixture. Stir to combine, and serve chilled in glasses, topped with a scoop of vanilla ice cream.

Plum syllabub

One of the simplest late summer desserts to throw together—star-anise-flavored plums served in a glass topped with frothy Chantilly cream. I make a similar recipe with rhubarb in spring and early summer. Both are good with almost any crisp cookies, particularly ginger (see page 412).

Serves 6 to 8
* Juice and grated zest of 1 orange
* ½ cup superfine sugar
* 1 pound ripe plums, pitted and sliced
* 1 bay leaf
* 4 star anise

For the syllabub
* 1 cup heavy cream
* Grated zest and juice of 1 large lemon
* 3–4 tablespoons sweet white wine
* ½ cup superfine sugar

Warm the orange juice in a pan and dissolve the sugar in it. Add the plums, orange zest, bay leaf, and star anise and cook until the fruit is soft (for about 10 minutes). Set aside to cool and infuse.

Using a slotted spoon, transfer the fruit to a bowl. Boil up the juice until it thickens. Return the plums to the pan, then allow to cool.

To make the syllabub, put the cream, lemon zest and juice, wine, and sugar into a bowl and beat for several minutes, until the mixture becomes thick and light.

Remove the star anise and bay leaf from the fruit. Spoon into individual glasses, adding the syllabub mixture over the top. Chill for a couple of hours before serving.

Scones with rosemary cherries

Scones are the epitome of a summer tea. I like them unusually small or large, so that you know they're homemade.

Yields 22 (1-inch) scones

For the topping
* Large handful of rosemary sprigs
* 22 cherries, pitted
* Geranium-scented strawberry jam (see page 225)
* 1 cup heavy cream, whipped

For the scones
* 1 ⅔ cups unbleached flour
* 1 tablespoon baking powder
* 2 tablespoons superfine sugar
* ½ cup (1 stick) cold butter, cut into chunks
* ½ cup milk
* 1 egg, lightly beaten, for glazing

First make the rosemary cherries. Preheat the oven to 325 degrees. Lay out the rosemary sprigs in a large baking tray and place the cherries over the top. Cook for 5 minutes, then allow to cool. Discard the rosemary sprigs.

Keep the oven on, but turn the heat down to 300 degrees. Grease or line a baking sheet with parchment paper for the scones.

Put the flour, baking powder, sugar, and butter in a food processor and blend until you have a breadcrumb consistency. Add the milk until the mixture comes together in a ball.

Pat out the dough on a floured surface to a thickness of 1 to 1½ inches. Cut out circles using a cutter and place them on the prepared baking sheet. Brush with the beaten egg and bake for 10 to 12 minutes, until risen and golden.

Cut each scone in half. On half of the scones, place a dollop of cream and a rosemary cherry on top. Spread the rest of the scone halves with strawberry jam and top with the cream.

Layered summer sponge

A really good sponge cake is hard to beat for a summer tea party. You make this light cake the old-fashioned way, mirroring the weight of the eggs to that of the butter, sugar, and flour. You can douse the sponge with any favorite liqueur to add flavor.

Serves 8 to 10
* 4 large eggs
* Butter (see method)
* Superfine sugar (see method)
* Self-rising flour (see method)
* Marsala wine (optional)

For the filling
* 2 teaspoons confectioners' sugar
* 8 ounces mascarpone cheese
* 1 cup heavy cream
* 3 cups mixed fruit, such as raspberries, strawberries (hulled and halved), and blueberries

Preheat the oven to 325 degrees. Line an 8-inch springform cake pan with lightly oiled parchment paper.

Weigh the eggs in their shells, then measure out the same weight each of butter, superfine sugar, and self-rising flour. Melt the butter over a low heat but do not brown it. Allow to cool slightly.

Separate the egg whites from the yolks. Put the whites into a large bowl and beat until they form stiff peaks. Add the superfine sugar, whisking all the time. Then carefully fold in the egg yolks and the melted butter with a metal spoon. Sift the flour into the mixture and stir in very gently.

Pour the mixture into the prepared pan and bake in the middle of the oven for 30 to 35 minutes, or until a skewer stabbed in the middle comes out clean. Leave to cool in the pan for a few minutes, then turn onto a wire rack to cool.

To make the filling, put the confectioners' sugar, mascarpone, and cream into a bowl and beat into soft peaks.

Cut the cake horizontally into 3 layers. Douse with the Marsala (if using). Spread the top of each layer with the whipped cream mixture and scatter with fruit. Stack the three layers on top of each other and serve.

Raspberry cupcakes with mascarpone frosting

This recipe comes from my friend Sarah Wilkin, who is a brilliant baker and does tiered chandeliers of these cupcakes for parties. I'm not normally one for a cupcake—they can be so dry—but these (and the Primrose lemon curd cupcakes on page 87—also her recipe) are fantastic. Blackberries can be used instead of raspberries, but take out the ground almonds, as those two flavors don't work so well together.

These cupcakes are good served on a cake stand, along with bread and cheese, at the end of a meal. Then some people can have savory and some sweet.

Yields 12 to 14 cupcakes
* 3 tablespoons butter, at room temperature
* ¾ cup superfine sugar
* 1 cup unbleached flour, sifted
* 2 tablespoons ground almonds
* 1½ teaspoons baking powder
* Pinch of salt
* 1 egg
* ½ cup milk
* ¼ teaspoon vanilla extract
* 1 cup fresh raspberries (set aside a few of the best for decoration)

For the frosting
* 5 ounces mascarpone cheese
* ⅓ cup confectioners' sugar, plus extra for dusting

Preheat the oven to 325 degrees. Line a couple of cupcake pans with 12 to 14 paper cases.

Put the butter, sugar, flour, almonds, baking powder, and salt in the bowl of a food processor or electric mixer and beat until you get a fine consistency. In a separate bowl beat together the egg, milk, and vanilla. Add this liquid bit by bit to the dry mixture until it's fully incorporated, but don't overmix. Gently fold in most of the raspberries, saving some for decoration.

Spoon the mixture into the paper cases until two-thirds full, then bake for 20 to 25 minutes.

The cakes should look golden and the tops spring back when touched. Transfer them to a wire rack and leave to cool.

To make the frosting, put the mascarpone in a bowl and beat until you get a creamy texture. Sift in the confectioners' sugar and mix until combined. Using either a piping bag or a spatula, apply the frosting to the cakes. Top with the remaining raspberries and dust with confectioners' sugar.

Upside-down raspberry cake

Halfway between a cake and a pudding, this can be served as it is, or with plenty of fresh raspberries over the top and softly whipped cream.

Serves 8
* 13 tablespoons (1 stick plus 5 tablespoons) butter
* 1 cup superfine sugar
* 1½ cups fresh raspberries
* 2 eggs, beaten
* ¾ cup plus 2 tablespoons unbleached flour
* ⅓ cup polenta
* 2 teaspoons vanilla extract
* 1 teaspoon baking powder

Preheat the oven to 350 degrees. Grease and line an 8-inch springform cake pan with parchment paper.

Melt 5 tablespoons of the butter and add ⅓ cup of the sugar. Heat gently until the sugar has dissolved. Add two-thirds of the raspberries and stir gently to coat. Arrange the raspberries in the bottom of the prepared cake pan.

In a separate bowl, beat the remaining butter and sugar to a creamy consistency. Gradually add the eggs, flour, and polenta, just a little of each at a time, beating as you do so. Add the vanilla and baking powder. Test the consistency of the mixture: it should drop off the end of a spoon in a big dollop. If it is too dry, add a little milk, until dropping consistency is reached. Spoon the mixture evenly over the raspberries in the pan.

Bake for 40 to 45 minutes, or until the cake is risen and golden. To test that it is cooked, gently press in the middle—the cake should bounce back into shape.

Allow to cool slightly in the pan before transferring to a wire rack. When nearly cooled, turn onto a large flat plate. Drizzle it with any syrup left in the pan and top with the remaining raspberries.

Devonshire honey cake with plum compote

With its quite dense texture and fantastic taste of honey, this cake almost makes you feel like you're eating straight from the comb. It's delicious but sweet, so serve it as a dessert with a sharp plum or blackcurrant compote and some fluffy cream. I got the original recipe from Joyce Collins of Kencol Farm Apiaries, who—until both my husband, Adam, and Bea, our gardener, became fiercely allergic—had bee hives at Perch Hill.

Serves 6 to 8
* 1 cup (2 sticks) unsalted butter
* 1 cup clear honey, plus a little extra for brushing
* ½ cup dark brown sugar
* 3 large eggs
* 2⅓ cups self-rising flour

For the compote
* 1 pound plums, pitted
* Juice and grated zest of 1 orange
* ½ cup superfine sugar, or to taste (damson plums often need more)

Cut the butter into pieces and drop it into a pan with the honey and sugar. Melt it slowly, then boil for 1 minute. Cool for 20 minutes.

Preheat the oven to 275 degrees. (The temperature needs to be very low as the high sugar content of the mixture makes it burn easily.) Grease an 8-inch springform cake pan.

Beat the eggs one by one into the honey mixture. Sift in the flour and beat until smooth. Pour into the prepared pan and bake for 50 minutes. Test if the cake is done by stabbing a skewer in the middle—it should come out clean. If not, bake for another 5 minutes and test again. When done, cool a bit in the pan, then turn onto a wire rack to cool a bit more. While still warm, transfer the cake to a flat plate and brush 2 tablespoons of warm honey over the top.

To make the compote, put the plums, orange juice and zest, and sugar into a saucepan and heat gently, stirring to melt the sugar. Cook for 5 minutes until the plums are soft. Serve alongside the warm cake.

Geranium-scented strawberry jam

Don't make strawberry jam in huge batches: it's harder to get it to set, and with endless boiling you lose the freshness of the flavor. Adding scented geranium leaves to the jam, as the Greeks often do, enhances the flavor. If you can't find them, adding black pepper is a delicious alternative—it cuts the sweetness of the jam.

Yields 2 pint jars
* 2 pounds fresh strawberries, hulled
* 4 rose or lemon scented geranium leaves, or a good grinding of black pepper
* Juice of 2 lemons
* 4 ½ cups granulated sugar, warmed in the oven

Place a saucer in the fridge, ready for when you come to test for setting point later on.

Put the strawberries and pelargonium leaves (or pepper) into a large, heavy-based, stainless-steel pan and use a potato masher to squash the fruit slightly. Don't push too hard—you just want some of the fruit to release a little juice, not to be completely flattened.

Stir in the lemon juice and bring to a boil for 2 to 3 minutes. Stir in the sugar and boil for another 10 to 15 minutes. Remove the leaves.

Pull the pan off the heat and test for setting point. Take the saucer from the fridge and place a teaspoonful of the jam on it. When cool, it should wrinkle when you push it with your finger. You could also use a jam thermometer here; when it reaches 220 degrees, the mixture will set.

Cool slightly and pour into dry, warm, sterilized jars (you can sterilize them in a very hot dishwasher, or boil them in a pan of water for 10 minutes). Seal each jar and process in a boiling-water bath according to jar manufacturer's instructions. Label with the date. This jam will last for several years. Once opened, store in the fridge.

Pickled cherries

Savory rather than sweet, these cherries are excellent to eat with any sharp cheese—a lump of Stilton or sharp Cheddar. Leave the stems on and keep them in pairs, if that's how they come, so you retain their amazing shape.

Yields 2 pint jars
* 2 cups cider vinegar
* 3 star anise
* 1 cinnamon stick
* 8 whole cloves
* 3 tablespoons dark or light brown sugar
* 1 pound fresh cherries with stalks (dark-colored ones are best)

Put everything, except the cherries, into a saucepan and bring to a boil. Simmer gently for about 10 minutes, until the sugar has dissolved. Add the cherries to the pan and take off the heat.

Cool slightly and pour into dry, warm, sterilized jars (you can sterilize them in a very hot dishwasher, or boil them in a pan of water for 10 minutes). Seal each jar and process in a boiling-water bath according to jar manufacturer's instructions. Label with the date. The cherries will last for several years. Once opened, store in the fridge.

Balsamic pickled onions

Good with any cold meat, particularly beef or ham, these onions are also great with sharp Cheddar. They're a satisfying thing to make one summer evening and store away because they make popular Christmas presents and keep for at least a year.

Yields 4 half-pint jars
* 2 pounds small pickling onions
* 3 tablespoons extra virgin olive oil
* 2 cups good-quality balsamic vinegar
* ¼ cup sugar
* 1 teaspoon coriander seeds
* 1 teaspoon cumin seeds
* 1 teaspoon fennel seeds
* 1 teaspoon mustard seeds

Preheat the oven to its lowest setting, ideally 275 degrees.

Top and tail the onions, taking care not to cut away too much root as you want them to hold together. Put them in a large bowl and cover with boiling water for 20 seconds to soften the skins. Drain, then cover them with cold water. Peel off the skin, putting the onions back in the water once they're done. This helps to stop your eyes from watering and the onions discoloring.

Once they are all peeled, drain and tip into a roasting pan. Add the olive oil and 5 tablespoons water. Place in the oven and, depending on the size of the onions, bake them for 1 to 1½ hours. They should be soft and translucent, but not brown, so check from time to time.

Scoop the onions into dry, warm, sterilized jars (you can sterilize them in a very hot dishwasher, or boil them in a pan of water for 10 minutes).

Put the vinegar, sugar, and seeds in a pan and bring to a boil. Pour over the onions. Immediately seal each jar and process in a boiling-water bath according to jar manufacturer's instructions. Label with the date. Leave for at least 6 weeks before eating. The onions will keep for a year or more. Once opened, store in the fridge.

Pickled garlic

If you want homemade pickled garlic that has a mild, but delicious flavor and keeps for ages, this is the recipe for you. It's very good served just as you would pickled onions, with cold meat or cheese and a hunk of bread, and lovely mixed with olives to serve with a glass of wine.

Yields 1 quart jar
* 5 large heads of garlic
* 1 large red chili, halved and thinly sliced lengthwise
* 7 cardamom pods
* 2 small sprigs of rosemary
* 1 teaspoon fennel seeds
* 1 cup rice vinegar
* ½ cup superfine sugar

Bring a large saucepan of water to a boil.

Meanwhile, peel the garlic and cut the larger cloves in half. Blanch for 1 minute in boiling water. Drain and place in a dry, warm, sterilized jar (you can sterilize it in a very hot dishwasher, or boil it in a pan of water for 10 minutes). Add the chili, cardamom pods, rosemary, and fennel seeds.

Put the vinegar and sugar into a saucepan over a low heat and stir until the sugar has dissolved. Bring to a boil, then take off the heat and allow to cool slightly.

Pour the vinegar over the garlic. Immediately seal each jar and process in a boiling-water bath according to jar manufacturer's instructions. Label with the date. The garlic will keep for up to a year. Once open, it's best stored in the fridge.

Thai spiced basil pesto

A summer classic with a Thai twist, this pesto is delicious on crostini, egg noodles, or pasta, or served with chicken or fish. Eat it right away, or store in a cold, dark room, fridge, or freezer.

Yields 1 pint jar
* ¼ pound fresh sweet basil
* ½ cup extra virgin olive oil
* ¼ cup pine nuts
* 2 garlic cloves, finely chopped
* Salt
* 2 ounces Parmesan cheese, grated
* 1 lemongrass stalk, outer leaves removed, finely chopped
* Juice and grated zest of 1 lime
* 1 red chili, deseeded and finely chopped

Put the basil, olive oil, pine nuts, garlic, and salt into a food processor or blender and blend, stopping from time to time to scrape the ingredients down toward the bottom of the bowl with a rubber spatula.

When evenly blended, pour into a mixing bowl and beat in the Parmesan, lemongrass, lime juice and zest, and chili by hand. Add a little more olive oil, if necessary.

If you want to store the pesto, put it into a dry, warm, sterilized jar (you can sterilize it in a very hot dishwasher, or boil it in a pan of water for 10 minutes). Smooth off the top with the back of a teaspoon and cover completely with a thin layer of olive oil. Seal and label with the date. Keep it in the fridge and it will last for two weeks.

After using some pesto from the jar, make sure there is still sufficient olive oil to cover the top completely. This will keep it fresh and prevent it from losing its color.

Beet and sweet potato relish

Here's a relish with wonderful color and flavor, good with broiled and barbecued meat, and nice heated and served warm with pork chops.

Yields about 3 pint jars
* 1 pound sweet potato, peeled and coarsely grated
* ⅔ pound raw beet, peeled and coarsely grated
* ⅔ pound red onions, thinly sliced
* 1 tablespoon peeled and grated fresh ginger
* 2–3 garlic cloves, finely chopped
* 1 red chili, finely chopped
* 1 teaspoon ground cumin
* 1 teaspoon cumin seeds, toasted
* Juice and grated zest of 2 limes
* 1¼ cups brown sugar
* 1⅔ cups cider vinegar

Put all the ingredients into a large, heavy-based, stainless-steel pan and gently bring to the simmering point. Simmer, stirring occasionally, for about 30 to 45 minutes, until the relish has thickened.

Allow to cool slightly, then spoon into dry, warm, sterilized jars (you can sterilize them in a very hot dishwasher, or boil them in a pan of water for 10 minutes). Seal each jar and process in a boiling-water bath according to jar manufacturer's instructions. Label with the date. This relish will keep for 6 months. Once opened, store in the fridge.

Quick elderflower "champagne"

This is the epitome of summer—a slightly fizzy, very lightly alcoholic drink with that unique taste of elderflower. You will need bottles with metal clasps on the top so that they don't pop as the liquid ferments.

Yields 4 quarts
* 3 cups superfine sugar
* 2 tablespoons white wine vinegar
* 30 large heads of elderflowers
* Grated zest and juice of 3 lemons
* 1 teaspoon dried yeast

Boil 4 quarts of water in a large, heavy-based, stainless-steel pan. Add the sugar and stir over the heat to dissolve. Allow to cool.

Add the vinegar, elderflowers, and lemon zest and juice to the pan. Sprinkle over the dried yeast. Cover with a kitchen towel and leave for 24 hours.

Strain through a fine sieve, then use a funnel to pour the liquid into bottles. The champagne will be ready in 10 days. Drink within 2 to 3 weeks. Don't be tempted to leave it longer as when it carries on fermenting, the fresh flavor of the elderflowers will be lost and it will start turning into wine.

Limeade

This is the lime equivalent of real English lemonade and I love it. It can be made either with still or sparkling water.

Serves 6
* 1/3 cup superfine sugar
* Juice and grated zest of 10 limes
* Plenty of crushed ice
* 1 lime, thinly sliced

Pour 2 quarts of water into a large pitcher and add the sugar, stirring until it has dissolved. Add the lime juice and zest. Put in the fridge to chill for a couple of hours.

To serve, fill tall glasses with crushed ice, pour in the limeade, and drop in some lime slices.

Lime cordial

While this is excellent diluted with fizzy water, it's best of all with really cold lager.

Yields 1 (750-ml) bottle
* **1¼ cups superfine sugar**
* **Juice of 8 limes and grated zest of 4**

Heat 2 cups water, add the sugar, and stir until dissolved. Add the lime juice and zest, then stir and allow to cool.

Keep in the fridge until needed.

Lemon thyme vodka lemonade

This is sharp, strong, and delicious.

Serves 1
* **Crushed ice**
* **1 shot lemon vodka**
* **4 teaspoons lemon juice**
* **¼ teaspoon sugar**
* **5 sprigs of lemon thyme**
* **Soda water**

Fill a cocktail shaker with crushed ice and add the vodka, lemon juice, sugar, and 4 sprigs of lemon thyme. Shake well, then strain into an ice-filled tumbler. Top up with soda and garnish with the remaining sprig of lemon thyme.

Negroni

Ideal on a warm summer's evening when eating out in the garden, and very cheering on a chilly wet one.

Serves 6
* Lots of ice
* 2 oranges, sliced
* 1 cup Campari
* ½ cup gin
* ½ cup sweet vermouth
* 1 cup freshly squeezed orange juice
* 2 ½ cups soda water (optional)

Fill a pitcher with ice. Add the orange slices. Pour in the Campari, gin, vermouth, and orange juice. When you are ready to serve, add soda water, or leave this out if you want something really powerful.

Strawberry and basil vodka cocktail

Quick, simple, and delicious, this drink has the intense summer flavors of strawberries and basil.

Serves 1
* Plenty of ice
* Double shot of vodka
* 8 strawberries
* 6 basil leaves
* Splash of cranberry juice (optional)

Put the ice, vodka, strawberries, and basil in a cocktail shaker and shake for quite a while to pulverize the fruit and herb and release their flavors. To decrease the sweetness slightly, add a splash of cranberry juice.

Strain into a martini glass.

Champagne cocktail

Here is a wonderful celebratory drink—bubbly, cheerful, and not too sweet.

Serves 12
* 1 bottle of Sauternes, chilled
* 1 cup brandy
* 2 bottles of champagne, chilled

Pour the Sauternes into a pitcher and add the brandy. When you're ready to serve, top up the pitcher with champagne and pour into champagne glasses.

Summer berry Bellinis

A simple and fantastically delicious summer cocktail consisting of fruit puree topped up with champagne or prosecco.

Serves 6
* 3 cups raspberries, blackberries, tayberries, or mulberries
* 1 teaspoon superfine sugar
* 1 bottle of champagne or prosecco

Puree the fruit in a food processor with the sugar, then strain to get rid of the seeds. Pour into a pitcher.

Pour a little pulp—no more than ½ inch—into the bottom of a champagne glass and top up with champagne or prosecco.

AUTUMN

In autumn the landscape is transformed with a rich, dense palette of colors: crimsons and mahoganies, and the velvet hues and textures of dahlias, salvias, and gladioli. We start to seek out food to follow suit—strong complex tastes, with plenty of fragrant spices and warming flavors. This is the moment for mulligatawny and spicy chickpea soup, pakoras in their jackets of chili, coriander, and cumin, mussels in a cream curry sauce, as well as big fat eggplants, pumpkins, pears, apples, chilis, sweet roasted peppers, corn on the cob, and lots of earthy beets eaten with horseradish.

It's good to have food you can shove in the oven and leave while you're in the garden or woods picking mushrooms, chestnuts, blackberries, rosehips, and sloes. I like going out as the day is coming to an end and spending a few minutes wandering down the lane harvesting blackberries for supper. There's always a particular corner as I go into the wood by the sunken stream that no one else seems to find, dripping with bulbous, black fruit.

Autumn almost sinks under its own abundance. In the garden you can feel overwhelmed by fruit and vegetables. Tomatoes are left unpicked, turning squidgy on the vine; fallen apples succumb to wasps; and old zucchinis pile up like giants' fingers. But that's part of autumn and what drives us to get on with a bit of preserving—picking and storing things away for eating through the winter. One of my favorite things at this time of year is to plan a weekend of preserving. We have a wonderful pick-your-own near us in East Sussex: Maynards, at Windmill Hill, Ticehurst, where we can pick autumn raspberries, damson plums, hazelnuts, apples, and pears. You can do it by yourself, but it's much more fun with children and friends, with several people peeling, coring, stirring, and bottling, then sharing out what's been made at the end of the day.

The heady aromas from a day of preserving are definitely a sign of autumn—as is the smell of a bonfire in the evening air. It's the time for tidying up our gardens, collecting everything together into a great pyre that can form the center of a Halloween or firework party, with everyone drinking and eating outside. For that, think of delicious things that will keep everyone warm and are easy to eat standing up. Sausage burgers are ideal, and I love Thai chicken burgers too. The recipes for desserts and homemade sweets, which might feel like too much of an effort to make for every day, are brilliant for a party.

Whether it's an autumn dinner with friends, or a big bonfire party, it's lovely to fill the room or the table with hanging garlands and bunches of corn on the cob, dahlias, and fat pumpkins. You can grow or buy some of those warty gourds to sit on the middle of your kitchen table through the autumn, and arrange big shallow bowls of crimson-black dahlias with a sprinkling of Chinese lanterns to keep them from looking somber. Life's all about fruitfulness and abundance at this time of year and hopefully, with these recipes, your food will reflect that.

Tomato and chili salsa with corn tortillas

A lovely, fresh-tasting salsa, which is very easy to make, and ideal for a Halloween party. This is good served with corn chips and it's a great side dish with Chili con carne (see page 280).

Serves 10 to 12
* 8 large ripe tomatoes (on the vine tomatoes are ideal for this)
* 4 large shallots or 1 red onion, finely chopped
* 4–5 green chilis or 1–2 red chilis, finely chopped
* Small bunch of cilantro, finely chopped
* 2 teaspoons superfine sugar or honey
* Juice and finely grated zest of 2 limes
* Salt and black pepper
* Tortilla chips, to serve

Peel the tomatoes, as described on page 125, then cut in half and discard all the seeds—they make the salsa too watery. Chop the flesh into small cubes.

Put the cubed tomato into a mixing bowl, add all the remaining ingredients (reserving a little lime zest for decorating), and mix thoroughly.

Keep the salsa in the fridge until needed. Sprinkle with lime zest, and serve with tortilla chips.

Spiced, toasted chickpeas

This makes an excellent quick and healthy party snack, brilliant for when you're feeding lots of people.

Serves 10 to 15
* 1 pound dried chickpeas, soaked overnight, cooked, and drained, or 2 (15-ounce) cans, drained
* 1 teaspoon cumin seeds, toasted and ground
* 1 teaspoon coriander seeds, toasted and ground
* Seeds from 15 cardamom pods
* Light dusting of paprika
* Light dusting of turmeric
* Salt and black pepper
* 1 tablespoon sunflower oil

Preheat the oven to 350 degrees.

Put the chickpeas into a roasting pan, add the spices, seasoning, and oil, and toss together. Spread them out in a single layer and roast for about 45 minutes, stirring halfway through their cooking time, until they become crispy. Serve in small bowls.

Squash hummus

I love this hummus, which has a sweeter, less garlicky taste than most. The squash gives it a vibrant orange color. It makes a great dip with Rosemary flatbread (see right) or slices of raw vegetables, and it's excellent with Grilled lamb chops or Slow-cooked lamb (see pages 61 and 64). It's also a good filling for peppers—hot or sweet (see page 62).

Yields enough to fill a large cereal bowl
* 1 small butternut squash (about ²⁄₃ pound)
* ½ pound dried chickpeas, soaked overnight, cooked, and drained, or 1 (15-ounce) can of chickpeas, drained
* 2 garlic cloves, coarsely chopped
* 2 tablespoons tahini paste
* 2 tablespoons olive oil, or more if you prefer a softer consistency
* Juice of ½ lemon, to taste
* Salt and black pepper

Preheat the oven to 375 degrees.

Wrap the squash in foil and bake for 1 to 1½ hours, until soft to the tip of a knife. Remove the foil and set the squash aside until cool enough to handle.

Cut the squash in half and discard the seeds and fibers. Scoop out the flesh.

Put the squash flesh into a food processor with the drained chickpeas and all the other ingredients and whizz until everything is well combined. Add a little extra olive oil if needed.

Rosemary flatbread

I included this quick and easy recipe in my *In Season: Cooking with Vegetables and Fruits* cookbook, and have included it again here because it is wonderful with so many things—hummus, any thick soup, or Cretan Baked feta (see page 182).

Yields 6 medium-sized flatbreads
* 1½ cups unbleached flour
* ½ teaspoon dried yeast
* A little rosemary, finely chopped, plus extra for topping
* 1 tablespoon extra virgin olive oil, plus extra for coating
* Salt

Sift the flour into a large bowl and add the yeast. Add ²⁄₃ cup tepid water, the rosemary, olive oil, and a pinch of salt, and start mixing it all together to form a rather sloppy dough. If your mix is too dry, add a little more water. If the mix is too wet, add a little more flour.

Once you have a ball of dough, take it out of the bowl and knead on a floured surface for 5 minutes, until it is elastic but slightly tacky. Leave the dough to rest in a warm place under a damp kitchen towel for 1 hour: it will rise until it has about doubled in size.

Preheat the oven to 400 degrees. Oil a couple of baking sheets.

Break off a golfball-sized piece of dough and roll it out on a floured surface to a thickness of about ¹⁄₁₆-inch. Repeat until you have used all the dough. Brush each flatbread with olive oil. Sprinkle with a little salt and rosemary.

Transfer to the prepared baking sheets and place in the oven for 12 to 15 minutes, until the surface of the breads starts to bubble and turn golden brown. Don't cook them too long or they'll turn into cardboard. Serve immediately.

Barbecued corn with chili and garlic butter

Here's a brilliant thing to eat when corn is at its very best in late summer and autumn. Pick or buy lots when it's in season, cook it, and shove it in the freezer. The corn loses its sugar quickly on storing, so you want to cook and freeze it as soon as you can. Then cook gently on a barbecue to make them sweet.

Serves 8

For the chili and garlic butter
* 7 tablespoons softened butter
* 1 red chili, deseeded and finely chopped
* 2 garlic cloves, very finely chopped
* 2 tablespoons very finely chopped fresh thyme

* 8 ears of corn, leaves and silks removed (keep the leaves for serving the ears after cooking)

Using a fork, mix the butter with the chili, garlic, and thyme in a bowl. Put the mixture in the fridge to harden a little, then roll it into a fat sausage, wrap in plastic wrap, and put it back in the fridge. You can then cut discs of flavored butter, one for each cob or person.

Cook the ears of corn in boiling salted water for 5 minutes. Plunge into cold water, then pat dry with paper towels. (If you're keeping the corn for later, freeze them at this stage.)

Put the ears of corn directly on a slow-burning barbecue, turning occasionally, for about 15 minutes.

Cut the cobs into chunks to make them easier to eat, place in a leaf for serving, and give everyone a disc of butter to melt over them.

Smoked mackerel pâté

An easy, inexpensive yet delicious pâté, perfect for feeding lots of people. Pep it up with fresh horseradish. It's fantastic on toasted Focaccia (see page 132) or on top of Quick caraway bread (see page 360). Top each slice with a peppery-tasting autumn salad leaf or a nasturtium.

Serves 15
* $^2/_3$ pound (about 10 ounces) smoked mackerel, boned and skinned
* 16 ounces cream cheese
* 1 cup heavy cream
* Juice of 1 lemon, or to taste
* 1 teaspoon freshly grated horseradish, or 2 teaspoons good bottled horseradish
* Black pepper
* Cayenne pepper

To serve
* Warm toasted bread
* Lemon halves

Put the smoked mackerel, cream cheese, and heavy cream into a food processor. Whizz briefly. Add the lemon juice, horseradish, and plenty of black pepper. Whizz again until the mixture forms a paste. Check the seasoning and add more pepper if necessary (you shouldn't need to add salt).

Pack the pâté into a dish and place in the fridge for 1 to 2 hours, until set. Just before serving, sprinkle with a little cayenne pepper. Serve with warm toast and lemon halves.

Pumpkin and apple soup
with chestnuts

Some pumpkin or squash flesh, an onion or two, and plenty of cumin: this is the basic recipe for a fabulous soup. I love the addition of apples—their sharpness cuts through the sweetness of the squash—and you can't go wrong in autumn with a topping of chestnuts.

Serves 8 as a starter, 6 for lunch
* 2 ¼ pounds (prepared weight) pumpkin or butternut squash, peeled, deseeded, and cut into chunks
* Olive oil
* 1 teaspoon chopped fresh rosemary
* Salt and black pepper
* 1 large onion, chopped
* 1 garlic clove, finely chopped
* 1 teaspoon ground cumin
* 2-inch piece of fresh ginger, peeled and chopped
* ½ pound tart cooking apples, peeled and chopped
* 3 cups good fresh vegetable or chicken stock
* 1 cup unsweetened apple juice

To serve
* Handful of cooked chestnuts (vacuum-packed are fine), chopped and warmed
* Crème fraîche (optional)

Preheat the oven to 325 degrees.

Place the pumpkin or squash pieces in a plastic bag, add a little olive oil plus the rosemary and salt and pepper and toss together. Empty into a roasting pan and cook in the oven for 45 minutes, or until soft and beginning to char around the edges.

Gently sauté the onion and garlic with the cumin and ginger in a large, heavy-based pan until soft but not colored. Add the roasted pumpkin or squash and the apples, mix well, then stir in the stock and apple juice. Reduce the heat, cover, and simmer gently for about 15 minutes, until the apples are soft. Check the seasoning and add more stock or apple juice to taste. Puree the mixture in a food processor or blender.

Reheat the soup, and add some chopped chestnuts and a dollop of crème fraîche (if using) to each serving.

Mulligatawny soup

This many-flavored and -textured soup is ideal for autumn. The chunks of chicken are crucial, and you can add more if you want. Have this from a vacuum flask on a picnic, or eat it for lunch. One big bowl makes a hearty meal.

Serves 8 as a starter, 6 for lunch
* 1⅓ cups red lentils
* 6 cups good chicken stock
* 1 teaspoon turmeric
* 2 medium-sized potatoes, peeled and cubed
* 2-inch piece of fresh ginger, peeled and coarsely chopped
* 4 garlic cloves
* ¼ cup vegetable oil
* 1 heaping teaspoon crushed cumin seeds
* 1 heaping teaspoon crushed coriander seeds
* ½ pound chicken breast meat, cut into 1-inch cubes
* Salt and black pepper
* Pinch of cayenne pepper
* Lemon juice, to taste
* Plain yogurt, to serve (optional)

Put the lentils, stock, and turmeric in a heavy-based saucepan, bring to a boil, and simmer slowly for 30 minutes, adding the cubed potatoes after 15 minutes. Puree in a food processor or with a wand whizzer, but leave some texture to the mixture.

Put the ginger and garlic in a food processor with a little water and blend into a sludge. Transfer to a saucepan and fry in the vegetable oil with the crushed cumin and coriander. Add the chicken, then a cup of water and simmer for 10 minutes or so, until cooked through.

Add the lentil mixture to the pan and season carefully with salt, pepper, and a pinch of cayenne, adding lemon juice to taste. Thin with more stock or water if you want it less thick.

I like to add a dollop of yogurt to each bowl of soup before serving.

Crab and red pepper soup

Here is a fantastic soup, especially in the early autumn when red peppers are in season and at their sweetest. The crabmeat makes this rich and filling, so serve it in small bowls or as a meal in itself. It's excellent topped with Fluffy croutons or with Cheese and fennel seed scones (see page 257).

Serves 8 as a starter, 6 for lunch
* 4 red sweet peppers (about 1 pound), quartered and deseeded
* 1 pound ripe tomatoes, halved, or 1 (14 ½-ounce) can of tomatoes
* 1 red onion, roughly chopped
* 3 garlic cloves, roughly chopped
* 1 tablespoon light brown sugar
* 1 red chili, deseeded and roughly chopped
* 2 tablespoons balsamic vinegar
* 3 tablespoons extra virgin olive oil
* 1 pound crabmeat
* 2 cups good fish stock
* 2 tablespoons Thai fish sauce
* Juice of 2 lemons
* Salt and black pepper

Preheat the oven to 350 degrees.

Put the peppers, tomatoes, onion, garlic, sugar, chili, vinegar, and oil in a roasting pan, and toss to make sure everything is well coated. Place in the oven for 45 minutes, or until they begin to char at the edges, turning them from time to time.

Put everything through a food mill or coarse sieve to get rid of the skins (or, if you don't mind the skins, whizz in a blender). Transfer to a saucepan, add the crabmeat, stock, fish sauce, and lemon juice and heat through.

Season with salt and freshly ground black pepper. Serve warm, not piping hot, to bring out the individual flavors. Add some cream if you like.

Porcini mushroom soup

This is a warming and fragrant autumn soup, with the distinctive taste of porcini mushrooms.

Serves 8 as a starter, 6 for lunch
* 1 ounce dried porcini
* 1 large onion, finely chopped
* 1 garlic clove, finely chopped
* 3 tablespoons butter
* 1 pound mushrooms (use button mushrooms, or a mixture, such as dried porcinis, chanterelles, and wild mushrooms), coarsely chopped
* Ground mace or freshly grated nutmeg, to taste
* 2 ½ cups good chicken or vegetable stock
* Large bunch of flat-leaf parsley, finely chopped
* 2 cups milk
* ⅔ cup heavy cream
* Splash of brandy
* Salt and black pepper
* Truffle oil or lemon juice (optional)
* Garlic bruschette (see page 168) or crusty bread, to serve

Place any dried mushrooms you are using in a bowl and soak them in 1¼ cups boiling water for 30 minutes.

In a large, heavy-based saucepan, fry the onion and garlic in the butter to soften but not brown. Drain the dried mushrooms, reserving the liquid in a separate bowl. Chop roughly and add to the onion mixture. Add the fresh mushrooms and cook together until soft. Add the mace or nutmeg to taste, and cook for another couple of minutes.

Pour in the hot stock and the reserved, strained porcini water and bring to a boil. Add half the parsley. Cover and simmer for 15 to 20 minutes. Puree the the soup in a blender and return to a clean pan. Season well. (When cool, you can freeze the mixture if you want to keep it for later.)

Add the milk. Bring gently to a boil, then simmer for a further 10 minutes. Take off the heat and add the cream, brandy, and seasoning to taste. Scatter over the rest of the parsley. The soup can be reheated gently, but do not boil once the cream has been added.

Add a little truffle oil or lemon juice for extra fla-vor, and serve with garlic bruschette or crusty bread.

Mary Berry's beet and coconut soup

A simple, delicious, and vibrantly colored soup inspired by the British cookbook author. Make this in the late summer and autumn, when beets are at their best. This is now one of our favorite soups to serve at a course lunch, and everyone—even if previously wary of beets—seems to love it. To make it a bit punchier, we add more curry paste than in Mary's original recipe.

If you prefer a milder version, add 1 tablespoon to start with and taste—you can always add more.

Serves 4
* 1 pound fresh beets
* 1 tablespoon sunflower oil
* 1 large onion, finely chopped
* 1–2 tablespoons Thai red curry paste, depending on its strength
* 1 (13 ½-ounce) can of coconut milk
* 1¼ cups chicken stock
* Salt and black pepper
* Juice of ½ lime
* 2 tablespoons chopped fresh flat-leaf parsley

Cut the leafy tops off the beets just above the bulbous root (keeping them for a salad), but don't trim the root or the color will bleed. Place in a heavy-based saucepan, cover with water, and bring to a boil, then simmer until tender—about 45 to 60 minutes, depending on the size. Drain and allow to cool, then peel and roughly chop. The beets can be prepared up to 24 hours ahead and kept in the fridge.

Heat the oil in a large saucepan over a medium heat. Add the onion, then cover and cook for about 5 to 10 minutes to soften. Add two-thirds of the beets to the onion, stir in the curry paste, and fry for couple of minutes over a high heat. Pour in the coconut milk and stock and season with salt and pepper.

Bring to a boil, cover, and simmer over a low heat for 5 minutes. Whizz in a food processor until smooth, then pour the soup back into the pan. Add the remaining beets (cut into small cubes) and the lime juice, and check the seasoning. Sprinkle with parsley and serve hot.

Cullen skink

Cullen is a town in the northeast of Scotland, and the word "skink" means "soup" or "stew." Cullen skink is traditionally made with potatoes, onions, and Finnan haddock. The soup is perfect for when the weather gets cold and you're feeding lots of hungry people.

Serves 6 as a starter, 4 for lunch
* 2 pounds undyed smoked haddock
* 4 cups milk
* 3 bay leaves
* 1 large onion, finely chopped
* 2 small potatoes, peeled, 1 finely chopped, the other cubed
* Black pepper
* Nutmeg and mace, to taste
* Small bunch of flat-leaf parsley, chopped

Put the haddock with the milk and bay leaves in a large pan. Bring to a boil, then immediately take off the heat. Let the fish poach gently and the flavors infuse for 5 minutes.

Remove the fish from the pan and skin it. Add the onion and the finely chopped potato to the milk in the pan and cook gently until soft. Discard the bay leaves and puree the milk mixture in a blender until you have a smooth, thickish cream.

Return to the pan, add a little more milk if necessary, and the cubed potato and cook until it is just soft. Flake the haddock into the soup. Season with plenty of pepper and nutmeg, and a little mace. (You probably won't want extra salt as the smoked fish usually provides enough.) Add the chopped parsley and serve.

Ham and lentil soup with green sauce

Just the thing for lunch after a good walk, this is a delicious, sustaining soup made with a smoked ham hock, lentils, plenty of vegetables, and parsley. Top each bowl with a swirl of green sauce—that's crucial—and serve with a hunk of bread and butter.

Serves 8 as a starter, 6 for lunch
* 1 medium-sized smoked ham hock (about 1⅓ pounds)
* 2 onions, finely chopped, plus 1 onion, coarsely chopped
* 2 carrots, peeled and finely chopped
* 1 carrot, peeled and coarsely chopped
* 2 garlic cloves, coarsely chopped
* 1 cup lentils, preferably green Puy lentils
* 1 parsnip, peeled and finely cubed
* Large bunch of flat-leaf parsley, coarsely chopped

For the green sauce
* Large bunch of flat-leaf parsley, coarsely chopped
* Small bunch of chives, coarsely chopped
* 1 garlic clove, coarsely chopped
* Juice and grated zest of 1 lemon
* 3 tablespoons extra virgin olive oil

Place the ham hock in a large saucepan and cover with water. Add the coarsely chopped onion, carrot, and garlic and bring to a boil. Cover, lower the heat, and cook together gently for 1 hour.

Strain off the liquid into a bowl, discard the vegetables, and remove the hock. Leave to cool, then skin the hock. Cut the meat from the bone and coarsely chop it.

Put the cooking liquid back in the pan. Add the lentils and cook gently for 20 minutes, or until they are beginning to soften. Then add the second group of vegetables: the finely chopped onions, carrots, and parsnip. Cook for another 10 minutes, then take it off the heat and add the parsley and chunks of ham.

To make the green sauce, quickly blitz the parsley, chives, garlic, lemon juice, and zest in a food processor with the olive oil.

Ladle the soup into bowls and drizzle green sauce on the top of each.

Cleopatra's tomato soup

In the summer I love to make a fresh-tasting, traditional Cream of tomato soup (see page 125), but in the autumn this intensely fragrant soup is hard to beat. It comes from Cleopatra's Mountain Farmhouse, a hotel in South Africa's Drakensberg Mountains owned by Richard Poynton, a passionate cook. I included the recipe in my *In Season: Cooking with Vegetables and Fruits* cookbook, but it's so good that it's worth repeating.

Serves 8 as a starter, 6 for lunch
* 3 1/3 pounds ripe tomatoes, whole
* 2 large onions, quartered
* 2–3 tablespoons olive oil
* Salt and black pepper
* 3 garlic cloves, crushed
* 2 teaspoons grated fresh ginger
* 1/2 small red chili, deseeded and chopped, or 1 dried chili, crumbled
* Bunch of cilantro, leaves and stems chopped, plus more to serve
* 1 1/4 cups tomato juice
* 2 (13 1/2-ounce) cans of coconut milk
* 1 heaping tablespoon brown sugar
* 2 tablespoons Thai fish sauce

Preheat the oven to 350 degrees.

Roast the tomatoes (you don't need to skin them) and onions in a roasting pan with a generous drizzle of olive oil, and some salt and pepper for about 30 to 40 minutes, until slightly browned on the edges.

Meanwhile, heat a little olive oil in a saucepan and cook the garlic, ginger, chili, and cilantro (leaves and stems) for 3 to 4 minutes.

Add the tomato juice and coconut milk, and cook for a few minutes.

Add the tomatoes, onions, sugar, fish sauce, and seasoning. Cover and simmer for 10 minutes. Blend in a food processor and serve with plenty of cilantro.

Spicy chickpea soup

I had this soup for lunch at Darina Allen's cookery school, Ballymaloe, in Ireland. It has become my favorite quick-to-throw-together, cold-weather soup, ideal for when people turn up unexpectedly to eat (in which case, I use canned chickpeas).

Serves 8 as a starter, 6 for lunch
* 1 pound package dried chickpeas or 2 (15-ounce) cans
* 6 cups vegetable or chicken stock
* 1 tablespoon coriander seeds
* 1 tablespoon cumin seeds
* 3 tablespoons butter
* 2 small onions (about 1/3 pound), finely chopped
* 5 large garlic cloves, finely chopped
* 1–2 red chilis (depending on the amount of heat you prefer), deseeded and chopped
* 1/2 teaspoon turmeric
* Salt and black pepper
* 1/3 cup heavy cream
* Juice of 1 lemon, or to taste
* Plain yogurt, to serve

If using dried chickpeas, soak them overnight in plenty of water.

Drain the chickpeas and put them in a saucepan, add the stock, and bring to a boil. Cover and simmer gently until soft (about 45 to 60 minutes for rehydrated chickpeas, 15 minutes for canned). Strain, reserving the liquid.

Meanwhile, toast the coriander and cumin seeds in a frying pan over a medium heat for 2 to 3 minutes, then crush with a mortar and pestle.

Melt the butter in a saucepan. Add the onions, garlic, chilis, and crushed coriander and cumin and cook gently for 5 minutes. Add the turmeric and cook for another couple of minutes. Remove from the heat, add most of the chickpeas (keeping some aside whole), and mix well.

Season with salt and pepper. Puree in a blender with the cooking liquid and cream. Return to a saucepan and simmer gently for 10 minutes, thinning with more stock as necessary. Add a little lemon juice to taste.

Serve with a dollop of plain yogurt and a few whole chickpeas scattered in each bowl for texture.

Mary's fluffy croutons

Here's a recipe of cookbook author Mary Berry's because I think her croutons are the most delicious things to have in a bowl of soup. You can make them in advance and freeze them uncooked, heating them straight from the freezer and adding 5 minutes to the cooking time given below. They are also fantastic as canapés for a party. In that case, use slightly thicker bread and mix half with a strong-flavored spice, such as caraway or cumin, and leave the other half cheesy and plain.

Yields about 30 croutons
* 2 ounces cream cheese
* 5 tablespoons butter
* 3 ounces Cheddar or any similar cheese, grated
* 1 large egg white
* 1 teaspoon cumin or caraway seeds (optional)
* Salt and black pepper
* 2 large slices white bread, 1-inch thick and ideally 2–3 days old, crusts removed

Preheat the oven to 425 degrees. Line a couple of baking sheets with parchment paper.

Place the cream cheese, butter, and Cheddar in a saucepan and melt over a low heat; it might look curdled, but don't worry.

In a bowl, whisk the egg white until stiff and fold this into the cheese mixture. Add the spices (if using) and season with salt and pepper.

Cut the bread into 1-inch cubes. Dip into the soufflé mix and lay out, quite well spaced, on the prepared baking sheets.

Bake for about 10 minutes, until puffy and golden.

Cheese and fennel seed scones

These are excellent with strong-flavored autumn or winter soups. They're perfect for lifting a bowl of soup from the everyday, and also make ideal rolls for sausages or chicken burgers at a party (see picture on page 288). They are quick and easy to do for lots of people, and they freeze brilliantly.

Yields about 6 scones
* 1 3/4 cups self-rising flour, plus extra for dusting
* 1 heaping teaspoon baking powder
* 1/2 teaspoon mustard powder
* 1/2 teaspoon paprika
* 1 tablespoon fennel seeds
* Salt and black pepper
* 3 tablespoons butter
* 5 ounces Gouda or Cheddar cheese, grated
* 2/3 cup milk, yogurt, or buttermilk
* 1 egg, beaten

Preheat the oven to 400 degrees and heat a baking sheet for 5 to 10 minutes.

Sift the flour and baking powder into a bowl.

Add the mustard powder, paprika, fennel seeds, and some salt and pepper. Using your fingertips, rub in the butter until the mixture resembles breadcrumbs. Stir in two-thirds of the cheese.

Add the liquid and, using your hands, gather the mixture into a ball and place on a floured surface. Knead lightly; scone dough must not be overworked. Roll out to a thickness of 1 inch and, using a round biscuit cutter or floured glass, cut out about 6 scones.

Transfer the scones to the preheated baking sheet. Brush each one with beaten egg and sprinkle over the remaining cheese. Bake for 10 to 12 minutes, until risen and golden brown.

Pumpkin cornbread

Serve this delicious savory bread with soup or strong cheeses, such as Stilton, sharp Cheddar, or a hard goat or sheep cheese, and put some Apple membrillo (see page 325) on the cheese board too. The bread is lovely toasted or grilled, and freezes well.

Yields 1 (1-pound) loaf

* ½ pound fresh pumpkin, peeled, deseeded, and cut into chunks
* 2 ¾ cups white bread flour
* 1 ½ cups yellow cornmeal, plus extra for dusting
* 1 teaspoon salt
* 1 heaping teaspoon dried yeast
* 1 tablespoon superfine sugar
* 1 ¼ cups lukewarm milk
* ⅓ cup vegetable oil
* ½ cup raisins
* ½ cup toasted pumpkin seeds
* ½ teaspoon ground cloves
* 1 ½ teaspoons baking soda

Preheat the oven to 400 degrees. Lightly oil a 1-pound loaf pan.

Put the pumpkin in a roasting pan and roast for about 40 minutes, until soft. When the flesh is soft, puree it and set aside. Turn off the oven.

Put the flour, cornmeal, salt, yeast, and sugar into a large bowl and add the milk. Mix with your hands until you have a smooth dough. Cover with a cloth and put the bowl in a warm place for the dough to rise for about an hour (it should double in size).

When the dough has risen, stir in all the remaining ingredients, including the pumpkin puree. Turn the mixture onto a board floured with cornmeal and knead for several minutes. Place in a clean bowl, cover with a kitchen towel, and leave to rise again in a warm place until doubled in size (about 1 hour).

Heat the oven again to 400 degrees. Place the dough in the prepared pan and bake for about 30 to 40 minutes, or until the loaf sounds hollow when tapped on the bottom. Allow to cool on a wire rack.

Pear, pancetta, and blue cheese salad

A simple salad with a classic combination of flavors, this is delicious with succulent autumn pears in decent slices, not slivers. To ensure that everyone gets a good scattering of ingredients, this salad is best made on individual plates. Serve for lunch or as a starter for a big autumn dinner.

Serves 6 as a starter or side salad, 4 as a main course
* Bunch of watercress, larger stems removed
* ¼ pound arugula
* ¼ pound small-leaf spinach
* 1 large or 2 small heads of Belgian endive, leaves separated and the heart sliced lengthwise
* ¾ cup walnut halves
* ¼ pound pancetta or bacon, cut into small strips
* 2 fat pears
* Juice and grated zest of 1 lemon
* ¼–½ pound blue cheese (depending on taste and waist), cut into thin slices
* Large bunch of flat-leaf parsley, coarsely chopped

For the dressing
* 2 tablespoons walnut oil (buy just a small bottle as it loses its flavor more readily than olive oil)
* 3 tablespoons extra virgin olive oil
* Juice of 1 lemon, to taste
* Salt and black pepper

Divide the watercress, arugula, spinach, endive leaves, and sliced endive heart among individual plates.

Lightly toast the walnuts for 5 minutes in a hot oven, or toss them over a medium heat on the stovetop. Don't burn them or they'll be bitter.

Fry or roast the pancetta or bacon strips in a pan until crunchy and golden.

Peel, core, and cut the pears into thick slices and squeeze the lemon juice over them to keep the flesh from discoloring. Lay the pear slices on top of the salad leaves, and scatter over the pancetta or bacon, walnuts, blue cheese, lemon zest, and parsley.

To make the dressing, mix the two oils with the lemon juice and season with salt and pepper. Dress the salad just before you eat.

Pumpkin, kale, and Parmesan salad

I would never normally think of eating raw kale, but in this salad the leaves are fabulous, providing a crunch that contrasts with the melony softness and sweetness of the pumpkin, the sharpness of the lemon juice, and the saltiness of the Parmesan. It's delicious served with bruschette rubbed with a cut garlic clove and drizzled with plenty of fruity extra virgin olive oil (see page 168). This salad is also fantastic with finely shredded raw Brussels sprouts in place of the kale.

Serves 6 as a starter or side salad, 4 as a main course
* 1 pound fresh pumpkin, cut into segments, peeled, and deseeded
* Juice of ½ lemon
* Flaky sea salt
* ½ pound kale leaves (curly kale or cavolo nero)
* Large handful of pumpkin seeds, toasted or oven-roasted
* 3 tablespoons freshly grated Parmesan cheese
* Black pepper
* Extra virgin olive oil

Cut the pumpkin segments into ribbons as thin as possible with a swivel potato peeler or mandoline. Put the ribbons in a bowl with the lemon juice and salt to marinate for a few minutes.

Meanwhile, remove the tough midribs from the kale leaves. Cut the leaves crosswise into fine strips, then spread them out on a large, shallow platter. Scatter over the marinated pumpkin ribbons and sprinkle with the seeds and Parmesan. Season with pepper, add a drizzle of olive oil, and toss it all together.

Fennel and apple salad with toasted pumpkin seeds

Fennel and apples are at their very best in the autumn. When choosing fennel, try to find the big, fat bulbs, not the tall, lanky ones (which are beginning to draw out and can be stringy). I like this salad as a starter, but it's also good with chicken, and delicious with almost any fish.

Serves 6 as a starter or side salad, 4 as a main course
* 4 fennel bulbs (about 2 pounds), plus tops
* Extra virgin olive oil
* Black pepper
* Juice and grated zest of 1 lemon
* 1 teaspoon toasted, crushed fennel seeds
* 3 tablespoons crème fraîche or fromage frais (or a mixture of crème fraîche and plain yogurt, or plain yogurt on its own, as lower-fat alternatives)
* 2 crunchy apples

For the roasted seeds
* 2 tablespoons pumpkin seeds
* 1 tablespoon extra virgin olive oil
* Good pinch of flaky sea salt
* ½ teaspoon cayenne pepper

Preheat the oven to 325 degrees.

Chuck away any tough or discolored outer layers from the fennel. Slice the bulbs as thinly as possible—a mandoline is the best tool for this—and finely chop the ferny tops, reserving a few to decorate. Arrange the sliced fennel and chopped tops in a deep bowl with a little extra virgin olive oil, black pepper, lemon juice and zest, and the fennel seeds. Fold in the crème fraîche, fromage frais, or yogurt.

Peel, core, and thinly slice the apples, then add them to the bowl. Fold gently to combine. Transfer to a shallow bowl or serving plate and decorate with the reserved chopped fennel tops.

Put the pumpkin seeds in a roasting pan and add a drizzle of olive oil, a pinch of flaky salt, and the cayenne. Toss them all together and roast in the oven for 5 to 10 minutes, until the seeds begin to brown. Scatter them over the salad and serve.

Roasted beet, pumpkin, and arugula salad

A similar salad to this is included in my *In Season* cookbook. In this recipe, I've added roasted cubes of pumpkin cooked with rosemary.

Serves 6 as a starter or side salad, 4 as a main course
* 1 tablespoon whole cloves
* 1 tablespoon black peppercorns
* 1 tablespoon cumin seeds
* 4 medium or 8 small beets, unpeeled
* 5–6 sprigs of rosemary
* 1 medium pumpkin or squash (red kuri or butternut are good) (about 2 pounds), deseeded, peeled, and cut into chunks (keep the pumpkin seeds to roast)
* Flaky sea salt
* 8 handfuls of arugula
* 2 handfuls of fresh mint leaves
* 6 ounces feta cheese, crumbled
* Bruschette (see page 168) or bread, to serve

For the dressing
* 3 tablespoons extra virgin olive oil
* Juice and grated zest of 1 lemon
* Salt and black pepper

Preheat the oven to 375 degrees.

Make a bed of cloves, peppercorns, and cumin seeds in a roasting pan. Place the beets on top and roast until soft to the point of a knife (about 1½ hours). Allow to cool a bit, then peel with your hands.

In a second roasting pan make a bed of rosemary sprigs and arrange the cubed pumpkin or squash on top. Roast until tender and beginning to char around the edges (about 45 minutes).

Meanwhile, wash the reserved pumpkin or squash seeds, removing most of the pith. Mix a good pinch of flaky salt with ¼ cup of water in a cup. Pour this over the seeds and roast in a third pan for about 15 minutes, until they just begin to brown.

Combine the dressing ingredients. Cover a shallow plate or bowl with the arugula and half the mint leaves. Place the beets, pumpkin, or squash and feta on top. Drizzle over the dressing and scatter the remaining mint leaves and seeds over the top just before serving with bruschette or good bread.

Tricolor pepper caponata

Make several jars of this sweet and sour mixture and store it in the fridge to eat through the autumn. Balsamic vinegar is a preservative, so it can be kept for up to a month. It's lovely with Grilled eggplant (see page 268), prosciutto, cold meats, and cheese, and excellent with just toast and salad.

Yields about 3 cups
* 3 mild peppers (1 red, 1 yellow, and 1 orange, about 1 pound in total)
* 1 large onion, finely chopped
* 2 garlic cloves, finely chopped
* 2–3 tablespoons olive oil
* Large handful of fresh basil leaves
* 5 tomatoes, skinned and coarsely chopped (see page 125), or 1 (14 ½-ounce) can of chopped tomatoes
* 2 tablespoons capers (salted capers have the best flavor, so find these if you can: drain and rinse them under cold running water, then dry on paper towels)
* 3 tablespoons balsamic vinegar
* 1 tablespoon dark brown sugar
* 1 teaspoon cocoa powder
* Handful of black olives, pitted and quartered
* Salt and black pepper

Preheat the oven to 350 degrees.

Put the whole peppers in a roasting pan and roast until they begin to char (about 25 minutes). Remove and place in a plastic bag to steam for 5 minutes so that the skin can then be easily peeled off.

In an ovenproof pan, gently fry the onion and garlic in the olive oil until transparent (about 5 minutes).

Slice or tear the peeled peppers into thin strips and add them to the pan. Tear up the basil leaves and add these to the pan with all the remaining ingredients. Cover and cook on the stove over a moderate heat for 15 to 20 minutes. Check to make sure that the mixture is not sticking on the bottom, adding a little water if necessary.

When the caponata has finished cooking, the mixture should look dark and rich, with most of the excess liquid absorbed.

Pour into dry, warm, sterilized jars (you can sterilize them in a very hot dishwasher, or boil them in a pan of water for 10 minutes), then seal and label with a date. Keep in the fridge and eat within a month.

Beet tart with horseradish cream

One of my favorite tarts with a sweet-savory flavor, this looks great with purple beets, and even better if you can find orange beets to alternate in stripes in the filling. The horseradish cream gives some added zip, but as horseradish root varies hugely in strength according to when it's dug up, it's impossible to be precise about quantities. If you can't find fresh horseradish root, use 2 tablespoons of good-quality bottled horseradish to about the same amount of crème fraîche (according to taste).

Serves 8

For the pastry
* 1½ cups unbleached flour
* A few sprigs of thyme, leaves finely chopped
* Pinch of salt
* 7 tablespoons cold butter, cut into chunks

* 4 medium-sized beets (I use 1 pound red and 1 pound golden beets)
* 2 large onions, finely chopped
* 2 tablespoons butter
* Splash of olive oil
* A few sprigs of thyme, leaves removed and finely chopped
* 3 tablespoons balsamic vinegar
* 1 tablespoon superfine sugar
* 2 eggs
* ⅔ cup heavy cream
* Nutmeg, freshly grated
* Salt and black pepper
* 3 or 4 sprigs of thyme, leaves picked, to decorate

For the horseradish cream
* Grated horseradish
* Heavy cream or crème fraîche
* A little mustard powder
* Pinch of white pepper
* Salt
* Lemon juice, to taste

First make the pastry. Sift the flour into a bowl and add the thyme and salt. Rub the butter into the flour, or pulse in a food processor, until the mixture resembles breadcrumbs. Add just enough chilled water for it to bind together as a dough. Roll into a ball and wrap in plastic wrap. Chill for an hour.

Meanwhile, boil the beets in salted water for at least 45 minutes, until soft. Drain, allow to cool a little, then peel. Grate the beets on the coarse side of a grater (keeping the two colors separate if you have them).

Preheat the oven to 350 degrees and heat a baking sheet until searing hot.

Roll out the dough on a floured surface to a thickness of ⅛ inch and use to line an 11-inch loose-bottomed tart pan, leaving the excess draped over the sides in case it shrinks.

Prick the base of the crust with a fork, line with parchment paper or foil, and weigh this down with baking beans or rice. Place on the hot baking sheet and bake for about 15 minutes. Remove the baking beans and paper and cook the crust for another 5 minutes to crisp the base a little. Take out of the oven and trim off the excess pastry. Keep the oven on and reheat the baking sheet.

Gently fry the onions in a pan with the butter and oil until translucent. Add the chopped thyme leaves and grated beets (if you have two colors, divide the onions and cook in separate pans). Add the vinegar and sugar and continue to cook gently for about 15 minutes, to reduce and make the mixture syrupy.

Fill the crust with the beet mixture, doing segments in different colors if you have them.

Whisk the eggs, cream, and nutmeg, and season with salt and pepper. Place the tart pan on the hot baking sheet in the oven, then pour in as much of the egg mixture as will fit easily over the beets. Scatter thyme leaves over the top, then bake for 35 minutes, until the top is starting to brown.

While the tart is cooking, peel and grate the horseradish. If you like it very strong, grate it just before you want to eat. It discolors quickly, so mix it with the other ingredients immediately.

Add enough heavy cream or crème fraîche to the grated horseradish to give a creamy consistency. Mix in a little mustard powder, white pepper, and salt, and finish by adding lemon juice to taste.

Grilled eggplant with fennel seeds and tzatziki

Autumn is the time for the last of the eggplants. Pull up the green calyx at the top and make sure that the flesh is white, not green. This means the fruits are ripe. If there are lots of seeds when you cut into them, it can mean that the eggplants are on the over-ripe side, but either way, you can still use them—the flesh will just be tougher, will suck up more oil, and take more cooking.

Serves 6
* 3 eggplants
* 2 teaspoons fennel seeds
* Salt
* 2 garlic cloves, peeled
* Extra virgin olive oil

For the tzatziki
* ½ cucumber
* 1 cup plain yogurt
* Large bunch of fresh mint, finely chopped
* 1 red chili, deseeded and thinly sliced (optional)
* 1 garlic clove, finely chopped (or 2 if you like strong tzatziki)
* 1 tablespoon extra virgin olive oil
* Salt and black pepper

To serve
* Salad leaves
* Tricolor pepper caponata (see page 264)
* Rosemary flatbread (see page 244) or pita bread
* Seeds of 2 pomegranates (see page 31)

Cut the eggplants lengthwise into slices ¾-inch thick. Score shallow diagonal cuts into the flesh using a serrated knife (which is less likely to cut right through than a sharp kitchen knife).

Toast the fennel seeds in a dry frying pan until they start to smoke (a couple of minutes). Transfer to a mortar, add a pinch of salt and the garlic, then grind with the pestle.

Heat a ridged grill pan for 3 to 4 minutes (until you can't count to 10 with your hand hovering just above it), or preheat the oven to 350 degrees.

Rub the garlic mixture into the cuts in the eggplant. Brush just the top side of each slice with 1 tablespoon olive oil (a lot, but this will make it creamy) and grill the slices for a few minutes on each side until slightly charred and tender to the point of a knife. Alternatively, place the grill pan in the oven and cook the slices for 15 minutes (this method is easier and less smoky than grilling on the stovetop). Keep warm.

To make the tzatziki, grate or cube the cucumber (you don't need to peel or salt it) and mix with the yogurt, mint, chili (if using), garlic, and olive oil. Season with salt and pepper.

Serve 2 or 3 eggplant slices on each plate with a good dollop of tzatziki, a few delicious salad leaves, some caponata, and flatbread. Scatter with pomegranate seeds.

Roasted red peppers with goat cheese

This is as simple as it gets, a brilliant, easy starter, ideal if you're cooking for lots of people and have limited time. You can use mozzarella instead of goat cheese for a milder taste.

Serves 6 as a starter
* 3 mild red peppers
* Basil pesto
* 12 cherry tomatoes, halved
* 2 garlic cloves, chopped
* 12 anchovy fillets (salted if possible—these have a better flavor than those in oil), chopped
* 24 capers
* 3–4 sprigs of thyme, leaves picked
* Salt and black pepper
* Extra virgin olive oil
* 2 goat cheeses (the little cakes), cut horizontally into 3 slices
* Pugliese sourdough bruschette (see page 168), drizzled with olive oil, to serve

Preheat the oven to 350 degrees.

Cut through the peppers from top to bottom, including the stem, and remove the ribs and seeds. Place the halved peppers in a roasting pan. Put a teaspoon of pesto in the bottom of each pepper, then add the different filling ingredients. Start with the tomatoes, followed by the garlic, anchovies, capers, thyme, a little salt and pepper, and a drizzle of olive oil.

Bake the peppers in the preheated oven for 20 to 30 minutes, until the edges are beginning to char. Take them out, put a slice of goat cheese on top of each one, and cook for a further 10 minutes.

These peppers are best eaten just warm, not straight out of the oven. Serve with sourdough bruschette.

Vegetable pakoras

Pakoras are mixed vegetables fried in spicy batter—the Indian version of garden tempura. They are fantastic as a starter if you're having a few people for dinner (not more than 6 to 8 or you'll spend too much time frying), or perfect with strong-flavored dipping sauces to eat with drinks. They can be made a bit in advance and reheated in the oven for 3 to 4 minutes at 400 degrees.

Serves 6 to 8
* 1 small cauliflower, cut into small florets
* 1 medium potato or sweet potato
* 1 parsnip
* 1 cup chickpea flour
* ½ cup rice flour
* 1 teaspoon flaky sea salt
* 2 tablespoons finely chopped curry leaves or cilantro
* 1 green chili, deseeded and finely chopped
* 1 teaspoon cumin seeds
* 1 tablespoon coriander seeds, coarsely ground
* Black pepper
* Sunflower oil
* Mango chutney and tzatziki (see page 268), to serve

Blanch the cauliflower florets in a pan of boiling water for 2 to 3 minutes, then drain.

Peel the potato and parsnip and thinly slice them both (⅛ inch in thickness).

In a large bowl mix the two flours with the salt, herb, chili, and spices, and season with some black pepper. Add 1 cup water and beat hard to make a medium-thick batter.

Fill a deep saucepan with enough oil to reach about one-third of the way up the side, and have a lid or splash-guard on standby to prevent the oil from spitting too much after you add each batch. Heat the oil until it reaches about 375 degrees, or until a cube of bread browns in 30 seconds.

Coat the vegetables in the batter and fry in batches until puffed, crisp, and golden. Serve with a good mango chutney and tzatziki.

Wild mushroom lasagna

If you find a stash of wild mushrooms, or see a great selection in a farmers' market or grocery, use them to make this lasagne—one of the very best autumn feasts. It's an ideal recipe for when you feel like spending a bit more time preparing food.

Serves 8
* 2 pounds mix of wild and farm-grown mushrooms
* 1 onion
* 1 garlic clove, finely chopped
* ½ pound bacon or pancetta (omit if vegetarian)
* 6 tablespoons extra virgin olive oil
* ½ pound lasagna sheets, fresh or dried
* A few chunks of butter, to finish

For the béchamel sauce
* 4 cups milk
* 6 tablespoons butter
* ½ cup flour
* 1 egg yolk
* 1 (8-ounce) tub of mascarpone cheese
* Freshly grated nutmeg to taste, plus a bit extra to finish
* Salt and black pepper
* ¼ pound Parmesan cheese, freshly grated

Preheat the oven to 350 degrees.

Slice the mushrooms, onion, garlic, and bacon (if using).

Heat the olive oil in a deep frying pan and cook the onion, garlic, and bacon (if using) on a gentle heat for 5 to 10 minutes, until the onion is soft, but not browned. Add the mushrooms to the pan. Cook gently for another 5 minutes, until the mushrooms are soft.

Meanwhile, make the béchamel sauce. Put the milk in a small pan and bring to a boil. In a separate pan, melt the butter. Stir the flour into the butter. Allow it to cook for a couple of minutes, then gradually add the hot milk. Add the egg yolk, then the mascarpone and plenty of nutmeg, stirring continuously. Season with plenty of salt and pepper.

Add almost all the Parmesan and stir until it melts. Make sure the sauce is fairly wet or the dish will become too thick and stodgy as the flour cooks more—you can always add more milk.

If using dried pasta sheets that need pre-cooking, boil the sheets in plenty of salted water, then allow them to dry flat on a clean cloth.

In an oiled 9 by 12-inch ovenproof dish, build up thin layers of mushrooms and bacon (if using), béchamel, then pasta, repeating in this order until you have two or three layers of pasta (depending on the size and depth of the dish). Finish with the béchamel and sprinkle with the remaining Parmesan. Dot the top with the chunks of butter and a light grating of nutmeg. Cook in the preheated oven for 35 to 40 minutes.

Mushroom risotto with truffle oil

You can't go through the autumn without having some kind of mushroom feast. A wonderful selection can be found, either by foraging (take care when identifying them), or buying from a good grocery or farmers' market. They look great all laid out on a plate. Admire them for a bit and then cook them. This risotto makes an excellent Sunday lunch, and is perfect for eating outside; even on quite a chilly day, it stays hot for ages. If you make too much, the leftovers can be made into risotto balls (though you may need to chop up some of the chunkier mushrooms for this). Roll the rice around chunks of good melting cheese (such as mozzarella or fontina), coat them in polenta, and fry them for supper the next day, served with a Rich tomato sauce (see page 277).

Serves 4 to 6
* 1 ounce dried wild mushrooms or porcini
* 3 tablespoons butter, for frying (or less if you prefer, but it won't be so creamy)
* 2 tablespoons olive oil
* 2 garlic cloves, finely chopped
* 4 shallots
* ¾ pound mixture of fresh wild mushrooms (such as porcini, chanterelles, and oyster mushrooms), chopped
* 2 cups Arborio rice
* 1 tablespoon chopped fresh thyme leaves
* 1 cup white wine
* 5–6 cups good chicken or vegetable stock
* Flaky sea salt and black pepper
* 3 tablespoons unsalted butter or mascarpone, for finishing

To serve
* Fresh shavings of Parmesan cheese
* Truffle oil
* Large bunch of flat-leaf parsley, chopped

Put the dried mushrooms in a bowl and soak in 1¼ cups boiling water for 30 minutes.

Heat the butter and oil in a large pan and sauté the shallots without browning. Add the garlic.

Drain the dried mushrooms, reserving the liquid, and chop roughly. Add them to the pan with all but a few of the fresh mushrooms and sauté with the shallots and garlic for a couple of minutes.

Add the rice and thyme and stir for a minute or two. Pour in the wine and stir until it has evaporated. Add the strained mushroom water (making sure it's not gritty) and a ladleful of hot stock, stirring constantly until absorbed. Keep adding the stock, still stirring constantly, allowing each ladleful to be absorbed before adding the next. After about 15 minutes the rice will be al dente. Season carefully. Remove from the heat and stir in the butter or mascarpone.

Quickly sauté the reserved wild mushrooms and sprinkle them over the risotto with generous shavings of Parmesan and a drizzle of truffle oil. Scatter over plenty of fresh parsley.

Curried shrimp with lentils

I love the texture and fragrance of this healthy dish. When you're making it for friends, don't buy the frozen bags of shelled shrimp: they go mushy and lose their shape so easily. Buy fresh unshelled shrimp and prepare them by hand for an infinitely nicer dish. Serve with tzatziki (see page 268), fruit chutney, and crunchy pappadams. It is also lovely served cold.

Serves 4
* 1½ cups lentils, preferably green Puy lentils
* Enough chicken, vegetable, or fish stock, or water, to cover the lentils
* ¼ teaspoon each of whole mustard seeds, black peppercorns, poppy seeds, and coriander seeds
* 6 cardamom pods, seeded
* 1 onion
* 2 garlic cloves, finely chopped
* ½-inch piece of fresh ginger, peeled and grated
* 2 tablespoons olive oil
* Juice and grated zest of 1 lime or lemon
* 1 teaspoon ground cumin
* 1 teaspoon ground turmeric
* 1 pound unshelled fresh shrimp, cooked
* Large bunch of flat-leaf parsley, coarsely chopped

Cook the lentils by bringing them to a boil in a pan of stock or water and simmering for 15 minutes, or until tender but not falling apart. Drain.

Meanwhile, roast all the whole spices together (mustard seeds, peppercorns, poppy seeds, coriander seeds, and cardamom) in a dry frying pan and crush them lightly with a mortar and pestle.

In a large saucepan, sweat the onion, garlic, and grated ginger in the oil with the roasted spices.

Add the lime or lemon juice and zest, ground cumin, ground turmeric, and lentils, and mix together. Leave to marinate in a covered dish for a few hours.

Peel the shrimp and fold them into the spiced lentils. Gently heat the mixture through. Pile lots of parsley on top to serve.

Mussels in a cream curry sauce

This is my favorite of all mussel dishes, good to eat slowly while you chat, and absolutely delicious. It is mellow, not sharp like moules marinière. Eat it with bread or rice to soak up the sauce. Mussels, like oysters, are generally thought to be best in the colder months of the year (those with an "r" in them).

Serves 6 to 8
* 4½ pounds mussels
* 4 shallots, finely chopped
* 2 garlic cloves, finely chopped
* 2 tablespoons butter
* 2 tablespoons olive oil
* 1 teaspoon dried chili, or 1 fresh red chili, deseeded and finely chopped (optional)
* 2 tablespoons mild curry powder
* 1 cup heavy cream
* Splash of brandy
* Lots of cilantro, chopped

Scrub the mussels and remove the fibrous beard that attaches each mussel to its rock. Don't use any that are cracked or open.

In a large pan sweat the shallots and garlic in the butter and oil. Add the chili, curry powder, and cream and cook until the onion is translucent (5 to 7 minutes).

Tip the mussels into the pan. Add the brandy, then cover and bring to a boil. Cook rapidly for 5 minutes. Take the pan off the heat and discard any shells that have not opened. Serve sprinkled with plenty of chopped cilantro.

Grilled scallops with corn puree

This is a particular favorite of mine, ideal for when you have people to dinner. You can make the puree—a dish from the London restaurateur Yotam Ottolenghi—beforehand and reheat it while you grill the scallops. Serve with Fennel and apple salad or Shredded Brussels sprouts (see pages 263 and 390).

Serves 4

For the corn puree
* 6 medium-sized ears of corn
* 3 tablespoons butter
* 6 ounces feta cheese, crumbled

* 12 slices prosciutto or thinly cut bacon (about 2 or 3 slices per person)
* 12 large scallops, preferably dived instead of dredged (about 3 or 4 per person)
* Salt and black pepper
* Fruity extra virgin olive oil
* 1 red chili, deseeded and finely chopped
* Small bunch of flat-leaf parsley, finely chopped
* 2 lemons, cut into chunks, to serve

First make the corn puree. Using a sharp knife, cut the kernels off the corn cobs. Place them in a large saucepan with 2 cups water and half the butter, bring to a boil, then simmer for 15 minutes. Strain over a large bowl, saving the water.

Put the corn into a food processor and whizz to a rough puree. Return the puree and reserved water to the saucepan. Stir constantly over a low heat until the mixture thickens (about 15 minutes), then stir in the remaining butter and the feta, stirring for a further couple of minutes. Set aside.

Bake or fry the prosciutto or bacon slices until crisp.

Heat a grill pan or heavy-based frying pan for 3 to 4 minutes (until you can't count to 10 with your hand hovering just above it). Season the scallops with salt and pepper, then grill or fry for a couple of minutes on each side. Remove from the pan, drizzle with olive oil, and sprinkle with chili and parsley.

Serve the scallops on a good dollop of corn puree, with the slices of crisp prosciutto or bacon on top and a chunk of lemon at the side.

Tomato and fennel squid

I love this Greek equivalent of Italian spaghetti alle vongole, which is usually eaten with macaroni-style pasta, but is also great with a hunk of bread. It's sweet, fishy, and rich, with a lovely anise flavor from the fennel and ouzo. Serve, as in Greece, with a very finely chopped cabbage salad topped with a little grated carrot, dressed with fruity olive oil and a squeeze of lemon. It's also excellent with Corn puree (see left).

Serves 6 as a sauce, 4 as a main course
* 1 pound squid
* ½ cup olive oil
* 1 medium onion, finely chopped
* 2 garlic cloves, finely chopped
* ¼ pound chorizo, sliced about ⅛-inch thick
* 1–2 red chilis, deseeded and finely chopped
* 2 (14 ½-ounce) cans of chopped tomatoes
* 1 fennel bulb, finely chopped
* 1 cup roughly chopped fennel leaves
* ½ cup roughly chopped parsley
* 3 ounces ouzo or raki (an anise-flavored spirit from the Balkans)
* Salt and black pepper
* 1 pound spaghetti

Clean the squid, removing the guts and transparent pen (or buy it cleaned). Cut into ½-inch rings.

Heat the oil in a large pan and gently cook the onion and garlic until soft. Add the remaining ingredients, apart from the spaghetti, and reserving some of the fennel leaves for decoration. Season with salt and pepper. Cover and cook gently for about 45 minutes until the squid is soft.

Meanwhile, cook the pasta. Drain, transfer to a shallow plate, and top with the squid mixture. Scatter over the reserved fennel leaves and serve.

Tarragon fishcakes with rich tomato sauce

These fishcakes contain no potato, so they are soft and light. You can use a mix of fish (as below) or just salmon. They take a bit of time to prepare, so make a double quantity and freeze half for another time (leaving out the eggs). I like them served with sautéed potatoes.

Yields 8 to 10 large (3-inch) fishcakes
or 16 to 20 small (2-inch) ones
* 1 1/3 pounds cod, haddock, pollack, or other white fish fillets
* 1 1/3 pounds fresh or hot-smoked salmon fillets
* 2/3 pound undyed smoked haddock
* Milk
* Salt and black pepper
* 2 bay leaves
* 2 hard-boiled eggs, roughly chopped
* 2 tablespoons chopped fresh flat-leaf parsley
* 2 tablespoons chopped fresh tarragon or 1 teaspoon dried
* 1 small onion, very finely chopped
* Olive oil, for frying

For the thick white sauce
* 4 tablespoons (1/2 stick) butter
* 1/2 cup flour
* Salt and black pepper

For the tomato sauce
* 2 (14 1/2-ounce) cans of chopped tomatoes or 10–12 fresh tomatoes
* 1/4 cup extra virgin olive oil
* 2 garlic cloves
* 1 red chili, deseeded and finely chopped
* Flaky sea salt and plenty of black pepper
* 2 tablespoons red wine vinegar, or to taste
* 1/4 cup crème fraîche

For the coating
* 1 egg, beaten
* 2 cups fresh breadcrumbs (a mix of white and brown is good)
* Seasoned flour

Put all the fish (except hot-smoked salmon, if using) in a large shallow pan and cover with milk (about 2 cups). Add a little salt and pepper and the bay leaves. Bring to a boil, then take off the heat and leave to stand for about 6 to 8 minutes.

Lift out the fish, reserving the liquid for later, and remove the skin. Using a fork, flake the fish into a large mixing bowl, keeping the flakes as generous as possible and removing any bones. If using hot-smoked salmon, flake this into the bowl too.

To make the white sauce, melt the butter in a pan. Using a wooden spoon or large whisk, stir the flour into the butter until lump-free. Allow to cook for a couple of minutes, then gradually add the reserved milk (about 2 cups) to create a thick sauce. Season with salt and pepper. Cook gently for 5 minutes.

Add the roughly chopped egg, parsley, tarragon, onion, and white sauce to the flaked fish in the mixing bowl and stir gently to combine. Season well with salt and pepper. Cover and place in the fridge to cool for at least 1 hour.

Meanwhile, make the tomato sauce. Put the tomatoes in a saucepan with the olive oil, whole garlic cloves, chili, salt, and pepper. Place over a low heat and slowly reduce to about half their volume, until the sauce is thick and rich.

Push the sauce through a coarse sieve and add the vinegar and crème fraîche. Keep warm until needed.

Put the beaten egg and breadcrumbs on two separate plates. Dust your hands with seasoned flour and shape balls of the fish mixture into cakes. Dip these into the beaten egg, then coat with the breadcrumbs. Shallow-fry in some hot olive oil until golden on both sides, or bake for 15 to 20 minutes in an oven preheated to 350 degrees.

Herb and garlic fried chicken

Gooey on the outside and moist in the middle, this fried chicken is laced with garlic, oregano, and thyme. Try it with Fig mashed potatoes or Cumin chunky fries (see pages 293 and 70) and green vegetables.

Serves 4
* 3 1/3 pounds whole chicken (organic or free-range), cut into 8 pieces
* Salt and black pepper

For the herb paste
* 4 garlic cloves, coarsely chopped
* 1/4 pound Parmesan or pecorino cheese, freshly grated
* 3 tablespoons olive oil, plus 1 tablespoon for frying
* 1 tablespoon chopped oregano, fresh or dried
* 1 tablespoon chopped thyme, fresh or dried

For the lemon gravy/dressing
* Juice and grated zest of 1 lemon
* 1 tablespoon chopped fresh oregano

Preheat the oven to 400 degrees.

Season the chicken well with salt and pepper and set aside (out of the fridge).

To make the herb paste, place the garlic, cheese, oil, and herbs in a food processor and blend until smooth.

Heat a little olive oil in a large cast-iron casserole or heavy-based non-stick flameproof pan over a medium–high heat. Add the chicken pieces, skin side down, and cook until golden brown (6 to 8 minutes). Turn the chicken and smear the skin with the herb paste.

Transfer the pan to the oven and cook the chicken, uncovered, until well browned and cooked through (20 to 25 minutes). Place on a serving plate and allow to rest for 5 minutes.

Drain the fat from the pan and add the lemon juice, zest, oregano, and a little water to it. Heat through, and serve this as a gravy.

Chicken fillets with cilantro and lime

My sister Jane gave me this recipe, which is ideal when you're having people to supper and feel like something quick, fresh-tasting, and healthy. It's good in the autumn, when cilantro is at its best. Serve with basmati rice cooked in bouillon and a dollop of tzatziki (see page 268). This is also delicious with Coconut and cilantro rice (see page 393) plus a tomato and scallion salad.

Serves 4
* Large handful of cilantro (about 1 cup once stalks removed), plus extra to serve
* Juice of 1 lime
* 1 garlic clove, coarsely chopped
* 3 tablespoons good olive oil
* 1 red chili, deseeded and finely chopped
* 2-inch piece of fresh ginger, peeled and chopped
* Seeds from 6 cardamom pods
* Salt and black pepper
* 4 chicken breasts, each cut into 3 or 4 pieces
* 3–4 tablespoons chicken stock

Put all the ingredients, except for the chicken and stock, into the small bowl of a food processor (or use a hand blender) and pulse until smooth. Smear the mixture over the chicken. Place in a covered dish in the fridge and leave to marinate and tenderize for at least 1 hour (or, better still, overnight).

Preheat the oven to 350 degrees.

Put the chicken pieces and all the marinade into a small casserole dish. Cover and place in the oven for 15 minutes, stirring halfway through the cooking time and adding the stock.

Remove from the oven and allow to rest for 5 minutes. Scatter with cilantro to serve.

Sussex stewed steak

An old favorite from British author Elizabeth David, this pot roast is incredibly quick and easy, perfect for putting in the oven before you go out for a walk or have a long gardening session. As it cooks slowly, it will be ready to eat almost whenever you want. It won't look elegant—you have to hack it to bits to serve—but the taste makes up for that. For variety, add a handful of dried porcini mushrooms.

Serves 4
* 2 ¼ pounds good braising meat (shoulder is ideal) in one piece, at least 1–2 inches thick
* 1 tablespoon seasoned flour
* 2 onions, thickly sliced
* ⅔ cup port
* ⅔ cup stout or dark beer
* 2 tablespoons red wine vinegar
* Salt and black pepper

Preheat the oven to 300 degrees.

Rub the meat with the seasoned flour and spread it out in a shallow lidded casserole. Scatter over the onions, then add the port, stout, and vinegar.

Cover tightly with foil, then the lid, and place in the oven for about 3 hours. Check it after 40 minutes or so, and if it's going too fast, turn the heat down so it only just bubbles. At the end of the cooking time the meat will be falling-apart tender.

Season to taste and serve with Fig mashed potatoes and Beet marmalade (see pages 293 and 292) or a very mustardy dressed green salad.

Chili con carne

The best chili is made with cubes of meat rather than ground, and is tastier cooked one day ahead—ideal when you are feeding loads of people, as you can get this main dish out of the way. Sour cream is a must to accompany the chili. Serve with rice or baked potatoes, and perhaps tortilla chips with melted cheese and Tomato and chili salsa (see page 243).

Serves 6
* 4 tablespoons olive oil
* 2 pounds good stew meat, cut into 1-inch cubes
* 2 large onions, finely chopped
* 2 sticks of celery, finely chopped
* 1 red pepper, deseeded and finely chopped
* 3 red chilis, deseeded and finely chopped
* 4 garlic cloves, crushed
* 2 bay leaves
* 1 tablespoon cumin seeds, toasted and ground
* 1 tablespoon dried oregano
* 1 tablespoon paprika
* ½ tablespoon chili powder
* ½ tablespoon ground cinnamon
* 1 tablespoon flour
* 2 (14 ½-ounce) cans of chopped tomatoes
* 1 tablespoon honey
* 2 (15-ounce) cans of red kidney beans, drained
* Salt and black pepper

Heat 2 tablespoons olive oil in a large, flameproof casserole dish and brown the steak in batches, stirring and turning to color it all over. As each batch is completed, transfer the meat and juices to a bowl.

Heat the remaining oil in the casserole dish, then add the onions, celery, pepper, chilis, and garlic. Cook over a medium heat until soft (about 10 minutes). Return the meat and juices to the casserole, adding the bay leaves, cumin, oregano, paprika, chili powder, and cinnamon, and sprinkling in the flour. Stir well, then add the tomatoes, honey, and ¾ cup water and simmer for 1 hour, stirring at regular intervals to prevent sticking, or cover and cook in the oven at 325 degrees for about 1 ½ hours.

Add the kidney beans, salt, and pepper and cook for a further 15 minutes before serving.

Fragrant Moroccan lamb shanks

Ideal for a big group, this is best made a day or two before needed and then reheated. This is good eaten with Lemon and lime couscous (see page 297) and Autumn roasted vegetables (see page 295).

Serves 4
* 1 tablespoon cumin seeds
* 1 teaspoon coriander seeds
* 1 tablespoon olive oil
* 2 onions, chopped
* 4 small lamb shanks
* 1 teaspoon ground cinnamon
* 2 teaspoons peeled and grated fresh ginger
* 1 teaspoon turmeric
* 2 garlic cloves, chopped
* 1 teaspoon smoked paprika
* ¼ pound dried pitted apricots, soaked (optional)
* 1 (14 ½-ounce) can of chopped tomatoes
* 2 cups vegetable or lamb stock
* Salt and black pepper
* ½ cup pine nuts, toasted
* Handful of cilantro or flat-leaf parsley, chopped
* Handful of fresh mint, chopped

Preheat the oven to 325 degrees.

Toast the cumin and coriander seeds in a heavy pan until they begin to pop. Using an electric coffee grinder or mortar and pestle, grind to a powder.

Heat the oil in a heavy-based ovenproof pan or casserole dish and cook the onions for a few minutes over a low heat. Transfer to a plate.

Place the lamb shanks in the pan and brown quickly over a high heat. Reduce the heat and add the ground cumin and coriander seeds plus the cinnamon, ginger, and turmeric, stirring to combine the flavors.

Return the onions to the pan and cook gently for 2 to 3 minutes. Add the garlic, paprika, apricots (if using), tomatoes, and stock. Season carefully. Cover and cook in the preheated oven for 2 to 3 hours. (You may need to add a bit more liquid to prevent it from drying out—check once or twice during cooking.)

When you are about to eat, scatter the pine nuts and fresh chopped herbs over the dish.

Pan-fried lambs' kidneys with lentils

For those who love kidneys this is hard to beat. Be careful not to overcook: to be at their most tender the kidneys should be just turning from pink to brown, which takes less than 5 minutes. This dish is delicious served with Squash puree (see page 293).

Serves 6

For the lentils
* 1⅓ cups lentils, preferably green Puy lentils
* 1 cup red wine
* 1 cup vegetable or chicken stock
* ¼ cup extra virgin olive oil
* 2 garlic cloves
* 2 red chilis, seeds left in, chopped
* 3 bay leaves
* Large sprig of thyme
* 2 heaping tablespoons crème fraîche
* Large bunch of flat-leaf parsley, finely chopped

* 2 tablespoons butter
* 1 tablespoon olive oil
* 14 lambs' kidneys (about 1 pound), halved and deveined

Put the lentils into a saucepan with the wine and stock. Add the oil, whole garlic cloves, chilis, bay leaves, and thyme and cook gently for about 20 minutes, until the lentils begin to soften but not collapse. Add a little more wine or water if necessary to prevent them from boiling dry.

Heat the butter and oil in a large frying pan and quickly fry the kidneys until just cooked (this takes less than 5 minutes).

Stir in the lentils and then the crème fraîche. Take the pan off the heat and add plenty of finely chopped parsley before serving.

Rabbit pie

I really enjoy rabbit pie, with crumbly, buttery pastry and lots of delicious juice. This recipe comes from Pauline Collins, who lives on a farm down the road from my house. I had one of her rabbit pies several years ago and it was memorably good. She also makes it with pheasant, chicken, and squirrel. Serve this with mashed potatoes, Roasted cumin carrots, and Creamed thyme leeks (see pages 290 and 296).

Serves 8 to 10

For the pastry
* 1⅓ cups unbleached flour
* 1 teaspoon salt
* 10 tablespoons cold butter, cut into chunks
* ⅓ cup lard or shortening

* 6 rabbits, skinned and cut into pieces
* 12 shallots, left whole
* 2 onions, quartered
* 3 bay leaves
* 3 carrots, peeled, left whole (depending on size)
* Salt and black pepper
* 3 cups unsweetened apple juice
* ½ cup (1 stick) butter
* ¾ cup flour
* Freshly grated nutmeg
* Sherry or white wine
* ¼ cup heavy cream
* Large bunch of flat-leaf parsley, chopped
* 14 ounces cooked, peeled chestnuts (vacuum-packed are fine), roughly chopped
* Egg and milk wash (1 egg beaten with 2 tablespoons milk)

First make the pastry. Sift the flour and salt into a bowl, then rub in the butter and lard until the mixture resembles breadcrumbs. Don't overwork; cold hands or a food processor work best. Add 1 tablespoon water, then gather the pastry into a ball. Cover with plastic wrap and chill for 1 hour.

Put the rabbit pieces, shallots, onions, bay leaves, and carrots in a large ovenproof pan with a lid. Season with salt and pepper. Cover with apple juice (topping up with water if necessary) and cook on the stovetop, or in the oven preheated to 325 degrees, until the rabbit is tender (about 45 minutes).

Allow to cool a little, then carefully remove the meat from the bones.

Remove the shallots, onions, and carrots from the stock and roughly chop them. Strain the stock and set aside.

Melt the butter in a saucepan, then stir in the flour and cook a little. Gradually add the reserved stock, stirring to make a smooth, thickish sauce. Season and add plenty of nutmeg, a splash of sherry or wine, the cream, and chopped parsley. Cook for 10 minutes, then add the rabbit and chopped, cooked vegetables, and stir in the chestnuts.

Put the mixture in a buttered dish (12 by 8 inches) and allow to cool. (The recipe can be done to this stage the day before.)

Preheat the oven to 375 degrees.

Roll out the pastry. Using a pastry brush, dampen the edge of the pie dish with a little water and place a thin strip of pastry all the way around the edge, pressing down with your fingers to secure it. Cut out a pastry lid to fit the top of the dish. Dampen the pastry strip with a little water and fit a lid on top of the dish. Pinch the edges to seal, and decorate the top with the leftover pieces. Cut a steam hole, then brush the top with a little egg and milk wash.

Bake until the pastry is browned and the pie contents are heated through (about 20 minutes).

Chorizo lentils with sausages

A friend often used to cook this for me when we were at university. It's filling, warming, and delicious, ideal for eating outside around a fire with a mustardy-dressed green salad.

Serves 6
* 12 good-quality, 4-inch-long pork sausages
* 1 onion, finely chopped
* 3 sticks of celery, finely chopped
* Olive oil, for frying
* 1 chorizo (½ pound), thinly sliced
* 10 slices of bacon or pancetta
* Juice of ½ lemon
* 1⅓ cups lentils, preferably green Puy lentils
* 1 cup red wine
* 1¼ cups vegetable stock
* 1 (14½-ounce) can of chopped tomatoes
* 2 whole garlic cloves
* 3 tablespoons extra virgin olive oil
* 2 red chilis, chopped
* 3 bay leaves
* Large sprig of thyme
* Pared and very thinly sliced zest of 1 lemon
* Pared and very thinly sliced zest of 1 orange
* Huge bunch of flat-leaf parsley, chopped
* Juice of 1 orange and 1 lemon
* 20–30 green olives, coarsely chopped

Preheat the oven to 325 degrees.

Prick and roast the sausages in the oven until they are cooked and brown all over (about 20 minutes).

In a large frying pan, gently fry the onion and celery until soft in a little olive oil. Transfer to a plate, then fry the chorizo and bacon in the pan until the bacon is slightly crunchy. Squeeze over the juice of half a lemon.

Pour the lentils into a heavy-based pan and cover with the wine, stock, and tomatoes. Add the cooked onions and celery, the whole garlic cloves, chorizo and bacon, 3 tablespoons olive oil, the chilis, bay leaves, thyme, and citrus zest and cook gently for about 20 minutes, until the lentils begin to soften but have not collapsed. Add a little more wine or water if necessary to prevent them from boiling dry.

Allow to cool for 5 minutes off the heat. Remove the bay leaves, thyme, and garlic cloves, then add the parsley (lots of it, to lighten the lentils), the orange and lemon juice, and the olives. Transfer the mixture to a large shallow plate, add the sausages, and serve.

Hungarian paprikash

A traditional, comforting dish, this is perfect for chilly autumn days. The lovage (or celery leaf) adds a crucial sharpness to the flavor. Eat this with little dumplings (see page 382) or, even better, make Parsnip balls (see page 292) to float on the top. They are lighter than dumplings and the parsnip's sweetness makes a good addition to the overall flavor.

It's important to use genuine Hungarian or Polish paprika for this recipe, as the Spanish sort gives the wrong flavor. I use one made by Prymat Polish, which comes in sealed packets.

As with all stews, this one tastes even better when reheated. If you're preparing it in advance, you can either freeze it before the sour cream is added, or refrigerate the finished stew for up to four days.

Serves 6 to 8

* 3 ⅓ pounds beef chuck or very good braising meat, cut into 1-inch cubes, with all gristle and fat removed (you can also use half beef, half pork)
* ¼ cup olive oil
* 2 onions, thinly sliced
* 2 medium carrots, peeled and thickly sliced
* 5 teaspoons sweet Hungarian paprika
* 2 teaspoons hot Hungarian paprika
* Salt and black pepper
* 1 tablespoon flour
* 3 ⅓ cups beef stock or consommé
* 4 garlic cloves, crushed
* 1 bay leaf
* Large bunch of lovage or fresh celery leaves, chopped
* 1 cup sour cream, mixed with 1 teaspoon flour, plus more sour cream to serve

Preheat the oven to 300 degrees. Dry the beef well with paper towels.

Place a large, heavy-based, ovenproof pan over a high heat. Pour in the olive oil. Add as much beef as will fit in one layer without crowding and brown well on all sides. Transfer to a bowl and fry the rest of the beef in the same way.

Gently fry the onions and carrots in the oil remaining in the pan (you might need to add a little more). Cover, stirring occasionally, until the vegetables are tender (5 to 7 minutes).

Stir in both paprikas and cook for a couple of minutes before adding the browned meat. Season generously with salt and pepper, then add the flour.

Add the stock, garlic, bay leaf, and two-thirds of the lovage or celery leaves. Bring to a simmer, then cover and cook in the middle of the oven for 3 hours. Check occasionally to ensure it doesn't dry out, adding a little more water if necessary.

Just before serving, stir in the sour cream and flour mixture, cooking gently on the stove for a few minutes to thicken the sauce.

To serve, add the remaining lovage or celery leaves, stirring until just wilted, and add a dollop of sour cream to each serving.

Sausage burgers

You might wonder, "Why not just have hot dogs?" Sausage burgers are much easier to eat, with the meat sitting safely in its bun, and nicer, with none of that sausage skin, slight sliminess, and worry about the pink middle when cooked on a fire or barbecue. The deliciousness of these burgers depends on the quality of the sausage meat.

Serve these, along with the Thai chicken burgers, right, at a party.

Yields 12 to 15 burgers (about 3-inch diameter)
* 2 ¼ pounds quality sausage meat (this could be squeezed out of prepared sausages)
* 1 red onion, finely chopped
* ½ teaspoon chili flakes (you can exclude this if cooking for young children)
* 1 tablespoon finely chopped fresh rosemary
* Salt and black pepper
* Flour, for dusting
* Olive oil, for frying

To serve
* Cheese and fennel seed scones (see page 257)
* Red pepper and onion relish (see page 327)

Put the sausage meat into a large bowl with the onion, chili flakes (if using), and rosemary and mix well with a fork. Season generously with salt and black pepper. Transfer the mixture to a floured surface and shape into burgers. (Have some flour on the side for dusting your hands.)

Heat some oil in a large frying pan or oil a barbecue grill and cook the burgers over a medium heat for about 3 to 4 minutes on each side. Serve with the relish inside the cheese and fennel scones.

Thai chicken burgers

I love chicken, particularly when it's smoky from the barbecue. The danger is that the chicken breast will be dry and rubbery, but these spicy chicken burgers are reliably tasty and moist. They're ideal for a party, but just as good for a family supper with a green salad. Cover them in breadcrumbs for a crunchier texture. Serve with tzatziki (see page 268) and Red pepper and onion relish (see page 327).

Yields 6 large burgers (3–3 ½ inches) or 12 medium burgers (2 ½–3 inches)
* 4 large skinless chicken breasts
* 1 tablespoon Thai green curry paste
* 1 small egg
* Salt and black pepper
* Flour, for dusting
* 2–3 tablespoons olive oil, for frying

Roughly chop the chicken breasts and put into a food processor with the Thai paste, egg, 2 to 3 good pinches of salt, and some pepper and whizz for a few seconds. (Be careful not to overprocess; you want the chicken to look like it's been minced, not pureed.) Don't worry if the mixture is quite loose—it firms up when frying.

Flour a work surface and your hands and shape the mixture into burgers.

Heat the oil in a large frying pan or oil a barbecue grill and gently cook the burgers for 5 to 6 minutes on each side, until they are golden and cooked all the way through.

Grated carrot, pine nut, and raisin salad

A carrot salad is perfect with stews and tagines. This one is also surprisingly good the next day—and even the day after that—as the flavors merge and deepen.

Serves 6 as a side dish
* 4 large carrots, peeled
* 1 tablespoon poppy or cumin seeds
* 1 tablespoon pine nuts or sunflower seeds
* 2 tablespoons raisins
* Salt and black pepper
* Really large bunch of cilantro, chopped

For the dressing
* Juice and grated zest of 1 lemon
* 3 tablespoons extra virgin olive oil
* 2 teaspoons honey (optional)

Grate the carrots on a medium-grade grater. (It's important not to grate them too finely, as you'll lose the important texture of the salad.) Set aside in a large bowl (essential for the thorough mixing that's needed later).

Now make the dressing. Put the lemon juice and zest and olive oil in a small bowl and mix together. Add the honey if the carrots are not as sweet as you'd like. Pour the dressing over the grated carrot.

Toast the poppy seeds and pine nuts in a dry frying pan, then scatter them, and the raisins, over the carrot. Season with salt and pepper. Stir everything together well, really mixing in the poppy seeds, and leave to marinate for a couple of hours.

Mix in the cilantro before serving.

Roasted cumin carrots

The beauty of these carrots is that you can make them the day before—they are just as good reheated. The slow roasting brings out all their sweetness, and finely chopped rosemary can be used instead of cumin seeds. Once cold, the carrots also make a great salad in Tahini dressing (see page 71).

Serves 6 to 8 as a side dish
* 2 ¼ pounds small to medium-sized carrots, peeled and left whole
* 1–2 tablespoons olive oil
* 2 tablespoons cumin seeds
* 2 tablespoons butter
* Salt and black pepper

Preheat the oven to 325 degrees.

Place the carrots in a roasting pan and drizzle with a little olive oil. Place in the oven for a good hour.

Once the carrots are cooked, toast the cumin seeds in a large dry pan to bring out the flavor. (If using rosemary, finely chop it but do not toast.) Add the butter and the roasted carrots to the pan and toss with the seeds or herb.

Season and serve immediately, or store in the fridge for reheating when needed.

Parsnip balls

A light alternative to dumplings, these parsnip balls are ideal for serving on their own with tzatziki (see page 268), or on top of Hungarian paprikash or Venison casserole (see pages 287 and 382). I use an almost identical recipe with zucchinis in summer (see page 149).

Yields 8 to 10 little balls
* 1 pound parsnips, peeled
* ½ teaspoon salt
* ½ teaspoon black pepper
* 1 hot green chili, finely chopped
* 1 small onion, very finely chopped
* 1 teaspoon peeled and grated fresh ginger
* 2 tablespoons chopped fresh cilantro or flat-leaf parsley
* ⅓ cup chickpea flour
* Oil, for frying

Grate the parsnips, discarding the core. Place in a bowl and combine with the rest of the ingredients, sprinkling the flour in last. Mix well and allow to sit for 10 minutes (this allows moisture to be released from the parsnips, which will help to form the balls). Using your hands, take walnut-sized pieces of the mixture and roll them into little balls.

Fill a deep saucepan with enough oil to reach about one-third of the way up the side, and have a lid or splash-guard on standby to prevent the oil from spitting too much after you add each batch. Heat the oil until it reaches about 375 degrees, or until a cube of bread browns in 30 seconds.

Add the parsnip balls and fry until they've browned all over.

Beet marmalade

This punchy, intense marmalade is good with red meat or game. If you prefer a gentler flavor, add the optional ingredients listed below.

Serves 6 as an accompaniment
* 4 medium-sized beets (about 2 pounds)
* 2 large onions, finely chopped
* 3 tablespoons butter
* Splash of olive oil
* 3 tablespoons balsamic vinegar
* 1 tablespoon superfine sugar
* 2 tablespoons Greek yogurt (optional)
* Grated lemon zest and juice, to taste (optional)
* 2 tablespoons dry-roasted poppy seeds

Boil the beets in a pan of salted water for about 40 minutes, until soft. Drain and allow to cool a little, then peel. Grate on the coarse side of a grater.

Gently fry the onions in a pan with the butter and olive oil until translucent. Add the grated beets, the vinegar, and sugar and continue to cook gently for about 15 minutes, to reduce and make the mixture syrupy.

If using the optional ingredients, mix the yogurt with a little lemon juice and zest. Once the marmalade has cooled a bit, stir in the yogurt and the seeds. Serve with red meat or game. Any left over can be kept in the fridge for 3 or 4 days.

Squash puree

Delicious with lentil dishes, this is also great with any roast meat or casserole. For a simple supper with a salad, try it on its own too, with cheese grated on top.

Serves 4 to 6
* 1 whole squash, such as acorn or butternut (about 2 ½ pounds)
* 4 tablespoons (½ stick) butter
* Generous bunch of fresh sage, finely chopped
* Salt and black pepper

Preheat the oven to 375 degrees.

Wrap the squash in foil and bake for 1 to 1½ hours, until soft to the tip of a knife.

Remove the foil and allow the squash to cool enough to handle. Halve lengthwise, then spoon out and discard the seeds and fibers. Scoop out the flesh and puree in a blender or food processor.

Put the puree into a saucepan with the butter and sage and reheat gently. Season before serving.

Fig mashed potatoes

There's nothing better than mashed potatoes made with a well-flavored floury variety. The sweetness of the figs and the crunch of the seeds make this ideal for eating with strong-flavored meat and casseroles.

Serves 6
* 7–9 dried figs, depending on size
* 2 ¼ pounds baking potatoes, peeled and cut into large chunks
* 3 tablespoons butter
* 3–4 tablespoons heavy cream or milk
* 2 tablespoons extra virgin olive oil
* 2 ounces Parmesan cheese, freshly grated
* Salt and black pepper

Place the figs in a bowl and pour boiling water over them. Leave to soak for 20 minutes.

Boil the potatoes in salted water until soft (15 to 20 minutes). Drain and mash them with the butter, cream, olive oil, Parmesan, salt, and pepper.

Drain the figs. Remove the woody stems and roughly chop the fruit. Add to the mashed potatoes. Mix well and serve.

Autumn roasted vegetables

Although great as a side dish, these vegetables are also good on their own, served on top of Lemon and lime couscous with plenty of fresh herbs, some Pickled ginger, and a dollop of tzatziki (see pages 297, 331, and 268). They are also excellent served with any hearty autumnal meat dish.

Serves 6 to 8 as side dish, 4 as main course
* 3 tablespoons olive oil
* 2 red onions, cut into quarters or eighths
* 2 red peppers, deseeded and cut into large pieces
* 1 yellow or orange sweet pepper, deseeded, and cut into large pieces
* 2 large carrots, peeled and cut into 2-inch chunks, halved lengthwise
* 1 pound squash, peeled, deseeded, and cubed
* 1 red chili, deseeded and finely chopped
* 2 unwaxed lemons, thinly sliced and seeds removed
* 2 sprigs of thyme
* Salt and black pepper

Preheat the oven to 425 degrees.

Measure the oil into a large plastic bag, add all the other ingredients, and season with salt and pepper. Toss together, then empty the bag into a large roasting pan. Place in the oven for about 40 minutes, turning from time to time, until the vegetables are just beginning to char at the edges.

Remove from the oven and allow to cool a little. Stir to mix the juices, then serve.

Warm eggplant and fennel salad

This is perfect with simple roast or fried chicken, and it's also good with fish. The soft creaminess of the roasted eggplant sets off the crunchiness of the raw fennel.

Serves 6 as a starter or side salad,
4 as a main course
* 3 plump eggplants
* 8 tablespoons extra virgin olive oil
* 2 fennel bulbs
* ¼ cup plain yogurt
* Juice and grated zest of 1 lemon
* Large bunch of fresh mint, coarsely chopped
* Large bunch of flat-leaf parsley, coarsely chopped
* Salt and black pepper

Preheat the oven to 350 degrees.

Cut the eggplants in half. Score the flesh lightly with a serrated knife. Brush 1 tablespoon olive oil into each cut surface of the eggplants, adding a little at a time until it is absorbed. Place in a roasting pan in the oven for 30 minutes, until soft and just beginning to char at the edges. Cut into large chunks and transfer to a serving bowl.

Cut the fennel into ¼-inch slices and add to the eggplant. Add the yogurt, the remaining 2 tablespoons olive oil, and the lemon juice and zest and mix while the eggplant is still warm. Scatter over the herbs and mix again. Season and serve.

Creamed thyme leeks

You can eat these classic creamed leeks with almost anything, but they work particularly well with Rabbit pie (see page 284).

Serves 6
* 4 medium-sized leeks
* ¼ cup (½ stick) butter
* 2 tablespoons olive oil
* 1½ cups heavy cream
* 2 teaspoons Dijon mustard
* Small bunch of fresh thyme, leaves picked and finely chopped
* Salt and black pepper

Chop the leeks as finely as you can—a mandoline is good for this. Fry them gently in a large pan in the butter and olive oil until just softening (not browning).

Add the cream, mustard, and thyme. Season with salt and pepper and continue to cook for a few more minutes.

Brussels sprouts salad with an orange and mustard dressing

The great thing about shredded Brussels sprouts is that you get lots of the green tender part, always the nicest bit of any brassica. That's particularly true when eating them raw, as here. Use the thinnest slicing blade on a food processor.

Serves 8
* 1 pound Brussels sprouts, outer leaves and stem bases removed, thinly sliced
* 2 large carrots (about ⅓ pound), peeled and grated
* 2 sticks of celery, thinly sliced
* 2 tablespoons raisins
* 2 tablespoons chopped cilantro, parsley, or mint (optional)
* ¾ cup mixed seeds (sunflower, sesame, and pine nuts), toasted

For the dressing
* Juice of 2 oranges and zest of 1
* Juice of ½ lemon
* 1 large shallot
* 1 tablespoon Dijon or grainy mustard
* 3 tablespoons extra virgin olive oil
* 1 teaspoon honey
* Salt and black pepper

Put all the salad ingredients into a large bowl.

Place all the dressing ingredients in a food processor and whizz until emulsified.

Pour the dressing over the salad, stir well to combine, and chill for 1 hour before serving.

Fennel and Parmesan gratin

Bulb fennel is one of my favorite vegetables—wonderful raw in salads and equally good in an oven-cooked gratin topped with crunchy bread–crumbs. This is the perfect accompaniment to fish or meat, particularly chicken.

Serves 6
* 6 fennel bulbs (about 2 pounds)
* ¾ whole nutmeg, grated
* Salt and black pepper
* ¼ pound Parmesan cheese, freshly grated
* 1¼ cups good vegetable stock
* ½ cup heavy cream
* 1 cup fresh breadcrumbs
* 3 tablespoons butter (for greasing the dish and dotting the top)

Preheat the oven to 350 degrees. Butter an ovenproof dish (12 by 8 inches)

Remove the outer scale of the fennel bulbs if coarse and stringy. Slice the bulbs and stalks as thinly as possible (a mandoline or the slicing disc on a food processor is good for this).

Pile a third of the fennel slices into the prepared baking dish. Add some grated nutmeg and a little salt and pepper on top, and scatter over a third of the Parmesan cheese. Repeat for the next third of fennel slices. Put in the final third of fennel.

Mix the vegetable stock and heavy cream together and pour over the top of the layered fennel.

Scatter over the breadcrumbs and the remaining Parmesan. (Don't worry if the baking dish looks rather full, it reduces down when cooking.)

Cover loosely with foil and bake for 45 minutes.

Remove the foil and dot on the remaining butter and return to the oven uncovered for a further 10 to 15 minutes, until golden brown. Allow to cool for 10 to 15 minutes before serving. The flavor is best when eaten warm.

Lemon and lime couscous

Here is a tasty side dish that I often use in place of potatoes or rice. As well as being an ideal accompaniment to lamb or roast vegetables, it is delicious with sausages, and with Chicken tagine (see page 167).

Serves 4 to 5
* 2 cups good vegetable stock or bouillon
* 1¾ cups couscous
* 2 tablespoons extra virgin olive oil
* Juice and grated zest of 1 lemon
* Juice and grated zest of 1 lime
* Salt and black pepper
* Generous handful of fresh mint, chopped
* Generous handful of flat-leaf parsley, chopped

Place the stock in a saucepan and bring to a boil.

Put the couscous into a deep bowl, pour over the olive oil, lemon and lime juice, and stock, stir just once, then cover and leave for 10 minutes to allow the grains to soften. Only then fork it through; done like this, your couscous should be dry, with each grain separate rather than a cloggy mush.

Season the couscous with salt and pepper, then add the chopped herbs and lemon and lime zest.

Mini sweet-scented geranium blackberry and apple pies

The idea of combining sweet-scented (geranium) leaves with blackberries originates from Elizabeth David. She said the leaf gives an incomparable flavor when cooked with blackberries for jelly (as they do in Greece), and it's an excellent addition to a classic apple and blackberry pie. You can make this as one big pie, or make miniature versions (as here), so that everyone gets their own.

Serves 8

For the pastry

* 1¼ cups unbleached flour
* Pinch of salt
* 2 tablespoons confectioners' sugar
* 6 tablespoons unsalted butter
* 1 egg yolk

* ½ pound tart cooking apples
* ½ pound sweet apples
* 2 cups blackberries
* Grated zest of 1 lemon
* ½ cup superfine sugar, plus extra for sprinkling
* 8 large scented geranium leaves (I grow *P. tomentosum*, which is peppermint-scented, but lemon or rose-scented would do as well)
* Milk, for brushing
* Cream or ice cream, to serve

First make the pastry. Sift the flour, salt, and confectioners' sugar into a bowl. Rub the butter into the flour by hand, or pulse in a food processor, until the mixture resembles breadcrumbs.

Add the egg yolk and just enough iced water to bring the mixture together into a ball. Wrap in plastic wrap and place in the fridge for 30 minutes while you prepare the fruit.

Peel, core, and slice the apples. Place in a saucepan with the blackberries, lemon zest, and superfine sugar. Mix and cook briefly until the sugar is dissolved and the juices start to run. Turn off the heat.

Add the geranium leaves and leave for about 30 minutes so that the flavors infuse.

Remove the leaves, then pile the fruit into 8 ramekins (arranged on a baking sheet) or into a small casserole dish.

Preheat the oven to 400 degrees.

Roll out the pastry as thinly as you can (about ⅛ inch). To make the pastry lids fit perfectly, using a pastry brush, dampen the edge of the ramekins or pie dish with a little water and place a thin strip of pastry all the way around each edge, pressing down with your fingers to secure it. Cut out a pastry lid to fit the top of each dish. Dampen the pastry strips with a little water and fit a lid on top of each dish. Pinch the edges to seal.

If you have any pastry left over, roll it out, press a geranium leaf on it to make imprints, then cut around the shapes. Use these to decorate the pies, sticking them down with a little water.

Pierce the top of each pie with the tip of a sharp knife, brush with a little milk, and scatter some superfine sugar over the top.

Bake in the oven for about 20 minutes, until the pastry is crisp and beginning to color, then lower the heat to 325 degrees and bake the ramekins for another 10 minutes and the large dish for another 20 minutes. Serve with cream or ice cream.

Toffee apple pie

It's fun to have toffee apples for an autumn party, but they are a pain to make and people rarely want to eat a whole one. I find a toffee apple pie (rather like a banoffee pie but without the bananas) is the perfect substitute. This recipe requires cans of condensed milk to be boiled in advance. To save time, you can now buy them pre-boiled.

Serves 6
* 2 (14-ounce) cans of condensed milk
* 8 Granny Smith apples (or any apple that keeps its shape when cooked)
* 7 tablespoons unsalted butter
* 1 tablespoon superfine sugar
* Juice and grated zest of 1 lemon
* 1 cup heavy cream
* Toasted sliced almonds, for decoration

For the cookie crust
* 18 Graham crackers (about 11 ounces), crumbled
* 7 tablespoons melted unsalted butter
* 1 teaspoon ground cinnamon

If your condensed milk is not pre-boiled, put the unopened cans into a large, flameproof casserole dish, cover with water, and bring to a boil over a high heat.

Meanwhile, preheat the oven to 275 degrees. Cover the casserole with a lid and place in the oven for 3½ hours. With this system, there is no danger of the casserole boiling dry, so it is safer than doing it on the stovetop. Set aside to cool overnight. When opened, the condensed milk will have turned into toffee.

To make the base, put the crumbled cookies into a food processor and whizz to a fine crumb. Transfer to a mixing bowl, add the butter and cinnamon, and stir together. Press the mixture into a 10-inch loose-bottomed tart pan and place in the fridge.

Peel and core the apples, cutting each one into 8 pieces. Melt the butter in a pan over a low heat. Add the apples and sugar and cook until golden brown and just softening but keeping their shape. Stir in the lemon juice and zest.

Open the cans of boiled milk and spoon the toffee onto the cookie crust (use a warm spoon that you keep dipping into a mug of hot water to prevent sticking). Arrange the apples evenly over the top.

Whisk the cream in a large bowl until just thick, then spread over the apples. Keep in the fridge until needed, and remove from the tart pan before serving. Sprinkle the almonds on top before you eat.

Baked figs with yogurt ice cream

Made when figs are plump and sweet, this is one of the best and easiest puddings. The figs are excellent served with just a spoonful of ricotta, but lovely with this ice cream, which is lighter and sharper than most, and goes well with any baked fruit.

Serves 6 to 8

For the yogurt ice cream
* 8 ounces mascarpone
* 4 cups plain yogurt
* 3 tablespoons honey
* Juice and grated zest of 1 lemon

* 12–16 fresh figs (depending on size)
* 3 tablespoons honey
* 2 tablespoons unsalted butter, cut into small cubes
* 5 tablespoons grappa or ouzo

First make the ice cream. Put all the ingredients for it in a food processor and blend quickly, or just mix well in a bowl. Pour the mixture into an ice cream maker if you have one. Freeze/churn for about 20 minutes, then pack into a plastic container and freeze for 2 hours. If you don't have a machine, place the mixture in a shallow container and freeze until half-frozen (about 1 hour). Remove and fork through, mixing the frozen edge into the middle to break up the ice crystals. Repeat twice.

Meanwhile, preheat the oven to 325 degrees. Stand the figs upright in a roasting pan and cut them with a cross shape. Drizzle over the honey, dot with the cubes of butter, and pour the grappa or ouzo over the top. Bake in the oven for 20 minutes.

Allow the ice cream to soften slightly in the fridge 15 minutes before serving.

Tarte tatin

You may already have a tarte tatin recipe up your sleeve, but this version, with a melting texture and an intense apple/caramel taste, leaves other recipes standing. I had it in America, cooked by a friend, and, even though I prided myself on my own tarte tatin, immediately asked for his recipe. The big difference is the long, slow cooking of the apple. Add an extra slosh of brandy if you want to cut through the sweetness.

Serves 6
* ½ cup light brown sugar
* ½ cup (1 stick) unsalted butter, cut into small chunks
* 9 apples (Granny Smiths are good), peeled, cored, and quartered
* Juice and grated zest of 1 lemon
* 2 tablespoons brandy
* 1 tablespoon vanilla extract
* 1 pound package of prepared puff pastry
* Whipped cream or vanilla ice cream, to serve (see opposite and exclude the cinnamon)

Cover the bottom of a tarte tatin pan or a 10-inch cast-iron frying pan (suitable for oven use) with the sugar and dot over the butter. Arrange the apple quarters on top in overlapping circles.

Place the pan on a very low heat, using a heat diffuser if necessary to ensure that the apples, butter, and sugar gently caramelize. This will take about 45 minutes. Stay nearby to make sure the apples don't burn, and don't be tempted to stir them.

Preheat the oven to 350 degrees.

Take the pan off the heat, pour over the lemon juice and zest, brandy, and vanilla extract.

Roll out the puff pastry and place over the apples, pulling it gently to the edges of the pan if necessary and cutting off the excess. Place in the oven for 25 minutes, or until golden brown.

Take the pan out of the oven and carefully invert onto a serving plate. The tart usually falls out intact; if not, just scoop up any apple left behind and add to the top of the tart. Allow to cool a bit before serving. Eat it warm or cool, with whipped cream or vanilla ice cream.

Baked apples with cinnamon ice cream

You can't go through autumn without having baked apples a couple of times. They are a favorite traditional dessert and irresistible with this gently flavored cinnamon ice cream. You can leave out the brandy or Calvados if you're making this for children.

Serves 6

For the cinnamon ice cream
* 1¼ cups milk
* ½ cup superfine sugar
* Splash of vanilla extract
* 1 (14-ounce) can of sweetened condensed milk
* Pinch of salt
* 2 cups heavy cream
* 1 heaping teaspoon ground cinnamon

* 6 medium-sized cooking apples
* 7 tablespoons softened unsalted butter, plus extra for greasing
* ½ cup brown sugar
* ½ cup golden raisins, soaked in Calvados or warm water
* ½ cup dates, pitted and chopped
* Juice of ½ lemon and grated zest of 1 whole lemon
* 2 tablespoons brandy or Calvados (optional)
* 2 tablespoons pine nuts or slivered almonds, toasted

First make the ice cream. Place the milk, sugar, and vanilla in a large, heavy-based saucepan and bring just to a boiling point. Remove from the heat and cool. Add the condensed milk, salt, cream, and cinnamon.

Pour the mixture into an ice cream maker if you have one. Freeze/churn for about 20 minutes, then pack into a plastic container and freeze for 2 hours. If you don't have a machine, place the mixture in a shallow container and freeze until half-frozen (about 1 hour). Remove and fork through, mixing the frozen edge into the middle to break up the ice crystals. Repeat twice.

Preheat the oven to 350 degrees.

Core the apples and score a line (just through the skin) right around each one about two-thirds of the way up. This will stop them from exploding in the oven as they expand during cooking. Place in a buttered shallow dish or on a silicone mat in a roasting pan.

Place the butter, sugar, golden raisins, dates, lemon juice, and zest in a bowl and mix together. Stir in the brandy or Calvados, if using. Fill the cavity of the apples with the mixture and pile the rest on top.

Bake for 30 to 40 minutes (covering with foil if the top starts to burn), or until soft when pricked with the tip of a sharp knife. If any syrup is left in the pan, spoon over the apples, then scatter with the toasted pine nuts or almonds.

About 15 minutes before the apples are ready, take the ice cream out of the freezer and allow to soften slightly in the fridge.

Let the baked apples cool a bit before serving with the ice cream.

Pear parcels with star anise

Breaking away from the usual pears poached in red wine, this recipe is quite easy and the pears look lovely brought to the table in their parcels. Big fat pears, such as Comice, that sit well on their bottoms are best. With skinny Anjou pears, you'll have to take a slice off the base for them to sit up straight. Serve with ice cream or, even better, with old-fashioned Baked egg custard (see page 405).

Serves 6
* 6 pears, peeled but with stems left on
* 12 star anise
* 12 whole cardamom pods, slightly crushed
* 12 whole cloves
* 12 tablespoons port
* 6 tablespoons honey

Preheat the oven to 350 degrees.

Cut 6 (12-inch) circles of parchment paper.

For each parcel, place a parchment circle in a small bowl (this keeps in the liquid when tying up the parcels). Place a pear in the middle of the paper. Add 2 star anise and 2 cardamom pods. Push 2 cloves into the pear (as these can sometimes pierce the paper when tying up). Spoon in 2 tablespoons port and 1 tablespoon honey. Gather the paper around the top of the stalk and tie with string. Transfer the parcel to a roasting pan. Repeat this step for each pear.

Bake for 45 to 60 minutes (depending on variety), or until soft to the tip of a knife. Serve still in the paper for each person to unwrap.

Baked blackberries and raspberries with mascarpone

Rose Gray, co-owner of London's River Café, demonstrated her blackberry and mascarpone recipe at our cooking school, and I've made it countless times since. This variation, with the addition of raspberries (which collapse more than the blackberries), is deeply colorful and tastes glorious.

Serves 6
* 4 cups blackberries
* 4 cups raspberries
* 2 vanilla pods
* 16 ounces mascarpone cheese
* 3 egg yolks
* 3 tablespoons confectioners' sugar

Preheat the oven to 400 degrees.

Wash the blackberries and raspberries and pick them over. Scrape the seeds from the vanilla pods.

Combine the mascarpone, egg yolks, vanilla seeds, and confectioners' sugar in a bowl.

Put the blackberries and raspberries in a small baking dish. Spoon the mascarpone mixture over them and bake for 5 to 10 minutes, until the mascarpone begins to brown.

Austrian curd cake

This is one of the quickest and easiest cakes you can make, which Debbie Staples, the cook at our Perch Hill school, had on a skiing holiday. It's perfect for teatime after an autumn walk, and excellent as a dessert served with autumn raspberries and heavy cream.

Yields 12 small squares
* 5 tablespoons unsalted butter
* ⅔ cup superfine sugar
* 8 ounces curd or cream cheese
* 2 eggs, separated
* Juice and grated zest of 1 lemon
* ¼ cup ground almonds
* 2 tablespoons semolina
* ⅓ cup raisins or dried cherries

To serve
* Heavy cream
* Raspberries

Preheat the oven to 300 degrees.

Cream the butter and sugar together in a bowl. Add the cheese and beat in the egg yolks. Add the lemon juice and zest, then the almonds and semolina.

In another bowl, beat the egg whites until stiff but not dry. Fold the whites and fruit into the cheesy mixture.

Put the mixture into a square or rectangular cake pan measuring about 8 by 8 inches. Bake in the preheated oven for about 30 minutes, or until a knife inserted in the center comes out clean. Watch carefully toward the end of the baking time as the top burns easily. Cover with foil if it shows signs of doing this. Cool in the pan.

When cooled, cut into squares and serve for tea or as a dessert with plenty of raspberries and cream.

Chocolate, beet, and orange cake

This dark chocolate cake tastes soft and rich while the beets add extra moisture and give it an incredible color. It is also easy to make.

The recipe comes from Jo Clark's mother, Rachel Dasent. Jo has been my right- and left-hand woman throughout the recipe testing and writing of this book.

Serves 6 to 8
* 1 medium beet (about ½ pound)
* 11 ounces dark chocolate (at least 70% cocoa solids)
* Juice and finely grated zest of 1 orange
* ½ cup ground almonds
* 3 eggs, separated
* ⅔ cup superfine sugar
* ½ teaspoon baking powder
* Cream or vanilla ice cream (see page 303 and exclude the cinnamon), to serve

Place the beet in a large pan of boiling water and cook for 30 to 40 minutes, until soft. Peel and coarsely chop.

Heat the oven to 350 degrees. Lightly oil an 8-inch loose-bottomed cake pan and line with parchment paper.

Melt about half of the chocolate in a double boiler.

Put the cooked beet into a food processor and whizz briefly, keeping some texture to it. Transfer to a mixing bowl and stir in the orange juice and zest. Now add the almonds, egg yolks, sugar, baking powder, and melted chocolate. Mix thoroughly.

In another bowl, beat the egg whites until stiff but not dry, and fold them into the chocolate mixture.

Spoon into the lined pan and place on a baking sheet. Bake for 35 to 40 minutes, then allow to cool in the pan.

Melt the remaining chocolate in a double boiler. To serve, pour melted chocolate over slices of cake, and top with cream or a dollop of vanilla ice cream.

Victoria sponge cake with fruit curd

The classic Victoria sponge cake is light and usually sandwiched together with jam, but it's very easy to serve it in other ways. For example, it can be stuffed with fresh raspberries or fruit compote, or filled with fruit curd and whipped cream, then topped with blackberries and quick-fried sugared apples, as suggested below.

Serves 6 to 8
* ½ cup (1 stick) unsalted butter, softened
* 1 cup superfine sugar
* 2 large eggs, lightly beaten with a fork
* 1 teaspoon vanilla extract
* 2 teaspoons finely grated lemon or orange zest
* ¾ cup self-rising flour, sifted

For the filling and top
* 1 cup heavy cream, lightly whipped
* 1 tablespoon superfine sugar
* 1 jar Blackberry and apple curd (see page 318)
* 1 cup fresh blackberries
* A few slices of apple, sautéed in butter (choose ones that keep their shape, e.g. Granny Smiths)
* Confectioners' sugar, for dusting

Preheat the oven to 350 degrees. Lightly butter the sides of 2 (7-inch) loose-bottomed cake pans and line the bottoms with buttered parchment paper.

Put the butter into a bowl and beat until soft. Add the sugar and beat again until light and fluffy (7 to 10 minutes by hand, or 3 to 4 minutes with an electric beater).

Using a wooden spoon, beat in the eggs a little at a time. Mix in the vanilla extract and lemon or orange zest, then beat in the flour until well mixed.

Divide the mixture between the prepared cake pans and level the tops. Place the cakes side by side in the middle of the oven and bake for 20 to 25 minutes. Turn out and cool on a wire rack.

Lightly whip the cream, then mix in the superfine sugar. Cover one of the cake surfaces with a thin layer of the cream mixture. Spread a layer of fruit curd over the second sponge and scatter with a little fresh fruit. Sandwich the two sponges together. Decorate the cake with the blackberries and buttered apple slices, and dust with confectioners' sugar.

Mary Stearns's apple cake

Mary Stearns is in her nineties, and brimming with vitality. She has lived on the farm at Sissinghurst—where I now live—almost all her life.

Her recipe for apple cake, thick with fruit, slightly fluffy and moist, is the best I have tried. It is quick and reliable enough for my youngest daughter, Molly, to make faultlessly. Serve it warm, straight from the oven, with sweetened whipped cream.

Serves 10 to 12
* 2 medium cooking apples, peeled and cored
* Juice of ½ lemon and finely grated zest of 1 lemon
* 1¼ cups sugar, plus extra for sprinkling over the top
* 1 cup (2 sticks) unsalted butter, softened
* 2½ cups self-rising flour, sifted
* ¾ cup hazelnuts, roughly chopped
* 1¼ cups golden raisins, soaked in hot water for 30 minutes
* 5 eggs, lightly beaten
* 1 tablespoon vanilla extract
* Whipped cream, sweetened with a little superfine sugar, to serve

Preheat the oven to 325 degrees. Butter a 9-inch square or round cake pan (buttering is not necessary if the pan is silicone).

Cut the apples into quarters, then cut each quarter lengthwise into 6 slices. Place in a bowl and gently mix in the lemon juice so that the slices are well covered.

In another bowl, beat the sugar and butter until light and fluffy. This can be done with a wooden spoon or electric beater. Add the flour, hazelnuts, golden raisins, eggs, lemon zest, and vanilla extract and, using a large metal spoon, stir to combine.

Spoon the mixture into the prepared pan, then push in the apple slices so that they are just showing. Sprinkle a little sugar over the top.

Bake in the middle of the oven for about 1 hour, or until a skewer or knife tip inserted in the center of the cakes comes out clean. If the cake starts to brown too quickly, place a piece of foil or parchment paper over the top. Allow to cool a little in the pan and serve with the sweetened whipped cream.

Caramelized sesame shortbread

The recipe here is based on Irish chef Darina Allen's almond squares, which we make with all sorts of seeds and nuts for tea break at the school. It feels particularly suited to autumn—a seedy, nutty time of year.

Yields 35 (2-inch) squares
* 1¼ cups unbleached flour
* 2 tablespoons superfine sugar
* ½ cup (1 stick) unsalted butter
* Drop of vanilla extract
* 1 egg yolk

For the topping
* ¾ cup sesame seeds
* ⅔ cup pine nuts
* 5 tablespoons unsalted butter
* ¼ cup light brown sugar
* 3 tablespoons honey
* 1 tablespoon heavy cream

Preheat the oven to 350 degrees. Grease an 8 by 12-inch Swiss roll pan.

Put the flour and sugar into a bowl, then rub in the butter. Add the vanilla extract and egg yolk and combine to form a dough. Press into the prepared pan. Prick the surface and bake for 10 to 15 minutes, or until golden. Remove and allow to cool for 10 minutes or so. (Keep the oven on for the next stage.)

Put all the topping ingredients, except the cream, into a saucepan and place over a low heat, stirring until the mixture is a pale straw color (about 2 or 3 minutes). Add the cream and cook for another 30 seconds or so.

Spread this mixture over the cooled base and smooth with a spatula. Bake in the oven for about 10 minutes, until golden brown. Allow to cool in the pan for 10 minutes, then transfer to a wire rack to cool completely. Cut into squares and triangles.

Scottish tablet

This is crumbly and dry rather than soft and squidgy. It reminds me of my childhood, quite a bit of which was spent on the west coast of Scotland, where we certainly ate plenty of fudge-like tablet. Don't be tempted to taste the mixture while cooking as it gets very, very hot.

Yields enough to fill a 12 by 10-inch baking pan
* ½ cup (1 stick) unsalted butter
* 5 cups granulated sugar
* 1 (14-ounce) can of condensed milk
* 1 teaspoon vanilla extract

Line a 12 by 10-inch baking pan with parchment paper and oil it lightly.

Put all the ingredients into a large, heavy-based, stainless-steel pan, adding half a can of water (measured in the empty condensed milk can). Bring slowly to a boil, stirring all the time, then simmer gently for 20 minutes, stirring regularly to prevent sticking. The mixture will darken in color and come away from the sides of the pan.

Take off the heat and beat for a couple of minutes with a wooden spoon until the mixture starts to crystallize and turn slightly gritty. As soon as this happens, pour or spoon it into the prepared baking pan. If you beat for too long, it will become stiff and over-crystallized.

Leave to set, then break up into chunks. Alternatively, cut into squares while the mixture is still a little soft.

Rose marshmallows

This is an adaptation of a recipe by my friend Hugh Fearnley-Whittingstall to which I've added rose flavor and petals. Don't be put off by people saying that homemade marshmallows are difficult to make. All you need is this recipe, a mixer or hand-held electric beater, and a jam thermometer. Eat the results within a day or two.

Yields enough to fill an 8 by 8-inch baking pan
* 1 tablespoon confectioners' sugar, sifted
* 1 tablespoon cornstarch
* 1 small raw beet, peeled and grated
* 3 (¼-ounce) envelopes gelatin powder
* 2 ⅔ cups granulated sugar
* 2 egg whites
* 1 tablespoon rose water
* 2 tablespoons finely chopped rose petals (pink, purple, or red)

Mix the confectioners' sugar and cornstarch together in a small bowl.

Line an 8 by 8-inch baking pan with parchment paper and oil it lightly. Sprinkle half the sugar and cornstarch mixture into the prepared pan.

Put the grated beet into a small bowl with ½ cup boiling water. Leave to steep for 1 minute. Strain the deep pink juice into another small bowl, discarding the beet, and add the gelatin. Stir, then allow to set.

Put the granulated sugar and 1 cup cold water into a medium-sized saucepan and bring gently to a boil, stirring to dissolve the sugar. Raise the heat and boil the mixture vigorously without stirring. Using a sugar thermometer to check the temperature, heat the mixture to 250 degrees. Remove from the heat and add the pink gelatin, stirring until well combined.

Place the egg whites in the bowl of a mixer and beat at high speed until they form stiff peaks. Then, with the mixer on a low speed, trickle in the pink sugar mixture, rose water, and rose petals, beating gently until the mixture turns really thick. When the beater is raised it should leave a ribbon trail on the surface. If it doesn't, beat for a little longer.

Pour the mixture into the prepared baking pan and leave to set for a couple of hours or more.

Cover a chopping board with the rest of the sugar and cornstarch mixture. Ease the marshmallow out of the pan and onto the board, then cut into chunks. Turn the chunks so that every side is dusted and they won't stick together.

Pumpkin seed and cinnamon brittle

A big flat plate of pumpkin seed brittle—like sesame seed snaps but with bigger seeds—is a great thing for any autumn party. It goes down well with children and adults alike, and will keep for a week or two in an airtight tin.

Yields enough to fill a 12 by 15-inch baking pan
* 1 ½ cups pumpkin seeds
* 1 ½ teaspoons ground cinnamon
* ½ teaspoon salt
* 1 teaspoon baking soda
* 1 tablespoon vanilla extract
* 3 cups granulated sugar
* 3 tablespoons unsalted butter
* 1 tablespoon honey

Oil an 11 by 15-inch shallow-sided baking pan.

Toast the pumpkin seeds in a hot frying pan for 3 to 4 minutes, stirring all the time while the seeds are popping.

Put the cinnamon and salt into a small bowl and mix together. In another bowl mix the baking soda with the vanilla extract.

Place the remaining ingredients in a heavy-based saucepan, add 1 cup water, and stir over a medium heat until the sugar has dissolved. Turn up the heat and boil rapidly for 20 to 30 minutes, stirring occasionally. The mixture should become golden brown and reach between 340 to 345 degrees on a sugar thermometer.

Remove the pan from the heat and stir in the cinnamon and vanilla mixtures and the toasted pumpkin seeds. The caramel will bubble up slightly.

Pour immediately into the prepared baking pan and spread it out swiftly and evenly. The brittle starts to set quite quickly and will be fully set after 30 to 40 minutes. It can then be easily released by gently twisting the baking pan. Break the brittle into pieces (I use the end of a rolling pin to do this) and serve.

Damson plum jam

Damson plums come and go so quickly that it's best to pick or buy some whenever you come across them. They make one of the very best jams, wonderful on toast and as a topping to porridge. If you have lots of fruit, make a batch as described below, and try another batch with 1 tablespoon finely chopped candied ginger or 1 whole vanilla pod. Both flavors are excellent with plums.

Yields 4 pint jars
* 2 ¼ pounds damson plums (or other red plums)
* 3 ¾ cups granulated sugar

Place a saucer in the fridge, ready for when you come to test for setting point later on.

Halve the damsons. Don't pit them at this stage—it's too much bother. You can take them out later as they rise to the surface.

Put the fruit and sugar into a heavy-based, stainless-steel pan with 1 ¼ cups warm water. Stir them all together, then allow to stand for 1 hour.

Place the pan over a gentle heat and warm slowly to dissolve the sugar completely, stirring regularly for 10 minutes. The pits will rise to the surface—remove them with a slotted spoon.

Turn up the heat to bring the fruit to a rolling boil. Keep stirring if it's sticking on the bottom and boil for about another 15 minutes.

Pull the pan off the heat and test for setting point. Take the saucer from the fridge and place a teaspoonful of the juice on it. When cool, it should wrinkle when you push it with your finger. You could also use a jam thermometer here; when it reaches around 220 degrees, the mixture will set.

Pour into dry, warm, sterilized jars (you can sterilize them in a very hot dishwasher, or boil them in a pan of water for 10 minutes). Seal each jar and process in a boiling-water bath according to jar manufacturer's instructions. Label with the date. This jam stores for at least a year. Once opened, it should be kept in the fridge and eaten within a month.

Blackberry and apple curd

Packed with delicious autumn flavors, this luxurious curd is great with homemade scones and clotted cream, or to fill a classic Victoria sponge cake (see page 308). Curds, which are made with egg, can't be brought up to boiling point because they would curdle, so they don't keep as long as jams and are best eaten within a week of opening.

Yields 6 to 7 small half-pint jars
* 2 ¼ pounds blackberries
* ⅔ pound cooking apples, peeled, cored, and roughly chopped
* ½ cup (1 stick) unsalted butter
* 6 eggs
* Juice and grated zest of 2 lemons
* Juice and grated zest of 1 lime
* 5 cups granulated sugar

Put the blackberries and apples into a large, heavy-based, stainless-steel pan with ⅔ cup water and bring to a boil. Reduce the heat and simmer for 20 minutes, until the fruit is soft. Put the fruit into a sieve and push the pulp through into a mixing bowl. Chuck anything left in the sieve.

Clean the pan, add the butter, and melt on a very low heat. Beat the eggs lightly and add to the pan, along with the remaining ingredients and the strained fruit. Cook the mixture, stirring almost continually, until it thickens (about 10 minutes).

Pour the curd into dry, warm, sterilized jars (you can sterilize them in a very hot dishwasher, or boil them in a pan of water for 10 minutes). Seal each jar and process in a boiling-water bath according to jar manufacturer's instructions. Label with a date. Unopened, the curd will keep for about 3 months in the fridge, or 6 weeks in a cool, dark place, such as a pantry. Once opened, keep in the fridge and eat within a week.

Chili jelly

Apart from having a pure, beautiful color, this savory jelly is delicious on grilled corn, with any meat or fish, or with bread and cheese.

Yields 4 pint jars
* 4 ½ pounds tart apples or crabapples, unpeeled
* ¾ cup cider vinegar
* 4 cups granulated sugar
* 6 jalapeño or medium-hot chilis, 3 red, 3 green, sliced into rings, deseeded if you want less heat

Place a saucer in the fridge, ready for when you come to test setting point later on.

Roughly chop the apples, core and all, and place in a large, heavy-based, stainless-steel pan with enough water to cover. Bring slowly to a boil. Cover and simmer until the apples are soft (about 20 minutes). Add the cider vinegar and boil for 5 minutes.

Strain overnight through a jelly bag or cheese-cloth into a large glass or china bowl. Don't be tempted to squeeze the bag as this will make the jelly cloudy.

Measure the juice (4 ½ pounds apples will yield about 1 quart of juice), and for every 2 ½ cups weigh out 1 pound of sugar. Pour the juice into a large, heavy-based, stainless-steel pan and add the sugar. Stir over a gentle heat to dissolve the sugar completely.

Add the chilis, then raise the heat and boil vigorously for about 15 minutes. Pull the pan off the heat and test for setting point. Take the saucer from the fridge and place a teaspoonful of the juice on it. When cool, it should wrinkle when you push it with your finger. You could also use a jam thermometer here; when it reaches about 220 degrees, the mixture will set.

Leave to stand for at least 20 minutes, then stir once more to ensure the chilis are distributed evenly through it. Taste to check that it's spicy enough— you can add a few more chilis at this stage, but remember that it will get hotter during storage.

Pour the jelly into dry, warm, sterilized jars (you can sterilize them in a very hot dishwasher, or boil them in a pan of water for 10 minutes). Seal each jar and process in a boiling-water bath according to jar manufacturer's instructions. Label with the date. Unopened, the jelly keeps for at least a year. Once open, store in the fridge and eat within a couple of weeks.

Chili sherry

Jane Dunn from Stone House, a lovely hotel near us in Sussex, gave me this recipe from India. Don't drink it, but use it in your cooking. One or two teaspoons makes all the difference to stews, sauces, and soups (it transforms a consommé).

Yields 2 pint bottles
* 1 (750-ml) bottle sweet sherry
* 10 hot chilis

Divide the sherry between 2 dry, warm, sterilized bottles (you can sterilize them in a very hot dishwasher, or boil them in a pan of water for 10 minutes).

Add 5 chilis to each bottle, then seal, label with the date, and leave to steep for 3 months. Once opened, use within 6 months.

Rosehip jelly

Rosehip jelly has a beautiful, slightly aromatic flavor. Try to gather your rosehips quite early on in the autumn, when they are lovely and fresh and full of vitamin C. This recipe can also be used to make hawthorn jelly, which is tart and tangy, excellent with strongly flavored meats, such as lamb and venison.

Yields 2 to 3 half-pint jars
* 2 pounds rosehips
* 3 1/3 pounds apples
* Juice and grated zest of 1 large lemon
* Granulated sugar

Place a saucer in the fridge, ready for when you come to test for setting point later on.

Wash the rosehips, but don't worry about removing all the stalks as everything is going to be strained later. Place the hips in a heavy-based, stainless-steel pan with just enough water to cover. Bring to a boil and simmer gently, stirring occasionally and topping up with water if necessary. The rosehips are cooked when soft and mushy: this can take up to an hour.

Now wash the apples and chop roughly, core and all. Place them in another heavy-based pan and add enough water to cover all the fruit. Add the lemon zest, then bring slowly to a boil and cook for about 20 minutes, until the apples are soft and mushy, adding a little extra water if necessary.

Put the cooked apples and rosehips into a jelly bag or cheesecloth and allow to drip overnight into a ceramic or glass bowl. Don't be tempted to squeeze the bag or the jelly will be cloudy.

Measure the juice and for every 2 1/2 cups weigh out 2 1/2 cups granulated sugar. Pour the juice into a clean saucepan, add the sugar and lemon juice, and allow to simmer, stirring to help dissolve the sugar. When the sugar has dissolved, turn up the heat and boil for about 10 minutes. Skim any scum off the surface.

Pull the pan off the heat and test for setting point. Take the saucer from the fridge and place a teaspoonful of the juice on it. When cool, it should wrinkle when you push it with your finger. You could also use a jam thermometer here; when it reaches 220 degrees, the mixture will set.

Pour or ladle into dry, warm, sterilized jars (you can sterilize them in a very hot dishwasher, or boil them in a pan of water for 10 minutes). Seal each jar and process in a boiling-water bath according to jar manufacturer's instructions. Label with the date.

Unopened, the jelly keeps for years. Once open, store in the fridge and eat within a couple of months.

Mint and apple jelly

Apple forms the base of many a fine herb jelly.

This classic mint jelly is a good color and delicious with lamb, but I also love it with sausages and couscous.

You can adapt this recipe to make rosemary, sage, or thyme jelly. For easy identification, put a sprig of the relevant herb (dipped for a second into boiling water to sterilize it) in the jars just before the jelly sets.

into dry, warm, sterilized jars (you can sterilize them in a very hot dishwasher, or boil them in a pan of water for 10 minutes). Seal each jar and process in a boiling-water bath according to jar manufacturer's instructions. Label with a date.

To give the mint flavor time to infuse, leave for a week or two before using. The jelly will keep unopened for up to a year, but once opened, refrigerate and eat within about a month.

Yields 4 pint jars

* 4 ½ pounds cooking apples, unpeeled
* Large bunch of fresh mint, coarsely chopped, plus 1 heaping tablespoon finely chopped mint
* ¾ cup white wine vinegar
* 3 ⅓ cups granulated sugar

Place a saucer in the fridge, ready for when you come to test setting point later on.

Roughly chop the apples (cores and all) and place in a large, heavy-based, stainless-steel pan with enough water to cover them. Add the coarsely chopped mint and bring to a boil. Pour in the vinegar and continue cooking until the apples are really soft (about 30 minutes).

Pour the mixture into a jelly bag or cheesecloth and leave to drip overnight into a large glass or ceramic bowl. Don't squeeze the bag as this will make the jelly cloudy.

Measure the juice and for every 2 ½ cups, weigh out 2 ½ cups of granulated sugar. (The amount of apple used here gives about 3 ½ cups juice.)

Put the juice and sugar in a large, heavy-based, stainless-steel pan and stir over a gentle heat until the sugar is completely dissolved. Boil vigorously for about 15 minutes, then pull the pan off the heat and test for setting point. Take the saucer from the fridge and place a teaspoonful of the juice on it. When cool, it should wrinkle when you push it with your finger. You could also use a jam thermometer here; when it reaches 220 degrees, the mixture will set.

Skim the surface with a spoon in order to get rid of any scum. Let the jelly stand for 20 minutes to cool, then stir in the finely chopped mint. Pour

Apple membrillo

Membrillo is a set fruit jelly traditionally made from quinces, but as quinces can be difficult to find, try making it with apples instead. It's fantastic on a cheeseboard.

Yields about 4 ½ pounds
* 4 ½ pounds cooking apples (or half apples and half quinces), peeled and cored
* About 5 cups granulated sugar
* 1 teaspoon ground cinnamon

Line a couple of shallow baking pans with parchment paper or oil a mold.

Roughly chop the apples (and quinces if you have them) and place in a pan with 1¼ cups water. Cover and stew gently until the fruit is soft (about 20 minutes).

Strain or mouli the fruit and measure the quantity. For each 2½ cups puree, weigh out 1⅔ cups sugar. Combine in a heavy-based, stainless-steel saucepan and heat gently until the sugar has completely dissolved.

Add the cinnamon, raise the heat, and bring to a boil. Stirring almost continuously to prevent it from catching, reduce by about two-thirds. As it reduces, it will spit, so cover your stirring hand with a cloth. Between stirs it's a good idea to put a wire splash guard over the pan. This does not seal in the heat, but stops the mixture from spitting all over the cooker.

Keep on the heat for about an hour (but it can be 1½ hours, depending on which fruit you use), stirring every few minutes, until the mixture turns a lovely reddish-brown and begins to come away from the side of the pan as you stir. When the spoon leaves a definite trail, pour the mixture into the prepared pans or mold. Cover with a kitchen towel and leave at room temperature for 2 to 3 days for the mixture to dry out a little.

Cut the membrillo into 6 by 6-inch squares. Wrap them in waxed paper and store in an airtight container. They will keep for at least a year.

You can cut smaller cubes if you wish and roll them in superfine sugar—delicious to eat as sweets or with cheese.

Apple chutney

Here is an excellent way of using up windfalls of fruit, or reducing the inevitable glut if you have an apple tree. This chutney is one of the best things to eat with a lunch of bread and cheese.

Yields 5 pint jars
* **4 ½ pounds cooking apples, cored, peeled, and chopped into small pieces**
* **3 cups golden raisins**
* **2 medium onions, finely chopped**
* **1 heaping tablespoon mustard seeds**
* **1 heaping tablespoon coriander seeds**
* **1 teaspoon chili powder or flakes**
* **1 tablespoon ground ginger**
* **1 teaspoon ground cloves**
* **3 ½ cups white wine vinegar**
* **4 cups brown sugar**
* **Juice and grated zest of 2 oranges**

Place the apples, golden raisins, onions, and spices in a large, heavy-based, stainless-steel pan with about two-thirds of the vinegar. Bring to a simmer, then cover and continue to simmer for about 30 minutes, until all is completely cooked.

Meanwhile, place the sugar in a small pan, pour the remaining vinegar over it, and heat gently until dissolved. Add to the apple mixture along with the juice and zest of the oranges. Simmer with the lid off until thick, stirring occasionally so it doesn't stick. Remember that chutney thickens if kept for a while, so err on the wet, sloppy side.

Ladle into dry, warm, sterilized jars (you can sterilize them in a very hot dishwasher, or boil them in a pan of water for 10 minutes). Seal each jar and process in a boiling-water bath according to jar manufacturer's instructions. Label with the date.

Unopened, this chutney keeps for years. Once open, store in the fridge and eat within a couple of weeks.

Zucchini and apple chutney

It's almost impossible to keep up with home-grown zucchinis and get to all of them before they turn too tough. Even if you're not growing them, zucchinis are among the cheapest vegetables in the late summer and autumn.

This recipe is a savory alternative to the traditional sweet zucchini and ginger jam. It's great with cold meats, pies, and a plate of bread and cheese. Leave out the chili for less heat.

Yields 3 pint jars
* **1 ½ pounds zucchini, peeled, seeded, and cut into 1-inch chunks**
* **1 ½ pounds apples, peeled, cored, and cut into 1-inch chunks**
* **2 ¼ cups light brown sugar**
* **1 large onion, finely chopped**
* **¼ cup finely chopped candied ginger**
* **1 ¼ cups cider vinegar**
* **1 teaspoon ground cloves**
* **2 teaspoons ground ginger**
* **1 teaspoon chili flakes**

Put all the ingredients into a heavy-based, stainless-steel pan. Place over a gentle heat and bring to a boil, stirring all the time to prevent the chutney from sticking. Simmer gently, uncovered, for 1 ½ hours, or until the chutney is thick, stirring frequently so it doesn't stick or burn.

Allow to cool slightly, then pour the chutney into dry, warm, sterilized jars (you can sterilize them in a very hot dishwasher, or boil them in a pan of water for 10 minutes). Seal each jar and process in a boiling-water bath according to jar manufacturer's instructions. Label with the date.

This chutney is best kept for a couple of months before eating as the flavor improves with storing. Unopened, it keeps for years. Once open, store in the fridge and eat within a couple of weeks.

Elderberry vinegar

This recipe is from Mary and John Stratton of Stratta oils and vinegars in Sussex. Elderberries are everywhere in the late summer and autumn, and make one of the best-flavored vinegars, giving a sweet sharpness to any dressing—a splash is excellent with Pigeon salad (see page 365)—and adds good extra flavor to duck or red meat gravies.

Yields about 2 pint bottles
* 1 pound elderberries
* 3 cups white wine vinegar
* 1¼ cups superfine or granulated sugar

Use a fork to strip the berries from their stalks. Place the fruit in a glass container and add the vinegar. Leave to steep for at least a week.

Strain off the fruit and discard.

Warm the strained vinegar and add the sugar, stirring until it's dissolved. Bring slowly to a boil and simmer for 10 minutes before pouring into dry, warm, sterilized bottles (you can sterilize them in a very hot dishwasher, or boil them in a pan of water for 10 minutes). Seal the bottles and cool. The vinegar can be stored for up to 2 years.

Red pepper and onion relish

I like the freshness of this relish—delicious served with burgers or sausages.

Yields 3 pint jars
* 7 sweet red peppers, deseeded and finely chopped
* 3 onions, thinly sliced
* 3 sticks of celery, finely chopped
* ¾ cup dark or light brown sugar
* 1½ cups cider vinegar
* 1 teaspoon peeled and grated fresh ginger
* 2 teaspoons smoked paprika (not hot)
* 1 tablespoon mustard seeds
* 3 garlic cloves, crushed
* 1 teaspoon salt

Put the vegetables and all the other ingredients into a large, heavy-based, stainless-steel saucepan or flameproof casserole. Bring gently to a boil, then reduce to a low simmer for 1 to 1½ hours. Stir the mixture regularly to prevent sticking or burning, as that would affect the flavor.

Pour into dry, warm, sterilized jars (you can sterilize them in a very hot dishwasher, or boil them in a pan of water for 10 minutes). Seal each jar and process in a boiling-water bath according to jar manufacturer's instructions. Label with the date.

This relish will last for several months. Once open, keep in the fridge and eat within a month.

Pumpkin and chili chutney

Late in the autumn you'll see pumpkins everywhere. As well as making Halloween lanterns from them, use at least one to make chutney. This recipe, from a friend, Pauline Tiplady, is particularly good when made with quite a densely textured pumpkin, such as Italian jam pumpkin or red kuri, and it's lovely with the widely available butternut squash.

Yields 2 pint jars
* 1 pound pumpkin, peeled, deseeded, and chopped into small pieces
* 1 cup white wine vinegar
* 2¼ cups light or dark brown sugar
* 1–2 red chilis, deseeded and finely chopped
* 1-inch piece of fresh ginger, peeled and finely chopped
* 6 garlic cloves, finely chopped
* 1 medium onion, finely chopped
* ⅔ cup raisins
* 1 tablespoon salt

Place the pumpkin in a heavy-based, stainless-steel pan with 2½ cups water. Bring to a boil and cook for about 15 minutes, until tender. Add the vinegar and sugar, stir well, and bring back to a boil. When the sugar has dissolved add the remaining ingredients and cook rapidly for 45 to 50 minutes, stirring well. Leave to cool.

Pour the chutney into dry, warm, sterilized jars (you can sterilize them in a very hot dishwasher, or boil them in a pan of water for 10 minutes). Seal each jar and process in a boiling-water bath according to jar manufacturer's instructions. Label with the date.

Store in a cool place for at least couple of months before opening as the flavors will improve. Unopened, it keeps for years. Once open, store in the fridge and eat within a month.

Bean chutney

A glut of Romano beans is almost inevitable if you grow them yourself, and they're cheap and abundant at greengrocers too, so it's handy to have a good pickle recipe up your sleeve. Some can be quite boring and others a little slimy, but not this one. It's excellent with pork pie and bread and cheese.

Yields about 3 pint jars
* 1¼ cups light brown sugar
* 3 medium onions, thinly sliced
* 1½ teaspoons mustard seeds
* ½ teaspoon ground black pepper
* 1 teaspoon salt
* 3½ cups malt vinegar
* 2 pounds Romano beans or regular green beans (or a mix), strings removed and thinly sliced (about ¼ inch) on the diagonal
* 2 heaping teaspoons turmeric
* 1 heaping teaspoon mustard powder
* 1 tablespoon cornstarch

Place the sugar, onions, mustard seeds, black pepper, salt, and half the vinegar in a large, heavy-based, stainless-steel pan and bring to a boil. Lower the heat and simmer gently for 10 minutes, or until the onions are soft.

In a separate pan, cook the beans in boiling salted water for 5 minutes, or until tender. Drain and add them to the onion mixture, along with the rest of the vinegar, and simmer for 20 minutes.

Place the turmeric, mustard powder, and cornstarch in a small bowl, add a little cold water, and stir to make a runny mixture. Add to the vegetable pan and simmer gently for a further 15 to 20 minutes, stirring until the cornstarch has thickened the mixture.

Allow the chutney to cool slightly, then pour into dry, warm, sterilized jars (you can sterilize them in a very hot dishwasher, or boil them in a pan of water for 10 minutes). Seal each jar and process in a boiling-water bath according to jar manufacturer's instructions. Label with the date.

This chutney is best kept for a couple of months before eating as the flavor improves with storing. Unopened, it keeps for years. Once open, store in the fridge and eat within a couple of weeks.

Spicy pickled beans

Rather than leaving them on the plant to toughen, pick beans when they're small and bottle them whole in preserving jars. Thin haricots verts are the nicest, but baby Romanos are also delicious. These spicy beans are fantastic in a bloody Mary, and I love eating them as an aperitif instead of olives.

Yields 2 pint jars
* 1 pound small green beans, ideally about 3 inches long, topped and tailed
* 1 tablespoon pickling spice
* 1 tablespoon black peppercorns
* 2 ½ cups white wine vinegar
* ½ teaspoon salt
* ¼ cup granulated sugar
* 3 bay leaves
* Large bunch of fresh dill, chopped
* 1 garlic clove
* Juice and thickly pared peel of 2 oranges
* 1 red chili, deseeded and chopped

Bring a large pan of water to a boil, add the beans, and boil for 1 minute. Drain well.

Place the pickling spice and peppercorns on a small square of cheesecloth and tie with string to make a bag. Place in a large, stainless-steel saucepan with the vinegar, salt, sugar, bay leaves, dill, garlic, orange juice, and peel. Cook the mixture over a low heat, stirring until the sugar has dissolved, then bring to a boil, reduce the heat, and simmer for 10 minutes. Remove the cheesecloth bag, bay leaves, and garlic clove. Leave to cool.

Pack the beans upright into dry, warm, sterilized jars (you can sterilize them in a very hot dishwasher, or boil them in a pan of water for 10 minutes). Make sure the beans are at least 1 inch below the top of the jars. Add the chili and pour in the vinegar mixture. Seal each jar and process in a boiling-water bath according to jar manufacturer's instructions. Label with the date.

These beans are best kept for a couple of months before eating as the flavor improves with storing. Unopened, they keep for years. Once open, store in the fridge and eat within a couple of weeks.

Pickled ginger

Many of us have been introduced to pickled ginger through eating sushi and other Japanese food, but it's fantastic with stir-fried cabbage, coarsely chopped Autumn roasted vegetables (see page 295), and as an accompaniment to Asian salads (see pages 32 and 168). In Japan they introduce a pink coloring from the deep purple form of an herb called perilla or shiso. As this may be difficult to find, I've suggested using beets instead.

Yields 2 pint jars
* 1 pound fresh ginger, peeled weight
* 2 cups rice vinegar
* 2 tablespoons granulated sugar
* 1 tablespoon salt
* 2 lemongrass stalks
* 4 star anise
* 2 slices fresh beets

Slice the ginger as thinly as possible (a mandoline is good for this, and quick). Place in a bowl, cover with boiling water, and allow to steep for 3 to 4 minutes. Stir a couple of times, then drain in a colander.

Put the vinegar, sugar, and salt into a heavy-based, stainless-steel pan and bring to a boil, stirring until the sugar and salt have dissolved.

Place the ginger, lemongrass, star anise, and slices of beets in dry, warm, sterilized jars (you can sterilize them in a very hot dishwasher, or boil them in a pan of water for 10 minutes). Pour over the vinegar mixture. Seal each jar and process in a boiling-water bath according to jar manufacturer's instructions. Label with the date.

Leave for a couple of days before using. Once opened, store in the fridge, where they will keep almost indefinitely. The vinegar may eventually turn cloudy, but this does not affect the flavor.

Blackberry and apple gin

Sloe gin has had a renaissance recently—even Gordon's, the distilling company, is making it now—so for a more unusual spirit, try adding some other fruits, such as blackberry and apple. After a couple of months, strain off the alcohol and eat the fruit with yogurt or ice cream. If you can't eat the whole lot in one go, return it to a clean bottle and top up with some new spirit. In this recipe the apple can be swapped for pear, and the gin for vodka, if you prefer. Serve as a delicious liqueur or as an aperitif mixed with tonic water and lots of ice.

Yields about 1 quart
* **1½ cups granulated sugar**
* **1 apple, peeled, cored, and finely chopped**
* **1½ cups blackberries**
* **1 (750-ml) bottle gin**

Using a funnel, pour the sugar into a large, sterilized bottle (you can sterilize the bottle in a very hot dishwasher, or boil it in a pan of water for 10 minutes). Add the fruit and then the gin. Seal tightly, then label with the date and store in a dark place. Turn the bottle as often as you can to dissolve the sugar gradually.

After 3 months, strain off the alcohol and place in dry, warm, sterilized bottles (prepared as described above). Seal and label with the date. The drink will keep for years.

Sloe or plum vodka or gin

Excellent for making a holiday party, this is also ideal as a Christmas present. The damsons left after the vodka is strained can be eaten with ice cream or yogurt.

Yields about 1 quart
* **1 pound sloes or plums**
* **1 (750-ml) bottle vodka or gin**
* **About 1¾ cups superfine sugar**

Remove any stems from the fruit and prick with a fork. If you're doing a large batch and can't face pricking every one, shove the sloes or damsons into the freezer overnight: this will break the skins, but doesn't affect the flavor.

Place the fruit in a large, sterilized preserving jar with the alcohol and sugar. (You can sterilize the jar in a very hot dishwasher, or boil it in a pan of water for 10 minutes.) If you prefer things less sweet, add less sugar (about 1¼ cups). You can always add a little more at the re-bottling stage, once you have tasted it.

Close the jar tightly and store in a dark place for 2 to 3 months, turning it as often as you remember—ideally every few days—until the sugar has completely dissolved. After 3 months, strain off the alcohol and pour into warm, dry, sterilized bottles (prepared as described above). You can add more sugar to taste at this point, if you like. Seal, label, and date the bottles. The contents will keep for years.

Elderberry robb

In northern Europe this non-alcoholic elderberry syrup is used regularly in the autumn and winter to stave off colds and flu. It's exceptionally high in vitamin C and generally very good for you. It's also deliciously versatile: try it drizzled over vanilla ice cream; drink it like kir with white wine or champagne; or splash it like bitters into a vodka and tonic.

Yields 2 half-pint bottles
* **2 ¼ pounds elderberries**
* **Granulated sugar**

Place the elderberries in a saucepan with 2 to 3 tablespoons water to prevent them from burning. Simmer slowly, crushing the berries until all the juice is extracted. Strain through a sieve into a bowl. Measure the juice, and for every 2 ½ cups weigh out 2 ½ cups of sugar. Place the juice and sugar in a large, heavy-based, stainless-steel pan and boil for 20 minutes: the mixture should become thick and syrupy.

Pour into dry, warm, sterilized bottles (you can sterilize them in a very hot dishwasher, or boil them in a pan of water for 10 minutes). Seal and label with the date.

Unopened, this syrup keeps for up to a year. Once open, store in the fridge and drink within a couple of weeks.

Danish glögg

This is the best of all spicy, hot red wine recipes to serve at a holiday party. I included it in my Christmas book, but it's here again because it knocks the socks off the usual over-sweet mulled wine or *Glühwein*.

Yields about 12 glasses
* **1 orange, studded with 10 cloves**
* **²/₃ cup raisins**
* **4–5 shot glasses of aquavit (if you can't find this, brandy, Madeira, or rum will do)**
* **2 (750-ml) bottles of red wine (as good as you can afford—good wine equals good *glögg*)**
* **2 cinnamon sticks**
* **1–2 tablespoons superfine sugar, or to taste**
* **Thickly pared zest of ½ lemon**
* **¾ cup whole, peeled almonds**

Place the clove-studded orange and the raisins in a bowl with the aquavit, cover, and marinate overnight.

Pour 1 cup of the red wine into a large saucepan and add the cinnamon sticks, sugar, and lemon zest. Heat up the mixture but don't allow it to boil. Meanwhile, drain the marinated fruit. Take the saucepan off the heat. Add the marinated fruit and the almonds. Cover and leave to steep for at least 30 minutes.

Add the remaining wine to the pan and heat up once more, again taking care not to let it get near boiling point. Serve in mugs or glasses, with a spoon in each to scoop up the nuts and fruit.

Blackberry champagne cocktail

Champagne with a shot of blackberry gin is perfect for an autumn party. It's equally good with elderberry or sloe gin.

Serves 1
* Blackberry and apple gin, bought or homemade (see page 333)
* Champagne or prosecco, chilled
* Sugar cubes (optional)

Put a small splash of blackberry gin into a champagne glass and top up with champagne. You can add a sugar cube in the bottom of the glass for extra potency, but I don't like it so sweet.

Spiced pear Bellinis

Fragrant with cardamom and cinnamon, this is an excellent autumn drink for a party. For a shortcut, buy bottled pear juice or puree, and add the spices before you pour in the champagne.

Serves 8
* 3 ripe pears, peeled, halved, and cored
* Juice and grated zest of ½ lemon
* ⅔ cup superfine sugar
* 10 cardamom pods, seeded
* Small cinnamon stick or ½ teaspoon ground cinnamon
* 1 bottle champagne or prosecco, chilled

Put the pears, lemon juice and zest, sugar, and spices into a saucepan with 2 cups water. Bring to a boil and simmer for 15 minutes, until the pears are soft. Allow to cool.

Put 4 of the pear halves into a food processor and whizz to a puree, adding 2–3 tablespoons of the cooking syrup.

Spoon 1 tablespoon of pear puree into each flute and top up with champagne or prosecco. Cut slices from the remaining poached pears and add one to each flute.

Ginger beer

The taste of ginger beer always makes me think of our autumnal firework parties. Drink it straight, or add beer to make it into shandy. For something more potent, mix with a shot of whisky.

Yields enough for 2 (1.5-liter) bottles
* 1 lemongrass stalk
* 2 tablespoons peeled and grated fresh ginger
* Juice of 2 lemons and thinly pared zest of 1
* 1¼ cups superfine sugar
* ½ teaspoon cream of tartar
* 1 teaspoon dried yeast
* Ice and fresh mint leaves, to serve

Give the lemongrass stalk a bash with a rolling pin. Put this, plus the ginger, lemon juice and zest, sugar, cream of tartar, and 5 cups water into a large pan. Heat gently, stirring to dissolve the sugar, then simmer for 5 minutes. Allow to cool a bit, then add 1 quart of water and sprinkle over the yeast. Cover with a lid and leave overnight.

Strain off the liquid and pour into plastic bottles (there is too much pressure for glass), leaving a space of 1½ to 2 inches at the top to allow for the fizz. Screw the lids on tightly and drink after 24 to 48 hours with loads of ice and fresh mint leaves.

Apple, ginger, and lime juice

A juicer is needed for this recipe, but it's worth having one anyway so that you can use up the tons of fruit around in the autumn. This apple juice is a great soft drink for a party, but can be mixed with vodka to make something stronger. You can store it in the fridge for a few days, but it's best drunk straight away. If you like a sharp juice, use tart apples. For something sweeter, choose Jonagold or Gala.

Serves 4
* 2¼ pounds apples
* 1 tablespoon peeled and coarsely chopped fresh ginger
* Fresh mint leaves (6–8 stems)
* Juice of 1 lime (if using sweet apples, you might want 2 limes)
* Crushed ice

Juice the apples with the ginger and mint (you should end up with about 2½ cups of juice). Add the lime juice and pour into glasses over crushed ice. Drink this straight away because, even with the lime juice, it will discolor in time.

WINTER

I enjoy winter, with the build-up to Christmas, and I've even come to like January. For many of us, it's a month to hibernate—spending those first few weeks of the year tidying up our lives, reading, planning, sleeping, and trying not to eat and drink as much as we have been.

That can't go on forever—life would be too boring—and by early February, most of us are ready to get back to seeing friends and cooking a few big weekend lunches and dinners. You need tempting food in February—it's the dreariest month of the year. It's my birthday and I know it's not the best month to have a big party. Everyone tends to feel gloomy and gray, but cooking—trying some new and enticing recipes—is an ideal way to lift the spirits.

When it's cold, you want hearty, meal-in-one soups—big bowls of cock-a-leekie or winter minestrone—and it's just the moment for traditional comfort food: a well-cooked fish pie, or a smoked fish and cheese soufflé, or, for meat-lovers, old-fashioned dishes such as toad-in-the-hole, cottage pie, or venison casserole. Finish off with a stalwart British dessert, such as queen of puddings or brandysnaps with ginger and lemon cream, and you'll be cheered by the people around your table.

Many of us crave interesting, strongly flavored food when it's cold. Indian, Moroccan, or Indonesian-inspired dishes, such as onion bhajis, the fragrant lamb soup harira, or a coconutty fish curry all come into their own now. These have plenty of fragrant, warming spices—turmeric, ginger, cumin, cinnamon, most with a spike of chili—just what you need in the depths of winter.

Our good intentions to purge ourselves of Christmas (or even a whole year's) excesses can linger into the early months, and many of us will be happy to be served salads and healthy beans and peas, deliciously cooked. Cold leafy salads don't hold much appeal in the winter, but warm salads with wilted greens, or winter flavors, such as duck and pigeon, are perfect, as are winter gratins, soups, and spicy stews using Puy lentils or chickpeas. It's nice to have a few partyish versions of these up your sleeve for big weekend dinners.

And this is the time of year for making marmalade—a great thing to do if you have friends for the weekend. It makes the house smell fantastic and everyone can help chopping peel, and then go home with a jar or two. January and February are the only times when the shops are full of bitter Seville oranges, as well as the very best tangerines and clementines. If you don't feel like making marmalade now, buy the fruit and put it in the freezer for when you do. Freezing the fruit does not affect the quality of the final marmalade.

Of course, winter also means Christmas, when everyone eats three times as much as they do at other times of the year. Some of us really go for Christmas. For others, it lasts only a day. Either way, brief or long, you want good food, straightforward, reliable, and easy to do, so that you—the cook—can actually enjoy the whole performance.

Prosciutto and arugula rolls

If you're having drinks before a lunch party, it's a good idea to make some quick and simple canapés to have at the same time. These I love—a salad in a prosciutto roll.

Yields 20 rolls
* 1 tablespoon poppy seeds
* 1/3 pound arugula (fine-leaved wild arugula is ideal)
* 20 slices prosciutto

For the dressing
* 3 tablespoons extra virgin olive oil
* 1 tablespoon lemon juice
* 1 teaspoon brown sugar
* Salt and black pepper

Toast the poppy seeds in a small pan over a medium heat for 2 to 3 minutes.

Combine the dressing ingredients in a clean, empty jam jar. Secure the lid and give it a good shake.

Put the arugula into a large bowl and pour over enough dressing to lightly dress the leaves. Add the toasted poppy seeds and toss.

Place a slice of prosciutto on a chopping board, sit some of the dressed arugula on it, and roll up. Serve immediately as the arugula will start to go limp if left sitting.

Grilled sweet potato on rosemary sticks

Although this recipe is included in my *In Season: Cooking with Vegetables and Fruits* cookbook as a vegetable side dish, I now like serving it as a canapé—small chunks of sweet potato spiked on rosemary sticks. While this is a bit fiddly, it's worth it, particularly if you have vegetarians to feed. Serve with napkins.

Yields 24 (1-inch) chunks
* 2 medium sweet potatoes
* 3 tablespoons extra virgin olive oil
* 12 rosemary stems or cocktail sticks

For the dressing
* Juice and grated zest of 1 lime
* Small bunch of cilantro, chopped
* 1 tablespoon honey
* 2-inch piece of fresh ginger, peeled and grated
* 1 mild red chili, deseeded and finely chopped
* 1 garlic clove, crushed
* Salt and black pepper

Peel the sweet potatoes and cut into chunky slices about 1/4-inch thick. Blanch in boiling water for a couple of minutes. Drain them and allow to dry. Put the slices in a bowl and, while still warm, smother with the olive oil.

To cook on the stove, preheat a cast-iron grill pan until very hot. Grill the sweet potato slices in batches for 3 to 4 minutes on each side, until soft and beginning to brown. Set aside and keep warm.

Alternatively, preheat the oven to 350 degrees. As you must cook the potato slices in a single layer, place them on 2 grill pans, or a grill and a baking sheet lined with a silicone mat and cook in the oven for about 8 minutes, or until soft and beginning to brown. This method is less smoky than grilling on the stove.

Mix all the dressing ingredients together and drizzle over the sweet potatoes while still warm. Cut into bite-sized chunks and spear a couple on each rosemary stick. These are at their best hot, but are also good cold.

Parmesan, Stilton, and black olive cheesy sticks

These cheesy sticks are so easy to make and have a delicious, intense flavor—a good mix of strong cheese and hot paprika.

Yields about 20 sticks
* ¼ pound Parmesan cheese, freshly grated
* ¼ pound Stilton cheese, grated
* 2 teaspoons cumin seeds
* 1 teaspoon hot paprika
* 20 black olives, finely chopped
* Salt and black pepper
* ½ pound packaged puff pastry
* Flour, for rolling out
* 1 egg, beaten

Preheat the oven to 400 degrees. Put out a couple of silicone mats, or oil a baking sheet, or line it with lightly oiled parchment paper.

Put the two cheeses, cumin seeds, paprika, olives, salt, and pepper into a bowl, stirring to combine.

Roll out the pastry on a floured surface to about 6 by 12 inches. Brush with a little beaten egg and sprinkle with a third of the cheese mixture, spread evenly all over the pastry. Fold the bottom third of the pastry up and the top third down to cover it. Roll out as before and repeat the process twice with the remaining cheese mixture. Finish by rolling the pastry into an 8 by 12 inch rectangle. Brush with a little beaten egg.

Starting parallel with one of the short ends, cut the pastry into strips ½ to 1 inch wide. Holding one end, twist the other end to give the strips a spiral shape. Place on the silicone mats or prepared baking sheet and bake for 10 to 12 minutes, until risen and golden brown.

Cool slightly, then place on a wire rack. These are best served warm.

Duck rillettes

I had this dish with my friend Kitty Ann at a party and have made it countless times since. Perfect for making several days in advance, this rich pâté is ideal served on little Crostini (see page 25) as canapés, and great on toast as a quick starter over Christmas. It also makes a lovely present, packed into a bowl and wrapped in cellophane and ribbon.

Serves 10
* 1 (5 ½-pound) duck, cut into quarters
* 3 ⅓ cups dry white wine
* 1 large onion, roughly chopped
* 8 juniper seeds, crushed
* 2 bay leaves
* Sprig of fresh thyme or 1 teaspoon dried thyme
* Salt and black pepper

Preheat the oven to 400 degrees.

Lightly prick the skin of the duck pieces with the tip of a sharp knife. Put them into a flameproof casserole and place in the oven, without the lid, for 40 minutes to melt the fat. Carefully drain away the fat and place the casserole over a low heat on the stovetop.

Pour in just enough wine to cover the duck. Add the onion, juniper, herbs, and a little salt and pepper. Cover and bring to a boil. Simmer gently for 1½ hours, or until the meat is falling off the bones.

Strain the juices into a mixing bowl, then skin the duck and shred the meat into the bowl of juices. Mix well and season to taste. Put into the fridge to chill, stirring every 30 minutes or so, until firm.

Spoon into a serving dish and freeze until needed, or pour a little clarified butter over the top, decorate with bay leaves and peppercorns, and store in the fridge for up to a couple of weeks.

Belgian endive boats filled with pantzarosalata

The contrast between the brilliant purple of the beet and walnut puree and the pallor of the Belgian endive makes this one of the best-looking winter canapés. It's also good in a mix of mezze to start a meal any time through the autumn or winter. Serve with bowls of stuffed vine leaves, tzatziki (see page 268), hummus, and pita or Rosemary flatbread (see page 244).

Yields 20 endive boats
* 1 large beet (about ⅓ pound)
* ¼ cup chopped walnuts
* 2 tablespoons white bread crumbs
* 1 garlic clove
* 6 tablespoons olive oil
* 4 teaspoons red wine vinegar
* ½ teaspoon salt
* 3 heads of Belgian endive

Cook the beet in boiling water for about 40 minutes, until soft to the point of a knife. Once cooked and cool enough to handle, peel it and chop coarsely.

Put the beet in a food processor with all the other ingredients apart from the chicory, and blend together until smooth.

Separate the chicory into individual leaves. Spoon a little of the beet mixture into each chicory leaf and arrange on a shallow plate.

Marinated olives

These are delicious served in a medium-sized bowl surrounded by a circle of endive leaves to scoop them up with. They are also great thrown into salad leaves for a quick tasty salad with crumbled feta cheese.

Serves about 15 to 20
* 1 pound large, plump green olives with pits in (these tend to be better quality)
* 2 garlic cloves, very finely chopped
* 2 large shallots, very finely chopped
* 2 sticks of celery, very finely chopped
* 3 tablespoons extra virgin olive oil
* 2 tablespoons white wine vinegar
* Pinch of chili flakes (optional)
* Grated zest of 1 lemon
* Juice of ½ lemon
* 2 tablespoons finely chopped fresh basil
* 1 tablespoon finely chopped fresh chives
* 1 tablespoon finely chopped fresh oregano or marjoram
* 1 teaspoon honey
* Salt and black pepper
* 2 heads of Belgian endive, to serve

Pit the olives if you have the time. If not, buy the best possible pitted olives.

Mix all the ingredients together in a bowl and stir thoroughly. Cover and leave in the fridge for 2 days.

Take out of the fridge a couple of hours before serving—olives are always best served at room temperature—and give another good stir.

Cock-a-leekie

With this traditional British soup, you usually cook the chicken with the vegetables—to give flavor—then take it out to eat cold at a separate meal. I think it's better with the chicken removed, carved, and then a chunk or two of meat put back in each bowl.

Serves 8 as a starter, 6 for lunch
* 1 large onion, thinly sliced
* 2 tablespoons olive oil
* 4 leeks, thinly sliced
* 3 sticks of celery, thinly sliced
* 2 large carrots, chopped
* ¼ pound smoked ham, diced
* 1 small free-range chicken (about 2 ½–3 pounds)
* 1 teaspoon ground allspice
* 1 bouquet garni (2 bay leaves, 1 sprig of rosemary, 1 sprig of thyme tied together with string)
* Salt and black pepper
* 10 pitted prunes, cut into quarters
* 2 tablespoons long-grain rice (optional)

To serve
* Freshly grated Parmesan cheese
* Parmesan and dill seed toasts (see page 359)

In a large saucepan, fry the onion gently in a little oil for 5 minutes. Add the leeks, celery, carrots, and ham and continue to fry gently for another 10 minutes.

Place the chicken in the pan and cover with plenty of water. Add the allspice, bouquet garni, and a pinch of salt and pepper. Bring to a boil, cover, and simmer very gently for 1 hour (or a little longer for a bigger chicken), skimming the top occasionally.

After 30 minutes, add the prunes—these give a delicious sweetness and are a traditional addition—and you can also add a little rice 10 minutes before the end of the cooking time. If the soup is too thick, add a little more water at this stage.

Taste and season. Take out the chicken and carve into generous chunks.

To serve, put a bit of chicken in the bottom of each bowl and cover with the soup. Top with a little grated Parmesan and serve with the toasts to make a good meal.

Avgolemono

This is a fresh, light, traditional Greek soup, using many of the same ingredients as British cock-a-leekie. It's comforting and deliciously tangy with the flavor of lemon and herbs. Add small chunks of chicken to make this a more substantial meal.

Serves 4
* 2 organic or free-range chicken breasts
* 4 ¼ cups good chicken stock, ideally homemade
* ¼ cup white long-grain rice
* 2 egg yolks
* ¼ cup lemon juice
* 1 tablespoon finely chopped fresh tarragon or chives, plus extra to decorate
* Plenty of flat-leaf parsley, roughly chopped

Cut the chicken into bite-sized chunks. Put into a saucepan, add just enough stock to cover, bring to a boil, and simmer gently for 5 minutes. Add the rice and the rest of the stock, and cook until the rice is soft. There should be enough liquid left to make it "soupy." Set the pan aside to cool down until lukewarm.

In a decent-sized bowl, whisk the eggs yolks and add the lemon juice. Carefully whisk in some of the lukewarm soup liquid, mixing well. Continue adding and stirring to equalize the temperature of the two liquids, then pour this concoction into the main pan.

Put the pan back on the heat, gently whisking until the soup thickens a bit. Take off the heat and add the tarragon and parsley. Taste and adjust the seasoning, and squeeze in some more lemon juice (as needed).

Ladle the soup into bowls, and decorate with some more tarragon or chives. Eat right away as this soup is tricky to reheat.

Winter minestrone

This recipe involves quite a bit of vegetable peeling and chopping, but a big pot of chunky minestrone makes the perfect lunch with homemade bread, and is ideal for feeding lots of people. Chervil is a winter-growing herb and, if you can find it, its delicate taste works well. If not, use parsley.

Serves 8 to 10
* 1 medium onion, finely cubed
* 1 leek, thinly sliced
* ¼ pound pancetta or bacon, cut into little chunks
* 3 tablespoons olive oil, plus extra for serving
* ¼ small rutabaga (about ¼ pound), peeled and cut into small chunks (optional)
* 2 carrots, peeled and cut into thin slices
* 3 large sticks of celery, thinly sliced
* Large bunch of chervil, chopped
* 2 quarts vegetable, lamb, or chicken stock
* 1 chili, deseeded and finely chopped (optional)
* 1 (14 ½-ounce) can of tomatoes
* 1 cup white or red wine
* ¼ pound spaghetti, broken up, or 1 (15-ounce) can of chickpeas, drained
* ½ pound cabbage or kale, stems removed and cut into thin strips
* Large bunch of flat-leaf parsley, coarsely chopped (stems included)
* Plenty of salt and black pepper
* Freshly grated Parmesan cheese, to serve

In a large pan, sweat the onion, leek, and pancetta in the oil for 7 to 8 minutes. Add the rutabaga, carrots, and celery, and cook gently for 5 more minutes. Add most of the chervil, keeping some aside for decoration, the stock, chili (if using), tomatoes, and wine. Bring to a boil and simmer gently for about 20 minutes.

Add the spaghetti (or chickpeas) and cook for a further 5 minutes. Throw in the cabbage for the last 3 minutes, and finally the parsley for the last few seconds. Taste, and season generously.

To serve, ladle into bowls, topping each one with a slurp of extra virgin olive oil, a little chopped chervil, and some grated Parmesan.

Cream of celery root and Jerusalem artichoke soup

This creamy, smooth-textured soup is lovely as a starter for a big winter dinner, but since it's so filling don't serve large bowls of it. This recipe would be plenty for eight people for a one-course lunch served with Parmesan and dill seed toasts (see page 359), and is fantastic with a swirl of truffle oil.

Serves 10 as a starter, 8 for lunch
* 2 onions, chopped
* 2 tablespoons olive oil
* 2 tablespoons butter
* 1 ½ pounds Jerusalem artichokes
* 1 ½ pounds celery root
* Bunch of flat-leaf parsley, finely chopped
* 2 quarts vegetable or chicken stock
* ½ cup heavy cream
* Salt and black pepper
* A little truffle oil, to serve
* Parmesan and dill seed toasts (see page 359), to serve

Fry the onions in the oil and the butter very gently until soft (about 10 minutes).

Peel the artichokes, discarding the knobby bits, and chop coarsely. Peel the celery root, cut into slices, and chop coarsely. Add both of these to the pan and sweat with the onion for 5 minutes. Add the parsley and stock and simmer for 20 minutes.

Puree well in a blender or with a hand blender. Add the cream and season carefully. Heat through, but do not allow the soup to boil.

Drizzle a little truffle oil on top of each bowl of soup as you serve, and put a plate of Parmesan and dill seed toasts in the middle of the table.

Curly kale and almond soup

For anyone who has cooked and liked Kale and chickpea curry, one of my favorite recipes from the *In Season: Cooking with Vegetables and Fruits* cookbook, this soup—using curly green kale, almonds, and chickpeas—is a must.

Serves 4 to 6
* 2 small red onions, finely chopped
* 3 garlic cloves, finely chopped
* 2 sticks of celery, finely chopped
* Extra virgin olive oil
* 1 (15-ounce) can of chickpeas, drained
* 2 cups good vegetable stock
* ¼ cup ground almonds
* 8 big leaves of curly kale or 12 leaves cavolo nero, stems removed if the leaves are large
* ¼ cup grated sharp Cheddar cheese

Gently cook the onions, garlic, and celery in a little olive oil until soft. Add the chickpeas and toss them in the oil, taking care not to break them up.

Add the stock and bring to a simmer. Stir in the ground almonds.

Roughly chop the kale and add to the pan, ensuring that everything is covered by the creamy stock.

Cover and cook gently for 5 minutes, or until the kale is just tender but still bright green. Puree half the soup in a food processor, and then combine with the coarser-textured half left in the pan. You might need to thin it a little with more vegetable stock.

Add the grated Cheddar, stir gently, and serve immediately.

Leek, sage, and lima bean soup

This is a substantial winter soup/stew—good with a sprinkling of crispy bacon or chorizo and fried sage leaves, as well as plenty of grated Parmesan.

Serves 8 as a starter, 6 for lunch
* 3 tablespoons olive oil
* 1 large onion, roughly chopped
* 3 leeks, roughly chopped
* 2 garlic cloves, roughly chopped
* 1 large parsnip, peeled and roughly chopped
* 3 sprigs of sage (about 30 leaves), half roughly chopped and half left whole
* 6 cups vegetable or chicken stock
* ⅓ pound dried lima beans, soaked overnight and cooked, or 1 (15-ounce) can of lima beans
* 1 teaspoon ground cloves
* Salt and black pepper

To serve
* ⅓ pound bacon, pancetta, or chorizo, cut into small chunks
* Olive oil
* Freshly grated Parmesan cheese

Heat the olive oil in a large, heavy-based pan and add the onion, leeks, garlic, parsnip, and chopped sage leaves. Cover and allow to sweat over a low heat for 10 minutes, stirring occasionally.

Add the stock, lima beans, ground cloves, and a little salt and pepper, then simmer gently for 15 to 20 minutes. Take off the heat and allow to cool a little to bring out the flavors.

Fry the remaining, whole sage leaves and bacon in a little olive oil until crisp.

To serve, ladle the soup into bowls and scatter the sage, bacon, and plenty of grated Parmesan over the top.

Moroccan harira with sorrel sauce

This is a traditional soup/stew—a meal in itself—eaten to break the month-long, daylight fasting of Ramadan. It's fragrant and spicy, typically served with little bowls of lemon juice to pour into the soup as you eat. It's also excellent with a swirl of sorrel sauce on the top. If you have leftovers, eat them with rice and yogurt the next day.

Serves 8 as a starter, 6 for lunch

For the stock
* Bones from the lamb
* 1 large carrot, halved
* 1 onion, quartered
* 1 stick of celery, halved
* 1 bay leaf
* 2 large sprigs of thyme
* Salt and black pepper

* 2¼-pound middle neck of lamb, filleted and boned (you want to end up with about 1 pound meat)
* ¼ cup olive oil
* 2 onions, chopped
* 2 sticks of celery, chopped
* 3 garlic cloves, finely chopped
* Small bunch of flat-leaf parsley, chopped
* 1 tablespoon peeled and finely chopped fresh ginger
* 24 ounces tomato puree
* ½ cup lentils
* 1 teaspoon turmeric
* 1 teaspoon ground pepper
* 1 teaspoon ground cinnamon
* 1 teaspoon smoked paprika
* 1 teaspoon ground ginger
* 1 tablespoon ground cumin
* 1 (15-ounce) can of chickpeas, drained
* Juice of 1 lemon
* Small bunch of cilantro, chopped
* Lemon wedges, to serve

For the sorrel sauce
* ¼ pound sorrel leaves, stems removed
* 1 cup plain yogurt
* 2 garlic cloves, crushed
* ¼ cup extra virgin olive oil
* Juice and grated zest of ½ lemon, to taste
* Plenty of salt and black pepper

Ideally, make the stock the day before so that the fat solidifies overnight and is easier to skim off the next day (there won't be much). Put all the stock ingredients into a large flameproof casserole with 3 quarts water. Bring to a boil and simmer uncovered until reduced by half (about 45 minutes to 1 hour). Strain the stock through a fine sieve, discarding the bones, vegetables, and herbs. Allow to cool. Pour into a bowl and set aside. If you wish, you could buy lamb stock (or make up vegetable stock) and skip this stage.

Chop about three-quarters of the meat into 1-inch cubes, and the rest into slightly larger cubes.

Heat the olive oil in the large flameproof casserole, adding the onions, celery, garlic, parsley, and fresh ginger and sweat for 5 to 10 minutes. Add the meat, stir to brown for 5 minutes, then add the tomato puree, lentils, and all the spices, and pour over the stock.

Stir well, bring to a boil, and allow to simmer gently for 1 hour, partially covered. Stir the soup every so often. You might need to add extra water if it becomes too dry.

Meanwhile, whizz up all the ingredients for the sorrel sauce in a food processor. Taste and season.

Add the chickpeas and lemon juice to the soup 15 minutes before the end of the cooking time. Taste and season, then mix in the cilantro.

To serve, ladle the harira into large shallow bowls, adding a dollop of sorrel sauce and a wedge of lemon on top of each one.

Cardamom parsnip soup with cilantro

The dominant taste in this creamy-textured soup is cardamom, with the addition of coriander, the brainwave of my younger daughter Molly, who loves it. A decent-sized bowl makes a good autumn or winter lunch and takes only 15 minutes to prepare. It's great with a dollop of tangy plain yogurt—better than cream—on the top.

Serves 6 as a starter, 4 for lunch

* 3 medium onions, chopped
* 1 tablespoon olive oil
* 2 tablespoons butter
* ½ teaspoon turmeric
* ½ teaspoon ground coriander
* 1–2 red chilis, deseeded and finely chopped
* Seeds from 8 cardamom pods (discard the husks)
* 3 medium parsnips, peeled and chopped
* 4 ¼ cups vegetable or chicken stock
* Medium bunch of cilantro, chopped

To serve

* Plain yogurt
* Cilantro, chopped

Fry the onions gently in the oil and butter until translucent (about 5 minutes).

Add the spices and fry for a couple of minutes. Add the parsnips and sweat for 2 to 3 minutes before adding the stock. Cover and simmer gently for 15 minutes, or until the parsnip is tender.

Puree the soup in a blender or food processor. Return to the pan and add the chopped cilantro.

Serve the soup with a dollop of yogurt in each bowl and a final scattering of cilantro.

Soda bread with sunflower and pumpkin seeds

Here's a very quick and easy recipe for when you want almost instant bread on the table. It does not use yeast, so there's no proofing—or waiting for it to rise. You can use white or brown flour, or half and half (as below). The toasted seeds add a nutty flavor. This is delicious with almost any soup, served warm with salty butter.

Yields 1 (1-pound) loaf
* 1¾ cups white bread flour
* 1¾ cups whole wheat flour
* 1 teaspoon salt
* 1 teaspoon baking soda
* 2 tablespoons pumpkin seeds, toasted
* 2 tablespoons sunflower seeds, toasted
* 2 tablespoons butter, melted
* 1¼ cups buttermilk, or plain yogurt thinned with milk

Preheat the oven to 350 degrees. Grease a baking sheet.

Sift the two types of flour into a large mixing bowl. Add the salt, baking soda (carefully measured, as more than a level teaspoon makes the bread slightly bitter), and seeds. Pour in the melted butter and buttermilk and mix well to create a soft dough.

With floured hands, shape into a round about 2 inches thick and place on the prepared baking sheet.

Using a sharp knife, mark into 4 or 6 wedges, then bake in the middle of the oven for 25 to 30 minutes, until the base of the loaf sounds hollow when tapped. Allow to cool on a wire rack.

Parmesan and dill seed toasts

These toasts—an adaptation of a recipe by the famous Scottish chef Claire Macdonald—make an excellent addition to soup, turning it from a starter into a meal. They are also ideal for serving with drinks as a simple canapé. For a change, try making them with half goat cheese, half Parmesan, with a little bit of roasted red pepper on the top.

Yields 24 mini toasts
* 6 thin or medium slices of 2-day-old white bread (don't use sliced white)
* ⅓ pound Parmesan cheese, freshly grated
* 2 tablespoons mayonnaise
* 4 scallions, finely chopped
* 2 teaspoons dill seed
* 2 teaspoons Dijon mustard
* A few drops of Tabasco (optional)

Preheat the broiler.

Use a 1½-inch biscuit cutter or glass to cut circles out of the bread (you should get 4 circles from each slice without using the crust). Put the circles on a baking sheet under the broiler and toast them on both sides for less than a minute (watch it—they burn almost instantly). These can be made a day in advance and stored in an airtight container.

Mix together all the other ingredients (except the Tabasco) and spread on to the toast circles, making sure they are covered as much as possible to prevent the toast underneath from burning.

Toast under the broiler until they are slightly puffed up and golden brown. Drizzle a few spots of Tabasco on to each (if you want) and serve right away.

Quick spelt and mixed seed bread

Spelt is an ancient type of grain, similar to wheat, but with a sweeter, nutty flavor. It creates a filling and sustaining bread that keeps hunger at bay for hours. The various toasted seeds included in this recipe make it delicious and healthy too, with flaxseed in particular being rich in essential fatty acids. The bread keeps well—about two weeks in the fridge in a plastic bag—so you can make several loaves at a time.

Yields 1 (2-pound) loaf
* ¼ cup sunflower seeds
* ½ cup sesame seeds
* ¼ cup flaxseeds
* 3 cups spelt flour
* 3 ½ teaspoons dried yeast
* 1 heaping teaspoon salt

Grease a 2-pound loaf pan.

Toast all the seeds in a dry pan for 5 minutes, tossing regularly to brown but not burn on all sides.

Mix the toasted seeds and all the dry ingredients in a large bowl. Add 2 cups warm water and mix well. This dough doesn't require kneading; just mix and scoop into the prepared pan

Leave to rise for about 1 hour, until it has doubled in size.

Preheat the oven to 400 degrees. Bake the loaf for 1 hour, then remove from the pan and bake for another 5 to 10 minutes. Allow to cool on a wire rack.

Quick caraway bread

Thrown together in an instant, this is one of the easiest and tastiest breads—an Elizabeth David recipe. It needs just one rise and makes a heavy, but wonderful bread. I love it for breakfast with marmalade, and it's excellent for cheese-on-toast fingers to eat for lunch with a big bowl of soup. For those that don't like the taste of caraway, replace it with sunflower seeds or chopped walnuts.

Yields 2 (2-pound) loaves
* 1 tablespoon dried yeast
* 10 ½ cups whole wheat flour
* 1 tablespoon sea salt
* 2 tablespoons caraway seeds

Put the flour and salt in a bowl and add the dried yeast. Add the caraway seeds and mix by hand or with a large fork. Slowly add 3 to 4 cups warm water (you might not need it all) until the dough has the consistency of cold, thick porridge.

Divide equally between two 2–pound loaf pans, or just shape into loaves and place on an oiled baking sheet. Cover and leave in a warm place for about 1 hour to double in size.

Preheat the oven to 400 degrees. Bake the loaves for 30 to 40 minutes. Allow to cool for a few minutes before removing from the pans and transferring to a wire rack to cool completely.

Wilted winter green salad

The colors here—crimson and brilliant green—look good, and when served warm, this is an ideal winter salad. It's excellent as a starter or as a side dish with meat and fish, and also works well as a main dish for a light lunch.

**Serves 6 as a starter or side salad,
4 as a main course**
* ½ pound radicchio or other red-leaf chicory
* ½ pound Savoy cabbage
* 1 tablespoon olive oil
* ⅔ pound prosciutto (about 8–10 slices), baked until crisp
* ½ pound blue cheese, cubed
* Seeds from 1 pomegranate (for removal technique, see page 31)
* ¼ pound arugula

For the dressing
* 1 tablespoon Dijon mustard
* 3 tablespoons lemon juice
* 6 tablespoons olive oil
* Salt and pepper

Tear apart the radicchio and cabbage. Remove and discard the chunkier stems, and cut or tear the leaves into 2½- to 3-inch strips. Place in a pan with a little olive oil and wilt together for a few minutes so that they are warm but still crunchy. Take off the heat.

Lay the wilted leaves out on a large plate and slightly crumble the prosciutto over them. Scatter the blue cheese and pomegranate seeds on top.

Whisk together all the dressing ingredients in a bowl. Just before serving, add the arugula, then dress and toss the whole salad.

Warm lentil, squash, and feta salad

This is something I make often, particularly in January and February, when I want a one-plate dish that's healthy and delicious. Add lots of herbs and individual salad leaves so it's light and leafy. You can replace the squash with 2 or 3 red peppers (roasted, peeled, and torn into strips—see page 264 for an easy technique), and I sometimes add baked or fried speck or prosciutto crumbled over the top. Either with or without the feta, this is also excellent as a side dish with roast lamb or beef.

Serves 8 to 10 as a starter, 6 as main course
* 1 large or 2 small butternut or chestnut squash, peeled, deseeded, and cut into large chunks
* 2–3 red onions, cut into eighths
* 2 tablespoons extra virgin olive oil
* 1 good sprig of rosemary, quite finely chopped
* Salt and black pepper
* 4 ounces vacuum-packed roasted chestnuts, roughly chopped
* 2 red chilis, deseeded and thinly sliced
* Juice and grated zest of 1 lemon
* 3 good handfuls of small-leaf arugula or similar salad leaf
* Large bunch of flat-leaf parsley, chopped
* Large bunch of cilantro, chopped
* 8 ounces feta cheese, crumbled

For the lentils
* 1½ cups lentils, preferably green Puy lentils
* 3 garlic cloves
* 1 good sprig of rosemary or 2 bay leaves
* 2 cups vegetable stock
* 1 cup dry sherry or wine
* 3 tablespoons extra virgin olive oil, plus 2 tablespoons to serve

For the dressing
* 2 tablespoons extra virgin olive oil
* Juice of ½ lemon
* Salt and pepper

Preheat the oven to 375 degrees.

Put the squash and onions into a plastic bag with the olive oil, chopped rosemary, and salt and pepper and toss together well. Empty into a roasting pan. Place in the oven for about 30 minutes, until soft and just beginning to brown on the cut edges. Add the chestnuts 5 minutes before the end of the cooking time to heat through.

Meanwhile, put the lentils into a medium-sized saucepan with the garlic and rosemary sprig. Pour in the stock, sherry, and olive oil and bring to a boil. Cook over a medium heat for about 20 to 25 minutes. Keep an eye on the pan, adding a little more liquid as necessary.

When the lentils are tender but not mushy, drain and remove the garlic and herbs. Add another tablespoon of olive oil, season with salt and freshly ground pepper, and leave to cool a little.

Add the chilis, lemon zest, and juice to the lentils, stirring everything together. Then add the arugula, parsley, and cilantro and lay out on a large serving plate. Check the seasoning.

Scatter with the roasted vegetables and crumbled feta.

Mix together all the dressing ingredients and dress the whole dish. This is best served warm, but also good cold.

Squab breast salad with juniper and pomegranate

I love the gamey taste of squab, and the breasts are what to go for. Cooked and then rested for 10 minutes until just warm, they are tender and delicious, perfect with the sharp, clean taste of juniper, the sweetness of pomegranate, and the strong-tasting peppery leaves. This is one of my favorite starters for a winter dinner, and it's lovely as a main course with mashed potatoes or Potato dauphinoise (see page 399).

Serves 8 as a starter or side salad,
6 as a main course
* 8 squab breasts
* 1 tablespoon juniper berries, crushed
* Flaky sea salt and black pepper
* 3 tablespoons olive oil
* ⅓ cup port
* 1 tablespoon red currant jelly
* Large handful of chicory or dandelion leaves or watercress
* Large handful of sorrel leaves or baby spinach leaves
* Large handful of arugula leaves
* Seeds from 1 pomegranate (for removal technique, see page 31)

For the dressing
* 3 tablespoons extra virgin olive oil
* 1 tablespoon Elderberry vinegar (see page 327) or red wine vinegar
* Salt and black pepper

Put the squab breasts in a bowl with the juniper berries and some salt and pepper. Stir and leave for 30 minutes.

Put the oil in a pan and heat for 2 to 3 minutes, until very hot. Add the whole squab breasts and sear for 2 minutes on each side. Add the port and jelly and stir together for 1 minute, over a medium heat.

Remove the breasts and wrap in foil to rest. Scoop out and discard most of the juniper berries, then reduce the remaining juice slightly and take off the heat.

Combine the dressing ingredients in a bowl and mix well. Wash and dry all the salad leaves, then dress them. Lay the leaves out on individual plates. Scatter the pomegranate seeds over them.

Carve each breast into about 7 or 8 thin slices and lay them out over the top of the leaves. Drizzle the warm reduced juice over everything and serve.

Duck and red cabbage salad with fragrant plum sauce

A brilliant-colored warm salad, with a mix of sweet and savory tastes, this is good for a party. I first made this with some leftover duck, but now do it regularly from scratch. There are quite a few different stages, but the flavors of the main salad improve if made the day before, and all except the duck can be prepared in advance.

**Serves 6 as a starter or side salad,
4 as a main course**
* 1 small red cabbage (about 1½ pounds), thinly sliced
* 4 medium carrots, peeled
* 1 bunch cilantro, roughly chopped
* ¼ cup roughly chopped fresh mint leaves
* 30 slices of Pickled ginger (see page 331)
* Juice of 3 limes
* 1 tablespoon rice wine vinegar
* ½ tablespoon fish sauce
* 1 tablespoon light soy sauce
* 1 tablespoon dark brown sugar
* Salt and black pepper
* 1 (5-pound) duck

For the plum sauce
* 1 pound fresh plums
* 3 garlic cloves, chopped
* 2-inch piece of fresh ginger, peeled and grated
* 1 red chili, deseeded and finely chopped
* 3 heaping tablespoons brown sugar
* 2 star anise
* 1 teaspoon ground cinnamon
* Salt and black pepper
* ¼ cup soy sauce
* 6 tablespoons red wine

To serve
* 1–2 tablespoons shredded Pickled ginger
* (see page 331)
* 3–4 tablespoons chopped cilantro

Discard any tired outer leaves of the red cabbage and cut the rest into quarters, removing the white core. Slice the cabbage very thinly and put into a large mixing bowl.

Using a vegetable peeler, peel and then ribbon the carrots into the same bowl. Now add all the herbs, flavorings, sugar, and seasoning. Stir well, then cover and refrigerate, preferably overnight, allowing the flavors and colors to mingle.

Meanwhile, halve the plums and remove their pits. Place in a heavy-based saucepan with all the other sauce ingredients plus ¼ cup water. Bring to a boil, then simmer for at least 30 minutes, until rich and thick, and most of the liquid has evaporated. As you need only about one-third of the sauce for this recipe, store the rest for another day. Pour the excess into a dry, warm, sterilized jar (you can sterilize it in a very hot dishwasher, or boil it in a pan of water for 10 minutes), then seal and label with a date. The sauce keeps very well in the fridge for a month, and freezes for up to a year.

Preheat the oven to 375 degrees. Rinse the ducks under cold water and pat dry. Put them in a high-sided roasting pan (as they release a lot of fat) and roast for 1 hour and 15 minutes. During this time, drain away the fat a couple of times.

Turn the oven down to 300 degrees and cook for a further 1 hour and 30 minutes, or until the meat is starting to come away easily from the bones.

Remove all the meat from the bones. While still warm, toss in a good coating of plum sauce.

Lay out the cabbage salad on a platter or in a shallow bowl and top with the plum-dressed duck. Scatter with the shredded pickled ginger and cilantro just before you serve.

Celery root salad with apple, pine nuts, and prosciutto

Here is one of the best winter salads, celery root remoulade, taken one step further. Ideal as a starter for a winter dinner or as the main dish for lunch, it's also fantastic topped with a slice or two of smoked eel.

**Serves 6 as a starter or side salad,
4 as a main course**
* Juice of ½ lemon (for acidulating water)
* 1 large celery root (1⅓ to 1½ pounds)
* 2 crunchy apples
* ⅓ pound prosciutto (about 16 thin slices)
* ½ cup pine nuts
* Large bunch of flat-leaf parsley, coarsely chopped

For the mayonnaise
* 2 egg yolks
* 2–3 tablespoons white wine vinegar, or to taste
* 1 tablespoon Dijon mustard
* 1 garlic clove, crushed (optional)
* Good pinch of salt and black pepper
* ¾ cup good sunflower oil
* ⅓ cup light olive oil plus 1½ tablespoons extra virgin olive oil
* 2 tablespoons fennel seeds
* 1 tablespoon chopped lemon thyme (or regular thyme)
* ⅓ cup Greek yogurt
* Lemon juice, to taste

Preheat the oven to 400 degrees. Fill a mixing bowl with water and add a good squeeze of lemon juice.

Peel the celery root and slice it as thinly as you can into big round discs. Slice these discs into julienne (matchsticks) as fine as you can make them. You can use a food processor for this, but you won't get the fineness and mix of shapes and sizes that you get when doing it by hand. The smaller and finer, the better—it's worth it. As you cut them, put the matchsticks into the bowl of acidulated water to keep them from turning brown.

Peel, core, and slice the apples into fine matchsticks and put them in the water with the celery root.

Oil a couple of baking sheets, or line them with parchment paper or a silicone mat. Arrange the prosciutto on them in a single layer and roast in the oven until just beginning to brown and turn crunchy (about 5 minutes). Toast in a pan or roast the pine nuts until they begin to brown. Set aside.

Now make the mayonnaise. Put the egg yolks, vinegar, mustard, garlic (if using), salt, and pepper into a blender, food processor, or mixing bowl. Whizz or whisk until the mixture becomes frothy. Add the oils slowly, one by one, in a steady stream, whizzing or whisking constantly until it thickens. Add the fennel seed and thyme, then mix the mayonnaise with the yogurt to lighten it a little. Add lemon juice to taste.

Drain the celery root and apple matchsticks, pat them dry carefully with a kitchen towel, and put a quarter into a serving bowl. Stir in just enough of the mayonnaise mixture to coat them. Then do another quarter, stirring with the mayonnaise, and continue until the whole lot is evenly and lightly dressed. (Julienned celery root sticks together so densely that if you try to mix a large amount with mayonnaise, you'll get undressed chunks in the middle. It's best to do it bit by bit.)

Stir in the parsley and pine nuts and lay the prosciutto over the top. This also works well individually plated, with two slices of ham or a little chunk of smoked eel over each serving (for a starter), or with three ham slices (for a main course).

It's a dense, filling salad, so don't serve huge portions.

Stilton and celery tart

One of the best winter tarts, with lots of strong flavors, this is best eaten at room temperature when all the tastes merge. The key with any tart is to have very fine pastry and not too much egg.

Serves 6 to 8

For the pastry
* 1⅓ cups unbleached flour
* Pinch of salt
* 7 tablespoons cold butter, cut into chunks

* 2 tablespoons butter
* Splash of olive oil
* 1 large onion
* 3 whole celery hearts (about 1 pound), thinly sliced
* 15 sage leaves, finely chopped, plus 10 whole small leaves for decoration
* Juice and grated zest of ½ lemon
* ½ pound Stilton cheese
* 3 whole eggs
* 1 cup heavy cream

First make the pastry. Sift the flour and salt into a bowl, then rub in the butter until the mixture resembles breadcrumbs. Alternatively, pulse in a food processor. Add just enough cold water for the mixture to bind together. Form into a ball, wrap in plastic wrap, and put in the fridge for at least 1 hour.

Preheat the oven to 350 degrees and preheat a baking sheet until searing hot. Grease an 11-inch loose-bottomed tart pan.

On a floured surface roll the pastry to a thickness of ⅛ inch and use to line the prepared pan, leaving the excess pastry draped over the sides in case it shrinks.

Prick the base of the crust with a fork, line with parchment paper or foil, and weigh this down with baking beans or rice. Place on the hot baking sheet and bake for 15 minutes. Remove the paper and beans and return the crust to the oven for another 5 minutes. Take out of the oven and trim off the excess pastry. Keep the oven on and reheat the baking sheet.

Put the butter and oil in a pan and fry the onion, celery, and chopped sage very slowly for 10 to 15 minutes, until the onions are translucent. Add the lemon juice and zest.

Fill the crust with the celery and onion mixture and crumble over the Stilton. Mix the eggs and cream and pour over. Scatter with the whole sage leaves, pushing them down into the tart a bit. Cook in the oven for 35 minutes, until the top is brown. Serve with a green salad.

Red onion, Parmesan, and rosemary tart

A simple and delicious winter tart made from standard fridge and pantry ingredients, this is ideal for when you want to cook for friends without having to shop. This is a descendant of an Elizabeth David rosemary and onion tart.

Serves 6 to 8
* 1 quantity shortcrust pastry (see page 370)
* 2 tablespoons butter
* 2 tablespoons light olive oil
* 3–4 large red onions, finely chopped
* 1 tablespoon finely chopped rosemary
* 3 eggs
* 1 cup crème fraîche or heavy cream
* 1/3 pound Parmesan cheese, freshly grated
* Black pepper

Preheat the oven to 350 degrees and preheat a baking sheet.

Roll out the pastry and use to make a crust (see page 370).

Put the butter and oil in a pan and fry the onions very slowly for 30 minutes, turning them regularly until you have a sweet and gluey heap. Add the rosemary.

Beat the eggs with the crème fraîche and all but 2 tablespoons of the Parmesan.

Spoon the sweet onions into the tart crust and pour over the cheese/egg mixture.

Sprinkle the remaining Parmesan and some black pepper over the top and bake in the oven for 30 to 35 minutes, until the tart is cooked and set in the middle.

Allow to cool a little before eating. This is good with a peppery-leaved green salad.

Winter garden fritto misto with winter herb green mayonnaise

This is one of my favorite things to have for a party—a plate of mixed tempura sitting in the middle of the table. Don't try to do this for too many people, and minimize what has to be done at the last minute. You can make the mayonnaise in advance and steam all the vegetables that need pre-cooking, but the tempura is best eaten straight from the pan to the table. Use all or just some of the vegetables listed below. The lemons are an interesting and key ingredient, taught to me by Rose Gray of the River Café.

Serves 8 to 10 as a starter

For the mayonnaise
* Large bunch of mixed winter green herbs, half flat-leaf parsley, the other half made up from chervil, sorrel, and/or fennel
* 2 egg yolks
* 2–3 tablespoons white wine vinegar, or to taste
* 2 garlic cloves, crushed
* ¾ cup good sunflower oil
* ⅓ cup light olive oil and 1½ tablespoons extra virgin olive oil
* Good pinch of salt and black pepper
* Lemon juice, to taste

For the batter
* 1 cup flour
* Salt and black pepper
* 2 tablespoons extra virgin olive oil
* 3 egg whites

* 1 sweet red pepper, sliced
* ½ butternut squash, peeled, quite thinly sliced and lightly cooked
* Small bunch of small or round carrots (about ¼ pound), lightly cooked
* Bunch of spring onions or scallions (about ¼ pound), lightly cooked
* Handful of Brussels sprouts (about ¼ pound), halved and lightly cooked
* ½ cauliflower, broken into small florets and lightly cooked
* 1 fennel bulb, cut into ¼-inch vertical slices, all with a bit of base to hold them together, lightly cooked
* 2 unwaxed lemons, cut into ⅛-inch slices, ends discarded
* Handful of sage tips
* Handful of flat-leaf or curly parsley
* Peanut or sunflower oil, for frying

First make the mayonnaise. Finely chop your herbs by hand or in a food processor. Add the egg yolks, vinegar, and garlic, and whisk for a few seconds. Still whisking, or with the motor running, add the oil in a slow stream, letting the mayonnaise thicken. Start with the sunflower oil, then the light olive oil, and finally the extra virgin olive oil for an extra depth of flavor. Season well and add lemon juice to taste. Set aside.

Now make the batter. Sift the flour, salt, and pepper into a medium bowl and make a well in the center. Pour in the olive oil and stir slowly, combining the flour with the oil. Slowly add enough warm water to loosen the paste, stirring all the time with a balloon whisk, until you have a batter the consistency of heavy cream.

Leave for at least 45 minutes before you use it. Just before cooking, beat the egg whites until stiff and fold gently into the batter.

Preheat the oven to 425 degrees and heat a pan of oil until very hot (about 350 degrees). Dip the vegetables, lemon, and herbs into the batter and shallow- or deep-fry in the oil—not too many at once. Stand back as you add each batch, or use a spit guard. Drain on paper towels, then keep hot in the oven as you work through the pile of vegetables. Scatter with plenty of salt and pepper and serve on a large plate, with the bowl of green mayonnaise sitting in the center.

Onion bhajis with pomegranate raita

This is the ideal starter before Cauliflower and chickpea curry (see right).

Serves 8 as a starter, 4 for lunch
(makes 8 large bhajis)

For the pomegranate raita
* 8 ounces Greek yogurt
* Seeds from 1 pomegranate (see page 31)
* Small bunch of fresh mint, chopped
* Grated zest of 1 lime
* Salt and black pepper

* 2 teaspoons cumin seeds
* 2 teaspoons coriander seeds
* 2 teaspoons yellow mustard seeds
* 2 black cardamom pods, split
* 2 dried chilis, roughly chopped
* 1 teaspoon salt
* 1 large onion, thinly sliced
* ¾ cup chickpea flour
* Juice of 1 lemon
* Small bunch of cilantro, chopped
* Black pepper
* Vegetable oil, for deep-frying

First make the pomegranate raita. Mix the raita ingredients together in a bowl. Season with salt and pepper. Cover and refrigerate until needed.

Place the seeds, cardamom pods, chilis, and salt in a mortar or electric spice grinder and grind to a coarse powder. Put the spices into a bowl with the onion and flour and mix thoroughly to combine.

Add the lemon juice and ¼ cup water and mix to form a sticky batter. Add the cilantro and plenty of freshly ground pepper and stir well.

Fill a deep saucepan with enough oil to reach about one-third of the way up the side, and have a lid or splash-guard on standby. Heat the oil until it reaches about 375 degrees, or until a cube of bread browns in 30 seconds.

Carefully drop spoonfuls of the batter into the hot oil and deep-fry for 2 to 3 minutes, or until golden brown and crisp. Remove from the oil with a slotted spoon and drain on paper towels. Keep them hot in oven while you cook the rest. Serve with the raita.

Cauliflower and chickpea curry

Based on a Prue Leith recipe, this is one of the best vegetarian winter curries, a delicious mix of flavors to eat with rice and/or pappadams, pomegranate raita (see left), and perhaps some flash-fried spinach with garlic and cumin.

Serves 3 to 4
* 4 garlic cloves
* 2-inch piece of fresh ginger, peeled
* 3 green chilis (optional)
* 2 tablespoons sunflower oil
* 1 medium onion, finely chopped
* ½ teaspoon ground black pepper
* ¼ teaspoon ground turmeric
* ¼ teaspoon ground coriander
* 1 teaspoon ground cardamom
* 1 teaspoon ground cumin
* 1 (14 ½-ounce) can of tomatoes
* 1 medium cauliflower, cut into even-sized florets
* 1 (15-ounce) can of chickpeas
* Salt
* Large bunch of cilantro, to serve

In a food processor or blender, combine the garlic, ginger, chilis (if using), and ⅔ cup cold water. Blend to a smooth paste.

Heat the oil in a medium saucepan and fry the onion until golden brown. Add the black pepper, turmeric, coriander, cardamom, and cumin and fry for 30 seconds. Now add the garlic paste and the tomatoes and stir until well mixed.

Add the cauliflower, chickpeas, and salt to taste. Bring to a boil, then cover and simmer for 15 to 20 minutes, until the cauliflower is just done—not too soft. Scatter with cilantro leaves and serve with rice, pappadams, and pomegranate raita.

Andrew's fish pie

An old friend Andrew Wallace's gentle fish pie, with a crumb topping. Serve with buttered broccoli.

Serves 6
* 3 ⅓ cups milk
* 3 bay leaves
* 1 ½ pounds fresh haddock fillets
* ⅔ pound undyed smoked haddock
* 9 tablespoons butter
* 1 tablespoon olive oil
* 3 leeks, thinly sliced
* ⅔ pound peeled shrimp
* 6 hard-boiled eggs (optional)
* ½ cup flour
* ½ cup chopped fresh flat-leaf parsley
* Salt and black pepper

For the topping
* 1 ⅔ cups breadcrumbs
* 2 ounces Parmesan cheese, finely grated
* ¼ cup chopped fresh flat-leaf parsley
* Finely grated zest of 1 lemon
* 5 scallions, thinly sliced
* 2 tablespoons butter

Preheat the oven to 325 degrees. Put out a rectangular baking dish 12 by 9 by 3 inches deep.

Pour the milk into a wide, shallow pan. Add the bay leaves and bring to just below a boil. Place the fish in the hot milk. Leave to stand, off the heat, for 5 minutes.

Put 2 tablespoons of butter and the olive oil in a pan and fry the leeks until soft (about 10 minutes). Spread over the bottom of the baking dish.

Remove the fish from the milk, discard the skin, and flake a little. Place it over the leeks. Top with shrimp. Peel and slice the eggs, then add these.

Melt 7 tablespoons of butter and stir in the flour, then the warm milk. Add the parsley and season. Cook for 4 to 5 minutes over a low heat. Pour into the dish, covering the fish.

Put all the topping ingredients except the butter into a bowl and mix. Melt the butter in a pan and stir the topping around in it. Sprinkle the mixture over the sauce. Bake for 30 to 35 minutes in the middle of the oven, until bubbling hot and golden.

Smoked haddock with Lord Dalrymple's top

For an easy Saturday lunch, this is one of my family's favorites. It's an Edwardian recipe from my aunt Fortune Stanley's cookbook, *English Country House Cooking*.

Serves 6 as a starter, 4 as main course
* ⅔ pound undyed smoked haddock
* ¼ cup (½ stick) butter
* ¼ pound spaghetti, broken into small bits
* ½ cup flour
* 1 ⅔ cups whole milk
* Salt and black pepper
* 1 tablespoon Dijon mustard
* Freshly grated nutmeg
* 6 eggs, separated
* ½ pound sharp Cheddar cheese
* 3 tablespoons finely grated Parmesan cheese

Preheat the oven to 400 degrees. Butter 4 large or 6 small ramekins, or an 8 by 3-inch soufflé dish.

Put the haddock in a shallow pan with 2 tablespoons butter and 1 to 2 tablespoons of water and poach gently until just cooked (about 5 minutes). Lift the fish out and flake into large pieces with a fork. Discard the skin.

Meanwhile, cook the spaghetti in boiling salted water for 3 minutes. Drain and add to the haddock (the pasta finishes cooking in the dish).

Melt the remaining butter in a saucepan, add the flour, and stir over a gentle heat for 1 to 2 minutes. Add the milk and fish broth. Season, add the mustard, and cook for 3 to 4 minutes, stirring continuously until the mixture is the consistency of thick heavy cream. Season again and add plenty of nutmeg. Take off the heat and stir in the egg yolks, then the cheese. Fold in the fish and spaghetti.

In a clean bowl, whisk the egg whites into stiff peaks. Stir in one-third of the fish mixture, then carefully fold in the rest with a metal spoon. Pour into the prepared ramekins or soufflé dish, not filling to the top. Bake the ramekins for about 15 minutes, and the large dish for 20 minutes, until browned and risen.

Serve straight from the oven, with a bowl of Lemon-and-anchovy-dressed purple sprouting broccoli (see page 394) and a green salad.

Indonesian fish curry
with mango salsa

Quick and easy to put together—about fifteen minutes from start to finish—this versatile curry can be made with almost any white fish. A minty cucumber salad and some slightly perfumed basmati rice (with a little garam masala added) go well with this.

Serves 4

For the salsa
* 2 ripe mangoes
* Juice and finely grated zest of 1 lime
* 1 small red chili, thinly sliced
* 1 teaspoon superfine sugar or honey (optional)

* 1 pound haddock, cod, or tilapia fillets
* Salt
* 2 tablespoons olive oil
* 1 large onion, chopped
* 2 garlic cloves, chopped
* ¼ teaspoon chili powder or flakes
* ½ teaspoon turmeric
* 1 bay leaf
* 1 lemongrass stalk, outer leaves removed and finely chopped
* 1-inch piece of fresh ginger, peeled and grated
* 2 tablespoons lime or lemon juice
* 1 (13 ½-ounce) can of coconut milk
* Small bunch of cilantro

First make the salsa. Run a sharp knife lengthwise around the mangoes, cutting either side of the long, flat seed. Make a criss-cross pattern in the flesh, being careful not to cut all the way through the skin. Pushing against the skin with your thumbs, turn the fruit inside out so you end up with a "hedgehog" shape. This allows you to easily cut away the cubes of mango from the skin.

Put the cubed mango into a bowl, add the rest of the ingredients, and stir well.

Cut the fish into generous chunks and lightly salt them.

Heat the oil in a pan and gently sweat the onion and garlic for 10 minutes. Stir in the spices, bay leaf, lemongrass, and ginger. Add the lime juice with a splash of water, and simmer until the onions are cooked through.

Add the fish and simmer for a further 5 minutes. Pour in the coconut milk and heat until it bubbles. Taste for seasoning and snip some cilantro over the top before serving with the salsa.

Halibut steak with lentils and a winter salsa verde

When you're in the mood for a hunk of fish, there's nothing better than a halibut steak or fillet doused with a tangy winter salsa verde and some fragrant al dente Puy lentils.

Serves 4

For the lentils
* Olive oil, for frying
* 1 onion, finely chopped
* 2 garlic cloves, finely chopped
* 1 fennel bulb, finely chopped
* 3 sticks of celery, finely chopped
* 1 tablespoon coriander seeds, coarsely crushed
* 1–2 red chilis, deseeded and finely chopped
* 1 1/3 cups lentils, preferably green Puy lentils
* 1 cup white wine
* 2 cups vegetable stock
* 3 tablespoons extra virgin olive oil
* Juice and pared zest of 2 lemons, chopped into strands
* 2 tablespoons capers, coarsely chopped

* 2–3 tablespoons flour
* 1 teaspoon ground cumin
* Grated zest of 1 lemon
* Salt and black pepper
* Olive oil, for frying
* 1 1/3 pounds halibut, cut into 4 (1/3-pound) fillets

For the winter salsa verde
* Large bunch of flat-leaf parsley
* 1/4 pound arugula
* 1/2 cup sorrel, if you can find it (alternatively use 1/4 cup fresh tarragon or chives)
* 2 tablespoons capers
* 2 tablespoons green olives, pitted
* Juice and grated zest of 1 lemon
* 3 tablespoons extra virgin olive oil

First prepare the lentils. Heat a little olive oil in a pan and gently fry the onion, garlic, fennel, and celery until soft. Add the coriander seeds and chili.

Pour the lentils into a pan, stir in the onion mixture, then cover with the wine and stock. Cook gently for about 20 minutes, until the lentils begin to soften but not collapse. Add a little more wine if necessary to prevent them from boiling dry. Add the extra virgin olive oil, lemon juice, zest, and capers. The liquid should be almost all absorbed by the end of the cooking time.

Meanwhile, preheat the oven to 325 degrees and combine the flour, cumin, lemon zest, and seasoning on a plate. Turn the halibut over in it to cover well.

Heat a drizzle of olive oil in a non-stick frying pan over a gentle heat for 2 to 3 minutes. In a good pan, this prevents sticking. Fry the fish on each side for 2 minutes, then transfer to the oven for another 10 minutes.

To make the salsa verde, stem and coarsely chop the herbs with the capers and olives. This is best done by hand with a large knife or mezzaluna so that the texture is not made too smooth. Place in a bowl and mix with the lemon juice, zest, and olive oil.

To serve, put the lentils on a large shallow platter with the fish laid out on top and a good dollop of the salsa verde on the side.

Red Thai curry mussels

Delicious, spicy, and fragrant. Use a good-quality red Thai curry paste. You can serve the mussels on their own, but they're even better with Coconut and cilantro rice (see page 393) to soak up the juice.

Serves 4 to 6
* 3 1/3 pounds mussels
* 3 tablespoons olive oil
* 1 onion, finely chopped
* 1 garlic clove, finely chopped
* 1-inch piece of fresh ginger, peeled and finely chopped
* 1 lemongrass stalk, thinly sliced
* 2 tablespoons Thai red curry paste
* 2 teaspoons dark brown sugar
* 1 1/2 cups fish or vegetable stock
* 1/2 cup white wine
* 2 teaspoons fish sauce (optional)
* Small bunch of fresh basil or cilantro, chopped
* Juice of 1 lime

Clean the mussels under cold running water. Discard any broken or cracked ones and remove the beards.

Heat the oil in a large flameproof casserole. Add the onion, garlic, ginger, and lemongrass and sauté gently for 3 to 4 minutes. Add the curry paste, stirring until you can really smell the spices, then stir in the sugar, stock, wine, and fish sauce (if using). Bring to a boil.

Reduce the heat to a simmer and cook the mussels, covered, for 5 to 6 minutes. Take off the heat and discard any mussels that have not opened.

Stir in all but a tablespoon of the chopped herbs and the lime juice. Serve with or on Coconut and cilantro rice (see page 393), and sprinkle over a little more chopped basil or cilantro.

Scallops in a cream chili sauce

This is a lighter version of the French classic Coquilles Saint-Jacques, a favorite of my father's. One of the first meals I remember cooking was this—for his birthday in December—from a battered book of Constance Spry's recipes. You can serve this in the scallop shells if you can get them from your fishmonger, or put everything together in a heatproof shallow dish.

Serves 6 as a starter, 4 as main course
* Butter
* 1 tablespoon olive oil
* 12 large scallops
* Lemon juice, to taste
* 3/4 cup heavy cream
* 1/2 red chili, deseeded and finely chopped
* A few basil leaves, torn
* Salt and black pepper
* 1 1/4 cups coarse white breadcrumbs
* 1 heaping tablespoon freshly grated Parmesan

Heat 2 tablespoons butter and the olive oil in a frying pan. Fry the scallops for 1 minute on each side. Squeeze over some lemon juice. Add the cream, chili, and basil and cook for 2 minutes. Season to taste.

Melt 1 tablespoon butter in another pan. Mix the breadcrumbs with the Parmesan and fry until crunchy.

Preheat the broiler. Meanwhile, divide the scallop mixture among 4 or 6 individual shells, or put them all into a heatproof baking dish. Scatter with the fried breadcrumbs and dot with tiny bits of butter. Put under the broiler for 2 to 3 minutes, until browned and bubbling.

Serve with mashed potatoes and some wilted spinach.

Jane's venison casserole
with no-suet dumplings

This is a recipe by my twin sister, Jane, and it's one of my favorite winter meals. The secret of this casserole is to let everything steep for a day. This brings out the flavor and makes the meat meltingly tender. Raw meat marinated in red wine dries out, but here the meat is sealed before marinating, which keeps it moist. These dumplings are lovely and lighter than most, but Parsnip balls (see page 292) can be added for a change.

This goes well with almost any winter vegetable: try it with mashed potato and Kale with juniper (see page 394). It freezes well too.

Serves 8 to 10
* 1 pound small shallots, peeled
* Olive oil
* ½ pound bacon or pancetta, chopped into pieces
* 4 large flat mushrooms, sliced
* 3 ⅓ pounds venison, cut into chunks
* 3 tablespoons flour, seasoned with a little salt and pepper
* 1 tablespoon crushed juniper berries
* 1 tablespoon crushed coriander seeds
* 1 tablespoon red currant jelly
* 2 tablespoons chopped fresh herbs, such as rosemary, thyme, and marjoram
* 1 (750-ml) bottle of red wine
* 3 ½ cups beef consommé
* Salt and black pepper

For 12 medium dumplings
* 1 ½ cups unbleached flour
* 2 teaspoons baking powder
* ¼ cup freshly grated Parmesan cheese
* 1 small pinch of ground cloves
* 1 small pinch of allspice
* 2 tablespoons chopped chives
* 1 teaspoon salt
* Pinch of black pepper
* 1 egg, beaten
* ½ cup milk

Fry the whole shallots in a couple of tablespoons of olive oil until they begin to soften. Add the bacon or pancetta and mushrooms and cook for about 5 minutes more. Transfer to a casserole that has a lid.

Roll the meat chunks in the seasoned flour and fry in the same pan until seared on each side. Transfer to the casserole and add all the remaining ingredients up to and including the salt and pepper. Cover and put aside to marinate for at least 12 hours.

Preheat the oven to 350 degrees. Cook the covered casserole for 1½ hours.

Meanwhile, make the dumplings. Sift the flour and baking powder into large bowl. Add the Parmesan, spices, chives, and salt and pepper. Mix in the egg and milk a little at a time. If the dough is a bit sticky, add some extra flour. Using wet hands, form the mixture into 12 small balls.

Take the casserole out of the oven 15 minutes before the end of the cooking time and add the dumplings, arranging them evenly over the top. Cover and cook for 5 minutes, then uncover and cook for 10 more so that the dumplings brown.

Venison fillets with rosemary and juniper

I was brought up on these. A bowl of venison steaks sitting in their marinade was regularly left in the fridge to tenderize for 2 to 3 days. I love them and could eat this at least once a week as a quick, thrown-together but special supper. Serve with Potato bonne femme, Aligot, or Potato dauphinoise (see pages 70 and 399), and crunchy broccoli or Baked red cabbage (see page 392).

Serves 4

For the marinade
* 1¼ cups white wine
* Juice of 2 lemons
* 1 tablespoon honey
* 3 tablespoons extra virgin olive oil
* 2 sprigs of rosemary, leaves finely chopped
* 10 juniper berries
* 3 star anise
* 3 garlic cloves, sliced

* 1¾ pounds venison fillets
* Olive oil, for grilling
* Salt and roughly ground black pepper
* 3 tablespoons red currant jelly

Put all the marinade ingredients into a plastic bag and add the meat. Seal the bag and put into a bowl. You can then turn the ingredients easily whenever you remember. Leave at least overnight.

Preheat a grill pan. Meanwhile, take the fillets out of the bag, reserving the marinade, and dry on paper towels.

Rub each fillet with olive oil, then season on all sides with salt and roughly ground pepper. Place on the grill pan and cook on each side for 2 to 3 minutes, depending on size. Take off the heat and wrap the meat in foil. Leave to rest for 10 minutes.

To make gravy, strain the marinade and pour 2 cups into a pan. Bring to a boil, then lower the heat and slowly reduce by about half. Add the jelly and stir until it has all melted. Season with salt and pepper.

Thinly slice the venison and arrange it on a large warmed plate. Pour over the gravy and serve.

Teresa's fresh cottage pie

There are a million recipes for cottage pie, but of all I've tried, this is the best—a recipe from Teresa Wallace, who has given me huge help, reading and commenting on every recipe in this book. This pie is bigger on vegetables than the traditional pie, making it less dense and very full of flavor. It's ideal for a big weekend winter lunch, served with boiled purple sprouting broccoli and Slow-roasted carrots (see page 397).

Serves 4 to 6
* 2 medium onions, chopped
* Olive oil
* 2 garlic cloves
* ¼ pound cremini mushrooms, sliced
* 2 medium carrots, peeled and finely chopped
* 2 medium leeks, finely chopped
* 1 or 2 sticks of celery, finely chopped
* 1 pound good ground beef
* 1 teaspoon tomato paste
* 2 teaspoons flour
* ⅔ cup red wine
* 1 bay leaf
* 1 sprig of thyme
* A few stalks of flat-leaf parsley, chopped
* Salt and black pepper
* Splash of soy sauce (optional)
* Pinch of cayenne pepper (optional)

For the topping
* About 1 pound baking potatoes, boiled, dried, and mashed with plenty of butter and hot milk
* Several small chunks of butter

In a casserole, fry the onions gently in a little olive oil for 5 minutes. Add the garlic and mushrooms and the rest of the finely chopped vegetables and cook for a further 5 minutes.

Add the meat, stirring to break it up, and brown a little. Add the tomato paste. Sprinkle on the flour and stir until absorbed.

Pour in the wine and enough water to ensure a slightly wet, sloppy texture. Tuck in the herbs, season, then cover and cook very gently for 1½ hours. By this time the mixture should be dark brown and of a thickish consistency. Taste for seasoning—you can add some soy sauce and a sprinkle of cayenne if it needs zipping up. Remove the thyme and bay leaf. Leave to cool for 20 to 30 minutes.

While the meat mixture is cooling, make the mashed potatoes.

Swirl the mashed potatoes on top of the meat using the back of a spoon (this looks nicer than fork marks). Scatter some chunks of butter over the top and it's ready for reheating (at 325 degrees for 20 to 25 minutes) when you want it.

You can make 2 or 3 pies at once as they freeze brilliantly.

Cured beef with beets and horseradish cream

An ideal dish to eat cold on a bright, sparkly winter day, fantastic with peppery and mustardy winter salad leaves and a drizzle of horseradish cream.

Serves 4
* ½ cup superfine sugar
* ½ cup coarse sea salt
* 2 garlic cloves, finely chopped
* Small bunch of thyme and rosemary, finely chopped
* 1 pound beef fillet
* Small bunch of rosemary, to make a "bed"
* 2 tablespoons coarse salt
* 8 small beets, leaves removed, but stems left on
* ¼ pound Balsamic pickled onions (see page 226)
* Handful of winter salad leaves—arugula, cress, ruby chard, and mustard leaves

For the horseradish cream
* 3 tablespoons crème fraîche
* 1 teaspoon Dijon mustard
* 1 tablespoon grated fresh horseradish or good-quality horseradish sauce
* Lemon juice, to taste

For the dressing
* 1 tablespoon honey
* 3 tablespoons extra virgin olive oil
* 1 tablespoon red wine vinegar
* Salt and black pepper

To make the cure, mix the sugar, salt, and garlic with the chopped herbs in a non-metal container. Add the beef—make sure it's completely covered—and leave overnight, or ideally for 24 hours.

Wash the salt mixture off the meat, then pat dry with paper towels. Although the meat is partly "cooked" by the marinade, if you don't like the idea of almost raw meat, it can be cooked a little more by searing in a hot pan for 2 minutes on each side if you wish. Wrap tightly in plastic wrap and place in the fridge until needed.

Preheat the oven to 325 degrees.

Make a bed of rosemary and coarse salt in the bottom of a roasting pan. Sit the beets on top and roast for about 1 hour, until soft to the tip of a knife. Cool a bit, then peel.

Meanwhile, mix together all the ingredients for the horseradish cream.

Cut the pickled onions in half and slice the beets into chunks. Combine the dressing ingredients in a bowl and mix well.

The finished dish looks most elegant served on individual plates. Slice the beef very thinly and put a few slices on each plate. Add a few chunks of beets, 2 or 3 onions, a few salad leaves, a dollop of horseradish cream, and a little dressing drizzled over the top.

Toad-in-the-hole with sage and red onions

This makes the best toad-in-the-hole, a classic English dish of sausages baked in batter. The sweetness of the onion and the smokiness of the sage are great additions. Serve with mashed potatoes and onion gravy (see below) and stir-fried cabbage.

Serves 4
* 1 tablespoon olive oil
* 8 large pork sausages (about 1 ½ pounds total weight)
* 1 large red onion, cut into eighths
* 8–10 fresh sage leaves

For the batter
* 1 ¼ cups unbleached flour
* 2 eggs
* Good pinch of salt
* Black pepper
* 1 ½ cups lowfat milk

For the gravy
* 1 onion, finely chopped
* 2 tablespoons butter
* 1 tablespoon olive oil
* 1 ⅔ cups beef consommé
* Splash of red wine

Preheat the oven to 400 degrees.

Put the oil and sausages into a 16 by 12-inch high-sided roasting pan and cook in the oven for 10 minutes.

Meanwhile, make the batter by putting the flour, eggs, salt, black pepper (a couple of grindings), and milk into a large mixing bowl. Whisk for a few minutes until there are no lumps. Put aside to rest.

Take the sausages out of the oven and turn up the temperature to 450 degrees. After 10 minutes, put the sausages back in the oven for 5 minutes, then pour the batter over them (leaving 2 tablespoons for the gravy). Scatter the onion chunks and sage leaves evenly over the top. Bake for a further 25 minutes, until nicely browned and well risen.

To make the gravy, sauté the onion in the butter and olive oil until soft. Add the consommé and wine and reduce over a gentle heat for 5 minutes. Stir in the remaining batter to thicken. Serve with the toad.

Shredded Brussels sprouts with ginger and toasted almonds

Even those who claim not to like Brussels sprouts will like this recipe. It's good hot, and almost as good cold, with a simple dressing of extra virgin olive oil and lemon juice.

Serves 6 to 8
* 2 ¼ pounds Brussels sprouts
* ¾ cup whole almonds, coarsely chopped
* 2 tablespoons peanut oil
* 2-inch piece of fresh ginger, peeled and grated
* 2 garlic cloves (optional), finely chopped
* Salt and black pepper

Discard the outer leaves of the Brussels sprouts, trim the stems, then grate or thinly slice what's left (the disc on the food processor is best for this).

Toast the almonds in a non-stick pan on top of the stove until they begin to brown, but not burn (2 to 3 minutes), tossing them around to toast all sides.

Heat the oil in a deep frying pan. Add the ginger and garlic and cook together over a medium heat for a couple of minutes. Add the shredded Brussels sprouts and toss in the oil. Sauté and keep turning the Brussels sprouts until heated through, but without losing their texture.

Remove from the heat while the Brussels sprouts are still a nice bright color. Season well and scatter over the toasted almonds.

Thyme-roasted Brussels sprouts with chestnuts

As simple as it gets—ideal for a frantic Christmas Day—these Brussels sprouts look and taste great, with a crunchy texture far removed from those soggy green balls of the past. The Brussels sprouts should be partially browned, which gives a lovely nutty flavor.

Serves 8
* 3 pounds Brussels sprouts
* Bunch of fresh thyme
* ½ cup extra virgin olive oil
* Salt and black pepper
* 7 ounces vacuum-packed chestnuts

Preheat the oven to 350 degrees.

Prepare the Brussels sprouts by pulling away a couple of the outer leaves and cutting a little slice off the base. Cut the Brussels sprouts in half and put into a mixing bowl with the thyme, oil, and salt and pepper. Stir briefly.

Tip the Brussels sprout mixture into a roasting pan in a single layer and roast for 20 to 25 minutes. Halfway through the cooking time, add the chestnuts, mix, and put back in the oven.

Baked red cabbage with apricots

There are masses of recipes for this classic Christmas lunch dish, which is delicious with turkey, but even better with duck. It's also excellent with roast pork or sausages. The version here is the easiest and tastiest of all I've tried. You'll find a little goes a long way with red cabbage. People seldom want to eat a great mound, so don't get carried away. The apricots (or blackberries) make a good Christmassy lunch addition.

Serves 8 to 10
* 2 ¼ pounds red cabbage, cut into ¼-inch slices
* 2 medium red onions, quartered and sliced
* 1 large cooking apple, peeled, cored, and sliced
* 3 tablespoons golden raisins
* 2 cups partially rehydrated dried apricots or defrosted blackberries
* 3 tablespoons balsamic vinegar
* 1 tablespoon dark brown sugar
* 1 teaspoon ground cloves
* 1 teaspoon ground cinnamon
* ¾ cup orange juice
* ¾ cup port
* Grated zest of 1 orange
* Salt and black pepper

Preheat the oven to 350 degrees.

Put all the ingredients into a casserole and stir well. Cover and put in the oven for 45 minutes, stirring and checking once or twice that there's enough liquid: if not, add a little more orange juice. When the cabbage is tender, taste, and season with salt and pepper.

This dish can be made up to a week in advance (the vinegar preserves it for ages) and reheated in the oven just before you want to eat. It also freezes well.

Slow-cooked cannellini beans

A good alternative to potatoes, these beans are ideal with any meat dish. Dried beans, soaked overnight, give a better, less slushy texture than canned, but you can use cans if you're in a hurry. I also like these beans served warm, as the center of a salad, served with lemon-dressed arugula leaves. To make them into a main course, add some fried chorizo slices dressed in lemon juice.

Serves 8
* 2 large onions, finely chopped
* 3 tablespoons olive oil
* 6 garlic cloves, finely chopped
* 1 small celery heart, thinly sliced
* 1 fennel bulb, outer leaves discarded and thinly sliced
* 2 red chilis, deseeded and finely chopped
* 4 sprigs of thyme, leaves chopped
* 3 sprigs of sage (about 20 leaves)
* 1 pound white cannellini beans, soaked overnight, or 2 (15-ounce) cans
* 2 cups vegetable, chicken, or beef stock or consommé
* 2 tablespoons Dijon mustard
* Salt and black pepper

Put the onions and olive oil in a shallow ovenproof pan and fry gently for 10 minutes. Add the garlic, celery, fennel, chilis, thyme, and sage and cook for another 10 minutes.

Preheat the oven to 350 degrees.

Add the beans to the pan and enough stock to cover everything. Bring to a boil on a gentle heat. Cover and transfer the dish to the oven for 2 hours (if using canned beans, cook for only 30 minutes), until the beans are soft but not collapsing. Halfway through the cooking time, check the dish in case the liquid has all been absorbed; if it has, add a little water.

Remove from the oven. Stir in the mustard and season to taste.

Fennel ratatouille

This slow-cooked, sweet ratatouille is particularly good with roast chicken or fish. Although it contains lots of ingredients, it's simple to make. It also becomes a wonderful soup—a sort of winter gazpacho—if pureed and thinned with vegetable or chicken stock.

Serves 6 to 8
* ¼ cup olive oil
* Sprig of fresh thyme
* 1 bay leaf
* 2 teaspoons fennel seeds
* 3 medium onions (about 1 pound), cut into quarters
* 2 sweet red peppers, deseeded and roughly chopped
* 2 garlic cloves, roughly chopped
* 4 fennel bulbs (about 2 pounds), outer leaves discarded and roughly chopped
* 2 (14 ½-ounce) cans of good-quality chopped tomatoes or 2 pounds fresh tomatoes, peeled (see page 125) and chopped
* ½ red chili, deseeded and finely chopped
* Grated zest of 1 lemon
* 1 tablespoon tomato paste
* 1 teaspoon honey
* Salt and black pepper
* Small bunch of fresh dill, roughly chopped
* Handful of black or Kalamata olives, pitted

Heat the oil in a large, heavy-based casserole with the thyme, bay leaf, and fennel seeds. Add the onions, red peppers, and garlic and sauté for 5 minutes. Add the fennel, tomatoes, chili, lemon zest, tomato paste, honey, and a little salt and pepper.

Cover the dish and simmer gently over a very low heat, stirring every so often, for an hour or more. Take the lid off and add the chopped dill and olives. Increase the heat slightly to reduce until the sauce becomes thick and syrupy. Taste, and season with a little more salt and pepper as necessary.

This can be served hot or cold, with a dollop of plain yogurt on the top.

Coconut and cilantro rice

Here's a fantastic rice dish, so full of flavor that I'd almost be happy to eat it on its own. It's lovely with Red Thai curry mussels (see page 381) and ideal with Cauliflower and chickpea curry (see page 374).

Serves 4 to 6
* 2 tablespoons vegetable oil
* 5 scallions, chopped
* 1 fresh green chili, deseeded and chopped
* ¾ cup dried coconut
* 1 ¼ cups jasmine rice
* 1 cup vegetable or fish stock
* 1 (13 ½-ounce) can of coconut milk
* Small bunch of cilantro, chopped
* Salt and black pepper

Heat the oil in a wok or large frying pan and stir-fry the onions, chili, and coconut until lightly browned.

Add the rice and fry for 2 to 3 minutes. Pour in the stock and bring to a boil. Add the coconut milk and simmer for 10 to 15 minutes, until the rice is tender (adding a little extra liquid if gets too dry). Take off the heat. Put the lid on and leave to steam for 2 to 3 minutes.

Stir in the cilantro. Taste, and season with a little salt and black pepper.

Kale with juniper

You can't go wrong with these two classic winter flavors together. They give an incredibly fresh and healthy taste. You can also add some thinly sliced chorizo (fried quickly in a little oil, then dressed with lemon juice) or pancetta to make a more substantial dish.

Serves 4

* 2 pounds kale, all stems removed and thinly sliced
* 1 tablespoon juniper berries, crushed
* 2 garlic cloves, chopped
* Sea salt
* 2 tablespoons peanut oil
* 1 red chili, deseeded and thinly sliced
* 1 tablespoon honey

Blanch the kale in salted boiling water for 3 to 4 minutes, until beginning to soften. Drain and squeeze all the water from the leaves.

Using a mortar and pestle, crush the juniper berries and garlic with the sea salt.

Heat 1 tablespoon of the peanut oil in a large frying pan. Add the chili and cook for 1 minute on a medium heat. Scoop the chili out and set aside.

Add the remaining peanut oil and the honey to the pan, then the kale and juniper mixture. Turn up the heat. Stir every minute or so for 3 to 4 minutes, until cooked.

Serve topped with the fried red chili, which brightens the whole thing up.

Lemon-and-anchovy-dressed broccoli

Purple sprouting broccoli is good just as it is, but the sharp dressing below improves it. The key thing with any broccoli is not to over- or undercook it. Place it in a deep pan of already boiling salted water (this cooks it more evenly than steaming) until the stems are just soft to the tip of a knife. Strain immediately into a colander and plunge into a bowl of cold water. Drain, dress, and serve.

Serves 4

* ¾ pound purple sprouting broccoli or broccolini
* ½ can of anchovy fillets (about 1 ounce)
* 2 garlic cloves, finely chopped
* 1 chili, deseeded and finely chopped
* 3 tablespoons butter
* Juice and grated zest of ½ lemon
* Black pepper

If using broccoli tips, remove the large outer leaves. If you have bigger stems, slice into 1 inch-ish strands.

Cook the stem sections (if you have them) in boiling salted water for 3 minutes, then add the tips, cover, and cook for another 3 minutes. Drain.

Fry the anchovies gently in their own oil until they start to dissolve. Add the garlic, chili, and the butter and just heat through. Add the lemon juice and zest.

Arrange the broccoli in a large shallow dish or on individual plates (both warmed) and toss with the anchovy mixture. Season well with pepper. You shouldn't need salt.

Serve with any strong-flavored casserole or fish.

Mixed root vegetables with a Parmesan and sesame crust

Here's a delicious vegetable dish that can be cooked the day before and then reheated in the oven (at 400 degrees) shortly before you want to eat.

Serves 8
* Olive oil, for roasting
* ½ pound parsnips
* ½ pound carrots
* ½ pound salsify (or replace with more of the other vegetables if you can't find it)
* ½ pound Jerusalem artichokes
* 2 ½ cups fresh brown or white breadcrumbs
* 2 tablespoons sesame seeds
* ⅓ pound Parmesan cheese, freshly grated
* Seasoned flour
* 3 eggs, beaten

Preheat the oven to 375 degrees. Put a lightly oiled roasting pan into the oven and allow it to get really hot.

Peel all the vegetables. Cut the parsnips and carrots into sticks, leave the salsify whole or cut in half, and cut the artichokes into chunks so that all the vegetables are a similar size. Place in a steamer and steam them for 10 minutes.

Mix the breadcrumbs with the sesame seeds and Parmesan. Dip the steamed vegetables in the seasoned flour, then in the beaten egg, and roll them in the breadcrumb/sesame mixture. Put them in the hot oiled pan and roast in the preheated oven for about 35 minutes, until tender and golden.

Slow-roasted carrots with garlic lemon butter

The best way to eat winter carrots is to slow-roast them whole for about an hour: it brings out their sweetness and flavor. This is an ideal vegetable to have on Christmas Day when time and oven space are short, as you can cook them the day before and then just sauté them on the stove with the garlic, lemon, and butter when you're ready to eat.

Serves 8
* 2 ¼ pounds medium carrots, peeled
* Olive oil, for roasting, plus a little for reheating
* 2 tablespoons butter
* 3 garlic cloves, finely chopped
* Juice and grated zest of 1 lemon
* Large bunch of flat-leaf parsley, finely chopped
* Salt and black pepper

Preheat the oven to 325 degrees.

Put the whole carrots into a roasting pan, drizzle a little olive oil over them, and roast for a good hour. Once cooked and cooled, put them in the fridge.

Just before you want to eat, put the butter and a little olive oil into a pan over a medium heat with the garlic, lemon juice, and zest. Add the carrots and toss for about 5 minutes, until warmed through. Scatter with the parsley, season, and serve immediately.

Crunchy rosemary roasted potatoes

This recipe is guaranteed to give you the crunchiest roasted potatoes you've ever had. Use a starchy variety since they make unbeatable roasted potatoes—crunchy on the outside and fluffy in the middle.

Serves 8
* 8 tablespoons goose or duck fat, lard, or olive oil
* 2 ¼ pounds potatoes, peeled and chopped into generous chunks
* Salt and black pepper
* A few sprigs of rosemary, chopped

Preheat the oven to 400 degrees.

Cover the bottom of a roasting pan with a thin layer of the fat (about 6 tablespoons) and put in the oven for 5 minutes to heat through.

Meanwhile, parboil the potatoes for 3 to 5 minutes (depending on variety) in boiling salted water. Drain, put them back in the pan, and dry them off over a low heat for a minute or two, shaking them around a bit to fluff up the outside.

Pour them into the roasting pan and toss in the hot fat or oil. Season with salt and pepper, and scatter the rosemary over them. Heat the remaining 2 tablespoons of fat in a pan and drizzle over the top to ensure that both the herbs and the potatoes are well coated; this will prevent the flecks of herb from burning. Place in the oven and roast for 45 minutes: the potatoes should be perfect.

If you're roasting a turkey in the same oven on Christmas Day, put the potatoes on the top shelf and, while the bird is resting, turn the heat up to 400 degrees for the remainder of the cooking time.

Leek, celery root, and potato gratin

I prefer this gratin to one made just with potatoes. It has a stronger, more interesting taste. I serve this with Christmas lunch, or top it with a grated sheep cheese (such as pecorino) to have with ham for Boxing Day lunch.

Serves 8
* 4 leeks, thinly sliced
* 1 tablespoon olive oil
* 3–7 tablespoons butter
* 1 pound celery root
* 1 pound potatoes
* 5 ounces prosciutto or pancetta
* ¾ cup heavy cream
* Freshly grated nutmeg
* Salt and black pepper
* Hard salty sheep cheese, grated (optional)
* 1 ¼ cups good vegetable stock

Preheat the oven to 350 degrees. Butter an ovenproof dish (approximately 13 by 9 inches).

Gently fry the leeks in the oil and a little of the butter until soft, but not browning.

Peel the celery root and potatoes, and slice them thinly (a mandoline or the slicing disc of a food processor is ideal for this).

Put a mixed layer of celery root and potatoes at the bottom of the prepared dish. Add a layer of leeks and snip over some strips of prosciutto or pancetta. Pour over the cream, then add some grated nutmeg and seasoning. Crumble over some of the cheese (if using), and dot with a little of the butter.

Repeat the layers, pour in the stock, and finish with a layer of cheese. Cover with foil and bake for 1 hour. Remove the foil, dot with the remaining butter if you omitted the cheese, and increase the temperature to 400 degrees to brown the top for about 10 minutes.

Allow to cool for 10 to 15 minutes before serving.

Classic potato dauphinoise

People might worry about the cream and butter content of this dish, but anyone you serve this to will love eating it—it's the potato classic for a party, delicious with any roast or casseroled meat. See also Potato bonne femme (page 70) for a less rich and fattening version.

Serves 6
* 1 cup heavy cream
* 3 bay leaves
* Grated zest of 1 lemon
* 1 shallot, roughly chopped
* 2 ¼ pounds small potatoes
* 3 tablespoons butter, softened
* 1 garlic clove, crushed
* Sea salt and black pepper
* 1 ¼ cups milk

Put the cream into a pan with the bay leaves, lemon zest, and shallot. Bring gently to a simmer, then take off the heat. Remove the bay leaves and allow to cool.

Peel the potatoes and cut into ⅛-inch slices (a mandoline is good for this). Plunge the slices into boiling water for 3 minutes. Drain.

Preheat the oven to 325 degrees.

Put the butter and garlic into a small bowl and mix well. Using about one-third of the mixture, grease a shallow baking dish (a ceramic tart dish is ideal). Arrange the potatoes in layers, sprinkling each layer with a little salt and pepper. Pour over just enough of the milk to cover the potatoes.

Dot the remaining butter mixture over the top and cover with foil. Put into the oven for about 1 hour, until most of the milk has been absorbed. Pour over the infused cream and put back into the oven, uncovered, for a further 30 minutes, until the top is golden.

Aligot

From the Auvergne, where it's served as a course in itself, this marvelous dish of mashed potatoes beaten with garlic, cream, olive oil, and lots of tomme de Cantal cheese (mild Cheddar or Caer-philly are good substitutes) is not for the faint-hearted. It's said that the strongest woman makes the best aligot because it requires a lot of elbow grease, lifting and mixing, lifting and mixing, until the potato is all glossy and smooth. Serve with any strong-flavored meat or fish, or on its own with a green salad. It's also excellent the next day as aligot potato cakes—rolled in quick polenta flour and fried.

Serves 6
* 2 pounds baking potatoes, peeled
* 3 tablespoons butter
* ½ cup light cream
* 3 garlic cloves, crushed and finely chopped
* ¾ pound cheese (see above), grated
* ⅓ cup extra virgin olive oil
* Salt and black pepper

Boil the potatoes in salted water until soft. Drain and mash them.

Heat the butter and cream in a large, heavy-based pan and add the potatoes. Mix well.

Add the garlic, cheese, and olive oil and beat together well for about 5 minutes with a large wooden spoon. Season and serve.

Queen of puddings

People love a traditional British pudding, and queen of puddings is a classic. You can use any fruit jelly or jam—black currant, gooseberry with elderflower, strawberry—but raspberry is the best.

Serves 6 to 8

* 1 ¼ cups fresh white breadcrumbs
* Grated zest of 1 lemon
* ½ cup superfine sugar, plus a little for sprinkling
* 4 eggs, separated
* 2 ½ cups milk
* 2 tablespoons unsalted butter
* 2 tablespoons fruit jam or jelly

Preheat the oven to 350 degrees.

Grease a not-too-shallow gratin dish (9 ½ by 11 inches or 8 by 12 inches) and put in the breadcrumbs, lemon zest, and a little of the sugar (you don't want too much sweetness underneath; the jam and meringue provide enough).

Put the egg yolks into a heatproof bowl. Heat the milk till not quite boiling. Add the butter and pour over the egg yolks, beating hard as you go. Pour this mixture over the breadcrumbs and bake in the oven for about 30 minutes, until the custard is only just firm. You can prepare ahead to this stage.

Warm the jam and spread it evenly and gently over the custard.

Beat the egg whites until stiff, add the remaining sugar (less than traditional meringues), and spread over the custard and jam base.

Sprinkle the top with a little superfine sugar and bake until slightly browned (15 to 20 minutes). This is best served piping hot.

Teresa's apple brown Betty

Lighter than a crumble or an apple Charlotte, this recipe from my friend Teresa Wallace has a delicious buttery crunch. Serve with lots of cream, or Cardamom and poppy seed ice cream (see page 402), which has a delicious nutty taste.

Serves 6 to 8

* ½ cup (1 stick) unsalted butter
* 3 ¼ cups white breadcrumbs
* 1 pound tart apples and 1 pound sweet apples, peeled, cored, and sliced
* ⅔ cup dried cranberries or raisins
* ½ teaspoon ground cloves
* 1 teaspoon ground cinnamon
* 1 teaspoon ground nutmeg
* 2 tablespoons superfine sugar
* 2 tablespoons dark or light brown sugar

Preheat the oven to 325 degrees.

Grease a baking dish (9 ½ by 11 inches or 8 by 12 inches) with about 1 tablespoon of the butter. Stick a good coating of the breadcrumbs onto the butter so that the dish is lined with them. (Save a few spoonfuls for topping the dish.) Melt the remaining butter and set aside.

Layer the apples with the cranberries, spices, and superfine sugar until they are mounded just below the top of the dish.

Scatter the remaining breadcrumbs on top so that they cover the apples. Pour over the melted butter, then sprinkle with the brown sugar. Cook in the oven for about 1 hour.

Cardamom and poppy seed ice cream

This slightly sharp ice cream is delicious at any time of year, but its nutty flavor is excellent with Teresa's apple brown Betty (see page 401), fruit crumble, or baked autumn or winter fruit (see page 305).

Serves 8
* 10 ounces mascarpone
* 5 cups plain yogurt
* 2 ½ cups superfine sugar
* Seeds from 15 cardamom pods
* 4 teaspoons poppy seeds, toasted
* Juice and grated zest of 1 lemon

Put the mascarpone, yogurt, and sugar in a food processor and blend them quickly, or just mix well in a bowl. Stir in the cardamom and poppy seeds.

    Pour the mixture into an ice cream maker if you have one. Freeze/churn for about 20 minutes, then pack into plastic containers and freeze for at least 2 hours before serving. If you don't have a machine, pour into a plastic container and freeze for 1 hour. Remove and fork through, mixing the frozen edges with the soft middle to break up the ice crystals. Repeat twice more at hourly intervals.

    Before serving, allow the ice cream to soften in the fridge for 15 minutes.

Baked egg custard

Egg custard is lovely warm or cold with plenty of nutmeg grated over the top. Serve it with buttered, sugared apples, or any winter fruit compote.

Serves 4
* **Unsalted butter, for greasing**
* **1 vanilla pod**
* **2 ½ cups milk**
* **2 strips of lemon rind, without pith**
* **2 whole eggs**
* **2 egg yolks**
* **1½ tablespoons superfine sugar**
* **Freshly grated nutmeg**

Preheat the oven to 350 degrees. Butter a shallow pie dish.

Using a sharp knife, split the vanilla pod and scrape out the seeds. Put the seeds and pod in a saucepan with the milk and lemon rind and heat to just below the boiling point. Remove from the heat.

In a large bowl beat together the eggs, egg yolks, and sugar. Pour the hot milk over the eggs and stir well. Strain the custard mixture into the pie dish and generously grate over the nutmeg.

Sit the dish in a bain-marie (a wide baking pan containing about 1 inch hot water). Bake the custard on the middle shelf of the oven for about 30 to 35 minutes, or until the custard is set.

Mango and apricot compote

Try this compote as a healthy winter dessert or breakfast—it takes just minutes to make. The dried fruit used here gives an intense, sweetly delicious flavor. Serve with honey and plain yogurt, a traditional Baked egg custard, or Bay-flavored pannacotta (see left and page 407).

Serves 4 to 6
* **1 ½ cups dried mango**
* **1 ½ cups dried apricots**
* **1 tablespoon brown sugar or honey**
* **4 star anise**
* **2 cinnamon sticks**
* **6 cardamom pods, slightly crushed**
* **Apple juice**

Put all the ingredients into a saucepan with just enough apple juice to cover the fruit. Poach gently on a low heat for 8 to 10 minutes.

Individual lime or lemon mousses

Both limes and lemons are at their very best in the winter and early spring—juicy, thin-skinned, and delicious. These individual mousses are perfect for a winter party, and this is the easiest recipe I've come across, with no getting in a fury beating eggs over hot water in a double-boiler. You can make them the day before and leave them somewhere cool, covered in plastic wrap. The fridge is too cold and will cause the gelatin to harden. Note that this recipe contains uncooked egg.

Serves 10
* 5 teaspoons gelatin
* 3 large or 4 medium eggs, separated
* ½ cup superfine sugar
* Grated zest and juice of 5 limes or 3 lemons
* 1 cup heavy cream
* Toasted sliced almonds or Ginger cookies (see page 412), to serve

Put the gelatin in a cup and pour on boiling water halfway up, stirring occasionally.

Using an electric mixer, whip the egg yolks with the sugar until silky and thick. Add the lime or lemon juice and zest.

Whip the cream into soft peaks and add to the yolk mixture.

Make sure the gelatin mixture is lukewarm and completely clear (or you'll get unappetizing little lumps of it in your mousse), then add it in a stream to the yolk mixture while continuing to beat. Stop beating as soon as it is all added so that you don't overbeat.

Rinse the beaters under the tap and dry, then beat the egg whites into stiff peaks in a separate bowl.

Immediately combine the two mixtures gently with a large metal spoon. Transfer to one large serving bowl or 10 individual dishes and leave to set in a cool place. When completely set, sprinkle with toasted sliced almonds or serve with ginger cookies.

Greek yogurt and bay-flavored panna cotta

Add some variety to your baked or stewed winter fruit with this creamy, fragrant panna cotta. It's very softly set—panna cotta at its most delicious—so leave in the ramekins. If you want to turn them out, line the ramekins with plastic wrap, but without adding more gelatin you won't get the most perfect circle. You could also serve this with cranberries (quickly cooked in a slosh of apple juice and sweetened with a little sugar) either put in the base of the ramekins or poured over the top.

Serves 6
* 1 vanilla pod
* 1 cup heavy cream
* ⅓ cup superfine sugar
* 4 dried or 2 fresh bay leaves
* 2 teaspoons powdered gelatin
* 12 ounces Greek yogurt

Using a sharp knife, split the vanilla pod and scrape out the seeds. Put the seeds and pod in a saucepan with the cream, sugar, and bay leaves. Bring gently to a boil.

Turn off the heat. Discard the bay leaves and vanilla pod, then whisk in the gelatin until dissolved, about 2 to 3 minutes.

Put the yogurt into a large mixing bowl and slowly pour the cream mixture on top, whisking to combine.

Spoon or pour into 6 ramekins or small bowls (lined with plastic wrap if you want to turn them out) and allow to set in the fridge.

Black fruit and apple tart

The black fruit puree used here is based on an Elizabeth David recipe, Black tart stuff, from *Spices, Salt and Aromatics in the English Kitchen*. It's a seventeenth-century recipe, and makes the most delicious and unusual dessert, ideal for any time in the winter, but particularly at Christmas. Black fruit puree is "sandwiched" between two layers of sharp apple puree in a sweet crust and topped with a circle of sweeter apples, a wonderful contrast of textures and flavors. The recipe makes enough black fruit filling for two tarts, but you could keep half in a jar as it's lovely with oatmeal or yogurt for breakfast, or as a filling for Sesame-seed brandysnaps (see page 413).

Serves 8 to 10
* ½ cup dried figs
* ½ cup dried prunes
* ½ cup dried apricots
* ⅓ cup raisins
* ⅓ cup golden raisins
* Pot of black tea
* 2 tablespoons finely chopped candied ginger
* 1 teaspoon ground cloves
* 1 teaspoon ground cinnamon
* 1 small glass of port (optional)
* 4–5 tart cooking apples (about 3 pounds)
* 1 heaping tablespoon brown sugar
* Grated zest of 1 lemon
* 2 apples (Granny Smiths are good), peeled, cored, and cut into ¼-inch slices
* 1 tablespoon apricot jam, warmed through
* Confectioners' sugar, for dusting
* 1 cup heavy cream, to serve

For the pastry
* 1¼ cups unbleached flour
* ½ cup (1 stick) cold unsalted butter, cut into cubes
* ¼ cup superfine sugar
* Pinch of salt
* 2 egg yolks

Remove the hard ends from the figs, then soak all the dried fruit overnight in enough tea to cover it well. The next day put the mixture over the heat and stew lightly for 10 minutes, until soft (add a little water if necessary). Strain, keeping the liquid.

Put the stewed fruit in a mouli or food processor. Add the ground cloves and cinnamon and puree it all together, using as much of the cooking liquid as you need to give a thick puree. You will then have what looks like a black sludge—the black tart stuff—with an intense, delicious flavor. Add the port (if using).

Cut the apples into chunks and place in a saucepan with ½ cup water. Add the sugar and lemon zest and cook gently down to a puree (10 to 15 minutes), stirring every so often to prevent sticking (add a little more water if it starts to dry out). Set aside.

To make the pastry, sift the flour into a bowl and rub in the butter until the mixture resembles coarse breadcrumbs. Alternatively, pulse in a food processor. Add the sugar and salt and then the egg yolks one by one, and mix/pulse again until the pastry comes together into a ball. Wrap it in plastic wrap and chill for 1 hour in the fridge.

Grate the pastry into a loose-bottomed 10-inch tart pan, pressing it down with your fingers and pushing it well up the sides. Chill again for 30 minutes. Preheat the oven to 350 degrees and heat a baking sheet until searing hot.

Prick the bottom of the crust with a fork, cover with a circle of parchment paper or foil, and weigh this down with baking beans or rice. Bake for about 10 to 15 minutes, then remove the beans and paper and bake for another 10 minutes to dry the pastry out a little (or until golden). Set the crust aside. Keep the oven on and reheat the baking sheet.

Pour half the apple puree into the crust and then half the total amount of black fruit puree. Add a layer of apple puree on top of that, then arrange the slices of apple in a spiral pattern over the top. Brush with the warmed apricot jam, then place on the hot baking sheet and bake for 15 to 20 minutes, until starting to brown.

Dust with confectioners' sugar and serve with plenty of thick cream.

Lemon and zucchini drizzle cake

You can make this cake at any time of year, but all citrus fruit is good in the winter and early spring. The zucchini adds a brilliant moistness and cuts through the sweetness of this sugary cake. This is my husband, Adam's, favorite.

Serves 10

* ½ cup (1 stick) unsalted butter
* ¾ cup superfine or granulated sugar
* 3 eggs, beaten
* ¼ cup milk
* 1¼ cups self-rising flour
* 2 medium zucchinis, grated
* 1 teaspoon baking powder
* Grated zest of 1 lemon

For the drizzle

* Juice of 2 lemons
* ½ cup superfine sugar

Preheat the oven to 350 degrees. Line a 9 by 9-inch brownie pan with parchment paper.

Beat the butter and sugar together until light and fluffy, then add the eggs and milk bit by bit. Fold in the flour, zucchinis, baking powder, and lemon zest. Pour the mixture into the prepared pan and bake in the oven for 25 minutes.

While the cake is baking, make the drizzle by mixing the lemon juice with the superfine sugar.

Once the cake is ready, remove from the oven. Allow to cool for 5 minutes, then turn out onto a plate. While still warm, pour the drizzle evenly all over the top. Allow to cool completely, then cut into rectangular fingers.

Spicy ginger cake

This is a luscious spicy ginger cake with nice big lumps of candied ginger. It's a recipe of Jo Clark's grandmother, who was brilliant at baking. Jo has helped me hugely with this book and many recipe ideas have come from her family and friends. You can substitute golden raisins for the ginger, or mix them half and half for a milder taste.

Serves 8

* ⅔ cup plus 2 tablespoons self-rising flour
* 2 teaspoons ground ginger
* 1 teaspoon pumpkin pie spice
* 1 teaspoon ground cinnamon
* 1 teaspoon ground cloves
* 2 tablespoons chopped fresh ginger
* 1 teaspoon baking soda
* 2 tablespoons corn syrup
* 2 tablespoons dark molasses
* 3 tablespoons unsalted butter
* ¼ cup dark brown sugar
* 1 egg, beaten
* Confectioners' or superfine sugar, for sprinkling

Preheat the oven to 350 degrees. Line or grease a square 8-inch cake pan.

Sift the flour into a large bowl. Add the spices, chopped ginger, and baking soda.

Heat the corn syrup, molasses, butter, and brown sugar in a saucepan until the sugar has melted, then pour into the dry ingredients. Mix well, then add the egg and ½ cup boiling water and mix again.

Pour the mixture into the prepared pan and bake for 15 to 20 minutes, until firm. Leave in the pan until cooled. Turn out, cut into squares, and sprinkle with a little confectioners' or superfine sugar.

Ginger cookies

These are good on their own with a cup of tea, and ideal for smartening up any dessert. Try them with Coffee mousse or Lemon mousse (see pages 73 and 407), or a bowl of ice cream.

Yields about 30 cookies
* 1½ cups unbleached flour
* 2 teaspoons baking powder
* 1 teaspoon ground cloves
* ¼ teaspoon cinnamon
* 2 teaspoons ground ginger
* ½ teaspoon salt
* 10 tablespoons unsalted butter
* 1 cup granulated sugar, plus a little extra for sprinkling
* 1 egg
* 3 tablespoons dark molasses
* 2 pieces of candied ginger, finely chopped
* 2 teaspoons ginger syrup (optional)

Preheat the oven to 400 degrees. Lightly grease a baking sheet.

Sift the flour, baking powder, spices, and salt into a bowl.

In a separate bowl cream the butter and the sugar together until pale and light. Add the egg, then stir in the molasses, chopped ginger, and ginger syrup if using. Fold in the flour mixture a bit at a time.

Take teaspoonfuls of the mixture and roll into large-grape-sized balls. Flatten them with a rolling pin or the palm of your hand and sprinkle with a little extra granulated sugar. Place on the prepared baking sheet and bake in the middle of the oven for about 10 minutes, until the surface of the cookies begins to crack.

Sesame-seed brandysnaps with ginger and lemon cream

Brandysnaps are traditional English things, which can be eaten as simple rolled cookies or filled with whipped cream and any soft fruit. To make them very Christmassy, fill with a little Black fruit and apple tart (see page 409) folded into whipped cream, in place of the ginger and lemon cream.

Here the brandysnap mixture is shaped into mini-baskets rather than rolls. These go soft within 24 hours (even in an airtight tin), so need to be made only a few hours before you want them. They aren't difficult to make, but you do need to concentrate.

Yields 20 mini-baskets
* 6 tablespoons unsalted butter
* ¼ cup corn syrup
* ½ cup superfine or granulated sugar
* ⅔ cup plus 2 tablespoons flour, sifted
* 1 teaspoon ground ginger
* 1 teaspoon cinnamon
* 1 teaspoon brandy
* 2 tablespoons sesame seeds
* Raspberries or other soft fruit, or Black tart stuff (see page 409), to serve

For the ginger and lemon cream
* 1 cup heavy cream
* Grated zest of 1 lemon
* 3 tablespoons candied ginger

Preheat the oven to 350 degrees. Set out a couple of silicone mats (brilliant for this) or lightly oiled baking sheets.

Put the butter and corn syrup into a saucepan and melt over a low heat. Stir in the sugar and take off the heat. Mix in the flour, ground ginger, cinnamon, brandy, and sesame seeds. Allow the mixture to sit for 5 minutes to solidify a little.

Put generous teaspoonfuls of the mixture on the silicone mats or prepared baking sheets, spacing them about 4 inches apart. This means you can do only 2 or 3 at a time because you must allow for spreading during baking.

Bake for 5 to 6 minutes, or until golden brown, keeping a close eye on them as they burn easily. Allow to cool for 2 to 3 minutes on the mats or sheets, then lift off with a spatula and drape over an upturned teacup (or the handle of a wooden spoon for rolls). If they harden before curling, heat through again in the oven for a few minutes to soften. Cool the shaped brandysnaps on a wire rack.

Repeat the baking and shaping process with the rest of the brandysnap mixture. You might need to wipe excess oil off the silicone mats between each batch because they release quite a bit of fat.

While the baskets are cooling, put the cream in a bowl and whisk into soft peaks. Stir in the lemon zest, ginger syrup, and chopped ginger.

To serve, fill the baskets partway with the cream mixture and pile lots of raspberries on top.

Cape gooseberry chocolates

I love the tangy flavor of this unusual fruit, which is related to the Chinese lantern. They look and taste good when half-dipped in rich, dark chocolate.

Yields 30 chocolates
* 3½ ounces dark chocolate (at least 70% cocoa solids)
* 2 tablespoons unsalted butter, softened
* 30 Cape gooseberries, papery cases pulled back but left on

Break up the chocolate into small squares and put into a double boiler over a gentle heat. Add the butter. Once the chocolate has melted, stir once (don't stir too often as this will make the texture grainy).

Cover a plate with waxed paper. Holding the fruit by the papery case, dip the fruit into the mix, lay out on the prepared plate, and put in the fridge to set for about 1 hour before serving.

Jane's strawberry and white chocolate truffles

These chocolates, invented by my sister Jane, are one of my very favorite things to make and eat from my Christmas book, so they had to reappear. One word of warning—don't make too many. They are utterly delicious, but incredibly rich.

Yields about 20 truffles
* ½ cup strawberries, fresh or frozen
* 1 ounce dried strawberries (from good gourmet shops)
* 7 ounces white chocolate
* 2 tablespoons unsalted butter, cut into chunks
* 1 ounce full-fat crème fraîche
* Milk chocolate flakes or drinking cocoa

Put the fresh or frozen strawberries in a saucepan and cook over a gentle heat until reduced to about 1 tablespoon of intensely flavored pulp. This will take about 30 minutes if frozen, less if fresh. Meanwhile, chop the dried fruit into the smallest possible pieces.

Melt the chocolate in a double boiler over a low heat. Try not to stir as that can make the chocolate grainy. Remove from the heat and add the butter, stirring until it has melted.

Add the strawberry pulp, dried fruit, and crème fraîche to the chocolate mixture and stir again. Allow to cool, then put in the fridge or freezer until firm enough to roll into balls.

Take spoonfuls of the mixture and roll into balls between the palms of your hands. Put the balls in a covered container, place in the fridge or freezer until hard, then keep in the fridge until you want to eat them. (They will last for at least a couple of weeks if kept chilled, and freeze well.)

Before serving, roll each ball around on a plate of chocolate flakes or drinking chocolate until coated.

Anna's thick-cut dark, dark marmalade

This recipe of my sister's makes a chunkily cut, not too sweet, deep-colored marmalade. You can use ordinary granulated sugar if you want a paler color and a less sweet taste.

Yields about 8 pint jars
* 3 1/3 pounds Seville oranges
* 1 teaspoon salt
* About 5 1/2 pounds dark brown sugar
* Juice of 2 lemons

Scrub the oranges under cold running water. Put them into a heavy-based stainless-steel pan, cover with 3 quarts of water, and add the salt. Put a lid on the pan and bring to a boil, then simmer for about 1 hour, turning the oranges once halfway through the cooking time. The fruit should be soft.

Strain, reserving the cooking liquid, and allow the fruit to cool completely. When cooled, cut the oranges in half and scoop the flesh and pits into a metal sieve set over a bowl. Reserve the orange rinds.

Using a metal spoon, stir and push the flesh through the sieve. Discard the membrane and seeds.

Cut the orange rinds into 1/8-inch strips, and then into pieces of the size you want.

Place a saucer in the fridge, ready for when you come to test for setting point later on. Add the rind to the sieved pulp and weigh it. For every 1 pound, measure 1 2/3 cups of the cooking liquid (if you don't have enough, make up the amount with water). Mix together, then weigh the mixture again and for every 1 pound measure out 2 1/2 cups sugar.

Put everything into the heavy-based stainless-steel pan along with the lemon juice. Heat slowly, stirring all the time, to dissolve the sugar completely. Increase the heat and bring to a rapid boil, then boil for 30 to 40 minutes, stirring only occasionally.

Pull the pan off the heat and test for setting point. Take the saucer from the fridge and place a teaspoonful of the marmalade juice on it. When cool, it should wrinkle when you push it with your finger. You could also use a jam thermometer here: when it reaches 220 to 225 degrees the marmalade will set.

When ready, take the marmalade off the heat and allow it to rest for 20 minutes, or the orange peel will float to the top of the jars. If any scum appears on the surface, a walnut-sized chunk of butter stirred into the marmalade makes it disappear instantly.

Stir once before pouring into dry, warm, sterilized jars (you can sterilize them in a very hot dishwasher, or boil them in a pan of water for 10 minutes). Seal each jar and process in a boiling-water bath according to jar manufacturer's instructions. Label with the date. This marmalade will keep for several years.

Clementine and lemon curd

Store-bought curd is often intensely sweet, which I don't like. This is sharper, good on really fresh bread, and lovely sandwiched in the middle of a Victoria sponge. It is best kept in the fridge and eaten fresh.

Yields about 2 half-pint jars
* 2 clementines, finely grated zest of both and juice of 1
* Juice and finely grated zest of 1 lemon
* 1 cup superfine sugar
* 10 tablespoons unsalted butter, cut into chunks
* 4 medium eggs, beaten

Put the juice and zest from the clementines and lemon into a heavy-based saucepan, add the sugar, and stir with a wooden spoon over a very low heat until dissolved.

Add the butter, stirring until it melts, then take the pan off the heat and whisk in the eggs. Put back on a very low heat and stir continuously for about 15 minutes. Do not allow the mixture to boil or it will curdle.

When the mixture has thickened (it will thicken further as it cools), pour into dry, warm, sterilized jars (you can sterilize them in a very hot dishwasher, or boil them in a pan of water for 10 minutes). Seal each jar and process in a boiling-water bath according to jar manufacturer's instructions. Label with the date. It will keep in the fridge for up to 2 weeks.

Crystallized ginger

Crystallized ginger lasts almost forever and has a fantastic, really intense flavor. A jar of this makes a brilliant Christmas present—you can go on eating it for months.

Yields 3 half-pint jars
* 1 pound fresh ginger
* 2 cups granulated sugar

Peel and slice the ginger into coin-shaped pieces about $1/8$-inch thick. Put into a pan, cover with cold water, and bring to a boil. Lower the heat and simmer gently for 35 minutes.

Drain the ginger and put into a large saucepan with the sugar and 3 tablespoons water. Bring to a boil, then lower the heat and simmer, stirring now and again until the ginger and syrup start to crystallize. This takes about 40 to 50 minutes.

Take off the heat and continue to stir the now-crystallized ginger for a minute or so to prevent it and the extra sugar from sticking on the bottom of the pan. Allow to cool for a couple of minutes, then stir again and put into jars. Seal with airtight lids and label.

There will be some sugar left in the bottom of the pan from the crystallizing process. This is delicious and useful, so keep it in a jar to sprinkle over a Lemon and zucchini drizzle cake (see page 410) or use for poaching dried fruit.

Roasted red onion and garlic chutney

Similar in flavor and texture to a really good red cabbage, this is perfect with cheese or pork pie. The quantities below make a big batch—enough to have some yourself and give some away as Christmas presents.

Yields 4 to 5 pint jars
* 9 pounds red onions
* 2 whole heads of garlic
* ¼ cup olive oil
* Salt and black pepper
* ¾ cup balsamic vinegar
* ¾ cup cider vinegar
* ½ teaspoon ground cloves
* 1 teaspoon ground allspice
* 1 cup light brown sugar
* 2 tablespoons roughly chopped fresh sage, or 1 tablespoon dried sage

Preheat the oven to 400 degrees.

Peel and thinly slice the onions. Separate and peel the garlic cloves, cutting any extra large ones in half. Place in a roasting pan, pour over the olive oil, and season with a little salt and pepper. Roast for 1 hour, stirring twice.

Put the onions and garlic into a large, heavy-based saucepan and add the remaining ingredients. Bring to a boil over a medium heat, then simmer very gently for about 45 minutes. Stir the mixture regularly to prevent sticking or burning.

Cool slightly, then pour into dry, warm, sterilized jars (you can sterilize them in a very hot dishwasher, or boil them in a pan of water for 10 minutes). Seal each jar and process in a boiling-water bath according to jar manufacturer's instructions. Label with the date.

This chutney will keep for up to a year. Once open, store in the fridge.

Cranberry and lime compote

Made with a mix of fresh and dried cranberries, this compote has a lovely sweet and sour flavor. It is best made at least a day ahead so that the flavors merge, but you can make it up to five days in advance.

Serves 10 to 12 (enough to fill a large serving bowl)
* 12 ounces fresh cranberries, defrosted if frozen
* ⅓ cup dried cranberries
* Grated zest and juice of 1 lime
* 2 tablespoons light brown sugar
* 6 tablespoons port
* 3 star anise
* 1 cinnamon stick

Put all the ingredients into a large saucepan over a medium heat, stirring as it comes to a boil. Lower the heat and simmer gently for 12 to 14 minutes. Pour into a bowl and allow to cool. Cover and put in the fridge until needed.

Before serving, discard the star anise and cinammon stick, and warm through slightly, adding a little extra port if you like.

Cabbage kimchi

This Korean pickled chili Chinese cabbage is delicious. Serve it with drinks, or as a starter with some smoked fish. It's wonderful with eel. You can eat it within a day or two of making it, or it will store for 4 to 6 weeks.

Yields a 1-quart jar
* 2 Chinese cabbages (about 9 pounds in total), split lengthwise
* 6 tablespoons salt
* 3 tablespoons crushed garlic
* 1 heaping tablespoon peeled and grated fresh ginger
* 1 tablespoon dried red chili flakes (add more if you like things fiery)
* 2 tablespoons dark brown sugar
* ¼ cup fish sauce
* 8 scallions, white and pale green parts finely chopped, green tops split and cut into 2-inch lengths
* ¼ pound peeled and julienned daikon (Chinese radish), or 1 kohlrabi, cut into rounds ⅛ inch thick, then into julienne strips 3 inches long

Pull the leaves off the cabbage one by one and place in 2 large mixing bowls. Put 3 tablespoons salt in each bowl, then add enough cold water to cover the leaves. Sit a weighted plate on top of each and leave overnight.

Drain the cabbage and rinse thoroughly under running water. Gently squeeze the leaves, then spread out on dish towels, patting with another dish towel to dry them.

Chop the cabbage leaves into 1½-inch pieces and put in a large bowl. Add the garlic, ginger, chili, sugar, fish sauce, and white parts of the scallions. Stir well to dissolve the sugar. Add the scallion tops and the daikon, mixing well.

Eat immediately as a salad, or pack the kimchi and all the liquid into a dry, warm, sterilized jar (you can sterilize it in a very hot dishwasher, or boil it in a pan of water for 10 minutes), then seal tightly and label. Allow to mature in the fridge for 4 to 6 weeks.

Winter apple, pear, and chestnut chutney

This is one of the easiest things to make, with everything put in one pan, cooked for about 45 minutes, and then poured into jars. It has a lovely crunchy texture from the chestnuts and an excellent taste. Make a couple of batches so that you can keep some yourself and give some away at Christmas.

Yields 6 pint jars
* 1⅓ pounds cooking apples, peeled, cored, and roughly chopped
* ¾ pound pears, peeled, cored, and roughly chopped
* 14 ounces vacuum-packed roast chestnuts, halved
* ⅔ pound onions, chopped
* ⅔ cup dried cranberries or golden raisins
* Juice and grated zest of 1 orange
* Juice and grated zest of 1 lemon
* 2 tablespoons pumpkin pie spice
* 1 tablespoon medium-hot curry powder
* 1 tablespoon coriander seeds
* 1¼ cups cider vinegar
* 1¾ cups light brown sugar

Put all the ingredients into a large, stainless-steel pan over a medium heat and stir well. Bring to a boil, then turn down the heat and simmer for 40 to 45 minutes, stirring occasionally until the mixture thickens.

Once it has reduced to a thick chutney consistency, stir more often so that it doesn't catch on the bottom of the pan, as the burnt flavor will affect the overall taste.

When the mixture has thickened, pour into dry, warm, sterilized jars (you can sterilize them in a very hot dishwasher, or boil them in a pan of water for 10 minutes). Seal each jar and process in a boiling-water bath according to jar manufacturer's instructions. Label with the date.

This chutney is best made a month before using and keeps well for up to a year. Once open, store in the fridge.

Jack Daniel's hot chocolate

This is the ultimate drink when you feel like something hot, sweet, and rich. You can have it in front of the fire after a cold walk or serve it as dessert.

Yields 1 large mugful
* 1 mug of milk
* 1 ½ ounces good-quality dark chocolate, plus a little extra for grating
* 1–2 teaspoons sugar
* 4 teaspoons Jack Daniel's whiskey
* 1 tablespoon stiffly whipped cream
* Freshly grated nutmeg or ground cinnamon

Pour the milk into a saucepan and heat to just below the boiling point. Break the chocolate into chunks and add to the milk, stirring until it dissolves. Add the sugar and stir again. Add the Jack Daniel's and pour the mixture into a mug or a little pot. Top with a spoonful of whipped cream. Sprinkle with a little grated chocolate and/or some spice.

Mulled pear cider

Pear cider is having a great renaissance in Britain at the moment because it's light on alcohol and packed with flavor. It's good served spicy and warm. I love this at a party—much lighter and less heady than mulled wine or even mulled apple cider.

Yields 6 to 8 glasses
* 2 (20-ounce) bottles of pear cider
* 3 tablespoons light brown sugar
* 2 pears, peeled, cored, and cut into small chunks
* ¾ cup fresh cranberries or blueberries
* 1 cinnamon stick
* 3 star anise
* ¼ whole nutmeg, freshly grated
* 10 cloves

Pour the pear cider into a large saucepan. Add the sugar and put over a low heat until the sugar has melted, stirring to stop it from catching.

Put the pears, berries, cinnamon, star anise, and nutmeg into the cider and cook until the fruit has just softened. Add the cloves. Bring gently to a simmer, then take off the heat.

Allow to sit for a few minutes for the flavors to infuse, but reheat if it sits too long as this is best drunk piping hot.

Pomegranate bellinis

Pomegranates are at their sweetest and best from late autumn through early winter, so make the most of them. You can squeeze the juice or buy it.

Yields 6 glasses
* 1¼ cups good-quality pomegranate juice
* 2 oranges, freshly squeezed
* 1 tablespoon sugar
* 5 cardamom pods, lightly crushed
* 3 tablespoons Cointreau or any other orange-flavored liqueur
* 1 bottle prosecco or champagne
* Seeds from ½ pomegranate (for removal technique, see page 31)

Put the fruit juices in a pan with the sugar, cardamom pods, and Cointreau and simmer for 6 to 7 minutes, until reduced to about 1¼ cups. Allow to cool, then strain into a pitcher, discarding the cardamom pods.

Divide the syrup equally among 6 glasses, top up with the prosecco, and serve with a few pomegranate seeds dropped in.

Asolano

In its purest form, this Italian party drink (included in my Christmas book) is a shot of Campari topped up by about three times that amount of prosecco. To avoid getting drunk too quickly, dilute with a splash of blood orange or pink grapefruit juice and fizzy water.

Yields 8 small glasses
* 3 ounces Campari
* Plenty of ice
* 1 cup freshly squeezed blood orange or pink grapefruit juice
* 20 ounces prosecco
* 10 ounces club soda

Pour the Campari into a pitcher of ice and mix in the orange or grapefruit juice. Add the prosecco and club soda and stir gently to combine. Pour into glasses and serve.

Roast turkey with lemon and herb butter

Get the best turkey you can, fresh rather than frozen, and free-range or organic. A turkey, properly and humanely reared, and hung for two weeks should have plenty of taste.

Here's a fuss-free recipe that produces a great-tasting, moist-fleshed roast turkey. The herb butter is pushed under the skin, and foil is used to cover the bird for half the cooking time, ensuring a lovely juicy meat with a fabulous golden color and fragrant flavor. If cooking a bird without the seasoned butter, do not use foil.

I recommend cooking the stuffing separately rather than stuffing the bird: fill the body cavity with just lemon, onion, and herbs.

Serves 10 to 12, allowing plenty for leftovers
* 1 (18-pound) free-range turkey with giblets
* 2 lemons
* 1 onion, quartered
* 2 sprigs of fresh sage
* 4 bay leaves
* 2 sprigs of fresh rosemary
* ½ cup (1 stick) softened butter
* 1 tablespoon coriander seeds, crushed
* Small bunch cilantro, tarragon, or rosemary, roughly chopped
* Salt and black pepper

Oven-ready weight roasting times
(allow an extra 30 minutes' roasting time and 30 minutes to rest on top of this)

* 9 pounds	2 hrs
* 11 pounds	2 ¼ hrs
* 13 pounds	2 ½ hrs
* 15 pounds	2 hrs
* 18 pounds	3 hrs
* 20 pounds	3 ¼ hrs
* 22 pounds	3 ½ hrs
* 24 pounds	3 ¾ hrs

Preheat the oven to 375 degrees.

Make sure you have removed the giblets from inside the turkey. Do not throw these away—you want them for the gravy.

Rinse the turkey under cold water and pat dry. Grate the rind of both lemons into a bowl. Cut the lemons in half and put inside the turkey cavity along with the onion, sage, bay leaves, and rosemary sprigs.

Add the butter, coriander seeds, and cilantro to the lemon rind and mix well. Season with salt and pepper. Gently push your hands under the skin of the turkey breast and press the butter onto the flesh, taking care not to tear the skin. Transfer the bird to a large roasting pan and season with salt and pepper. Cover with a double layer of foil and roast for 3 hours, or the time recommended in the table opposite, removing the foil halfway through.

As ovens vary, check if the turkey is cooked about 30 minutes before the end of the cooking time by piercing the thigh with a sharp knife: the juices should run clear, with no signs of pink. Alternatively, insert a meat thermometer halfway through the thickest part of the breast: if the bird is cooked, it should register 165 degrees. If not cooked, continue cooking for 15 to 30 minutes, repeating the knife or thermometer test.

Take the cooked turkey out of the oven and allow to rest for 30 minutes—covered with foil or a clean kitchen towel—before carving. This allows the juices to settle and keeps the bird warm (it should stay hot for up to 45 minutes). Reserve all the juices that ooze out while the bird rests and add them to the gravy (see page 428).

Serve with the gravy, Crunchy roasted potatoes (see page 398), Slow-roasted carrots (see page 397), Baked red cabbage (see page 392), Roasted red peppers with macadamia and apple stuffing (see page 428), and Bread sauce (see page 433).

Turkey gravy

To make life easier on Christmas Day, it's a good idea to make the giblet stock for the gravy the day before and store it in the fridge until needed.

Serves 10 to 12
* 1 tablespoon olive oil
* 1 turkey neck (from the giblets)
* 1 large red onion, chopped
* 1 stick of celery, chopped
* 1 large carrot, peeled and chopped
* 3 slices of bacon, chopped
* 1 cup white wine
* 1 bay leaf
* 2 sprigs of fresh thyme
* 2 garlic cloves
* Salt and black pepper

To finish on Christmas Day
* 2 tablespoons softened butter
* ¼ cup flour

To make the stock, heat the oil in a large saucepan. Add the turkey neck, vegetables, and bacon or lardons and sauté for 10 minutes. Add the wine, 4 cups of water, the herbs, garlic, and a little salt and pepper. Bring to a boil and allow to simmer gently for 45 minutes. Strain into a pitcher, allow to cool, and store in the fridge overnight.

When the turkey has been taken out of the oven and the fat drained from the roasting pan, mix the softened butter and flour together in a small bowl and stir into the roasting pan juices over a medium heat. When thoroughly combined, add the prepared stock and the juices from the resting turkey. Bring to a boil, stirring, then simmer gently for 5 to 10 minutes.

Taste the gravy and add salt and pepper as needed. When you are ready to serve, pour it into a pitcher, or two pitchers—one for each end of the table.

Roasted red peppers with macadamia and apple stuffing

Most people in the know do not recommend stuffing turkeys. You get much more even, and therefore safer, cooking without it, so cook the stuffing separately. The roasted red peppers and macadamia nuts add a lovely sweet flavor to this stuffing, and if you leave the nuts whole, you get plenty of texture too. This is an ideal recipe if you happen to have vegetarians for Christmas lunch.

Serves 8 to 10
* Olive oil, for frying and drizzling
* 1 large red onion, chopped
* ½ cup pecans
* ¾ cup macadamia nuts
* 2 ½ cups fresh breadcrumbs
* 2 bunches of flat-leaf parsley, chopped
* 2 tablespoons chopped fresh thyme
* ½ teaspoon ground cloves
* ½ teaspoon ground cinnamon
* Grated zest and juice of 2 oranges
* 2 large cooking apples, peeled, cored, and chopped
* 4 sticks of celery, chopped
* 3 garlic cloves, finely chopped
* 3 tablespoons melted butter
* Sea salt and black pepper
* 2 orange peppers, halved and deseeded
* 2 sweet red peppers, halved and deseeded

Preheat the oven to 350 degrees.

Heat a little olive oil in a pan. Add the onion and sweat over a low heat until soft. Allow to cool.

Roast the pecans and macadamia nuts for 2 to 3 minutes in a dry frying pan.

In a large mixing bowl combine the breadcrumbs with the chopped herbs, spices, orange zest, apples, celery, nuts, and garlic. Add the onion and the orange juice. Stir in the melted butter and season well.

Fill the pepper halves with the stuffing mixture, drizzle with a little olive oil and roast for 25 to 30 minutes.

Slow-roasted duck with fruit and herb gravy

Delicious sweet, fall-off-the-bone duck with crispy skin is a wonderful alternative to turkey if you want a change from the usual Christmas bird. And it's easy to cook, even in a small oven. If you are feeding 4 to 6, you should have two birds for generous portions. Serve with a sharp, thin gravy made from the herby, orangey juices, or Fragrant plum sauce (see page 366) or a tart compote of cranberries and lime (see page 420)—all are good with the rich, dense taste of duck. Drain and keep the duck fat in the fridge for roasted potatoes.

It's unlikely you'll have much—or indeed any—duck left over, but if you do, use it to make the Duck and red cabbage salad (see page 366).

Serves 4 to 6
* 2 free-range ducks, about 4–4 ½ pounds each
* 2 oranges, satsumas, or clementines, cut in half
* 2 onions, cut in half
* 4 sprigs of rosemary
* 2 sprigs of sage
* 4 small sticks of celery, with leaves (optional)
* Salt and black pepper

For the gravy
* 1 heaping teaspoon flour
* 4 teaspoons apple juice or cider
* 2/3 cup chicken stock

Preheat the oven to 375 degrees.

Rinse the ducks under cold water and pat dry. Fill each body cavity with 2 orange halves, 2 onion halves, 2 rosemary sprigs, 1 sage sprig, and 2 sticks of celery. Season with salt and pepper.

Put the birds into a high-sided roasting pan (as they release a lot of fat) and roast for 1 hour and 15 minutes. During this time drain away the fat a couple of times.

Turn the oven down to 300 degrees and cook for a further 1 hour and 15 minutes, or until the meat is starting to come away easily from the bones. Transfer the ducks to a warmed carving plate and set aside to rest for 15 minutes. Do not cover or the skin won't stay crisp.

Drain off all the fat in the roasting pan. Spoon the oranges, onions, and herbs out of the resting ducks and place in the roasting pan with all the juices and ducky bits left on the bottom. Place the roasting pan over a low heat. Add the flour and stir it all around with a wooden spoon.

Add the apple juice and stock and bring to a gentle simmer, stirring constantly. While stirring, squash the oranges with the back of the spoon to release all the juices. Add a little water if necessary.

Taste the gravy and season with salt and pepper. Strain through a coarse sieve into a pitcher and serve immediately with the duck.

Bacon-wrapped chestnut stuffing rolls

These sweet stuffing rolls are lovely with duck or turkey.

Yields about 12 medium or 24 small rolls
* 2 medium onions, chopped
* 1 stick of celery, finely chopped
* 3 tablespoons butter
* 1 pound bacon
* 1 tablespoon juniper berries, crushed
* 2 garlic cloves, finely chopped
* 20 fresh sage leaves, chopped, or 1 teaspoon dried sage
* ¾ cup chopped dates
* 7 ounces vacuum-packed or canned chestnuts
* 2 ½ cups good fresh white breadcrumbs
* Small bunch of flat-leaf parsley, roughly chopped
* Grated zest of 1 orange
* Grated zest of 1 lemon
* ½ teaspoon grated nutmeg
* 1 large egg, beaten
* Sea salt and black pepper

Preheat the oven to 350 degrees. Oil a baking sheet, or line a baking pan with a silicone mat.

Sweat the onions and celery in the butter over a low heat for 10 minutes. Chop ⅓ pound of the bacon and add to the pan with the juniper berries, garlic, and sage and cook for a further 5 minutes.

Put all the remaining ingredients, apart from the seasoning and bacon slices, into a large bowl and add the onion mixture. Mix well to combine. Season with salt and pepper.

Stretch out the bacon slices with the back of a knife. If making small rolls, cut the bacon in half, put a walnut-sized dollop of the stuffing on one end of each piece, and roll up. If making medium rolls, put a tablespoonful of stuffing on one end of each piece and roll up. If you have any stuffing left over, roll it into balls.

Place everything on the prepared baking sheet or pan and bake for 20 to 25 minutes, until the stuffing is just browning and the bacon is a good golden brown.

Bread sauce with chunky red onions

In an ideal world, as well as serving the turkey with gravy, it's good to have bread sauce and a cranberry compote (see page 420) to go with the meat too. The onions and hazelnuts in this bread sauce give it great texture and flavor. This is delicious served with turkey, chicken, duck, or any game.

Serves 10 to 12
* 10 cloves
* 2 garlic cloves
* 5 cups whole milk
* 2 bay leaves, fresh or dry
* 1 sprig of fresh rosemary (about 4 inches)
* 10 peppercorns
* 2 medium red onions, cut into eighths
* 4–5 cups fresh white breadcrumbs, or 2-day-old loaf cut into chunks
* Full handful of hazelnuts
* ¼ teaspoon freshly grated nutmeg
* 2–3 tablespoons crème fraîche
* Sea salt and black pepper

Stick the cloves evenly into the garlic cloves and place in a saucepan with the milk, bay leaves, rosemary, and peppercorns. Bring slowly to a boil, then turn off the heat, cover the pan, and leave for 30 minutes so that the flavors infuse.

Strain the milk into a clean saucepan, add the onion chunks, and cook on a low heat for 20 minutes. Add the breadcrumbs, hazelnuts, and nutmeg and simmer on a low heat for another 5 minutes.

Remove from the heat, stir in the crème fraîche, then taste, and season with salt and pepper. Serve immediately, or cool, cover, and store in the fridge until needed. This sauce can also be frozen.

When reheating, you might need to add a little extra milk or crème fraîche so that the sauce is not too stiff.

Turkey tonnato

If you have duck or goose for Christmas lunch, you're unlikely to have leftovers, so it's for turkey that one needs a few ideas. Turkey tonnato, which I included in my Christmas book, is a winter version of the classic summer buffet dish Vitello tonnato. Served with baked potatoes, a Fava bean pilaf (see page 174), and plenty of salad, it's ideal for a big lunch on any of the days after Christmas. The flavor improves with keeping, so, if possible, make this the day before you are going to eat it.

Serves 6

For the mayonnaise
* 2 egg yolks
* Juice of ½ lemon, or to taste
* 1 teaspoon mustard powder
* ¾ cup good sunflower oil
* ⅓ cup olive oil
* Good pinch of salt and black pepper

* 1 (5-ounce) can of good tuna in olive or sunflower oil
* 5 anchovy fillets
* 3 tablespoons lemon juice or vinegar
* 3 tablespoons capers
* 2 pounds cooked white turkey meat, chilled

To serve
* Olives
* Whole capers, chopped
* Flat-leaf parsley or chives
* Lemon slices

First make the mayonnaise. Put the egg yolks, lemon juice, and mustard powder in a bowl. Froth up with a whisk. Add the oils in a gentle stream, whisking constantly, until the mixture thickens. Season to taste with salt and pepper.

Put the tuna, anchovies, lemon juice, and capers in a food processor and pulse until creamy. Mix with the mayonnaise. Thin the mixture to the consistency of light cream by adding a little boiling water if necessary.

Slice the meat very thinly and carefully. Place a little of the mayonnaise sauce in the bottom of a large, deep platter or a baking pan that will fit in the fridge and arrange alternating layers of meat and sauce over it. Keep a little sauce in reserve for when you serve the meat. Cover well with foil and put in the fridge for several hours or up to 3 days.

Serve at room temperature on a large flat serving plate. Cover with the reserved sauce and decorate with the olives, capers, parsley, or chives and lemon slices.

Turkey and Parmesan gratin

I first ate this excellent, now slightly adapted, Elizabeth David chicken recipe (Poulet au gratin à la Savoyarde) cooked by my great friend Pip Morrison, who keeps a yardful of chickens. I think it's also one of the best ways to use up any leftover turkey after Christmas.

Serves 4 to 6

* 3 tablespoons butter, plus a little extra for the topping
* 3 tablespoons flour
* 2 cups hot turkey or chicken stock, strained
* 1 cup heavy cream
* 2 heaping teaspoons dried tarragon or 4 heaping teaspoons fresh
* 4 teaspoons Dijon mustard
* Salt and black pepper
* 2 tablespoons freshly grated Parmesan cheese (the traditional Savoy dish uses Gruyère, but Parmesan or a Parmesan/Cheddar mix is best)
* 2 pounds cooked turkey or chicken, cut into pieces
* ¾ cup breadcrumbs

Preheat the oven to its highest temperature.

Melt the butter in a saucepan and stir in the flour. Cook for a minute or two, then add the hot strained stock, whisking all the time. Pour in the cream a little at a time and, once all added, let it cook very gently for 5 minutes. Add the tarragon, mustard, and salt and pepper to taste. Stir in the cheese. Cover and set aside for 10 minutes for the flavors to infuse.

Pour a layer of sauce into the bottom of a 7 by 9-inch heatproof gratin dish that will be okay under a hot broiler. Add the chicken or turkey and pour the rest of the sauce over the top. Sprinkle with the breadcrumbs, dot with butter, and put on the top shelf of the oven for 5 minutes.

Preheat the broiler. Toast the gratin dish under the broiler for 2 minutes so that the top is crunchy and golden.

Christmas bubble and squeak

We almost always have leftover vegetables after Christmas, and this is the perfect dish to use it all up. Roasted potatoes, Brussels sprouts, carrots, even red cabbage all work well here, but I don't give quantities as you will use whatever you have. This is delicious with cold ham and a mustardy dressed green salad, and also lovely with Turkey and Parmesan gratin (see previous recipe).

* Goose fat or olive oil
* Leftover vegetables (potatoes must be 50 percent of the mixture)
* 1–2 tablespoons coriander seeds, crushed
* Salt and black pepper

Preheat the oven to 400 degrees. Cover the bottom of the biggest roasting pan you can fit in your oven with a thin layer of goose fat or olive oil (about 3 tablespoons) and put in the oven for 5 minutes to heat through.

Break up the potatoes a bit in a bowl with a knife or large fork. Cut the carrots into 1-inch chunks. Mix the potatoes, carrots, and Brussels sprouts with the coriander seeds, then quickly stir in the red cabbage.

Scatter the mixed vegetables into the hot pan (a thin layer is key for getting a good crunch) and roast in the oven for 20 to 30 minutes, until beginning to turn crisp and brown. Season and serve.

Turkey croquettes

An old-fashioned dish, which my children absolutely love, ideal for using up leftover turkey or chicken.

Serves 6
* 1/3 pound smoked bacon or ham, finely chopped
* Oil and butter, for frying
* 1/2 pound cooked turkey meat, white or brown
* 1 onion, finely chopped
* 1/4 cup flour
* 1 cup turkey, chicken, or vegetable stock
* 2 tablespoons heavy cream
* 1 egg, beaten
* Juice and grated zest of 1 lemon, to taste
* Small bunch of parsley, chopped
* Small bunch of tarragon, chopped
* Salt and black pepper

For the crust
* Instant polenta
* 1 egg, beaten
* 2 cups toasted breadcrumbs

Fry the bacon or ham in a drop of oil over a gentle heat until cooked but not crunchy (about 5 minutes).

Chop up the leftover turkey in a food processor, pulsing just a couple of times so that it's not too mushy. Alternatively, finely chop it by hand. Fry the onion gently in a little butter. Add the flour and then the stock, bacon, cream, chopped turkey, egg, and a little lemon juice and zest. Add the chopped herbs and season with salt and pepper.

Spread the mixture onto a large plate, cover with plastic wrap, and leave to cool and thicken in the fridge for an hour or two.

Roll the mixture into 12 cylinders about 3 inches long. Roll these first in the polenta, then the egg, and, last, the breadcrumbs. Fry until golden in a little oil and butter for about 5 minutes, turning regularly, and keep warm in a low oven (300 degrees) until they are all ready to serve. You can freeze any of the mixture you don't use.

Individual Christmas cakes

Christmas cake never seems to get eaten in our house, so I tend to make several small ones rather than a single big one. These are also great for presents and for putting in people's stockings. If you have a small oven, you might want to bake the cakes in two batches.

Yields 10 ramekin-sized cakes
* 2 cups flour
* 1½ teaspoons pumpkin pie spice
* Good pinch of salt
* 1 cup (2 sticks) unsalted butter, softened
* 1 cup brown sugar
* 4 large eggs
* 1 tablespoon dark molasses
* 1 teaspoon vanilla extract
* ¼ cup chopped mixed citrus and lemon peel
* ¼ cup dried currants
* 1⅓ cups raisins
* ⅔ cup dried cranberries
* ⅓ cup blanched almonds, toasted or oven-roasted and roughly chopped
* Grated zest of 1 lemon
* Grated zest of 1 orange
* 2 tablespoons brandy

To decorate
* Apricot jam, warmed
* Marzipan (optional)
* Icing (optional)

Preheat the oven to 300 degrees. Cut out 10 (8½ to 9 inch) circles from parchment paper. Brush lightly with oil and push into 10 deep ramekins about 3½ inches in diameter.

Sift the flour into a bowl, add the pumpkin pie spice and salt, and set aside.

Cream together the butter and sugar in a large mixing bowl until pale and light. By hand this will take 7 to 10 minutes; with an electric mixer about 3 to 4 minutes.

Put the eggs, molasses, and vanilla extract in another bowl, whisk lightly, then beat a little at a time into the creamed mixture. Add some of the flour along with the last few additions of egg to prevent the mixture from curdling (if it does curdle, don't worry, just carry on).

Put the peel, fruit, and nuts in another bowl and stir in 2 tablespoons of the flour.

Using a metal spoon, fold the remaining flour into the egg mixture, then add the fruit and nuts and grated citrus zest. Stir in the brandy.

Spoon the mixture into the prepared ramekins, place on a baking sheet, and bake in the oven for 1 to 1½ hours, or until a skewer stabbed in the center of the cakes comes out clean. Leave to cool in the ramekins, then turn out and remove the parchment.

To decorate, brush with a little warmed apricot jam, then cover with marzipan and icing, if you fancy it. Top with decorations as you like. Then—if they're presents—wrap the cakes in clear cellophane and tie with twine or ribbon.

Peter's Banbury cake mincemeat

A recipe from Peter Weedon of the Paternoster Chop House that I included in my Christmas book, this is my favorite of all mincemeats, good and orangey with lots of nutty texture. It's not as sweet as most, so go for the more conventional recipe (see page 442) if you prefer things sweet. If you can't find damson plums, use cranberries instead.

Yields 1 pint jar or 15 to 20 Banbury cakes (see right) or mince pies
* ⅔ cup hazelnuts
* ¼ pound plums or cranberries
* ¼ cup light brown sugar
* ⅓ cup raisins
* ½ cup dried currants
* ⅓ cup suet (vegetarian or meat)
* Juice of ½ lemon
* 1 apple, peeled, cored, and diced
* A dash or two of Sloe or damson vodka or gin, store-bought or homemade (see page 333), or whisky or brandy if you can't find these

Mix all the ingredients together in a bowl.

Ladle the mincemeat into a dry, warm, sterilized jar (you can sterilize it in a very hot dishwasher, or boil it in a pan of water for 10 minutes). Seal each jar and process in a boiling-water bath according to jar manufacturer's instructions. Label with a date. Alternatively, keep it in a bowl covered with foil somewhere cool (the alcohol content makes it safe to store) until you want to use it.

You can use the mincemeat right away, but it's even better if left to age and marinate for 4 to 6 weeks. Eat within 3 months of opening.

Banbury cakes

Containing the slightly less sweet mincemeat, these Banbury cakes are brilliantly versatile. They are lovely as a dessert with heavy cream, or for tea, and absolutely delicious with a lump of crumbly Stilton or Lancashire cheese anytime before or after Christmas.

Yields 15 to 20 cakes
* 1 pound puff pastry, store-bought, but made with butter
* 1 quantity Peter's Banbury cake mincemeat (see left)
* 1 egg white
* A little superfine sugar

Preheat the oven to 400 degrees. Lightly oil, or place a silicone mat on, a baking sheet.

Roll out the pastry thinly (¼ inch) and use a 4-inch cutter or floured glass to cut out rounds (you can make much smaller ones for canapés). Put 2 teaspoons of the mincemeat mixture in the center of each round, gather up the pastry to make a shape like a mini purse, pinch firmly together, and cut off the excess. Turn the little cakes upside down and flatten slightly with the palm of your hand. Cut 3 quite deep slits in the top of each one.

Mix the egg white with some superfine sugar and brush this glaze over the cakes. Put them on the silicone mat and bake for 10 minutes to get a lovely crisp, crystallized finish.

Once they've cooled, freeze them, or store in a sealed tin. Kept airtight, they will be fine for up to a month.

Cointreau butter

Here is an excellent alternative to the Christmas classic made with brandy, and children generally prefer it. Have it with mince pies as well as Christmas pudding.

Serves 8
* 1 cup (2 sticks) unsalted butter, softened
* 1 cup superfine sugar
* Grated zest of 1 orange
* ¼ cup Cointreau (or brandy)

Beat the butter and sugar in a bowl until light, pale, and creamy. Fold in the orange zest. Mix in as much Cointreau (or brandy) as you wish. Chill in the fridge.

If you are making this in advance, either wrap it well and freeze it, or keep it in a covered container in the fridge.

Mincemeat

It's always worth making your own mincemeat because it has better texture and depth of flavor than store-bought.

Yields 2 pint jars
* 2 tablespoons chopped candied orange and lemon peel
* ⅓ pound apples, peeled, cored, and chopped
* ⅓ cup golden raisins
* ½ cup pitted dates
* ½ cup soft dried pitted apricots
* ⅓ cup seedless raisins
* ⅓ cup dried currants
* ¼ cup blanched almonds, roughly chopped
* 2 pinches each of freshly grated nutmeg, ground ginger, and pumpkin pie spice
* ⅓ cup brown sugar
* ⅓ cup suet (vegetarian or meat)
* Grated zest and juice of 1 lemon
* 2 tablespoons brandy

Put the candied peel into a large mixing bowl with the chopped apples. Put the golden raisins, dates, apricots, and raisins into a food processor and pulse briefly. Add this to the mixing bowl with the currants, almonds, spices, sugar, suet, and lemon zest and juice. Mix well and cover. Leave overnight.

Stir the mixture and add the brandy. Spoon into dry, warm, sterilized jars (you can sterilize them in a very hot dishwasher, or boil them in a pan of water for 10 minutes). Seal each jar and process in a boiling-water bath according to jar manufacturer's instructions. Label with a date.

Store in a cool place for at least 4 weeks before using. The mincemeat is best used within 3 months.

Mince pies

These classic mince pies (a recipe from my Christ-mas book) are good eaten just as they are, and they're even better with a dollop of crème fraîche or soft goat cheese tucked under the pastry top before you heat them. The orange-flavored pastry is also delicious; sometimes I swap this for lemon.

Yields about 25 pies

For the pastry
* Pinch of salt
* 3 cups unbleached flour, sifted
* 1 cup (2 sticks) unsalted butter or half butter and lard or shortening

* Grated zest of 2 oranges (or lemon)
* 1 tablespoon confectioners' sugar (optional)
* 2 egg yolks
* Ice-cold water

* 1 quantity Mincemeat (see opposite)
* Cream cheese, soft goat cheese, clotted cream, or full-fat crème fraîche
* Superfine sugar, to taste
* 1 egg, beaten, for egg wash
* 1 tablespoon confectioners' sugar, for dusting

Preheat the oven to 425 degrees.

To make the pastry, add the salt to the sifted flour. Rub the butter—or butter and lard—into the flour lightly with your fingers, or pulse in a food processor, until the mixture resembles breadcrumbs. Stir in the orange (or lemon) zest (and a little confectioners' sugar if you want a sweeter pastry). Mix the egg yolks with a very little ice-cold water, and add just enough to bring the mixture together in a ball. Cover the pastry in plastic wrap and allow it to rest for half an hour in the fridge.

Flour your work surface and roll out the pastry. Using a cutter, make rounds slightly bigger than you need to fill the dimples in your tart pan and cut the same number of slightly smaller rounds for the tops. Line the tart pan with the larger rounds and put about a small spoonful of mincemeat in each. Add a teaspoon of cream cheese, soft goat cheese, clotted cream, or full-fat crème fraîche, slightly sweetened, on top. (You can't freeze the mince pies if you use light or less than full-fat cream cheese or crème fraîche.)

Wet your fingers with water and lightly dampen the edge of each round before putting the top on and gently pressing the edges together. Make two small slits in the top to let the steam escape, and lightly brush with a little egg wash.

Freeze the pies in their pan at this stage, or bake in the preheated oven for 15 minutes. Mince pies also freeze well once cooked, but try to avoid reheating them more than once, as they dry out easily. They can be cooked from frozen, but will need about 5 minutes' more cooking. Allow them to cool in the pan for a few minutes, before transferring them onto a cake rack to cool a little.

Serve warm, dusted with confectioners' sugar.

Apple and mincemeat strudel

For this recipe you can buy mincemeat and add a couple of tablespoons of brandy to the mixture, or use homemade (see page 442), which has great texture and taste and is quick and easy to make. The quantities below are for one big strudel, so you could make two and freeze one for later. It's wonderful with homemade ice cream, such as vanilla, cinnamon (see page 303), or Cardamom and poppy seed (see page 402).

Serves 10 to 12
* 1 cup pecans, roughly chopped
* 1 (29-ounce) jar good-quality low-suet brandy mincemeat, or homemade (see page 442)
* 3 apples, peeled, cored, and grated
* 1 cup dried apricots, roughly chopped
* 13 ounces pre-rolled puff pastry
* 1 small egg, beaten
* 1 tablespoon sesame seeds
* Superfine sugar

Preheat the oven to 350 degrees. Lightly oil a large baking sheet.

Put the pecans in a small baking pan and toast in the oven for 3 to 4 minutes. Allow to cool. Mix together the mincemeat, grated apples, apricots, and pecans.

Unfold the pastry and place on the prepared baking sheet. Spoon the mincemeat mixture lengthwise along one half of the pastry to within 1 inch of the edges (you might be left with a little mincemeat in the jar). Brush some of the beaten egg around the margin, then fold the pastry over to seal in the mixture. Gently fork down the edges.

Brush the strudel with the remaining beaten egg, sprinkle over the sesame seeds and some superfine sugar, and cut several slits in the top of the pastry. Bake in the middle of the oven for 30 to 35 minutes, or until golden brown.

Chocolate and mincemeat brownies

Lovely and rich, with a gooey middle and nutty texture, these are good served with basil leaves to cut through the richness of the chocolate.

Yields 16 medium brownies
* 7 ounces high-quality dark chocolate (at least 70% cocoa solids)
* ¾ cup light brown sugar
* 1 cup (2 sticks) unsalted butter
* 4 eggs
* ½ cup self-rising flour
* Heaping ¼ cup good-quality mincemeat
* ¾ cup Brazil nuts, walnuts, or pecans, roughly chopped
* 1 teaspoon pumpkin pie spice
* Pinch of salt
* Small bunch of basil, to serve
* Confectioners' sugar

Preheat the oven to 350 degrees. Lightly oil a 9 by 9-inch brownie pan or shallow baking pan, or line with lightly oiled baking parchment, or use a silicone mat.

Melt the chocolate, brown sugar, and butter in a saucepan over a low heat, stirring all the time. Allow to cool slightly.

Beat the eggs in a large mixing bowl and stir in the melted chocolate mixture. Add the flour, mincemeat, nuts, pumpkin pie spice, and pinch of salt and combine thoroughly, using a wooden spoon or spatula.

Spoon the mixture into the prepared pan and bake for 20 to 25 minutes, or until just set in the center. Leave to cool in the pan, then cut into small squares.

Top each brownie with a basil leaf, and sprinkle with a little confectioners' sugar before serving.

Christmas pudding

This recipe, adapted from one by Constance Spry (the best of many I tried, and included in my Christmas book) makes a pudding with unbeatable texture and flavor, including whole almonds and masses of dried fruit. Try to make it a few weeks before D-day, as the flavors improve on storing.

Yields 1 large pudding (serves about 10)
* ¾ cup self-rising flour
* 3 cups fresh white breadcrumbs
* 1 ½ cups currants
* 1 ½ cups golden raisins
* 1 ½ cups raisins
* 6 ounces suet (vegetarian or meat)
* 2 tablespoons chopped candied lemon and orange peel
* ¼ cup almonds, slivered
* 1 small apple, grated
* Grated zest and juice of 1 orange
* ½ teaspoon pumpkin pie spice
* A little freshly grated nutmeg
* ½ teaspoon salt
* 3 eggs, beaten
* ⅔ cup brown ale or milk
* 1 cup light brown sugar

To serve
* Plenty of boiled coins
* A sprig of holly
* A little brandy

Mix all the ingredients together in a large mixing bowl. Lightly oil a medium (1 ½-quart) Christmas pudding basin or pudding mold and fill with the mixture. Cover with a double layer of parchment paper, secure with string, and then boil or steam.

If boiling, use a huge saucepan with a cushion of crumpled foil in the bottom. Sit the pudding basin on the cushion and pour in enough boiling water to reach two-thirds of the way up the basin. Cover tightly and simmer for 5 to 6 hours, topping up with boiling water when necessary. If steaming, put the basin or mold in a double saucepan or steamer and steam for 5 to 6 hours, again topping up the water when necessary.

When cooked, allow the pudding to cool, then re-cover it with another double layer of parchment paper secured with string. Now cover with foil (it mustn't touch the pudding itself as the fruits will react with the aluminum) or cheesecloth and store in a cool pantry, fridge, or freezer until you need it.

On Christmas Day, boil or steam the pudding as described above for another 3 hours. Once it's hot, stuff a few coins into the pudding for children to discover, pushing them right into the middle with a skewer.

Turn the pudding out of its bowl onto a large, flat plate and top it with a sprig of holly.

Heat some brandy briefly in a pan or ladle, light carefully with a match, and pour it over the pudding. Carry to the table and serve with Cointreau or brandy butter (see page 442) or straight cream.

A

B

ABOUT THE AUTHOR

Sarah Raven is an expert on all things to grow, cut, and eat from the garden. She is a prize-winning garden writer and her *In Season: Cooking with Vegetables and Fruits* cookbook was named Cookery Book of the Year in 2008 by the Guild of Food Writers. She is a passionate teacher, running cooking, flower-arranging, and gardening courses at Perch Hill, the East Sussex farm she owns with her husband, the writer Adam Nicolson. She is also a presenter on BBC's *Gardeners' World* and is currently filming a BBC series about the restoration of wildflower habitats and the cultivation of biodiversity. Sarah writes weekly for the *Daily Telegraph* as well as for several leading magazines. Sarah has two daughters and three stepsons.

www.sarahraven.com

ABOUT THE PHOTOGRAPHER

Jonathan Buckley has been collaborating with Sarah Raven, taking photographs at Perch Hill, for thirteen years. His work has been widely published in books, magazines, and newspapers worldwide. He was named Photographer of the Year and Features Photographer of the Year by the Garden Writers' Guild in 2006.

This book was a team effort with ideas thrown around between many people, but drawing particularly on the love of food of four cooks: Jo Clark, Debbie Staples, Liz Wood, and Teresa Wallace. Jo worked with me on this almost every day for over a year, brainstorming, recipe testing, and then reading and re-reading every recipe many times at all the different proof stages. There wasn't a day when working with Jo wasn't enjoyable and I am hugely grateful.

Debbie Staples and Liz Wood were also part of the ideas sessions and did much of the recipe testing and cooking for our food photography shoots. Teresa Wallace, Jane Raven, Clare Smith, and Kate Hubbard also read and commented on all the food ideas and many of the words. Without these people, this book would not have gotten to the end—and turned into something that makes me feel as proud as it does. I also want to thank the Perch Hill school and garden team—Tessa Bishop, Colin Pilbeam, Bea Burke, Denise Betteridge, Liz Craig, and Ben Cole—who often shopped, grew the ingredients, harvested, tasted, and commented, providing the backup which made it fun.

A hugely affectionate thank you goes to Jonathan Buckley. This is now our sixth book together and we both feel it is the best we've ever done. His photographs are exactly what I hoped for: beautiful and tempting, relaxed yet real, with a sense of the places—Perch Hill and Innibeg, our holiday house in Scotland—the colors and almost the smells. I can't imagine working with anyone else.

Caroline Michel, my agent at Peters Fraser and Dunlop, always makes me feel that the fraughtness and deadlines that go with writing any book are one hundred percent worthwhile, and remains brilliantly upbeat at all times—that's so encouraging, and I'm very grateful to her. I want to thank Trish Burgess for her copyediting skills, and Natalie Hunt at Bloomsbury, who has ironed out and pinned down the ambiguities, and has been both totally supportive and enthusiastic throughout the pulling together of this large and complicated cookbook. Huge thanks to her and to Richard Atkinson for his belief. Thanks also to Xa Shaw Stewart, who helped coordinate text and photographs, Sarah Barlow, who proofread, and Penny Edwards, who organizes the incredible quality of printing of Bloomsbury books. For how the book looks I am grateful to Stuart Smith, Victoria Forrest, Namkwan Cho, and Selina Swayne from Smith Design, with clear and definite direction coming again from Richard in creating the dazzling look.

RECIPES

Many thanks for specific recipes also go to Ronald Kunis, executive chef of restaurant De Kas in Amsterdam for the Celery salt (page 18) and Bay leaf ice cream (see page 73), and to Carien van Boxtel for translating; Francis Hamel for the idea of the Pea and spinach timbale (page 40); Tam Lawson for the Salmon carpaccio (page 43), Pumpkin and apple soup (page 248), and her recipe for Mince pies (page 443); Fiona Isaacs for the Persian jewelled rice (page 67); Debbie Staples for Orange and passion fruitade (page 105), Jamaican rum punch (page 107), and the Basil meringues (page 210); Catherine Jago for the Summer berry Bakewell tart (page 214); Liz Wood for the Grapefuit and cranberry spritzer (page 105) and Upside-down raspberry cake (page 223); Lucinda Fraser for the Shrimp, melon, and tomato salad (page 142); Rose Gray for the idea of the Summer garden fritto misto (page 146) and Beef carpaccio with fennel (page 163); Sam Bibby for the idea of Grilled summer vegetables with goat cheese (page 148); Willie Athill for Larb moo (page 165); Ivan Samarine for Scallops cooked on the fire (page 192); Kitty Ann for Chicken breast stuffed with garden herbs (page 198) and Duck rillettes (page 348); Sarah Wilkin for Balsamic pickled onions (page 226); Richard Poynton, who owns Cleopatra's Mountain Farmhouse in the Drakensberg Mountains, for Cleopatra's tomato soup (page 255); Jane Dunn for the idea of the Beet tart (page 267); Teresa Wallace for Curried shrimp with lentils (page 274) and the idea for Sussex stewed steak (page 280), Indonesian fish curry (page 378), for introducing me to Black fruit and apple tart (page 409), Turkey croquettes (page 437), and many other recipes and ideas; Mrs. Titley for the Tarragon fishcakes with rich tomato sauce (page 277); Caroline Wood for Chorizo lentils with sausages (page 286); Deborah Needleman for Fig mashed potatoes (page 293); Hugh Van Dusen for Tarte tatin (page 302); Sue Thomas for the Bean chutney (page 328); Sybille Russell for Danish glögg (page 334); Tony Dasent for the Marinated olives (page 351); The Whitehouse Restaurant Lochaline for Curly kale and almond soup (page 355); Miles Nelson for the idea of the Parmesan and dill seed toasts (page 359); Sybille Wilkinson of Gilchesters Organics for Quick Spelt bread (page 360); Juliet Glaves for the idea of the Cauliflower and chickpea curry (page 374); and of course Jo Clark and her family for many recipes and food ideas.

To my wonderful husband, Adam,
who has learned to like a good dinner,
Rosie and Molly, and Tom, Will and Ben

First published in the United States of America in 2011 by
Universe Publishing,
A Division of Rizzoli International Publications, Inc.
300 Park Avenue South
New York, NY 10010
www.rizzoliusa.com

Copyright © Sarah Raven 2010
Photography © Jonathan Buckley 2010

First published in the United Kingdom as
Food for Friends & Family
by Bloomsbury Publishing Plc
36 Soho Square
London W1D 3QY

2011 2012 2013 2014 / 10 9 8 7 6 5 4 3 2 1

Text adapted for the United States by Stephen Orr

Printed and bound in China by C&C Offset Printing Co., Ltd.

ISBN: 978-0-7893-2230-2

Library of Congress Control Number: 2010937480